Villy Sørensen, philosopher and author, has been a member of the Danish Academy since 1965. He was nominated for the Nobel prize for literature in 1978 and has won many distinguished awards for his writing. In addition to books on Kafka, Nietzsche, and Schopenhauer, Sørensen writes fiction illustrating his philosophical thoughts and writings.

W. Glyn Jones is Professor of Scandinavian Studies at the University of Newcastle upon Tyne. His works on Danish literature have been published widely.

SENECA

the humanist
at the court of Nero

VILLY SØRENSEN
translated from the Danish by
W. Glyn Jones

———————

THE UNIVERSITY OF
CHICAGO PRESS

PA
6675
.S613
1984

Originally published by Gyldendal as
Seneca. Humanisten ved Neros Hof
© 1976 by Villy Sørensen

The University of Chicago Press, Chicago 60637
Canongate Publishing Ltd, Edinburgh

Translation © 1984 by W. Glyn Jones

The Publishers acknowledge the financial assistance
of the Amalienborg Foundation
in the publication of this volume

Library of Congress Cataloging in Publication Data
Sørensen, Villy, 1929–
Seneca, The Humanist at the Court of Nero.
Translation of: Seneca, Humanisten ved Neros Hof.
Includes index.
1. Seneca, Lucius Annaeus, CA. 4 B.C. – 65.
2. Nero, Emperor of Rome, 37–68.
3. Humanism.
4. Rome – History – Nero, 54–68.
5. Stoics.
6. Authors, Latin – Biography.
7. Philosophers – Rome – Biography.
8. Statesmen – Rome – Biography.
I. Title.
PA 6675S613   1984   188   [B]   84–18
ISBN 0–226–76827–9

Printed in the United Kingdom
93 92 91 90 89 88 87 86 85 84 54321

CONTENTS

Translator's Note

Villy Sørensen is a highly conscious stylist who delights in using words, often in paradoxical settings, so as to give new meaning to otherwise stock expressions. He does so many times in this book. One stylistic feature of the original Danish is the strict and consistent use of Greek forms for Greek names, and Latin forms for Roman names. I have maintained this distinction in the English translation — though with a few minor modifications — with the result that some Greek names appear in slightly unaccustomed forms. Not to have done this, however, would have spoilt some of the effect of the chapter on Seneca's tragedies.

Some of Seneca's dramas are readily available in the Penguin Classics, in a translation by E. F. Watling. Where appropriate, I have quoted from these translations, indicating them by the simple reference *Tragedies*, and indicating the relevant page in this edition.

W.G.J.

I. MYTH AND PHILOSOPHY

Myth and history

Seneca, who was a contemporary of Jesus, seems modern in many ways. The problems he encountered as a statesman at the court of Nero, and about which he wrote as a poet and philosopher, the conflict between *Realpolitik* and humane ideals, between the demand for political commitment and the desire for self-realisation in peace and tranquillity, are problems relevant to our time; his humanist ideals are so natural to us that we easily forget that they were less natural and more original in his day.

If Seneca appears to be more modern than many philosophers who are closer to us in time, it is, of course, partly because present-day Europe has more in common with the city of Rome than with the more limited and enclosed society of pre-industrialised Europe. With its worship of quantity, its lack of common spiritual values, its wealth and its poverty, its enjoyment of life and its spleen, its search for entertainment and for salvation, its individualism and its mass psychosis, Rome was the great precursor of our own urban civilisation. Therefore, while we can understand Seneca in the light of our own time, we can perhaps better understand our own time in the light of his, and so a knowledge of history turns out to be useful after all. The similarities between the two epochs will occasionally be put into relief by the differences between them.

The greatest difficulty has been brought about by time. Everyone bears the stamp of the age in which he lives. However, in the ancient world time passed more slowly than it does now, and to Seneca time was longer than it is to us. The Stoic philosophy which he professed had been developed three hundred years before him; in his philosophy of nature he makes random use of thinkers from the first century A.D., to which he himself belonged, and as far back as the sixth century B.C.. He might well criticise older theories with his logical powers of reason and believe in the power of knowledge, but he had no scientific, objective criterion for what was right and wrong; for him there was not *one* science whose latest results outdate older theories, and to whose supreme and objective authority it is necessary to defer. This indicates that, however modern Seneca's humanist ideas otherwise were, there were two modern ideas which he (like the rest of the ancient world) never acquired: the ideas of objectivity and progress — the two principles which are essential to our modern, scientific and technical civilisation, and which denote a definitive break with primitive mentality.

As it is natural science which prepares the way for the belief in progress, these two ideas are closely tied to each other. The unscientific feeling that there is something behind natural phenomena makes man reluctant to interfere with them; if it is established that there is a meaning built into things from the start, it is obvious that man can scarcely create new things which are even better. The Utopia of the Romans was not in the future, but in the past, in the Age of Gold when in Seneca's view people lived in harmony with themselves and each other, when they had all things in common and the best members of society as their leaders — not as leaders who exercised power, but leaders who served the people. It was private possessions which brought about the change and prepared the way for greed and the desire for power, which were thus the products not of nature, but of civilisation.

However, this pessimistic view of culture stands in clear contrast to the cultural self-confidence which persuaded the Greeks and subsequently the Romans to call all other peoples barbarians. In another context Seneca himself had to admit that powerful and determined characters like, for instance, the Germanic tribes tend to be aggressive before becoming civilised: 'Their strength is imperfect as is the case with everything which springs from a fertile nature but is yet without culture.' Strictly speaking, these two ways of looking at things are mutually exclusive, and so it is tempting to reject the one as 'mythical' and accept the other as 'historical'. Firstly, however, the ancient world does not make a particularly clear distinction between myth and history, and secondly it is probably just as one-sided to give either nature or civilisation all the honour for what is good, or all the responsibility for what is bad in human life. Cultural pessimism and cultural optimism are, to use a pair of fashionable modern terms, complementary or dialectical, and they can be reconciled to each other if it is assumed that man is not 'barbaric' by nature, but that he easily appears to be so if he does not develop in step with cultural change. In the beginning, man projected his own unconscious soul into the things around him, which he felt to be alive; likewise he experienced the history of his own society through the natural cycle. As he grew more conscious of himself, he extracted his soul from things and created new things instead. In other words, he created history in the scientific understanding and exploitation of nature. The last decades have shown that nature in the long run does not tolerate being considered and treated as merely an object to be exploited; what is true of external nature seems also to be true of human nature: there is a limit to what human beings can adapt to without placing their own nature at risk. Against this modern background the mythical view that the development of civilisation was a fall from nature is not *so* primitive that it has only historical interest. Nor were the attempts of the Stoic philosophers to seek the foundations for the law of men in a natural order which has been obscured by the development of society. Myth tells not only something of the way in which primitive man experienced things, but also of the primitive way in which man experiences things; the view that man is only fashioned by his own time and not also by history can no longer be accepted as scientific.

The Romans were not created for the civilisation which they created. It is from the resultant conflict that humanist ideas arise as ideas about a social order different from that which is no longer felt to be the natural order. Philosophy — Greek philosophy — originated from the idea that things could be different — or rather from the thought that in reality, by nature, from the start, they were different from what they have become — and what they have been understood to be. The closeness between the Greeks and the Romans and the original state makes it natural to begin this account of a Roman humanist who was inspired by Greek ideas by going back to the very beginning, firstly to the emergence of Greek thought from a world of mythical ideas (Chapter I) and secondly with a look at Roman history and mythology (Chapter II).

The Age of Gold and civilisation: Hesiod

With the myth about the Age of Gold which existed at the beginning of time, ancient man clung to an — admittedly romantic — memory of a social order which in fact can be called a natural order, when primitive man lived in closer contact with nature than does civilised — i.e. urban — man. The transition from a society tied to the natural order, in which everything remains unchanged, to an urban society in which many things are new, is *the* great advance in civilisation which first gave man a sense of the instability of all things. In the beginning time was not like a line constantly pointing to something new, but like a circle constantly enclosing itself. The cultic festivals of tribal society were repetitions, repetitions of what happened in the beginning, and the myths told the story of this. They were illustrations, not theories, of how things began. And the individual member of society has just as little history as does society itself: he is only himself when he is placed outside himself, when in cultic ecstasy he repeats prescribed patterns of behaviour: 'In every *real* action, i.e. in every repetition of an archetypal action, profane time and its passage are suspended.' So writes Mircea Eliade in 'Le Mythe de l'Eternel Retour', which includes a wealth of examples of the resistance to time and history in primitive societies and even in the great cultures of the ancient world. The myth of the Age of Gold is in itself an expression of such a psychological resistance, and of course it was only formulated when everything was no longer the same.

The idea of a human race constantly deteriorating throughout the ages of gold, silver, copper and iron respectively was formulated (in the 7th century B.C.) in *Hesiod*'s poem 'Works and Days', one of the first, most confused, profound, primitive and revolutionary poems in world literature. For a large part it consists of a farmer's advice as to how and when to do things in the fields and home: for Hesiod it was still natural to expect everything to be in the natural order. Meanwhile, he also undertakes to give good advice on seafaring, though he heartily disapproves of it; he argues that there is no need to go to sea if society is just, because then a fertile earth will bear plentiful fruit. From this it can be deduced that seafaring and trade are only necessary if society is no longer just.

And Hesiod's society is no longer just. His poem seems to be partly inspired by a quarrel over an inheritance which he had had with his brother, who had used bribery to ensure the support of powerful men. We have to imagine these powerful men as something similar to the kings in the Iliad, but in Hesiod's work they are seen in a much less flattering light than the splendour with which they are portrayed by (the slightly older) Homer. Homer's heroes easily feel wronged and are quick to seek revenge, and when they go too far they can say with true Homeric innocence that, 'Zeus is to blame'. Hesiod, on the other hand, is the little man in society who finds it more difficult to assert his rights, and so he has to *threaten* his opponents with the wrath of Zeus: 'House and family wither away when Olympic Zeus so decides; he turns their mighty armies to dust and lays waste their walls, and their ships he strikes on the sea' — if they are not just.

But this belief that justice pays and that the unjust are punished is in clear contrast to Hesiod's designation of his epoch as the 'age of iron' in which might is right, and the evil-doer is praised, when kinsmen fight each other and there is no help against evil. Things were different in the Age of Gold when everyone lived on the fruits of the earth and knew no evil. The distant Age of Gold has obviously arisen in Hesiod's imagination as a contrast to the present age: the sense of injustice precedes the idea of justice.

The strange thing is, of course, that in the Age of Gold it was not the righteous god Zeus who reigned in heaven, but his father Kronos, whom Zeus put out of a job. While we are told that the first human beings lived like gods, without worries or problems and without knowing death as anything but a short sleep, we cannot help noticing that the gods at that time really lived more like human beings in the Age of Iron, something which Hesiod discreetly keeps to himself in this context but recounts at length in another poem, 'The Theogony' (The birth of the gods). Here we learn that the inoffensive Kronos castrated his father Uranos and then devoured his own children who were later to become the Olympic gods: it is quite obvious that the divine fathers objected to their children's getting on in the world and taking over power from them. When Zeus made it and came to power, he, too, made similar arrangements, but a remarkable thing happened in his time, something over which the myths do not linger: time comes to a standstill in the world of the gods. The gods remain the age they are now and only beget children with mortals. If we look more closely to discover what becomes of time, we see that these mortals, these human beings, have had to assume the burden.

Human beings were created by Prometheus, and it may be that Zeus saw in them a threat to his supremacy. Whatever the case may be, he froze them, so that Prometheus had to steal fire for them from the fireplace of the gods. Zeus realised that he would have to live alongside human beings, but he cunningly had the smith god Hefaistos make a female for them (so far all human beings must have been men) and sent this woman, Pandora, to Prometheus's somewhat dull brother, Epimetheus. Like another Adam he allowed himself to be beguiled by the woman and her dowry, Pandora's box, from which all conceivable torments issued into the human world, leaving only hope behind. But hope creates a link between man and future time, and it was in fact time and mortality which Pandora gave to men, who in any case could strictly speaking only multiply with the help of woman. Generation conflicts arose among human beings as they subsided among the gods: in the Age of Iron fathers cannot agree with their children, or children with their fathers, or brothers with brothers, writes Hesiod.

Thus there are two contrary lines of development in Hesiod's mythical stories: human beings become more bellicose and the gods more peaceable with the passage of time, until the gods rise above time on Olympus and live as carefree an existence as did human beings in the Age of Gold, when everything was unchanging. Admittedly, Hesiod has difficulty in sketching this latter development: he tells his Pandora myth in 'Works and Days' in continuation of his attack on the greedy men of power who 'do not know how much a half is more than a whole'. It would be easy for human beings to obtain enough in a day to last for a whole year if Zeus, in anger at Prometheus's strategem, had not hidden the necessities of life from men and allowed sorrow and trouble to descend on them. Zeus, the father of justice with whom Hesiod elsewhere threatens the powerful men, seems to throw in his lot with them when it comes to making life unbearable for ordinary people.

In fact the Olympic gods are created in the image of a prince rather than of a human being; this is more obvious in Homer than in Hesiod. Their divine power over mortal men is established at the same time as differences in the human world emerge between ruling families and other mortals — who sometimes have to go to sea because their fields no longer bear fruit. In Homer, the Olympic gods, Zeus, Hera, Athene etc., have turned into one large family, a dominant clan, after originally being primitive local gods. Kronos, whom Zeus displaced as the head of the clan, was, according to Robert Graves, originally a god of corn who was mown down each year like corn in the field. In this he resembled the 'divine king' in certain primitive communities, who was sacrificed at the end of his reign so that his strength could be absorbed in the natural cycle. (In the course of time a male child was sometimes sacrificed instead of the king, which might be the reason why Kronos in the myth devours his own children). Zeus's usurping power from Kronos reflects the transition from the primitive tribal society, whose king so to speak was sacrificed for the community, to a larger society based on the family, in which the king and the ruling family assume power over society. As this transition leads to greater social differences but away from the barbarism which human sacrifice betokens, it can be regarded as a 'fall' and as 'progress'. In his own primitive way Hesiod was dialectical. And when in his myth of the Age of Gold Seneca maintained that leaders did not exert power at first, but sacrificed themselves for the people, there was a grain of history in it.

Nature and law: the philosophers of nature

The moral protest against prevailing injustice is expressed wherever trade breaks down the framework of a society based on agriculture and kinship, and leads to a greater discrepancy between rich and poor; it also leads to more demands on the part of the citizens and to the establishment of the rule of law instead of absolute monarchs. At such a time the prophets in Israel, like Hesiod in Greece, threaten the unjust rulers with divine retribution. To say 'Vengeance is mine, saith the Lord', is the same as saying that it is not for the rulers, and that there *is* a higher justice than the law of revenge and violence which is theirs. Solon, the lawmaker of Athens, who was also a poet, continues Hesiod's moral criticism of the rulers, but he is not content to threaten them with a just Zeus; he seeks, with the help of the law, to impose limits on the arrogance of the great.

Hesiod says somewhere that the riches which the gods give are

15

better than what man can take for himself. Solon repeats this distinction and states clearly that it is the insatiable hunger of the great, or, in blunt terms, their greed which is evil. It is trade and an economy based on money which leads to this epoch-making discovery: that there is a difference between financial profit and moral profit, between good things and the Good (concepts which language still tends to confuse). In Homer a good man is a man with possessions, and in Israel, too, riches were a sign of divine favour. Society loses its (Homeric) innocence when riches and power are no longer seen as the expression of divine favour, but of men's lust for money and power.

It was this significant new departure which Nietzsche called 'the slaves' moral revolt': the weak, who could not oppose might with might, took their revenge by calling the powerful evil and themselves good. Morals and the law resulted in the savage instincts, which until then had been allowed free rein, being turned inwards into man, and the soul became that part of man which did not express itself. Nietzsche is right in arguing that the idea of the soul is contemporary with the moral concepts of good and evil, but he ignores the fact that it was not the grandiose warlike activities of the great which caused this moral protest: it was their greed. It was first and foremost material possessions which were disparaged, not the body and its instincts. But once the distinction is made between material goods and the good, it does not take long to recognise the fact that material values in general are inferior, and that goodness is a purely spiritual thing. The 'spirit' or the 'soul', which originally meant 'breath', is now — by the time of Pythagoras in the 6th century B.C. — seen as man's innermost being, which in ecstasy can liberate itself from the body and on the death of the body will enter another body: the transmigration of souls is the way to ultimate salvation and to union with the divine.

If the good is purely spiritual, then God must also be 'pure spirit', as Xenofanes puts it at about the same time. Xenofanes talks ironically about the amoral Homeric gods who are created in a human image, just as oxen would create gods in the image of oxen. Just as Homer's divine family corresponds to the tribal society with its right of revenge, the one, spiritual God of Pythagoras and Xenofanes corresponds to a society founded on law — and to the individual. At the same time as the law liberates the individual from the tribe and makes him responsible for his own actions, the individual becomes increasingly homeless in the more 'civilised' urban society, in which philosophies and religions emerge offering salvation to the individual. Individual ecstasy replaces the collective ecstasy of the tribal society. If the mythical fall from nature is to be dated historically, it must be fixed at the time when civilisation underwent the great change to a society based on the town, trade and law. It may seem surprising that the introduction of a — written — law and legal system can be considered as a 'fall', but the Apostle Paul said that, 'The law entered that the offence might abound', while Plato (and the Introduction to Jutlandic Law from 1241) argues that the perfect society needs no law. A sense of injustice and of lawlessness precedes law and the demand for it; or, as Seneca writes in his discussion of the fall from nature and the Age of Gold, 'Then vices made their entry, and kingship became tyranny. The introduction of laws became more and more necessary, and at first they were indeed formulated by wise men.'

The seven wise men of the ancient world, who gained the reputation of being the first lawmakers, included not only Solon of Athens, but also *Thales* from Milet, the first 'philosopher of nature'. It is no coincidence that it was in the largest of the Greek colonies in Ionia on the coast of Asia Minor, in the port and trade centre of Milet, that a philosophy arose explaining the natural manner in which things came into being. Mainland tradition was not so well established there; the Ionian philosophers of nature, who were practical men of the world, were less prejudiced in their views and had more than a theoretical interest in studying the elements which as seafarers and traders they were dependent on.

Basing society on law and not on tradition is the same as basing it on reason; reason turned against the irrationality of the traditional social order and from the mythical understanding of the world which had been passed on for generations; the moral criticism of the unjust rulers was also applied to the amoral gods and the myths of creation in which their barbaric family life played its part. Even Hesiod had sought in Zeus the justice which he failed to find in the social order, the world order, and for him justice, *Dike*, was not an abstract idea, but a goddess, the daughter of Zeus. Law and justice were at first not just thought of as customs to be *accepted*, but as something which is *discovered*: the philosophers of nature tried to found law and justice on the laws of nature and natural justice, and it is from society that the concept of law has been applied to nature.

The important thing is not really that Thales believed water to be the prime element from which everything has developed (through condensation and dilution), or that Anaximenes believed it to be the air and Heraclitus fire: (No one found it in the fourth element, earth). The important thing is their common belief in the possibility of understanding nature by means of reason, which in Greek is *logos* and in Latin *ratio*, thereby implying that nature is 'logical' or 'rational', i.e. that it conforms to laws. The logical understanding of nature was the recognition of the fact that there is a natural explanation of how everything comes into existence; the Greek word for nature, *fysis*, means growth, while the Latin word *natura* simply means birth. The Greek (and Roman) view of nature was anything but objective: in their eyes inorganic nature was also full of life, 'full of gods', as Thales is said to have put it.

The philosophers in the Greek city states, where homogeneity had been replaced by change and variety, were faced with the philosophical problem of the relationship between the changeable and the unchangeable, and between unity and diversity. Nevertheless, Parmenides (c. 500 B.C.) still felt it natural to assert that only the unchangeable was real. That the first philosophers found the idea of evolution just as alien as the idea of objectivity is apparent from *Anaximander's* famous fragment (from before 550 B.C.): 'On their disintegration, existing things must of necessity return to their origins. For according to the dictates of time, they must all suffer punishment for their injustice.' Pythagoras, too, is said to have maintained that at the end of an epoch everything returns to exactly what it was before, and in Heraclitus (c. 500 B.C.) we find the idea of existence as an eternal fire which is lit and extinguished as appropriate, and which purifies and renews itself in the world conflagration. In one sense this corresponds to the periodic renewal of the primitive society, which now, in urban society, comes to be applied to the entire universe, to cosmos.

Meanwhile, it must have been more difficult to apply the harmony of cosmos to a society in which growing conflicts formed the social background to a moral revolt. Heraclitus, who saw the universe as a unity of opposites and war as the father of all things, was also profoundly aware of social disharmony: he could wish that his fellow

18

citizens in Ephesus should keep their riches, so that their moral turpitude could become clear to all; and he wanted to see them hanged because they had exiled their best citizen on the ground that no one should be outstanding among them. Then there is his saying that, 'It is also a law to follow the will of one individual,' and the anecdotes telling how he wept over the foolishness of men. These things make Heraclitus the first of the early philosophers of whom we can form a picture; he must have been a pessimistic intellectual who had understood the problem of democracy: that the idea of a community of citizens, no longer naturally based on tradition but founded on law, presupposes reasonable citizens. A couple of his more obscure fragments put the problem quite clearly: 'Speaking with understanding, one ought to base oneself on what is common to all, just as a state should base itself on its laws — indeed, even more so. For all human laws derive nourishment from the one divine law; that reigns supreme insofar as it wishes, and satisfies all men and supersedes all things.' However: 'Although thought (logos) is what is common to all men, they live for the most part as though they all had their own private reason.'

Although everything else might be in a state of flux, one thing was absolutely fixed for Heraclitus: the law governing the entirety, which can only be recognised with the help of reason — though only few people are equipped with sufficient reason to do so. Half a century later, when (as Heraclitus had said) the citizens no longer needed 'to fight for their laws as they would for the city walls,' but when law and citizenship had triumphed and Greek democracy was fully developed, it became more difficult to see how the law of society was founded on the sole, divine, natural law. In the democratic state law does not mean obeying the will of one individual, but asserting one's own will as far as the laws permit; the *Sophists*, the teachers of worldly wisdom, made it their task to teach citizens how best to do this. They drew the consequences of the fact that different people in reality do not come to the same view of the same thing — and so decided that reason in the abstract does not exist, but only as the 'private reason' of the individual. With his famous dictum that man, the individual, is the measure of all things, *Protagoras* (c. 450 B.C.) emerged as the proponent of a relativism in values and morals which could be dangerous for social morals, but which would promote the individual's consciousness

19

of his own freedom. The Sophists coined the often-quoted expression, 'To live in harmony with nature'; but by nature they did not mean external nature, cosmic harmony, on which the older philosophers of nature sought to found the law. On the contrary, they meant the natural urges and needs which the law seeks to restrain. For the Sophists the law was only a convention, something generally accepted, an arbitrary arrangement in the interests of the ruling class; they are the first radically anti-authoritarian thinkers. For the first time intellectual activities could be regarded as a threat to society: in 432 B.C., the year before the Peloponesian War broke out, a law was passed in Athens aimed at combatting blasphemy: it was directed against the philosophers of nature and the Sophists.

The good and the state: Socrates and Plato

In seeking to base the right of the individual on his natural impulses and rejecting general criteria for an absolute right, the Sophists ultimately risked finding themselves defending the right of the strongest. However, we owe most of our knowledge of the Sophists to *Plato*, who opposed their principle of relative values and perhaps for this reason emphasised it; in his dialogues he presented *Socrates* in a heated discussion with the Sophists, whose opinions and arguments he reduced *ad absurdum*.

Socrates did not preach morals as opposed to the Sophists' concept of the relativity of morals, but he sought to demonstrate that it was logically untenable to renounce the absolute moral concepts (of good and evil, right and wrong) as they are necessary as the basis for a meaningful discussion (or for regulating people's behaviour towards each other). It was in this Socratic spirit that Plato chose the dialogue form: conversation distinguishes itself from monologue by not preaching private opinions, but allowing common ground to be seen: Socrates did not preach the good or the true, but he let them emerge — or be conspicuous by their absence, so that all came to nought.

Socrates' ironic use of dialogue (which is the basic meaning of the word dialectics) appears to have been more negative in its effect than the persuasive art of the Sophists. After the defeat of Athens by Sparta (404 B.C.) in the Peloponesian War it was natural for the Athenians to find a hidden cause of their defeat in moral decay, and Socrates, who wished at any price to 'avoid acting contrary to the law', was accused of believing in other gods than those of the State and of teaching youth to do the same. Although he denied his guilt, he did not deny that there was a difference between the State's view of the gods and his own, saying to his fellow citizens that, 'Despite all possible respect and esteem for you, I will obey the commands of God rather than yours.' In his defence speech he directed the severest possible accusation against the State: 'He who really wishes to fight for justice must necessarily — if he wants to redeem his life even for a brief second — work in his private capacity and renounce participation in public life.'

Ironically enough, Socrates, who opposed the Sophists' view of the law as an arbitrary arrangement, admitted in this way that they were right: what passed for law and justice in the state was in fact arbitrary; and that was the trouble. Consequently, it was the duty of the individual not to seek the best for himself under the prevailing circumstances, but to seek the Good. In so doing he would be in conflict with those evil circumstances which reduce the good to the opportune, to what is good for oneself. If, in his fight for what is right, the individual has to oppose the state, he must ultimately be *above* the state: in its way Socrates' individualism was more radical than that of the Sophists, to whom he indeed was counted as belonging in his day.

According to Hegel, Socrates was the inventor of morals; before him the Greeks had no idea of an absolute moral standard or of an absolute good, but only of social morality. In the struggle to base the state on law and reason instead of privileges and tradition, the citizens had had no sense of the difference between the social law, according to which an individual can be judged, and the moral law, according to which the state can be judged. Only when the state is in crisis is the question raised as to the ideal from which it is deviating. In democracy it is natural to strive for what is good for oneself and, with the Sophists, to see it as natural to do so. On the basis of Socrates' concept of the Good as what in any circumstances is good for anyone, it was better to suffer injustice than to be the cause of it: a good man can scarcely avoid suffering injustice, but, 'No evil can befall a good man.'

Socrates said that an inner voice, a 'demon', prevented him from doing anything wrong, and although he was presumably being ironical in suggesting that in his ignorance he needed a demon to tell him what

21

anyone could know for himself, this naturally irritated his fellow citizens. If the individual in general is not the measure of good and evil, then it is undemocratic for one single individual to be that measure. If it is not man or the state which determines what is moral and just, then these things must be determined *a priori*; good and evil must be enshrined in the nature of things. However, for the ordinary citizens Socrates' idea of the good as being different from what the State thought to be good must have appeared to be rather up in the air — and Aristophanes did in fact place Socrates up in the clouds in his comedy. Plato, the disciple of Socrates, tried to discover the ideal from which the State had deviated, and to relate the social order to the eternal order of things: he raised Socrates' idea of the good to the Idea of the Good, by which he meant a superior, indeed the supreme, reality. Nevertheless, he had to construct an ideal state in order to let the idea of the Good and the Just come to its right *within* the state.

So Plato's 'state' is a utopia, but it is typical that he should write about the ideal constitution of a state as though it had actually existed at some time in the past and disintegrated because of an increasing tendency to deviate (in the procreation of children!) from certain cosmic number combinations, resulting in growing psychological and social disharmony. Plato sees changing forms of government as a consistent cycle: the rule of the best men (i.e. the nobility) was natural in the beginning when everything was new; what is ideal cannot be improved, but only undermined, and so in Plato's view change is 'something particularly pernicious'.

However, if the best is to be found in the beginning of time, the absolute Good must be outside time altogether. Mircea Eliade argues that primitive man suspends time in the cultic repetition of prescribed patterns of behaviour, adding in this connection that the primitive view of the world has a 'Platonic structure'. Using the same words, this means that Plato's view of the world has a primitive structure; so while the relativist idea of the Sophists can be said to be the first expression of a 'modern' mentality, Plato can be regarded as 'the philosopher of a primitive mentality'.

Plato retained, so to speak, the memory of the primitive experience of reality, i.e. the experience of a reality beyond time in an age when it was no longer a social reality. In the city state, despite city festivals and tragedies (cf p246), a collective re-creation of what was eternally the same was not possible. Thus it became the philosophical task of individuals to revive the 'ideas', the eternal patterns of transient things, which in themselves are nothing but reproductions, shadow pictures. However, they can remind us of a hidden reality: a thing or things of beauty can kindle a reminiscence of the Beautiful, the idea of the beautiful. (In its original sense the idea is something seen, not something thought). They can raise the soul in erotic ecstasy, something which is only possible because the soul ultimately belongs to the world of ideas, just as the body belongs to the world of the senses. Immortality, which the creation myths reserved for the gods in an age when time was beginning to make itself felt in human society, is something which the mortals in Plato's philosophical myths can recapture by freeing themselves from the senses and sensuality and by recognising what is eternal and unchanging. To achieve understanding is for Plato a moral action: 'Virtue is knowledge.'

The individual has to make a great effort if spiritual reason is to triumph over greed and what is unreasonable. Likewise, the unreasonable members of the state, the greedy tradespeople, must be kept in check so that the reasonable members, the philosophers, can rule. In the just state spiritual powers are so justly distributed that the greatest mental gifts are reserved for the highest strata, and the least are directed to the lowest class; in fact the just state ensures for its citizens the life in harmony with their nature which the Sophists had propounded, except that, in contrast to them, Plato insisted that human beings are different by nature and not on account of their social status. In Greece, as in other ancient communities, it was normal to see slavery as 'natural', as founded in the inferior natures of the slaves; it was also usual to see the physical work often carried out by slaves as inferior, but not to conclude that it was the work which made the slaves inferior. But Plato does appear to believe that there are occupations which could be damaging to the soul: 'Commerce and shopkeeping ... give rise to cunning and unreliability in the soul' he argues in his last great work, the 'Laws'.

The perfect society needs no law because it is based on nature's own law. In the 'Laws' the conversation is no longer centred on the ideal state, in which everything is common to all, but on the best achievable, in which everything is equitably distributed and where every man has his plot of land. Admittedly, the differences which exist between people make it necessary to divide them into four classes according to wealth; however, they 'must not strive for great profit through base business transactions, usury or the fattening of poor cattle, but on the contrary for all that can be achieved by the cultivation of the soil.' And even this should not be done to such an extent that the principal object of it all, the well-being of the soul and the body, is neglected. The city must not be situated too close to the sea, which will tempt the citizens to seafaring and trade; this brings gold and silver money to the country, and that is referred to as 'the greatest misfortune that can befall a state.' Elsewhere Plato says that the greatest misfortune for a state is 'When young men enjoy special recognition if they are always producing something new', for that transforms the character of the young, making them despise the old and value the new. Change is particularly damaging to society, in which every man has his plot, and the number of plots and families must be kept constant if the social balance is to be maintained. Plato's society, based on the idea of the city in the country, is a consistent nil-growth society in a state of balance, something which does not seem so 'reactionary' today as it was in the optimistic age when all hopes were placed on progress. Plato had seen the disintegration of the city state and had bad experience of progress; progress had in a way shown him to be right, though his eternal ideas could not slow it down.

On the other hand Plato has made a greater mark on Western thought than any other philosopher, and he has sometimes been blamed for the unfortunate development which some people believe it has undergone. According to Heidegger he made truth into a question of man's correct relationship to things rather than a question of the fundamental character of things, thus preparing the way for man's domination of the material world. Yet, according to the historian of science, Farrington, his low opinion of material things was a brake on technical and scientific development. Both of these views can be equally wrong. It is, however, certain that Plato's *dualism*, the distinction he drew between the senses and the spirit, was a precondition for the natural science which first emerged in Christendom (cf p231). The Greek philosopher who at the time of Socrates went furthest towards an 'objective' view of nature was *Democritus*. He maintained, like Plato, that the real cannot immediately be discerned by the senses; but for him the real was not 'ideal' but material, atoms in empty space. With this, the distinction between philosophical idealism and materialism was established. However, to ascribe to Plato all the honour or all the responsibility for the idealistic view that there is something behind visible phenomena is to go too far, even for Plato. He discovered rather than invented the 'Platonic structure' of primitive experience; he was very much aware of the original state, and if, thanks to his poetic gifts, he has been able to raise fallen souls ever since, it is presumably because they, too, have retained a recollection, albeit less intense, of that same thing.

Cultural optimism and cultural pessimism

The ideas of progress and the objective understanding of nature are closely connected. If it is atoms and their movements and relationships which have set everything going, it is more impressive that things have gone as far as they have than if it is all only a shadow of a glorious past. Democritus, who was the originator of this atom theory, also described how people at first lived like wild animals but gradually learned from their mistakes and were spurred on by necessity and created tools to cope with their needs. The rationalist Sophists apparently tended towards cultural optimism, and the great tragedians expressed the same view. In Aischylos' 'Prometheus Bound' the hero, who according to legend created man and procured fire for him, is given the honour for our entire culture:

> (I) first yoked the wild animals to the plough . . .
> and it was I who gave them the ship . . .
> The countless hidden treasures
> in the bosom of the earth:
> ore, iron, silver and gold — does anyone maintain
> that he brought them to light before I!

In one of the chorus' songs in Sophocles' 'Antigone', 'Great things exist, but greatest is Man in his deeds', seafaring is also praised, but mostly the fact that man 'enclosed the lands with laws and defences'. In other words, the great cultural transition to the community based on trade and law, which Hesiod saw as moral decay, was seen as progress by the poets of the great age of Athens. But at the time of war and

25

crisis at the end of this, the fifth century, there was no longer any basis for an optimistic view of progress, and at the same time the interest in nature gave way to political and human problems. Socrates, writes Farrington, clouds 'the optimistic picture of man engaged in an attack on external nature'.

Even when Farrington wrote this, in 1944, the year before Hiroshima, the attack on external nature was still seen as the only natural thing; what needed explaining was not that the scientific and objective interpretation of nature only triumphed in Christian Europe, but that it did *not* get anywhere in Greece, despite the lead given by the philosophers of nature. According to Farrington it was due to the division of society into masters and slaves, which led to the separation of scientific and practical work and prevented technical progress — and which expressed itself in the dualism of the philosophers. Certainly Aristotle rejected the idea of his teacher, Plato, that there was something behind natural phenomena, but he maintained that there is something *within* them, that the material is only the raw material of a creative principle, in the final analysis of God, which sets the whole thing in motion for the sake of certain eternal purposes. Thus, Aristotle subordinated the scientific, causal view which sees phenomena as the effects of what has gone before, to the teleological view, which understands them on the basis of the object (*telos, finis*) which they serve or strive towards. Farrington also derives teleology from the master-slave realtionship: 'The new concept of nature, which sees nature as a force with an object in view, is a thought which arose in the mind of a master who ruled over slaves.' But this materialistic explanation, which paradoxically enough ascribes an exaggerated importance to the ideas of the philosophers, is not tenable: from the beginning of time man has projected his own soul into things and seen natural phenomena as the expressions of a will; even for the philosophers of nature, nature was the work of the gods. Democritus was the only one to approach a causal interpretation of nature — and even that was not until the time of Socrates and Plato. He would rather find one causal explanation than take over the whole of the Persian empire, he said — thereby implying that so far no one had found one! Hitherto men and even philosophers had, as it were, understood nature and themselves under one heading; the interest in external nature faded when, in the age of crisis in the city state, men discovered

26

themselves as problems.

It was the Sophists who had first directed their attention to human nature rather than external nature and seen it in contrast to law and convention; Diogenes, who is still famous for living in a barrel in the 4th century B.C., intensified this contrast and put into practice the 'life in harmony with nature' which, particularly for the Sophists, was so far only a theory. Aristotle said it was impossible to talk of human nature independently of society, as man is a social creature by nature; he is a *zoon politikon*, a creature living in a *polis*, a city state. But in Diogenes' opinion the whole of city civilisation was an arbitrary arrangement created by and giving rise to artificial needs which cannot be satisfied by natural means and therefore lead to dissatisfaction; natural needs are few and small — and the satisfaction derived from them all the greater. Diogenes distanced himself from the city state by calling himself *kosmopolites*, a citizen of the world, and he proved by deed that, even if practice, *askesis*, was required, it was possible to get rid of the artificial needs. In other people's opinion he led a dog's life, but he referred to himself as a dog, *kyon*, and it is from this that the word Cynic, the name of his school of thought, is derived. Whether or not Diogenes' dog's life was in accordance with nature or not, he was at least in harmony with his age, for the individual was no longer naturally anchored in the city state, and the philosophical interest in human nature was becoming diluted into a sentimental interest in man as a child of nature. One of Aristotle's pupils, Dikaiarkos, wrote a history of civilisation in which even the transition from the collecting to the hunting stage is viewed as a fall from nature; another of Aristotle's pupils, Alexander the Great, shattered the political horizon with his conquests and in his way agreed with Diogenes by declaring that if he were not Alexander he would be Diogenes. In the tempestuous times after the death of Alexander, when empires rose and fell, when everything was to be feared, and when chance, *tyche*, was the preferred deity, the two philosophical schools which were to dominate Rome arose: Epicureism and Stoicism, the declared aims of which were peace of mind and fearlessness.

27

Individual and society: Epicure and Zenon

There had from the start been a certain correspondence between the distribution of power in Heaven and on Earth. Corresponding to the tribal society's divine king there was Kronos; to the society based on kinship there was the corresponding Olympic family of gods; and to the society founded on law and justice corresponded the one just God. It was in the well-ordered cosmos that the philosophers of nature found the basis for social law and order, but the divine reason ordering the world, which had replaced the arbitrary Homeric gods, was in its turn replaced by a superior arbitrariness, and it is not a coincidence that fortune, *tyche* became the dominant deity in the period of crisis in the city state. In the first of the three great tragedians, Aischylos, it is fate, *moira*, which rules the world, strictly but justly, while in the last of them, Euripedes, *tyche* plays a far greater role. Similarly, in the first historian, Herodotus, who describes the war successfully waged by the Greeks against the Persians in the first half of the 5th century, it is *moira* which reigns, while *tyche* 'appears to be the only one of the old Greek gods whom Thucydides has kept.' (Leo Hjortsø). Thucydides described in his work the catastrophic Greek civil war in the second half of the 5th century B.C.. At a time of instability, when the individual lost his security and confidence in the state, in *polis*, he felt himself at the mercy of unseen powers: *tyche* was the name given to them by the intellectuals, but the ordinary people feared them under the names of many other gods.

At the end of the unstable 4th century B.C. Epicure looked at the contemporary world and concluded that the world must have come into existence by accident. While Aristotle had seen a divine purpose in the universe, Epicure's world knew of no such purpose, though his philosophy did: its object was to liberate man from fear and to show the way from surrounding disharmony to harmony within; the theoretical precondition for putting this psychological freedom into practice was the conviction that man in fact, by nature, is a free being, and not at the mercy of metaphysical forces. Epicure then took over Democritus' atoms and used them to construct a world in which there was no place for gods (Epicure's gods were naturally enough Epicureans and did not worry about the world), but Epicure differed from Democritus by allowing his atoms to depart from the straight

28

movement which Democritus ascribed to them — thus providing the possibility of chance — and of human freedom. Since, according to Democritus, the soul was also an atom (which in Latin came to be called *individuum*, indivisible), the atom theory was a very natural basis for a philosophy which like Epicure's no longer took the whole, *cosmos*, but the individual as its point of departure.

Epicure, who in his way was not far from a 'modern' concept of nature, was not originally interested in it, but he interpreted it according to need; for him nature was first and foremost human nature, the natural human needs, the satisfaction of which provides happiness. Like the Cynics he insisted that the sufficient is the most satisfying and that the superfluous is the most unsatisfying; it was thus a misconception when gourmands and lechers were later called 'pigs from the sty of Epicure'. Nevertheless, it was not entirely without justification that good Greek citizens saw the Epicureans as bad citizens, since Epicure had to recognise the fact that the service of the state disturbed philosophical calm and thus encouraged his disciples to 'live in hiding'. Epicure took the consequence of the fact that the individual was no longer naturally anchored in the city state: he allowed him to be himself.

Epicure founded his school of philosophy in Athens in 306 B.C.. A few years previously, his philosophical rival and antithesis, Zenon from Cyprus, had come to Athens where he visited the various schools of philosophy, Plato's Academy, Aristotle's Lykeion, but particularly learned from Krates the Cynic before starting his own school in the colonnade, *Stoa*, from which Stoicism derived its name.

Zenon's philosophical aim, 'Stoic' calm, was not very different from that of Epicure; through his philosophy he, too, offered the individual liberation from his surroundings. However, while Epicure had been content to observe that man is not a political animal by nature, but an individual, Zenon had no intention of severing the natural ties between the individual and society. Under all circumstances man is a social creature, and if the circumstances are so bad that the individual cannot achieve his rightful place in society, he still has a natural urge to work for the common good; therefore a good man like Socrates will emerge in opposition to a bad state. Zenon, who was not a born Athenian, was the right person to emphasise the difference between the state in which man is born by chance and the human society to which he belongs by birth. He was thus able to conclude the long philosophical discussion as to whether law is based on nature or convention by distinguishing between the law and the legal system valid in the individual state, *polis*, and the one, natural, law which applies to the entire human community, *kosmopolis*, and which by nature makes all men equal. It is this natural equality which is at the root of the Stoic idea that every man, irrespective of his station, has the possibility of realising himself or, to use the Stoic term, of 'becoming wise'. The wise man is not a product of his surroundings, but is master of them.

That man is born to wisdom, though by no means born wise, means in its turn that man is by nature not only a social but also a rational being; it is precisely the social instincts and the propensity for reason which give to the human being who by birth is the weakest the possibility of becoming the strongest, and which give human life a *moral* goal. The animal is what it is by nature; man must become what he is by dint of his reason. In this we find the second essential difference between Epicure and Zenon, a difference which is closely connected with the first: that the object of human striving is not (individual) happiness, but the moral attitude which benefits human society as a whole — though it may not suit any one random state.

For Zenon being wise means 'being in harmony' — with oneself and thereby with Reason. Zenon's successors as leaders of the school in Athens, Cleanthes and Chrysippos, modified the expression to 'being in harmony with nature', thus modifying also the meaning of this old Sophist concept, which the Cynics had practised in a somewhat anarchical manner. To the Stoics nature does not mean natural, selfish instincts, but rational nature, the logical cosmos which because of his reason man can be more in harmony with than can unreasoning creatures. For Zenon and his successors it was obvious that the universe was regulated by purpose and reason, and the thought that it had come into being by accident was scandalous to them. This is the third decisive point of disagreement with the Epicureans. In the Stoic view fortune influences the external world, but not the wise man: to become wise is to liberate oneself from one's surroundings and to fulfil one's mission, which is preordained — by God or Fate or reason or nature, for to the Stoics all these are one and the same thing. Unlike the Epicureans the Stoics do not place God outside the world, and unlike Plato and Aristotle they do not place him above the world, but they identify the divine and the natural and thus replace Plato's dualism with a monistic theory.

In the course of time a discrepancy has certainly arisen between the eternal intention of Fate and the more arbitrary intentions of human beings, between natural law and the prevailing conditions of justice — for there would be no need for Stoicism if conditions still made it easy for man to realise himself. Like Plato and Aristotle, Zenon, too, wrote a 'state', a *Politeia* (which like the other writings of the early Stoics has been lost and is only known from quotations and references by others); in it he, too, places the ideal society at the beginning of things, when the law of nature still prevailed, and when differences between men had not appeared. But even in the progressively increasing divergency from nature, which comes with civilisation, there is still a certain element of harmony; for the moral decline is an attendant phenomenon of the cosmic process which will finally result in the world conflagration in which the universe will purify itself and begin afresh. Eternity is not, as with Plato, above time but in it, and the wise man has eternity within himself when in Stoic tranquillity he lives in time but is raised above time: in the beginning everything was the same, and the wise man is still the same. It was not for nothing that the Stoics liked to compare the untroubled progress of the wise man with that of the heavenly bodies.

In this way Zenon and his successors were able to gather the various threads of Greek philosophy into a coherent pattern at a time when coherence was not clearly to be seen. The Stoic philosophy, which fixed the eternal in time, did so successfully in the sense that this became the dominant train of philosophical thinking for half a millenium, for the period normally called 'Hellenism', which is usually thought of as a time of disintegration. In the ancient world time, even a time of disintegration, went slowly: great catastrophes did not give people a different view of things, but they made them believe that the end was near. Christianity, which more or less unnoticed arose in the midst of it all, at the time of Seneca, and which, with its moral concepts was not uninfluenced by Stoicism, nevertheless contained a new view of nature and history, and with its radical distinction between time and eternity led to the definitive break with the primitive concept of reality — and to the modern view of science and history.

II. HISTORY AND MORALS

History and fate

There is the all-important difference between ancient civilisations and our modern industrial civilisation that the ancient ones favoured what was old, while our modern world prefers what is new. 'The customs of our forefathers' was the supreme expression of moral quality for the Romans; they were always on the look-out for a precedent, which is really quite remarkable as, despite Alexander the Great, there was no precedent for their own conquest of the world. The tiny community of peasants which Rome had originally been, gradually extended over most of the known world; this demanded different customs of the Romans from those of their forefathers, and it led to internal crises. When, in 146 B.C., the last important enemy, Carthage, had been overcome, Rome divided against itself. However, in the opinion of the Romans themselves this was not because they had continued to observe the primitive practices of their forefathers, but because the customs of their forefathers had been forgotten.

However fond the Romans were of writing and creating history, they never got hold of the idea that men create their own history. Admittedly, there are a couple of old Roman proverbs saying that everyone is the architect of his own fortune, or that fortune favours the brave, but what they actually say is that through bravery man can ensure the favours of fortune; he can fashion his own fortune, but not create it. Thus the brave Romans were the tools of fortune, *fortuna*, and if fortune deserted them this was seen in a diminution of bravery and a decline in morals.

In the middle of the 2nd century B.C. a Greek by the name of *Polybios* set about describing how almost the entire world came under Roman domination within less than fifty years. In his opinion this was because of the moral superiority of the Romans and thanks to their constitution, which he considered the best in the world. But showing how this happened meant to him 'giving readers a general view of the workings of fortune,' for he saw the achievement of the Romans as 'the most wondrous and beneficial work of fortune'.

Polybios thought that he could already discern the seeds of moral decay in victorious Rome, but he did not see in this a *reason* why fortune should let Rome down, but rather a sign that it was doing so. To argue that fortune determines the progress of history is tantamount to saying that the same law of natural necessity can be applied to history as to nature. Everything which originates in time must decay in time, and the State, like anything else, is subject to a natural cycle; if it is not destroyed from outside it will disintegrate from internal causes just when, like Rome, it has achieved a position of unassailed superiority.

What Polybios described as a general historical pattern Roman historians believed they had experienced a hundred years later. At the time of Julius Caesar *Sallust* wrote: 'When the State through hard work and justice had become great, when mighty kings had been conquered in battle, when wild tribes and great nations had been brought to their knees, when Carthage, Rome's great rival for power, had been completely destroyed and lay open to Rome by land and sea, then *fortuna* began to rage and reduce everything to chaos. For men who had easily borne toil and danger, doubt and difficulty, peace and the luxury which at other times would have been desirable became a burden and a misery. First came the desire for money, then the desire for power, and they formed, so to speak, the basis of all evil.'

This was written under the impression of the civil wars which had devastated Rome for a hundred years. But when Octavian had brought the civil war to an end and had been given the title of Augustus, and when peace reigned over all, *Livy* nevertheless found the time ripe to enquire what qualities led to Roman domination of the world and how it was that morals then steadily declined until they reached their lowest point in his day. In Livy's opinion, too, luxury had brought greed in its train: it was as though the luxury and power which had been won because of the good qualities had then resulted in the bad ones, in greed and ambition. This seems to be a good materialistic explanation: it was easy enough for their forefathers to be frugal as long as their circumstances did not permit anything else. The luxury which had flowed to Rome especially from the conquests in the East at the time of the civil wars changed the economic and political structure of Roman society and played its part in undermining the old social virtues. But even if the historians could indicate a connection between

33

luxury and moral decay, the only cause which they could find for the moral decay was — that manners had declined because *fortuna* had begun to rage. This fatalism was so deeply rooted in the Romans that they never thought of looking for material causes for the pernicious greed for material goods which they called *luxuria*. In Livy's opinion the strange thing was not that morals were decaying, for that is the law of history, but that it was so long before the decay set in in Rome: 'In no other state did greed and luxury assert themselves so late; in no other state have poverty and frugality been so highly esteemed for so long.'

If it is assumed that fate has decreed what is to happen, it is natural to try to discover what is to come. Omens were considered before any decisions of public concern were made in Rome: the auguries read signs in the behaviour of birds, the haruspices in the entrails of sacrificial animals. Of course, anyone who has gained insight into the future can speak with greater authority than those who have nothing to cling to except their own opinion, and the right to consult the omens, the *auspicium*, was quite reasonably reserved for the highest authorities in the state. It was a political weapon, and the Romans knew enough about *Realpolitik* to be able to manipulate the sacred omens when it suited their political ends. A high-ranking official could thus prevent a popular assembly by maintaining that he had heard thunder. From this it should not be concluded that high-ranking members of society did not themselves believe in the omens which they sometimes got by cheating; innocents who have cheated in order to win a game are quite likely to forget that they have cheated and to remember only that they have had luck on their side. Even an outstanding person such as Julius Caesar, a man who more than any other Roman might well be suspected of ignoring things to which others attached importance, believed at least in his own *fortuna*.

Romulus and Pythagoras

At that important moment when the twin brothers Romulus and Remus were about to found Rome they had, of course, to read the omens. Remus saw six vultures, but Romulus saw twelve and therefore considered that he was right in founding the city. These twelve birds were later thought to be an omen concerning the age of the city: Rome's days were thus numbered from the start, though it was not quite certain how the sum was to be done. When Caesar had reformed the calendar to give the year 365 days, there were those who thought that each bird must represent a month in an *annus magnus*, and as Rome was invaded and almost destroyed by the Gauls 365 years after the founding of the city, i.e. in 388 B.C. there were grounds for fearing a new crisis at the end of the second *annus magnus* in 23 B.C., especially with the renewed outbreak of civil war after the murder of Caesar in 44 B.C..

It was a bad omen that Romulus murdered his brother when he founded Rome. In general Romans did not bother too much about the odd fratricide here and there, but at a time of civil or fratricidal war, when some were looking for and others fearing the strong man who could unify the divided state, Romulus became a contentious figure. He was, of course, still the founder of the city and its first great warrior, but at the same time he was a king, and once the Romans had turned out their last king (c. 500 B.C.) they were inclined to think of freedom as being freed from a king. In the year of Caesar's death Cicero thought it necessary to maintain that Romulus had put aside brotherly love and humanity in favour of what he saw as his own interests; the fact that Remus had upset him — by jumping over the puny city wall which Romulus had begun to build — only gave him an outward appearance of having been justified. Meanwhile, Romulus' people took after their ancestor: they were easily upset and inclined when angry to take the law into their own hands; the civil war was the consequence of that.

The transition from a society based on kinship to one founded on citizenship, from the law of vengeance to the rule of law, was not easy for the Romans, who always had the dual task of maintaining peace at home and waging war abroad. According to Livy even Romulus' successor, King Numa, was faced with this problem; he belonged to a different tribe from Romulus and encountered the difficulties which naturally arise when several tribes who so far have waged war against each other are brought together and have to learn to live with one another. 'By means of law and justice and good morals' says Livy, 'Numa wanted to re-found the city which had been created by the force of arms. But he saw that the men who had been hardened by

35

military service could not accustom themselves to these virtues. Therefore he built the Temple of Janus as a witness to war and peace, for he believed that he must reduce his people's desire for war and turn them away from the use of arms. The open temple was a sign that the state was prepared for war; the enclosed temple signified that the Romans were living at peace with their neighbours. After Numa's reign it was twice closed, once after the Punic War (against Carthage, 264 - 41 B.C.) . . . and once after the Battle of Actium (31 B.C.). The Gods allowed our age to experience this: then the Emperor Augustus achieved peace on land and sea.'

King Numa was considered to be a pupil of the Greek philosopher Pythagoras, and although this does not agree with the chronology, since Numa is supposed to have ruled about 700 B.C. and Pythagoras lived in the 6th century B.C., there is a good logic in connecting the legendary prince of peace with Pythagoras, who is said to have been the first man to call himself a philosopher. At any rate he was one of the Greek philosophers who proclaimed a new moral code in the great period of transition, when 'law was to be king', replacing the will of the absolute ruler. Pythagoras had travelled in Egypt and Babylon and then been active in Greek colonies in southern Italy; several cities there could trace their laws back to him. Thus there was an obvious geographical reason why Pythagoras should be the first philosopher to exert an influence on Rome. Like other philosophers at the time he sought to found law on the natural laws of the universe; his observation of the numerical connection between pitch and the length of the vibrating string led to the theory that the universe in general is determined by numerical relationships; in Rome *mathematici* became the name for Pythagoreans — and astrologers.

When society took away from the individual tribe the right to assert the law, it meant that vengeance, previously a duty, was now a crime. But it was, and still is, a contradiction in terms to maintain that it is a crime to kill a fellow citizen but a heroic deed to kill members of another tribe or nation; or it would be a contradiction if solidarity within the community were not a precondition for external strength. Pythagoras, as far as is known, was one of the first to make the epoch-making discovery that under any circumstances at all it is evil to kill a fellow creature. In consequence of the doctrine of the transmigration of souls, Pythagoras also counted animals as fellow creatures, and so his view could only seem heretical in the extreme in Rome, where animal sacrifices and the interpretation of the entrails of sacrificial animals was at the very heart of the state religion. Strictly speaking a moral code which forbids killing must mean death to a society which is always at war.

Nevertheless, in the second half of the 4th century B.C. a statue of Pythagoras was erected in the Forum in Rome, and it was even maintained that he had been a Roman citizen. At that time the Romans were engaged in extending their power over the whole of Italy and thus came into closer contact with the Greeks (in southern Italy), whom they regarded with mixed feelings. It may well be that the Romans felt that they were on their way up and the Greeks on their way down, but the Roman upstarts could not help seeing that the Greeks had something which they themselves lacked. In order to put this right they simply identified their own somewhat dull gods, Jupiter, Juno, Minerva etc. with their livelier Greek counterparts, Zeus, Hera, Athene etc., and they traced their own history back to the Troy which the Greeks had conquered in the Trojan War of which Homer had written in 'The Iliad'; in this way they acquired a respectable past — and an old defeat to turn to their victory.

The transitional period between a society based on kinship and one based on law, which in Greece had produced the philosophers, produced no original thinkers in Rome. Just as the first Roman laws — the Laws of the Twelve Tablets from 451 B.C. — bore the stamp of Greek law, so the Romans also had to import a Greek philosophy of law. And the myth of the Pythagorean King Numa stems from the time when the Romans felt they had to create for themselves a respectable past in order to hold their own against the Greeks; so Numa was after all younger than Pythagoras. But Pythagoras' Roman citizenship was problematical: in 181 B.C. some Pythagorean writings which were ascribed to King Numa were burned after a decision of the Senate; even Julius Caesar, who was otherwise afraid of nothing, banished the leader of the Pythagoreans; Augustus, Tiberius and Claudius followed his example. It was probably less the pacifism of the Pythagoreans than their preoccupation with astrology as a means of predicting the future that worried those in power; they believed so firmly and unswervingly in the future that they wanted to reserve the knowledge of it for themselves.

Vengeance and Law

Roman law, often said to be Rome's outstanding gift to succeeding generations, was not compiled until after the fall of the West Roman Empire. In the field of law, too, the Romans preferred to keep to precedent rather than rules, and the first primitive laws, the Laws of the Twelve Tablets from 451 B.C., were and remained the foundation of their law.

Since law in principle limits power, those in power are in principle not interested in the law and only legislate when the people acquire sufficient social significance to insist on their demands. In Rome, as in Greece, it was trade with other tribes which led to a more demanding citizenry. Rome's development from a primitive peasant society to a primitive urban society took place under Etruscan rule; when the last Etruscan king had been dethroned by the oldest families, whose 'fathers' — *patres* — had seats on the council, the Senate, such sharp divisions appeared in the population that two words had to be coined to distinguish between them: *populus* which betokened the privileged patrician families, and *plebs*, the common run of tradespeople, artisans and smallholders with no political power. The state gods Jupiter, Juno, Minerva, who were given their temple on the Capitol in 509 B.C., were the gods of the patricians, but the plebeians were powerful enough to erect a temple for the more earthbound gods Ceres, Libera, Liber (Demeter, Persefone, Dionysos) on the Aventine in 493. The patricians were in control of the Senate and Assembly, and the plebeians formed their own counterblast to the Assembly and chose their own representatives, the popular tribunes; when, at a critical moment, the *plebs* threatened a collective exodus, the patricians felt compelled to recognise the popular tribunes, who were given the right to intervene if a (patrician) civil servant abused his power over a plebeian; in time they were given the right of veto over all decisions affecting the public at large, except for war and peace. The tribunes succeeded in establishing this limitation on the arbitrary exercise of power betokened by the publication of the Laws of the Twelve Tablets.

These laws do not signify a final transition from a law based on family and vengeance to one more fully founded on civil justice, but rather a transitional phase from which the Romans never quite emerged: it is against this background that Seneca's human legal concepts must be understood. From time immemorial the father of the household had had unlimited authority over all his house, *familia*, which was originally a self-sufficient unit; many matters, for instance immorality by female members of the family, were even at the time of the emperors still under the jurisdiction of the family father; right until A.D. 374 he had the right to expose unwanted children. In Seneca's day it was possible for a son to take his father to law, but Seneca also mentions a case of a father whipping his son to death, which led to no other punishment than that the *people* fell upon him in the Forum, so that the emperor had to protect him!

The fact that the Roman state interfered as little as possible in the private lives of its citizens must not be seen as an expression of a 'liberal' ideology, but as a continuation of traditional family justice. The state had no means of enforcing the law, not even a police force. Admittedly, the Laws of the Twelve Tablets forbade private vengeance, but the injured party could put his case to an official, who could then permit him to take his revenge. In reality the principle of retaliation still applied, even if the law recommended reconciliation. Taking the law into one's own hands, especially when it came to defending one's own property, was allowed for a long time in Imperial Rome: 'People will not allow others to take possession of their property,' writes Seneca, 'and at the slightest disagreement over property boundaries they resort to stones and weapons, but they do let others involve themselves in their lives; indeed they drag them in and let them become masters of them.'

The legal term for claiming one's right was *vindicare*, which often simply means to take revenge. Cicero, who otherwise condemns cruelty by one citizen to another, nevertheless considers *vindicatio*, the urge to avenge physical violence or any other form of insult, as a natural instinct, just like piety, a sense of duty, gratitude, respect and truthfulness! It was beneath the dignity of the Romans to tolerate *injuria*, a concept which was of enormous importance and extremely widespread in Rome; apparently the old Romans only allowed themselves to be insulted by deeds, but at the time of the emperors they could also be insulted by words. Consequently the violent attacks on people which were common at the time of the Republic are no longer found in the works of authors from the time of the emperors. Strangely enough, the Laws of the Twelve Tablets only prescribed fines for *injuria*, but death for singing lampoons. However, to sing lampoons outside the door of an official was the way in which the general populace could express its discontent; as the people were now protected by the law, this popular form of retribution was strictly prohibited.

Since the responsibility for punishment for an insult rested with the injured party, it is obvious that it was more of a risk to insult a great man than a little man; moreover, an important man would be more likely to feel an insult to his dignity. In reality the little man had no possibility at all of asserting *his* rights unless he secured the help of an important man. So the lesser members of society sought legal protection from the powerful, as their *clients*, and the standing of an important man was to some extent assessed on the basis of the numbers of his clients. So Roman society was not merely divided 'horizontally' into classes, but also 'vertically' into 'families', and while there was no class solidarity there was a strong feeling of solidarity in the families, as they were based on mutual interest; the clients received material support from their 'patrons' and in return they supported them in elections. The result of this was that the internal conflicts in Rome, once *plebs* were given equality with *populus*, took on less the character of a class struggle than of a conflict between powerful men with their dignity to defend and their insults to avenge. Julius Caesar's reason for throwing the dice and marching on Rome was that he had sustained an insult to his dignity; he had, he wrote, in no way come 'to commit evil, but only to defend himself against the malice of his opponents . . . and to vindicate freedom for himself and for the Roman people who had been oppressed by a clique.'

Even if Imperial Rome limited the right to take the law into one's own hands — which had undermined the Roman republic — the attitudes of great and small remained unchanged. They are parodied by Petronius in his novel 'Satyricon' from the time of Seneca; in it the young lady Quartilla has prayed to the god Priapus for a remedy for a cold and been referred to the puppies who are the principal characters in the novel; she assures them that an entire regiment would have 'avenged the insult and defended her dignity' (injuriam meam vindicaret et dignitatem) if they had not obliged her. In similar circumstances the well-to-do could have called on a whole regiment of clients.

The classes

Classis originally means call-up and subsequently becomes the designation for those who have the right to be called up, for in Rome it was a privilege to serve in the army. At first *plebs* were outside the class; later the entire population was divided into five classes according to the equipment they could manage. The equestrians, who provided two horses, were the first class, while those who owned nothing and only served to maintain society by producing children, the *proletarii*, were classless. All those citizens who served in the army made up the popular assembly which elected the top officials, consuls and prætors. Since these 'honorary positions', *honores*, were unpaid, a certain level of wealth was necessary before it was possible to accept them, and as those in the popular assembly always voted according to their class, the rich always had the final say. The best qualification for being appointed to the administration was — for the Romans who were so conscious of the past — that one's forefathers had done so before; it was almost always the same families' members who were elected — and who filled the Senate, in which retired civil servants were automatically given a seat. Formally the Senate was an advisory body for the consuls, who had executive power, *imperium*, but as both consuls and the popular assembly were elected annually, while the Senators were appointed for life, only the Senate was able to carry out a long-term policy. In times of war the Senate strengthened its position at the expense of the people, and as it was always a time of war, a powerful élite gained control of Rome at the same time as Rome gained control of most of the world. Rome was still a society based on families, even though it was the size of one's fortune as well as kinship which now decided rank.

In a way Rome was really also still a peasant society, as the ownership of land was considered to be the only respectable form of property, and commerce and skills were considered less dignified means of assuring a livelihood. It was beneath the dignity of the Senate aristocracy to take part in business transactions; from 218 B.C. it was also prohibited by law, something which indicates that they did not always take their dignity so seriously. The constant growth of the empire, however, also expanded the market and the need for merchants, and as the wealth which merchants could earn qualified

41

them to do military service as equestrians, the word equestrian gradually came to mean the well-to-do middle class. The equestrians often formed a sort of limited company, acting as contractors for the state, being given responsibility for the erection of public buildings, for roadmaking and for mines. By dint of their profits and connections the equestrians could also earn their way into the Senate, although it was not easy for a 'new man', *homo novus*, to get so far; of the 108 consuls in the years between 200 and 146 B.C. only eight came from 'new' families.

From the start, Rome's expansion was not carried out from imperialist motives and — until the destruction of Carthage and Corinth in 146 B.C. — only partly from economic interests. As late as the 2nd century B.C. there was an obvious reluctance to annex foreign territory; the Romans were content to turn enemies into allies, an art which they understood better than other nations either before or since, and they were not interested in having armies stationed in foreign countries. The army was largely based on the free farmers, and it could therefore only be strengthened at the expense of agriculture.

That is what happened during the second century. The farmers had to spend longer periods in the field, while the import of cheap corn from Sicily and Africa (which became Roman provinces in 241 and 146 B.C. respectively) made corn production less profitable; prisoners of war were cheap labour for the landowners. The logical consequence was that they bought up smaller farms and ran their growing estates by means of slave labour. Instead of corn they produced wine and olives for export and thus developed a financial interest in beating their rivals; it was in fact a great landowner, the elder Cato, who wanted Carthage destroyed. Another senator believed that the city should be spared, as an enemy was necessary to strengthen Roman solidarity; even the conqueror of the city, Cornelius Scipio Æmilianus, was filled with grim forebodings of the destruction of Rome when he saw the ruins of Carthage.

Sallust said that it was after the destruction of Carthage that *fortuna* began to rage. Wealth, which it was easier to conquer than to create, made the rich more interested in fresh expansion and the poor more numerous; constant military service prevented the farmers from cultivating their land; the middle class of free peasants was reduced in numbers, so that the efficiency of the army decreased; slave rebellions

42

in the provinces made it plain how risky it was to be dependent on the work of slaves.

It was against this social background that two tribunes, the famous brothers Tiberius and Gajus Gracchus, suggested that land should be made available to those who owned none, partly by the establishing of 'colonies' in the provinces, partly by parcelling out *ager publicus*, the common land which had been annexed by the conquest of Italy, and which the tenants, men of the Senate aristocracy, had grown accustomed to considering as their private property. The opposition of the Senate made especially Gajus Gracchus see it as his task to break its power and to return power to the popular assembly. With that object in view he sought not only to win the people but also the equestrians for his cause and to turn them against the Senate; he managed to get a law passed on the sale of cheap corn to the poor of Rome; he gave the equestrians access to the Bench, which hitherto had been reserved for Senators, and he gave the equestrian companies in the provinces the right to gather taxes. These measures lasted longer than the Gracchus brothers, and their effect was not what was intended. The advent of cheap corn made the landless less interested in joining the colonies in the provinces and, indeed, it even attracted some of the rural poor to Rome. And the senators, who as vice-regents in the provinces were looking after their own financial selves, were now assisted by the equestrians: in their new dignity as tax gatherers, these 'publicans', who appear as sinners in the Gospels, further helped to bleed the provinces and to stimulate imperialist policies.

Civil war: fighting for honour – and the army

The fact that the Romans had no concept of progress makes it difficult to distinguish between progressive and conservative Roman politicians. Strictly speaking the reform programme of the Gracchus brothers was conservative, as the consequence of it would have meant the return to a city state democracy incapable of ruling a world-wide empire. This does not mean that the idea of colonies was not far-sighted, as other influential Romans could see. But the more influence they had, the greater must be their fear that others should acquire greater influence than they; as influence depended on the number of backers, of clients, no far-sighted statesman who wanted to improve the lot of the people could avoid the suspicion of trying to win the people for himself. Therefore they had to be opposed. This was the fate of the Gracchus brothers: they were murdered by the Senate's men in 133 and 121 B.C. respectively.

A conflict arose between those who wanted to break and those who wanted to strengthen the power of the Senate. The former came to be known as *populares*, demagogues, by the latter, who called themselves *optimates*, the best; the two words can best be 'translated' as the people's party and the Senate party, but in reality the conflict was not so much between parties, not to say classes, as between programmes. It was fought between military leaders intent on honour and influence — and on control of the army which not even a military leader can do without.

Romans had never qualified themselves for a political post by their political ideas, but always by dint of family relationships and connections, which euphemistically were called 'friendships', and by their moral qualities. It was a dogma that the best should rule (and so the rulers called themselves the best) and that success was the reward for virtue. As has already been remarked: fortune favours the brave. Virtue, *virtus*, was the bravery appropriate to a man, *vir*, and the success he received as the reward for virtue was the glory, *gloria*, which he achieved in the field of glory. But significantly enough, *gloria*, which originally meant reputation gained through great achievements, gradually acquired the secondary meaning of seeking for fame, and at last the entirely negative sense of ambition; thus Seneca talks of, 'the ambition which is repulsive, but common to many rulers, to demonstrate their power by means of terror.' This reflects a social-psychological development: the good old Romans had gone to war to achieve honour in the service of the State; now the upper class started one war after another purely for gain, and the military men who conducted the wars did not only aim at winning glory and the spoils of war, but also used the spoils of war in an effort to gain the support of the army. The immediate cause of the civil war was the question of who was to lead a campaign in the East; Gajus Marius, the candidate of the people's party, or Cornelius Sulla, that of the Senate.

Gajus Marius was a 'new man' who had made his way by earning a fortune as a 'publican' and by marrying into one of the ruling families, the Julian family. He had gained honour as a military leader in Africa, and when the Cimbrians from Jutland and the Teutons from Northern Germany threatened Rome the Senate felt obliged to accept him as consul for a number of years running. Marius threw back the Germanic tribes, but with an army which, unlike the old Roman armies, did not consist of landowners. He took the consequences of their no longer being numerically strong enough to make up the army, and he called the proletariat to arms with promises of wages and land after they had finished their service. By an irony of fate it was former soldiers, veterans, who came to populate the colonies which the Gracchus brothers had wanted to establish precisely in order to avoid this development. It turned out to be inevitable and fatal: the soldiers were now the clients of their commander, more loyal to him than to the State.

Sulla had brought an end to the war started by Rome's allies in Italy, who were embittered at having to fight for Rome without enjoying Roman citizenship; it ended with their winning citizenship but no real influence. A single tribe, the Samnites, refused to accept the conditions and fought in the civil war on the side of Marius; after Sulla's victory, he lured 7000 Samnites to Rome with a promise of free conduct. Seneca tells of their fate: 'Sulla was at a meeting nearby ... and when he heard the screams from the thousands suffering under the sword, he said, "Let us continue, Senators; it is only a few rebels being executed on my orders." Nor was this a lie: to Sulla this was not a great number.'

Both parties proceeded with such ferocity that they had equal cause for revenge when the opportunity offered itself; and the opportunities came when first Sulla, then Marius, then Sulla again gained power in Rome. Sulla has the honour of having introduced 'proscriptions', lists of people whom all were entitled to kill. But he was also generous: he freed thousands of his opponents' slaves and made them his own clients. He was the only Roman commander who voluntarily relinquished power and gave it back to the Senate, having broken the power of the popular assembly and the equestrians. But the power of the Senate depended on the army, and the army was no longer in the hands of the State, but of the military commanders. Sulla's arrangement was overturned by two generals, Crassus and Pompejus, who had fought on his side and whose power the Senate feared — as a consequence of which they allied themselves with the equestrians and the people's party in order to achieve the consulate in 70 B.C..

As a young man Pompejus had raised an army of his own clients and had started for himself. In the 60's, with the support of the people's tribunes and the equestrians, he was entrusted with a large number of extraordinary military powers; in Asia Minor he created two new provinces and various vassal states; the equestrians had been extremely dissatisfied with his predecessor, Lucullus, who had been too honest in the way he had acted as vice-regent. Pompejus opened vast areas for them to exploit, and for the soldiers to plunder. In 62 B.C., when he returned from the East, the Senate feared that he might assume dictatorial powers, but Pompejus entered Rome as a private individual; through this gesture he obviously expected to win the confidence of all and to be entrusted with the power which he would not arrogate; but he was met with distrust both by the Senate and the people's parties.

In Rome Julius Caesar, into whose Julian family Marius had married, inherited his clientele; he sought to win the people's support through such lavish entertainments that the Senate had to pass a law limiting their extent. In this way he acquired an enormous debt which Crassus, the richest man in Rome, paid. Crassus was admittedly Pompejus' 'friend', but he was jealous of his success; he himself had not gained any honour since 71 B.C., when he had put down the last great slave rebellion, the Spartacus rebellion, and had 6000 slaves crucified along the Appian Way. As Pompejus felt rejected by the Senate he sought an understanding with Caesar and sealed the 'friendship' by marrying his daughter Julia, so now Crassus had nothing to do except support both the great men; in 60 B.C. they entered into a private alliance which is called the first triumvirate (rule by three men) and thus ruled the State but not each other.

Caesar managed to be elected consul in 59 B.C. and in the following years he got hold of the vice-regency in Gaul and thereby an army; with this he won a long series of victories over the Gauls and the Germanic tribes which he himself immortalised in his accounts of the Gallic Wars. In Rome both his enemies and his 'friends' were equally appalled at his successes. Crassus tried to do something similar and went to war against the Parthans, a Persian tribe in control of Persia, but be suffered a humiliating defeat and a miserable death. Although vice-regent in Spain, Pompejus dared not leave Rome, where anarchy reigned. In 52 B.C. the Senate found itself compelled to give him dictatorial powers simply to establish law and order; Pompejus marched his army into Rome, where no army had ever before been stationed in peacetime. Relying on Pompejus' army, the Senate was emboldened to challenge Caesar and called him home, but Caesar refused to give up his army unless Pompejus did the same. As usual, Pompejus wanted to keep on good terms with both parties and assured Caesar that he had always put the State above private connections. Quite apart from this, the private connection between them had been weakened on the death of Julia in 54 B.C.. Caesar, however, felt that his great achievements were not being recognised; out of consideration for his own dignity and the freedom of the people he marched on Rome in 49 B.C.; the following year Pompejus was defeated at Farsalos in Greece and murdered in Egypt, where he had sought refuge. Thereafter Caesar ruled as an absolute dictator in Rome.

Caesar and Cato

Caesar's real antithesis was not Pompejus, who 'was no better, but more furtive', but *Cato the Younger*, a senator who saw it as his duty to oppose those states within the State which the powerful men with their clients really were. He described the state of affairs in Rome with words which have been used of social economy in a later age: 'public poverty, private wealth', and according to Sallust he addressed his fellow senators as: 'You, who always have put houses, estates, statues and paintings above the State ...'

His idea was that all should be the clients of the State; Caesar drew the consequences of the fact that the State in practice had been dissolved and saw the victory of one will, his own, as the only solution. Cato consistently condemned all illegal methods, whereas Caesar consistently employed any means which suited his sole purpose. If Søren Kierkegaard is right in thinking that purity of the heart is to will one thing, then Sallust could rightly praise both Cato and Caesar as men of 'enormous moral strength' (*virtus*) — in contrast to Pompejus, who would have preferred to use legal means to achieve illegal power. Pompejus had in fact at one time sought Cato's 'friendship' and wanted to marry *his* daughter before he landed in Caesar's forecourt. In his

47

otherwise very positive biography of Cato, Plutarch argues that he should have been less uncompromising on this one point in order to avoid greater misfortunes; but as the moral guardian of the State Cato was forced to reject any connection with the man who at that time was the greatest danger to the State.

The confrontation between Cato and Caesar came when the Senate was sitting in judgement on Catalina, an impoverished aristocrat who, with Caesar's support, had attempted to become a consul; when he was not elected he had started a conspiracy which had been broken by Cicero, who was consul in 63 B.C.. Cato wanted to apply the death penalty, but Caesar reminded him that what is called anger in others is called arrogance and cruelty in those in power, and maintained that those who are in the highest positions can take fewest liberties. On that occasion Cato gained the support of the Senate, but when in power Caesar lived up to his words, and even turned them into a programme: 'Because of their cruelty our predecessors could not avoid incurring hatred and could only enjoy the fruits of victory for a short time, apart from the one man whose example I do not want to follow, Sulla. The new rational view in victory (*ratio vincendi*) must be that we arm ourselves with mercy (*misericordia*) and generosity (*liberalitas*).'

Caesar's gentleness, *clementia*, amazed everyone. Cicero, who after some hesitation joined Caesar's opponents, had previously declared him to be 'the only man on whose victory no one has lost his life, except in battle.' Later he asserted that Caesar had won over his opponents by 'a show of mercy'. But Caesar himself did not pretend his gentleness was more than it was seen to be; in his Gallic War he had not hidden the fact that he could be cruel when the situation demanded it. But apparently Caesar was psychologically more balanced than those who had gone before him, less prone to personal spite and more aware than they that victory demanded that the evil chain of vengeance should be broken.

Meanwhile the morals of gratitude were just as typical of the moral Romans as the sense of injury and the desire for vengeance. Seneca writes, significantly though perhaps with some exaggeration, 'There are murderers, tyrants, thieves, lechers, robbers, blasphemers, traitors — but the ungrateful man is the lowest of all.' It was through gratitude for help received that the client was tied to his patron; anyone who gave something to someone else placed him in his debt, and a debt of

Bronze bust, thought to be Seneca, from the 1st century, found in the Papyrus Villa in Herculanum. Museo Nazionale, Naples.

The Younger Cato (95–46 B.C.). Bronze bust fround in Morocco this century. Musée des Antiquités Pré-Islamiques, Rabat.

gratitude was a debt of honour. By granting his opponents their lives, Caesar made them all his clients and in fact put into practice Cato's idea that everyone should be clients of the State. Only the State happened to be Caesar. The enemies to whom he had shown mercy could not oppose him without being classed with or below murderers and traitors. No one realised this more clearly than Cato. After the defeat of Pompejus he, together with the rest of the army, had been sent to Africa; when Caesar had defeated this army in Thapsus in 46 B.C. he committed suicide in Utica: 'He would not be bound in gratitude to one who showed mercy to men over whom he had no rights.'

There were others who took a more liberal view of morals. However, through his demonstrative suicide Cato became the martyr of freedom and a moral challenge to the republicans, who had accepted the new order of things; in particular it was a challenge to his nephew and son-in-law, Marcus Brutus, who had fought on the side of Pompejus at Farsalos and allowed Caesar to show mercy to him. He wrote a book about Cato, and Caesar must have seen a danger in the Cato cult, for he took the time to write an Anti-Cato. This did not prevent Cato, who professed Stoicism and used to prepare himself for meetings of the Senate by reading the Stoic classics, from becoming the model for later Roman Stoics, the image of the Stoic man of wisdom.

Just over half way through the first century B.C. Stoicism had been introduced into Rome by the leader of the Stoic school in Athens, Panaitios, who had gained a good deal of influence over the powerful group of people around Scipio Æmilianus, the conqueror of Carthage. Panaitios had the same view of the State as the slightly older historian Polybios. As already seen, Polybios considered the Roman constitution to be the best in the world, because by dividing power between the consuls, the Senate and the popular assembly it combined monarchist, aristocratic and democratic elements. In *his* work on the state, Plato had shown how government by the best can degenerate into an oligarchy, which in its turn degenerates into government by the masses and this again into tyranny. Polybios, too, saw the 'fixed cycle' of constitutions as subject to the natural order of things. But as constitutions decline when one of the elements in the state gains the ascendency, it is precisely the 'mixed' state which is the best state, *res publica mixta*, which Panaitios and subsequently Cicero supported. What turns a large number of individuals into a community state is a general agreement as to what is just and socially useful; Cicero wanted *res publica*, the state, to be thought of as the 'cause of the people': that is what the leader of the state must serve.

It is a classical Stoic idea, first formulated by King Antigonos of Macedonia (276-29 B.C.), who was a pupil of Zenon himself, that the greatest should serve the least, that government is 'superior slavery'. Panaitios formulated a princely ideal characterised by justice, magnanimity and mercy towards conquered enemies. As it was a similar programme to that expressed by Caesar in his 'new rational view in victory', there is a terrible irony in the fact that the 'ideologist' behind the conspiracy against him, Marcus Brutus, was himself an adherent of Stoicism.

But the natural right of the people to murder a tyrant was part of Stoic thinking. In the eyes of the conspirators, who admittedly did not belong to the people but to the disenchanted Senate aristocracy, and who were led by the two prætors Brutus and Cassius, Caesar was not the servant but the tyrant of the people. The fact that after murdering him on the 15th March 44 B.C. they did nothing to gain power for themselves shows that they — or at least Brutus — did not wish to follow in Caesar's footsteps; however, it also shows that they — or Brutus — had not realised that the disintegration of the republic had not been brought about by Caesar but by the states within the State. Brutus, who assumed the cause of Pompejus, also assumed his lack of consistency: it was a contradiction in terms to bring down the tyrant but allow his arrangements to stand unaltered — as though *they* had been useful and not tyrannical.

Ever since that 15th March there has been a lively debate as to whether or not Caesar had a great political vision which he failed to realise. It has rightly been pointed out — by Erik Wistrand — that if he had such a vision he himself never indicated it with one word, even if he did energetically comment on his own cause: 'Everything indicates that the aim of his policy was his own *dignitas* and *gloria*, the traditional objective of all Roman aristocrats.' However, even if Caesar's policy was only a means to this end, it still meant that he had to try to get the State working again; first and foremost he had to break the power of the Senate aristocracy, which he did in principle by giving all citizens access to the Senate, by limiting the exploitation of the provinces, by securing the borders — and by procuring land for the soldiers and the proletariat. The arrangements made by Caesar were largely what the situation — and not merely the tyrant — demanded. Caesar's murderers soon had to realise, as Cicero, who sympathised with them, said in a letter (9th April, 44 B.C.): 'that regaining freedom was not the same as re-establishing the republic.' It was the same as a renewal of anarchy.

Brutus sought an understanding with Caesar's fellow-consul, Marcus Antonius, who at first appeared to be conciliatory. Then Caesar's adopted son and principal heir, the eighteen-year-old Octavian, appeared and claimed his inheritance, which Antonius had partly appropriated. Cicero, who at the critical moment when Brutus and Cassius had had to leave Rome, had made himself the leader of the Senate and attacked Antonius in a number of speeches, was of the opinion that the Senate could use Octavian against him, but Octavian saw through the plan and sought an understanding with Antonius — just as Pompejus had done with Caesar before him. In 43 B.C. — together with Lepidus, one of Caesar's officers — they formed the second triumvirate and had resort to the proscriptions which Sulla had introduced. Cicero was one of the many victims.

Cicero and humanitas

In the speeches from the beginning of his career directed against the vice-regent Verres, Cicero had attacked the way in which the ruling classes were exploiting the provinces. By the end of his life the great orator was the leader of the Senate aristocracy. It was thus no accident that he was an adherent of a 'mixed' state. He was and remained, for better or for worse, a 'new man', snobbish and self-centred; he was always boasting that in 63 B.C., when he was consul, he had put down the Catalina revolt, boasting 'not without reason, but without end', comments Seneca. But at the same time he was passionately concerned to work towards a state in which a new man *could* make his way and in which personal achievements weighed more heavily than inherited rank or 'friendship' and wealth: 'There is no more repulsive kind of state than that in which the rich are considered to be best,' he wrote in

51

his book on the State. In the same book he says, 'Anyone who has put himself at the disposal of the optimates and leaders loses the serious and dignified quality of his voice and his personal behaviour.'

He himself sometimes lost the dignified quality, but never his passionate commitment. The ambitious Cicero's greatest weakness was his desire to run the State himself, even if he was no statesman, but his greatest ambition was to create a new moral foundation for the State. In the age of imperialism and positivism it was not considered good form to provide a moral foundation for political thinking. In our century no one has been more ridiculed than Cicero, by scholars who were more inclined to praise glorious Caesar then hesitant Cicero. Compared with Caesar, Cicero was certainly the little man, the 'new' man, and his delight at the death of Caesar is almost embarrassing. Yet Caesar was great enough to know better than his 20th century admirers that, 'It is better to have extended the boundaries of the Roman spirit than of the Roman empire.' He was referring to Cicero. The Romans had extended their empire without asking themselves why; their historians could bewail the fact that the *virtus*, the moral strength, of their forefathers, which had created the empire, was not sufficiently alive to maintain it. But Cicero had a vague idea of something which Seneca understood better: that there was a need for a moral strength of quite a different order. And in his works *virtus* appears in happy union with a new concept, *humanitas*.

During Caesar's dictatorship, when Cicero felt excluded from politics, he wrote a long series of philosophical works in which he aimed at a more human version of the Roman warrior ideal. At the same time as working on his furious onslaught on Antonius, he wrote a book 'On friendship' and sought once more to give the concept of 'friendship' — which of course in Rome had come to mean useful connections — its rightful meaning of mutual kind feelings. Even though Cicero did not profess any one philosophy, but with an impressive universal view of Greek philosophy chose the best in it, it was especially the Stoic teaching of natural sympathy as the basis of the state which formed the basis of his own view of the state; it was through Cicero that the Stoic idea of the natural rights of man found its way into the American Declaration of Independence. Cicero does not occupy an important place in the history of philosophy, where it is the great and idiosyncratic systems which are most in evidence, but nevertheless he had a greater influence than most philosophers, less of course because of his moral weakness than by dint of his moral inspiration.

In Roman writers one often comes across the idea that a state based only on power is no different from a tribe of wild animals. The Stoics, who proclaimed a life 'in harmony with nature', argued that human nature is not naturally determined like animal nature but results from a moral challenge. It is in the work of meeting this challenge, of forming and fashioning oneself that *humanitas* arises which makes man, *vir*, into a human being, *homo*, and not merely a warrior. In the 2nd century B.C. Terence, the writer of many comedies, basing himself on the Greek Menander, had formulated the famous dictum, presumably inspired by Stoicism: *Homo sum, humani nil a me alienum puto* — I am a human being, and I consider nothing human to be alien to me. It is not Roman Law, but this humanism which Cicero and Seneca advocated, that is Rome's outstanding legacy to later ages.

Vergil and the Age of Gold

In 42 B.C. Octavian, and more especially Antonius, beat Cassius and Brutus at Filippi in Macedonia. This is the somewhat abbreviated way in which this is usually put, for it would be going too far to name all the soldiers — and in any case they are not known. But in spite of their anonymity the soldiers played an important part in the civil war; on several occasions they refused to give battle, and the most urgent problem for the victors of Filippi was to find land and wages for over a hundred thousand soldiers. Octavian seized vast areas in Italy for them; the former owners had to get out. In the first of the bucolic poems, 'Bucolica', which he wrote about 40 B.C. Vergil depicts a shepherd leaving his ship, talking to another whom Octavian has allowed to remain behind. Apparently Vergil attaches more importance to the good fortune of the one remaining than to the unhappiness of the one leaving, despite the fact that he himself had to leave his family estate in Mantua. The sacrifice was not too great a price for the peace which now seemed a reality.

One of the soldiers who had fought on the wrong side in Filippi was later to become famous — Horace. He wrote a bitterly ironic poem called 'The 16th Epode' exhorting his fellow citizens to leave Rome, which was collapsing under its own strength, and to go to sea and find the island of the blessed where Kronos, who had ruled in the Age of Gold, and whom the Romans called Saturnus, was thought still to rule. Presumably the poem was written after the peace again had been broken — and before Antonius and Octavian concluded another one in Brundisium (Brindisi) in 40 B.C.. As was customary, the pact between them was sealed by a marriage, between Octavian's sister, Octavia, and Antonius, despite the fact that he was already living with the Egyptian queen, Cleopatra.

Perhaps Vergil imagined that the fruits of this marriage would ensure peace for all time; perhaps the conclusion of peace in itself was sufficiently miraculous to remind him of strange thoughts of the prince of peace who had also been prophesied in the East. His famous fourth bucolic poem on the child redeemer is like a reply to Horace's suggestion that Rome should be given up: Vergil, too, dreamt of the Age of Gold replacing the Age of Iron, but to him it was a lofty and serious idea, not a bitter joke. It must still be remembered that Rome's days were numbered from the beginning and that the second *annus magnus* was approaching its end; the civil war and the moral decline were seen as symptoms of the end of time, and the prophecies ascribed to the priestess of Apollo, the Sibylla of Cumae, whose advice was sought in critical situations, also pointed to it. It is against this background that the enormous relief at the Peace of Brundisium must be understood; Vergil broke into song, dedicating the result to one of the consuls, Asinius Pollio, in this memorable year 40 B.C.:

Rustic muses, raise your voices.
We will sing in more powerful tones.
Not everyone is satisfied with scrub and stunted thicket;
our song is for the tall forest:
It shall reach the ears of the Consul.

Now is the age foretold by the Sibylla at its end.
Now are born new centuries.
Justice will return with the glorious days of old.
New things are blossoming, and their shoots are rooted
in heaven above.

A boy is born before whom the age of iron will
disappear, and from him will come a golden age
throughout the world.
Preserve him at his birth, O goddess.
Now reigns thy brother, O Apollo.
In your consulship, Pollio, arises the pride of our age,
glorious months are now beginning their procession.
In your consulship every trace of our shame will be
erased, and the earth will be freed from its eternal
fear.
He shall receive life like a god, he shall see heroes
consort with the gods, and he shall himself be seen
among gods, reign over a world at peace amidst the
virtues of former generations.

In the 30's B.C. Octavian consolidated his position in Italy, and
Antonius saw to his in the East. Octavian paved the way for the
coming show-down with a propaganda campaign which appealed to
Italic national sentiments: the West had to be defended against
Antonius who, it was said, was in Cleopatra's power and intended
removing the capital to Alexandria and making free Roman citizens
into the subjects of an oriental despotism. During these ten years
Vergil wrote his great poem 'Georgica', in praise of agriculture and
rural life and Italy. Just as his advent poem showed Hesiod's Age of
Gold and his goddess Justice, *Dike*, returning unexpectedly, his
Georgics are to some extent written in reply to Hesiod's 'Works and
Days': as Vergil presents it, work on the land is not a curse, but also a
work with man, throwing his virtues into relief: the moral decline in
the city is something in which the farmer has no part; despite the
pressures of the Age of Iron, his life still has something of the glory of
the Age of Gold about it. Since moral decline was said to be a symptom
of the end of time, the still extant peasant virtues of the forefathers still
provided a basis for arguing that a new start was possible. Vergil read
his poem to Octavian after he returned victorious from his final
confrontation with Antonius in the naval Battle of Actium in 31 B.C..
    In 27 B.C. the Senate honoured Octavian with the name of
Augustus, a word related to *auctoritas* which can be interpreted as 'he
who has (superior) authority'. He was now faced with the same task as

the mythical King Numa: turning rough warriors into a peaceful population. Meanwhile, the empire had become so vast that world peace had become necessary for internal politics unless Rome was again to be torn apart by quarrels between military leaders; so an obvious thing to do was to proclaim peace, *pax romana*, which was a necessity for Rome as Rome's special contribution to civilisation. Vergil formulated it in his epic, 'The Æneid':

> You, O Roman, remember that you must conquer nations;
> that shall be your art, and the law of peace you shall give,
> defend and protect the weak and vanquish the proud.

'The Æneid' is the story of how Æneas, the son of the goddess Venus (from whom Julius Caesar also boasted descent), after many battles and torments founded the Roman family. His final battle for the country in Latium he fought against Turnus, who represents both the original population and the ancient Roman martial virtues. He is savage and sensitive of his honour, seeks to confirm his *virtus* by gaining *gloria* — and it is no coincidence that it is only in the portrayal of the noble but primitive Turnus that Vergil relates these two traditionally related concepts to each other. His victor is a hero of a quite different type; he is constantly referred to as *Pius* Aneas, which in Christian tradition is usually translated by 'pious Æneas', but it is a piety which consists in putting the common good before private comfort, of renouncing one's own desires in favour of loftier demands — as Æneas must renounce his love of Dido because of the task which fate has given him. Thus *pietas* means family feeling, filial respect, etc., but Vergil applies it to the entire Roman family; it is precisely a *family* Æneas is to found, the family which in the Age of Iron had been split up, and which in the Age of Gold was again to be united.

In 'The Æneid' Vergil continued to prophesy the Age of Gold and presented the events of his day not merely as a result of past actions, but as their objective: Augustus was the man who was to come; this was clear already to the founder of the family:

> Here is the man, here is he who so often was
> promised, Caesar Augustus, that child of Caesar

who once more will create a golden age
for the land of Latium once rule by Saturnus.

It is no surprise that a poet should flatter someone in power; it had happened before Vergil, and it has happened since. It is more surprising that such an inspired poem as 'The Æneid' could contain everything that a ruler could desire; the poet could well have had his scruples. In his great novel, 'The Death of Vergil', Hermann Broch suggests that it was perhaps for this reason that Vergil wanted his uncompleted poem destroyed on his death. It was certainly not from any desire to please on the part of Vergil or the direct result of the wishes of Augustus — things of that kind have never been particularly inspiring. It was because Augustus corresponded to the 'mythical' awareness of the age: he *was* the man who was to come. Horace, too, who began by suggesting that people should leave Rome for the isles of the blessed, ended by placing the Age of Gold in Rome. Peace must have had a miraculous effect on a generation which had never known anything but war and which had a 'mythical' fear that the end of time was approaching.

In 'The Æneid' Vergil lets Jupiter himself belie the theory that Rome's days were numbered: 'Romans shall not be restricted by moving times or boundaries; I will give them power without end.' No gospel could be more welcome to Augustus. He knew how to make the most of the spirit of the age. In 17 B.C., six years after the end of Rome's second *annus magnus*, he found the time ripe to celebrate the beginning of a new epoch. It happened in a twelve-day long 'festival of the century', in which all Rome took part; perhaps this was the one and only occasion on which it was possible to gather the entire Roman family in a celebration with a spiritual content, just as had been done in the festivals of the old tribal society. On this occasion, two years after the death of Vergil, it was Horace who had composed the advent hymn, *carmen sæculare*; it was sung by a double chorus of Roman boys and girls, expressing the wish that the Age of Gold should return and be yet more golden and last for ever. From now onwards, Rome, whose days had been numbered from the start, was called the eternal city.

A large society can scarcely maintain the same community of mind as can a small one; this was one of the reasons for the increasing internal difficulties in the growing Roman empire. The problems were the same as faced by the mythical King Numa: difficulties arise as soon as several tribes find themselves living together in a community based on law and justice and not family feeling. As families which originally were self-sufficient are absorbed into a society divided by specialised work and class, they all become more dependent on one another — but at the same time their sense of unity is weakened. It is no coincidence that the first temples to the state gods were built in the first years of the republic: in Rome the state religion was a political tool intended to ensure the unity of the State. No one has expressed it more clearly and cynically than Polybios:

'I think that what is criticised in other peoples keeps the Roman state together; I mean their fear of the gods. For it is manipulated and introduced both into private and public life as much as is humanly possible. It might seem strange to many people, but I believe that they have done it for the sake of the vast majority. For if the task were to form a state of wise men such things would not perhaps be necessary, but as the great mass of people are easily swayed and constantly demand things contrary to the law, moved by foolish urges and violent passions, the only thing to do is to keep them in check through fear of the invisible and by outward show. Therefore I do not believe that it was in thoughtlessness or by mere chance that people in times past were given the idea of gods and an underworld, but am more inclined to the view that our own age is foolishly and short-sightedly trying to drive these concepts out.'

State religion had been neglected during the decline of the republic, which is a clear indication that it was of greater concern to the men in power than to oppressed citizens, who in times of trouble sought refuge in eastern religions promising some form of salvation, in Stoicism or Neo-Pythagoreanism. But even if the intellectual élite could adopt a slightly ironical attitude towards the traditional gods and could express their allegiance to them with a reservation like that of Ovid: 'It is a good thing there are gods, so let us believe in them;' — it is not correct to say, as is often maintained, that religion in general had lost its power over minds in the age of the emperors. All the Romans of whom we have any knowledge, from the coarse ex-slaves in Petronius' novel to Ovid himself, had retained the original feeling that there is something behind natural phenomena, though they had different ideas as to what it might be.

The ancient Roman gods were personifications or rather abstractions of everyday tasks, especially the tasks of the farmers, and they were particularly related to those important moments in life — birth, marriage, death — for which the mythical imagination has always had a predilection. According to John Ferguson nineteen gods went into action at a birth — and they only existed in and for this function. With all their special gods for this, that and the other, the Romans had as it were formalised the primitive means of experience and systematised a fear of the gods, transforming it into a fear of not observing the rules; legal pedantry is typical of Roman religious practice — and there was no room for any form of ecstasy. Many of the festivals of the primitive peasant society still lived on in more or less corrupted form; the Saturnalia, celebrated on the 17th December, was an ancient new year festival and, like the festivals of the old tribal society, represented a return to a primeval age, the Age of Gold, when Saturnus reigned and all men were equal. The social norms were suspended, and the fruitful chaos of the beginning of things broke out afresh as a reminder of the arbitrariness of all human institutions. But the Saturnalia, which gave the individual the possibility of stepping outside his role in society (the slave became the master and the master the slave) was really a reversal of the ancient tribal festivals in which the individual in fact realised his own supra-individual role in society. It was entertainment and licentiousness rather than an expression of unity and ecstasy; the same was true of the more bloodthirsty public entertainments which enjoyed their heyday during the age of the emperors.

Augustus, who obviously could not arrange a centenary festival every year, tried in many other ways to rally the Romans around the idea of Rome and the task with which it was entrusted. He also sought to rally them around himself. One of his initial moves was the restoration of the state religion; he re-founded 82 temples and emphasised the close relationship between the gods and himself by building a temple for Apollo, the god of light, next to his own residence on the Palatine; likewise he built a temple to Venus in Caesar's Forum (for the Julian family was, of course, descended from Venus), and for Mars in his own Forum, for Mars was the father of Romulus and thus of the entire Roman people. Throughout the empire the Goddess *Roma* was worshipped, together with *Vesta*, the goddess of the hearth and the home; to these could be added the Emperor's *genius* or guardian spirit. Just as individual families cultivated the genius of the father (and the *juno* of the mother), the intention was that the entire Roman family should cultivate the genius of the 'father of the fatherland' Pater Patriae — an honorary title which the Senate gave to Augustus in A.D.2.. 'We have called him thus,' writes Seneca, 'so as to indicate to him that it is the authority of a father which has been given to him, the authority which demands the greatest restraint in caring for one's children and the neglect of one's own interests in favour of theirs.' The neglect of one's own interests in favour of those of the family is precisely the *pietas* which Vergil praised in the head of all the family, 'pious Æneas'. On Augustus' shield of honour, which was put up in the popular assembly, his *virtus* was specified as *clementia, justitia, pietas*: clemency, justice and a sense of community.

Augustus

When Augustus assumed power there were, as there had been when Caesar assumed power, those who complained of a lack of freedom; however, these people were not the ordinary people, who had known neither freedom nor security for over a hundred years, but the leading families. It was to other circles that Augustus originally looked for support, but by 38 B.C., through his marriage to Livia, he had married into the Claudian family, one of the oldest in Rome. He did not repeat Caesar's glorious mistake of showing mercy to his opponents and thus insulting them, but he first terrified the powerful and then appeased them by reforming Caesar's Senate and giving the Senate nobility its privileges again. By 27 B.C., only four years after his victory over Antonius, he could take the risk of declaring that the State, *res publica*, which in name was the same as the republic, had been re-established, and of laying down his extraordinary powers — only to get them back from the Senate under other names. After this he could maintain that he did not have greater power, but — as Augustus — greater authority than others; he did not have the title of Emperor — Caesar, of course, was his name — but he had the status of the first man in the Senate, *princeps*, from which the Romans' own word for the empire, the Principate, is derived.

Until 23 B.C. Augustus had been annually elected consul by the popular assembly; when in that year he declined to allow himself to be re-elected, this caused a good deal of consternation, as it was obviously thought that the title of Consul was all-important. For the people it was still a case of Augustus or chaos; therefore it was not felt to be as meaningless as it in fact was that in return Augustus was made a tribune for life; as such he was formally protecting the people from the abuse of power, but in practice his authority as a tribune gave him power over all legislation. On top of this, the Senate had in 27 B.C. given him *imperium*, i.e. the supreme civil, military and judicial authority in all the border provinces. This was only a formal confirmation of the fact that Augustus' authority depended on the army, which was garrisoned in the border provinces. Before the final show-down with Antonius Augustus had made the army take an oath of allegiance to him personally; as one of the main reasons for the civil war had been that the armies had become too big and too closely tied to their leaders, an urgent task had been to reduce numbers to the least possible and to prevent the close relationship between the legions and their officers. This Augustus sought to do by means of limited appointments and by frequent re-postings; the first of these tasks meant that a limit had to be put on expansion along the natural borders. Some historians have believed that Augustus actually went too far in his efforts to reduce the size and power of the army; in a precarious situation, such as arose during a rebellion in some eastern provinces in A.D.6, 'this absence of a strong central reserve of troops nearly proved fateful.' (H.H. Scullard).

The memories of the army which Pompejus in his day had ordered into Rome were still sufficient to frighten people; in Rome it was a case of maintaining the illusion that the authority of the prince of peace was not dependent on the army. But as the lack of forces of law and order in Rome had also turned out to be fatal, Augustus garrisoned the imperial praetorian guard close to the city; in Rome itself a city prefect, who acted as the emperor's deputy during his absence, was in charge of the three 'city cohorts', a sort of military police, while another prefect, *præfectus vigilum*, commanded corps of firemen and watchmen. The prefects were taken from the equestrians and were directly responsible to the Emperor. So was the prefect of Egypt, which in contrast to the other provinces was the Emperor's 'private' domain. The imperial border provinces were administered by Augustus' personal representatives, while the remaining provinces were to be the responsibility of the Senate and administered by vice-regents, usually former consuls, who — in contrast to earlier practice — were highly paid, so that they were less keen to exploit their provinces. As Augustus also had the administration of the Senate provinces supervised by his personal procurators and the responsibility for demanding taxes removed from the tax gatherers and given to local officials instead, the exploitation of the provinces was limited and their wealth increased; the condition of the empire was quickly improved; most people felt themselves more secure, and very few felt themselves less free.

It was Augustus's political genius that he left forms unchanged and was content to alter the realities of the situation. Although the Senate was subordinate to the Emperor, and although the popular assembly had no power (and ceased to exist under Tiberius), the old institutions were functioning again, and officially it was not only the State, but also the republic, which had been re-established. This ambiguity was the reason why under Augustus it was possible to be a 'Pompeian' and why the memory of Julius Caesar was certainly honoured — though as time went on it was kept a little in the background. As Caesar had been given divine status and a temple dedicated to his *clementia*, Octavian had assumed the name of *Divi filius*, the son of the Divine, and had thus emphasised his right to inherit Caesar's power and clientele. But as Augustus he ensured that his life-style was very different from that of his predecessor: if the State had been Caesar, Augustus was the (personification of the) State, or the man who modestly put himself on one side for the benefit of the State. He emphasised this by turning the imperial city, which had been a city built of tile, into a city of marble, but he did not turn his own residence, on the Palatine, into a palace.

In everyday life Augustus did not indulge in any great imperial pomp and circumstance, preferring to present himself as the ancient Roman *pater familias*, an example to follow on the path of virtue leading back to the customs of their forefathers and seriously concerned with creating order in the Roman family, something which he tried to do with his laws against immorality and luxury. He also exhorted Roman men to found families — if Roman citizens were to retain their privileges in the administration and the army, there must be enough of them; (as far as the army was concerned, the problem had to be solved simply by giving Roman citizenship to the soldiers in the legions). Augustus, who had dethroned the aristocracy, was himself more middle-class than princely in his outlook, and so it may appear surprising that in the eyes of his subjects he was divine as well. It must have demanded considerable ingenuity to combine bourgeois simplicity with divine authority.

On the last day of his life, in the month which was called after him, in A.D. 14, he is said to have asked those closest to him if he had not played his part well. In this some will see a confirmation of the view that Augustus was conscious of his political role, but that he did not believe in his divine mission. If this were true, Augustus would have an infinitely wider horizon than others of his time, but nothing indicates that he was of such mental stature. The classical work on the Roman revolution leading to the principate is by Ronald Syme. In his opinion it was a class revolution since it removed the power from the Senate — though admittedly no other class assumed that power. Syme is so keen to emphasise the limitations of Augustus, with whose weakliness he even seems to reproach him, that it is completely inconceivable that such a weakly, hypocritical man could achieve anything at all in this harsh world, let alone found a world-wide empire which despite its inbuilt weaknesses nevertheless lasted for half a millenium. The explanation given is the unlikely one that it was due to a series of improbable strokes of luck.

Even if this were the explanation, good luck, *fortuna*, was for the Romans a fate which favoured the brave; good fortune was not in contrast to personal merits, but it was a reward for them. The borderline between the human and the divine was not in ancient times so scientifically determined as in the modern age; the man who achieved great things did so thanks to the decree of fate, the sanction of the gods and the divine spark within himself, and therefore Caesar and Augustus were deified after their deaths. Augustus scarcely felt that it was due to him personally that he had succeeded in bringing about peace; it was not for nothing that an altar was erected to good fortune, *fortuna*, as well as one to peace on the Field of Mars in Rome, which was the centre of Augustus' architectural activities. Augustus had been lucky enough to bring about peace; it was his achievement and the will of fate, and so in all modesty he could feel himself to be the tool of the gods; and that is probably what he did.

Ovid and the new age

However, the attitude towards peace and *fortuna* gradually changed.

If peace is a reality, it cannot in the long run awaken the same enthusiasm as when it was established; while it can be a relief that bad times are changed into good ones, it can become a matter of course that good times should become even better. The great prosperity of the Empire was thus just as difficult to reconcile with the thrift of earlier generations as peace was with martial virtues. So it was not surprising that Augustus, with his friend Maecenas acting as a personified art foundation, carried out a conscious cultural policy and tried to involve poets in keeping people's spirits and morale high, something which Horace did in his odes in praise of the ancient Roman virtues. But it is a contradiction in terms continually to praise the past when the present has officially the status of an Age of Gold, and there was a younger poet, Ovid, who would not allow himself to be used, but struck up an entirely new tone:

> Let him praise the past who will! But happy am I who
> was born now, in the age to which I am suited in
> every respect! Not because it is now that gold is being
> extracted from the earth, or because pearls are coming
> to us from distant shores, or because marble is being
> wrested from diminishing mountains, or because the
> blue waters are being contained by the walls of the
> dam, but because we are blessed with the good things
> of culture, and that coarseness which was so fixed in
> our forefathers' beings is now gone.

Augustus had every reason to be content with a poet who was so

Augustus (63 B.C. – 14 A.D..; Emperor from 31 B.C.). Marble bust found in Egypt. Ny Carlsberg Glyptotek, Copenhagen.

*Tiberius (42 B.C. – 37 A.D.; Emperor from 14 A.D.). c. 20 A.D..
Ny Carlsberg Glyptotek, Copenhagen.*

*Private instruction in more comfortable surroundings than in school. The
pupil in the chair on the right is reading from a scroll, and the one on the far
right has his folding writing slate in his hand. Relief from tomb in
Neumagen, c. 200 A.D.. Landesmuseum, Trier.*

enthusiastic about his own time, but his pleasure was not unmixed. It was unheard of to speak so disrespectfully of the peasant virtues of former times, which Vergil had praised; moreover, these words were to be found in the poem called 'The Art of Love', which could equally well be called the art of seduction, and the implication of which was in absolute contrast to Augustus' laws on morality. There was a generation between Vergil and Ovid, who was born after the death of Caesar, and that made a difference. Vergil prophesied an Age of Gold, while Ovid rejoiced because the gold was being dug from the earth; Vergil founded history in myth, while Ovid reduced myths to psychology; he was humorous, where Vergil was highflown, and he adopted an ironical attitude towards the ancient Roman festivals, *fasti*, which he described in the poem of that name.

Ovid was more interested in the happiness and unhappiness of the individual than in social morals; there was a different spirit in his work from the Roman spirit which Augustus wanted to awaken with the help of the poets. Admittedly, his principal work, the 'Metamorphoses', an interlinked series of Greek and Roman legends on the theme of metamorphosis, finishes with the apotheosis of Caesar and with the wish that it will be a long time before Augustus, too, goes to heaven as a god. To all this, however, Ovid adds a prophecy of eternal fame, not for Rome but for his own poem; in his eyes not only is the individual seeking his own advantage, but art, too, has begun to glorify itself, and for it Rome is a subject like anything else. The mythical history of Rome is included on a level with any other myth in the 'Metamorphoses', and the person seen most in the cantos on Rome is neither Æneas nor Augustus, but Pythagoras, from whom King Numa according to legend sought enlightenment. Pythagoras is not mentioned by name, for the Pythagoreans merely referred to him as Him, but it is left to him to pronounce the serious moral of this humorous poem: that everything is changed into everything, human beings to animals, animals into human beings, and that it is a crime to sacrifice fellow creatures, something which of course was part of Roman cultic practice. Pythagoras' explanation of why there is no longer an Age of Gold on earth is that a taste for meat has made men kill animals, and that animal flesh gives human being the characteristics of animals.

It is usual to call the author of 'The Art of Love' frivolous and superficial, but the 'Metamorphoses' contains a more profound psychology than any other Roman poem. In 'The Art of Love' Ovid adopts an ironical attitude towards moral norms, but in 'Metamorphoses' it is the tragic confrontation between norms and natural urges which leads to the metamorphoses: man, who cannot find his place in the social order, is drawn into the natural order of things. There is a certain consistency in the fact that Ovid, obviously under the inspiration of Pythagoras, is looking for a way from the individualism which underlies 'The Art of Love' to a greater sense of community or brotherhood than that afforded by the state; in both cases he went too far for Augustus' taste. Augustus exiled him to Tomi (Constanza) on the Black Sea; the official reason was his immoral 'Art of Love' which, however, had appeared eight years before his exile, but there were more and secret reasons for it: Ovid had been present at something he was not entitled to be present at, possibly a Pythagorean seance in which knowledge of the imperial family was sought by astrological means. But whatever the reason, the spirit in Ovid's work was a symptom that something had been unsuccessful. Augustus exiled the symptom.

The Age of Gold continued to be the name given to literature from the time of Augustus. Ovid was the last of the great Roman poets, and the inspiration for his work is no longer Roman in the old sense. Strangely enough, although in 'The Art of Love' he had expressed an inappropriate enthusiasm for his own time, he returned to Hesiod's old view of history at the beginning of 'Metamorphoses'. Seneca, who somewhere approvingly quotes Ovid's description of the Age of Iron, revealed the same ambivalence half a century later. At times he could remark, even with delight, that his forefathers had not been much better (for it is man, not the age, which is responsible for evil), and he, too, after attempting to identify the Age of Gold with his own time nevertheless ended by placing it in the dim distant past.

The historians and the idea of decline

It became official Roman ideology that the Emperor, whoever he was, had brought about the Age of Gold and created prosperity. Strictly speaking, this only meant something if an Age of Iron had gone immediately before, and it is easy to understand that the worse his predecessor had been, the more enthusiastic was the reception given to a new Roman emperor. As predecessors had often been bad, the expectation of an Age of Gold stood more and more radiant against a darker and darker background; the prevailing mood was sombre in the glorious age of the emperors, and the ancient idea of moral decline was at the very centre of the works of Roman historians. One of them wrote:

'Rome had its earliest infancy under Romulus, its founder and provider; then it had its childhood years under other kings; when it reached the age of discretion it could not tolerate slavery, and after having learned to do without the child's play it preferred obeying laws to obeying kings. This youthful stage ended with the Punic Wars; then Rome's mature strength developed, and its age of adulthood began. When Carthage, which had long prevented it from reigning supreme, was brushed aside, it really spread its power over all the world, on land and sea. But when all kings and nations were subjugated and Rome no longer had any need to wage war, it abused its powers and was thus finally exhausted from within. This was the beginning of old age when, torn asunder by civil strife and struck by internal crises it again resorted to a monarchic government as though in a second childhood. Indeed, after the loss of freedom ... Rome aged as though it had not the strength to maintain itself without seeking the support of monarchs.'

These are the words of Seneca's father, also called Seneca, written in his high old age at the time of the Emperor Caligula, which explains his negative view — if not of the old age of Rome, then at least of the rule by emperors. The weakness of the regime founded by Augustus was that it depended on one man and his army; despite all formalities, the emperor had absolute power, and that, in the opinion of the elder Seneca, was not so much extended *ad absurdum* as taken to its utmost consequence by Caligula's rabid unpredictability as a ruler.

The emperor's unpredictability made it difficult to think of good fortune and luck as rewards for moral deserts, especially as under Tiberius and Caligula rogues were raised to positions of high honour. To Seneca *fortuna* has become a negative concept which — as the term applied to all the external circumstances over which man has no control — stands in contrast to *virtus*, which at the same time changes

meaning and comes to stand for the moral strength with which man —
e.g. Cato — is able to endure sufferings in his fight against injustice.

To the great historian of the imperial age, Cornelius Tacitus, who still clung to the ancient Roman ideals, the absence of the *virtus* which reaps honour in the field of battle meant that Rome no longer had good fortune on its side and was moving towards its destruction. For him as for the elder Seneca the monarchy in itself was a symptom of moral decay; despite his aversion for the monarchy and his sympathy for the republic, he saw the republic as a thing of the past.

Tacitus still assumes that history is decided by fate, but he asks the question, very relevant in his day, whether *everything*, including the emperor's likes and dislikes, is preordained, or whether man's own attitudes and actions have any influence on his ability to live his life without disasters if he steers a middle course between stubborn insubordination and abject submissiveness. Tacitus does not hide the fact that he himself, having been both a senator and a praetor (in A.D. 88) under the tyrant Domitian, had felt forced to comply in a manner obnoxious to him. This is in itself an example of how difficult it could be precisely for the most distinguished men in the Roman empire to preserve their dignity. Just as insulted dignity lay behind Caesar's march on Rome, it is possible to discern injured dignity behind Tacitus' indignant portrayal of the Roman emperors and their henchmen; it is worth keeping this background in mind, since his 'Annals' are a principal source of much that is in this book. For the Romans moral strength (or its opposite) was and remained the driving force in history, and therefore their historians were always inclined to moralise. This also applies to another source of information about the imperial age, Suetonius, even if he did not express any opinion on the course of history or see things in relation to each other; for a long time he was private secretary to the Emperor Hadrian, and in his biographies of the emperors (from c. A.D. 120) he considered, as it were, the emperors from the point of view of a valet. While Tacitus could hardly see the empire for emperors, Suetonius had difficulty in seeing the emperors for their deeds, qualities and, especially, vices. And so the history of the age of the emperors has been handed down very largely as stories of imperial vices.

III. EDUCATION AND CAREER

The Annæus family and oratory

Lucius Annæus Seneca was born in Corduba in c. 4 B.C.. He was thus a Spaniard, as the Spanish still like to point out: they called a conference of philosophers in 1965 on the 1900th anniversary of his death and demonstrated the link between Seneca's philosophy and later Spanish thought. The practical and political interest, the humour and the easy-flowing style are things which Seneca certainly has in common with the best Spanish thinkers, whether or not they were influenced by him or simply related in temperament. A certain — Spanish — pride cannot be denied in Seneca, although on the other hand he never refers to himself as a Spaniard or shows any trace of Spanish national feeling. In Corduba, which had been the capital of the province of Baetica since 197 B.C., and where the citizens were also Roman citizens, the Latin spoken was as good as that in Rome. Seneca's father, who bore the very same three names, had moreover spent at least a part of his youth in Rome and also wanted to spend his old age there; together with all his family, he moved to Rome while Seneca was still so small that he could be carried in the arms of his aunt.

The elder Seneca was born about the middle of the last century B.C., and lived to be almost 90. He had experienced the death agonies of the republic and wrote a history of Rome with a republican leaning — a work which has been quoted above but is otherwise no longer extant. As an introduction to it Seneca wrote a biography of his father, but this has been lost as well; elsewhere he speaks of him with great respect, though he also talks of him as 'stiff and old-fashioned', which was the reason why the mother, Helvia, was deprived of the chance of following her intellectual interests: 'If only my father, outstanding and excellent man as he was, had been less devoted to the customs of our forefathers and wished that you should be taught and not merely informed about the fundamental principles of wisdom.'

Seneca was the second of three brothers, and it was presumably especially out of consideration for the education and careers of his sons that the father moved to Rome. There was, of course, no systematic provision of schooling in Rome any more than there was in Cordova. In the good old days when it was sufficient to be able to read, write and add up, the most elementary teaching was done by the father himself or by a 'pedagogue' chosen from among the slaves. However, the division of labour during the last couple of centuries of the republic had made it a special though not particularly distinguished job to knock the elements of learning into children's heads. And after the Romans in the 2nd century B.C. had subjugated Greece, and Greek culture in return had begun to make its mark on Rome, private schools were opened to teach Greek and Latin. No use was made of school books as such; the pupils read the best writers, in particular Homer and Vergil in Seneca's day, and thus acquired the skills needed to understand the text — and nothing else: school subjects and specialised teachers were unknown; *grammaticus* was sufficient.

Greek influence was most apparent in the third stage of education, at the schools of rhetoric where the language of tuition was at first exclusively Greek. Rhetoric was of course of great importance in a society where all public debate was oral, and where a politically gifted individual could not make any impression without some skill in public speaking, and where lawyers could acquire all the respect and popularity necessary to be elected to political office. In the Greek city states governed by a popular assembly, training in rhetoric had thus had a practical purpose. In ancient Rome fathers had taken their sons along with them to the Forum where lawsuits were fought, so that at an early age they could learn from the great orators. In the schools of rhetoric training was more theoretical, and at first, in the 2nd century B.C., a good deal of old-fashioned Roman opposition to these unfortunate Greek practices made itself felt.

The pupils in the schools of rhetoric, most of whom were of grammar school age, had on the one hand to produce written drafts for speeches which mythical or historical figures could be imagined to have made at decisive moments, and on the other to make oral *suasoriæ*. These were arguments for and against a decision, and again they were decisions which mythical or distant historical heroes had been forced to take; for instance, whether Agamemnon ought to sacrifice his daughter in order to placate the gods. Moreover, the pupils had to compose *controversiae*, speeches for the prosecution or defence in lawsuits — not real ones, but imaginary ones designed to give special scope for incisiveness and hairsplitting.

In his youth in Rome the elder Seneca had heard the great orators from the last years of the republic and had himself seen how oratory had lost its political significance and degenerated into exercises in fair words, to 'declamation'. When an old man, he was persuaded by his sons to write his recollections of the orators of his day and their *suasoriæ* and *controversiæ*; his memory was so impressive that he was able to rattle off 2000 names alphabetically and 200 verses backwards! The rhetorical arguments were concerned with matters of high drama; the principal themes of art are sometimes said to be love and death: those of rhetoric were rape and murder. Roman brutality made itself very obvious in rhetoric. In the Middle Ages, when men had no historical sense and when moreover they thought that the elder and the younger Seneca were one and the same person, they took the fictitious conflicts as historical events and produced a popular version entitled *Gesta Romanorum*, the deeds of the Romans — an entertaining piece of popular literature which was much read and provided the material for a great deal of later poetry and fiction.

As an example of a controversy we can take a résumé from the 4th century dealing at least with a tangible problem: Can a person be condemned for thought or only for deeds? The accused is one of the vestal virgins whose task it was to look after Vesta's sacred fire in the hearthplace of the city and who had undertaken to live a life of chastity; if a vestal virgin was found guilty of unchastity she had by law to be buried alive, though this had not happened since 216 B.C.. A vestal wrote this verse:

> Happy the bride!
> I will lay down my life
> that a wedding is beautiful.

She was accused of unchastity.

First party: ' "Happy the bride," says the woman who wants to be one. "I will lay down my life," says the woman who maintains it. "that a wedding is beautiful": either you swear what you know or you swear falsely what you know not. Neither becomes a priestess. For you the magistrates dip their *fasces*[1]; for you consuls and praetors step aside: Is this too small a reward for your virginity? A vestal should seldom swear to anything and never by anything but her own Vesta. "I will lay down my life" — presumably because the eternal fire has gone out? — "I will lay down my life" — presumably because you have been asked in marriage? I ask you, Vesta, for the supreme punishment; let your cruelty match the hatred of your priestess. Read your poem aloud, so that I can hear what it is about. *Must* you write a poem? *Must* you make your words delightful by writing verse? *Must* you with your verses and rhythms relax the strict rule which you owe to your temple? If you must sing the praises of marriage, then tell of Lucretia[2]; write of her death before you swear by your own. How deserving you are of the supreme punishment, you for whom something is more delectable than your dignified station as a priestess! It is "beautiful"! How directly you put it, and how these words come from the depths of your soul, though from a soul which longs for what it knows not instead of rejoicing at what it knows. Impure is she also who is not unchaste but longs for unchastity.'

Second party: 'She is reproached for a single verse, not even for the whole poem. But, you say, it is unfitting for her to write a poem. There is a great difference between what you can reprove and what you can punish for. No one can be condemned for unchastity whose body has not been ravished. Do you think that poets really can be identified with what they write? She has lived in purity and chastity; her manner of life has not been dissolute, and her speech with men has not been licentious; I will admit to you that she is guilty of one crime: she has imagination! Why should she not envy Cornelia[3], why not envy the woman who gave birth to Cato, or those women whose children become — priestesses?'

An important feature in controversy was *colour*, the different speakers' different presentations of the background to the conflict; an inventive mind could sometimes make the entire case look different by ascribing other motives to the parties in dispute; this, of course, may have

---

1. The bundles of rods which the lictors carried before a high magistrate and which from ancient times had symbolised the power to dispense justice.
2. Lucretia was such an exemplary wife that she took her own life after being raped by Sextus Tarquinus; according to legend this led to the fall of the Tarquins and the monarchy.

intensified the sense of dramatic effect, but perhaps it may also have increased psychological awareness. Seneca asks on one occasion what benefit can be derived from untying knots which you have tied yourself, but he admits that it can sometimes be amusing and stimulate shrewd, clear thought. Subsequent ages, for which teaching has often meant particularly the passing on of — often useless — information, have nevertheless been critical of the Roman concept of education as a training in eloquence, and have expressed surprise that the Romans who were practical in their approach to things in general could not work out a more practical form of education.

One of those most thoroughly acquainted with ancient Rome, the French historian Jérôme Carcopino, rejects everything in Roman schooling, including the fact that boys and girls were taught together in the lower classes. Curiously enough, however, he finds the cause of the unpractical teaching provided by the Romans in their 'overdeveloped practical sense': 'Always on the look-out for immediate profit, the Romans never saw the long-term advantage of disinterested research.' Originally the Greek system of training in rhetoric had had the practical aim of enabling Roman officials to be a match for the Greeks they were to rule over; and Latin rhetoric which was introduced in the beginning of the first century B.C. was originally suspect in the eyes of the authorities because it spread the privilege of eloquence to more and more of the people. But eloquence became less significant as the popular assemblies withered away and the Senate merely said what the Emperor wanted it to say. Rhetoric became an object in itself and 'increasingly devoid of serious content' says Carcopino.

Strangely enough, this useless rhetoric was enormously popular. The great orators were much admired in Rome and attracted attention wherever they went; when they spoke in the Forum, the public went to listen to them in great numbers. This was not merely because the teaching provided by the grammarians, which both upper and middle class children profited by or suffered under, had shown how to appreciate an elegant formulation, but also because the rhetoricians had taken account of public demand:

3. Cornelia was the mother of Tiberius and Gajus Grachus.

'The grammarian stamped his pupils, developed their taste, fed their memories: in short he created a broad public capable of understanding and taking part in the literary life of the day. The orator submitted to the tyranny of the public, worked in accordance with its orders and took its demands into consideration. His willingness to comply had important consequences. From the start Roman literature had shown a tendency to isolate itself within intellectual circles ... When it comes to oratory, it is the public at large which steps forward and creates for itself the literature it dreams about ... All that was necessary was some gifted men who understood the public and could satisfy it at the same time as raising it above itself, and this would be a literary turning point ... Seneca was one of those geniuses. It is impossible to say whether this highly sophisticated Stoic consciously wrote for the general public. But as he, too, was brought up on oratory, an instinctive understanding between him and his public was more or less pre-ordained.'

Thus writes A. M. Guillemin; and it is a fact that Ovid and Seneca, the two authors most obviously influenced by rhetoric when in the age of the emperors it became an object in itself, were also the most popular. Ovid himself talks of his popularity, and this is confirmed by the incriptions in Pompeji. Seneca's widespread popularity and influence is betokened by the many gravestones on which are quoted words of consolation and wisdom, and also by later authors who deprecated it. Thus Quintilian, who was professor of rhetoric at the end of the first century, recalls that in his day Seneca was the only author read by young people, which of course was because of his unfortunate propensity for scorning Cicero's classical prose, the variety of styles and his predilection for striking maxims.

The elder Seneca had already made the same objections to the orators of the imperial age as did Quintilian. He had had special praise for the speakers from the time of the republic, particularly Cicero, whom he unfortunately had not heard himself — not because he was too young (he was about 12 years old on the death of Cicero) but because the civil war kept him at home in Cordova. 'All the qualities with which Roman eloquence can compete with and surpass boastful Greece blossomed at the time of Cicero; all those gifted men who have contributed to the glory of our intellectual life were born at that time,' he writes, and then goes on to talk of the decline of morals: they become inferior day by day, whether because of the luxury of the time — 'for nothing is so fatal to the spirits of gifted men as luxury' — or an eternal law according to which the most sublime qualities degenerate into the most abysmal. It seems to be an eternal law that fathers experience the culmination of intellectual life in their own youth, but the elder Seneca's conservatism had the future before it: his and Quintilian's rhetorical ideals dominated the whole of the late imperial age. The younger Seneca was not rated particularly highly by the authors of the 2nd century, who speak of a 'vulgar style' which pleased the uneducated. It is only in the first Christian writers that we find a more positive evaluation of him.

When the elder Seneca wrote his rhetorical memoirs the younger Seneca had not, as far as can be judged, yet begun his philosophical writing, though he had probably started his career as a speaker. There is a hint of disagreement between them once when the father addresses his sons: 'You will probably not be offended by unpolished style and uneven composition before you reach my age; for the moment I do not doubt that even offensive lapses of good taste will amuse you.' — The sons were not as young as all that at this time; it emerges from the father's prefaces to his books that the two eldest were embarking on a career in the service of the State; and to be appointed to the lowest rank in the state service, that of quaestor, you had to be 25 years of age. The youngest son, *Mela*, had no ambitions; on the other hand his father thought him the most gifted, as emerges from some particularly paternal words he addressed to him: he will not encourage him to do anything he does not want to do; he is happy to know that Mela is content with his father's (equestrian) rank, and as the path chosen by his brothers is full of danger as well as hope, he is glad to know that the youngest of the brothers has chosen a safer course. But he still encourages him to study rhetoric, as it will open the way to other fields.

From the letter of consolation which Seneca wrote some years later to his mother it appears that the eldest brother, *Novatus*, has meanwhile been given an official appointment, while the youngest, Mela, has become so wise that he has decided not to seek a career; Seneca flatters his mother by saying that Novatus will do her honour while Mela can spend all the more time on her, and this was probably not only flattery, for the feeling of kinship was strong in the Annæus family. Tacitus admittedly believes that Mela was more interested in money than in honour and that he thought he could earn more as an imperial procurator (of the equestrian class) than as a senator. He moreover maintained his connection with Cordova and there became father to *Marcus Annæus Lucanus*, who subsequently made a name for himself as a poet. At one time Novatus was adopted by the orator Junius Gallio and took his name: adoption to the Romans was not a question of providing a family for orphan children, but of providing sons — usually adults — for childless families. Under the name of Gallio, Novatus became consul and then, in A.D. 52, proconsul in the province of Achaea (Greece): in the course of his duties in this office he was according to the Acts of the Apostles confronted by the Apostle Paul, who was accused by the Jews of Corinth — but Gallio refused to be a judge in such matters.

On various occasions Seneca expressed devotion to his brothers, especially to Novatus-Gallio, to whom he dedicated two of his works and in a third praised for his immunity to flattery. In an epigram he expresses the wish that his brothers may survive him and that his death will be the only sorrow he will ever cause them, that they will only rival each other in affection — and that little Marcus, who now gives them pleasure with his delightful infant gurgling, will one day compete in eloquence with his orator uncles.

From philology to philosophy

It might seem surprising that it should be just Seneca who was criticised by the orators for placing form above content, for no Roman ever criticised the orators for just this more than Seneca — which might well be the reason for their aversion to him. Seneca takes over the good old Socratic distinction between the skills which (perhaps) make people better *at something*, and the life skill, philosophy, the love of wisdom, which alone can make better people. He is critical of all specialists who in some strange way all consider the particular profession by which they live as the only one worthy of attention, and he is particularly critical of grammarians and philologists who turn reality into words — and not words into reality. It may well be all right for a grammarian to teach Homer and Vergil, for there are a lot of good things to be found in Homer and Vergil; but when Vergil writes that 'time flies irrevocably', it makes the grammarian think not of the fact that he should not waste time, but make the observation that Vergil always uses the expression 'flies' when speaking of time. It is not surprising that a grammarian and a philologist should get different things from Cicero's 'State' than a philosopher does, for 'in the same material everyone finds what is suited to his profession: in the same field a cow looks for grass, a dog for a hare, a stork for a lizard.' It is, however, more surprising that a philosopher often gets no more out of it than a philologist or a grammarian. This is because philosophers also want to be specialists and: 'have become envious of grammarians and mathematicians: everything superfluous in their branches of learning they have adapted to their own. That is why they know how to speak better than how to live.' From the beginning, from the hand of nature, pupils have a great desire for the good, but their teachers form their intellect, not their souls: 'Therefore, what was philosophy has become philology.' This dictum was transformed by Nietzsche in his inaugural lecture as Professor of Philology in Basel in 1869, when he expressed his intention of turning philology into philosophy. Seneca concentrates all his criticism of Roman education in another famous saying, likewise often inverted when it is quoted: 'We learn not for life, but for school'.

In his youth Seneca himself moved from the philologists to the philosophers, and he discusses and quotes his masters on various occasions in his epistles to Lucilius, which he wrote in the final years of his life. One of them, *Papirius Fabianus* — 'who was not one of those lectern philosophers, but a true philosopher in the old sense of the word' — had himself renounced the art of speaking in favour of philosophy. Seneca's father, who was not exactly enthusiastic about this development, nevertheless mentions him as an example of how the art of speaking can lead to other arts; Seneca himself calls him: 'a man who distinguished himself both in his manner of life and his learning and also, less importantly, in his eloquence.' A criticism of his style, such as expressed by his correspondent Lucilius, Seneca answers by saying that Fabianus did not seek to fashion words but souls, his words were well chosen but not affected — and if he was not perfect as a speaker, then at least he was truly able to fire the enthusiasm of his pupils and encourage them to follow in his wake without dampening their enthusiasm from the start.

Meanwhile, Seneca seems to have had his introduction to philosophy from the Stoic *Attalus*; when he heard him speak about mankind's self-inflicted sufferings he felt gripped by pity for all mankind — and by admiration for a philosopher, who is raised above all those things beneath which others are crushed. From Attalus Seneca learned to distinguish between natural and unnatural urges — and to keep off oysters and mushrooms, ointments and perfumes, hot baths and soft beds. The Neo-Pythagoreans were also of importance to Seneca in his youth. He had not heard *Quintus Sextius* but he had read him with enthusiasm, and from him he had learned the Pythagorean custom of ending the day by examining his conscience; Sextius' pupil, *Sotion*, had taught him that cruelty becomes a habit in those who kill animals, and that eating animal flesh is harmful to the body and the soul. He was not entirely convinced by the doctrine of the transmigration of souls, but Sotion had been liberal in his views and said that even if you did not share the belief of the master that when eating animals you were eating former human beings, it is nevertheless good to live frugally and to seek other eating habits than those of lions and vultures. 'That', writes Seneca, 'encouraged me to avoid meat, and before a year had passed it had become not only an easy habit but actually a pleasing one, too. I seemed to be intellectually more active, though today I dare not maintain that I really was. You ask why I did not persist? My youth coincided with the first years of the reign of the Emperor Tiberius. At that time efforts were made to drive out foreign cults, and one of the pointers to superstition was abstinence from the flesh of certain animals. On the request of my father, who was not afraid of gossip but disliked philosophy intensely, I returned to my former habits. And it was not even difficult to persuade me to partake of better meals.'

In A.D. 17, when Seneca was about 20 years old, some Neo-Pythagoreans who had been found guilty of using astrology to study the future were deported; in A.D. 19 the Senate exiled those adherents of the Egyptian and Jewish religions who were not willing within a certain time to renounce their superstitious beliefs. Apart from the fear of being accused of un-Roman activities, however, Seneca had another good reason for eating more substantial food: he suffered from tuberculosis for many years:

'As long as I was young, I could stand the suffering and defy the

78

illness. Later I succumbed to it; I always had a cold, and I was all skin and bone. I often felt tempted to put an end to it all, but consideration for my dear old father prevented me, for I was less concerned with whether I had the strength to die than whether he had the strength to stand the loss. . . I will tell you what was a comfort to me then, though I assume that what gave me comfort in fact acted as a powerful medicine. Food for the soul also serves as a medicine, and what uplifts the spirit also benefits the body. I was saved by my studies; I owe my recovery to philosophy. I owe my life to it, and that is the least thing for which I am grateful to it.'

Seneca owed his recovery not only to philosophy, but also to his aunt: 'I have to thank her gentle, motherly care for my recovery after a long illness.' She was married to a Roman equestrian who from c. 16-31 was prefect in Alexandria. Egypt had a special place in the Roman Empire: it was the Emperor's private domain and administered by an imperial official drawn from the equestrian class. Seneca was obviously in Egypt to convalesce during his last years in the state service. He tells how his uncle died on the way home, and how he himself saw his aunt do all she could to save his dead body — presumably from being thrown into the waves during a storm, something which superstitious practice demanded. Otherwise he tells nothing of his stay in Egypt, apparently the only foreign country he visited, although in the bibliography to his 'Natural History' Pliny lists a work by Seneca entitled 'On the geography and religious customs of Egypt' and also a similar work on India. In his youth Seneca also wrote of minerals and fish and earthquakes, possibly during his stay in Alexandria. All these works have been lost, but their titles at least indicate his interest in nature — and possibly in the wisdom of the East.

Rome under Tiberius

The ageing Seneca writes, in his 49th Epistle: 'So much seems to have happened only recently when you immerse yourself in your memories! Only recently, as a boy, I sat at the feet of the philosopher Sotion; only recently I began to conduct lawsuits; recently I lost the desire — and recently the ability — to do so.' Seneca does not have much more to say of his eventful career as an orator; and he says nothing at all of his political career, as quaestor, praetor, consul, tutor and minister to the Emperor. Nor do we know whether because of ill health he was excused the otherwise compulsory military service which the sons of senators and equestrians could do as officers (tribunes) for six months. Seneca does sometimes use martial images in his writings, but he shows no particular interest in or experience of military life. Perhaps it was Seneca's Spanish pride that forbade him to speak of his own merits — in this he is the absolute opposite of Cicero — but at the same time it could well be dangerous for him to say too much about the political life which he knew so intimately.

Seneca's career as an orator began towards the end of the reign of the Emperor Tiberius. Tiberius, who was *princeps* from the death of Augustus in A.D. 14 to A.D. 37, from his 56th to his 79th year, found it difficult to follow in the footsteps of Augustus, whose stepson he was, due to the marriage between his mother, Livia, and the Emperor. Tiberius had distinguished himself as a soldier but not achieved the same popularity as his brother Drusus; he had also been unfortunate in his marriage, while Drusus' son Germanicus had been favoured by fortune both in battle and in marriage: he had three sons and three daughters by Agrippina, the granddaughter of Augustus. Rumour had it that Augustus himself had wanted to see Germanicus as his successor but that Livia had forced through the claims of her own son, though, let it be noted, only when the first four of Augustus' candidates for the throne were already dead. For years Tiberius had felt passed by and he took his bitterness with him to the throne. His claim to it was that he had been adopted by Augustus, against whom he felt a good deal of ill will, and whose commanding presence he lacked; he reacted against the worship of the Emperor, which had fallen to Augustus' lot, and he wanted the Senate to be more independent of the Emperor; at the same time he felt slighted at not being treated with the same respect as his predecessor.

In A.D. 19 Germanicus died, presumably from natural causes. However, it was rumoured that Tiberius had had him poisoned, and his death gave rise to such sorrow and bitterness that Tiberius and Livia found it unwise to take part in the funeral ceremonies, something to which the people took yet greater exception. The popular urge to love or to hate was a political factor in imperial Rome; for the members of the upper strata of society this implied a merciless either-or: they were regarded either as being superhuman or inhuman. Augustus, who had created the new Age of Gold, had been deified after his death — but popular wit said of Tiberius: 'You, O Caesar, have corrupted the Saturnian Age of Gold. Your days, all your days, will be of iron.'

When, weary of the flattery of the great and tired of the hatred of the masses, Tiberius withdrew to Capri in A.D. 26, rumours arose about his incredible excesses, of which we can read in Suetonius. Tiberius had good reason to be misanthropic and suspicious, but his very suspiciousness constantly fed his misanthropy. Someone who distrusts everyone may tend to put his faith in a single person, often someone completely unworthy of it. Thus Tiberius, who was otherwise so meticulously conscientious, appointed as his representative in Rome the completely unprincipled prefect of the guards, Sejanus, who demonstrated his strength by garrisoning the praetorian guard in Rome itself and exploited his power by ridding himself of the Emperor's closest relatives. Agripinna and Nero, her and Gemanicus' eldest son, were exiled, while the second son, Drusus, was kept a prisoner in the imperial palace. Nero died in suspicious circumstances, after which Sejanus took over his widow and thus, although he was the 'new man', became consul and in reality the heir to the throne. But he could not wait for the Emperor to die, and when at last Tiberius understood the danger, Sejanus had achieved such power that he had to be brought down by a coup. Seneca could use Sejanus as a moral example of the fate of those lustful for power: 'On the selfsame day as he had had the Senate as an escort of honour, the people tore him to pieces.' It happened in 31, the year Seneca returned from Egypt.

The fall of Sejanus, however, did not lead to a change; Tiberius, who had seen his trust abused, could now trust no one, least of all his closest relatives; he had Drusus put to death in prison; as for Germanicus' youngest son, Gajus, who was now next in line for the throne, he had taken him with him to Capri to keep him out of harm's way. In Rome the reign of terror continued; Seneca, who in one place praises the early years of Tiberius' reign for their good qualities, writes thus of his last years: 'Under the Emperor Tiberius the fashion of making accusations against other members of society was very widespread, almost commonplace, and in a time of peace it plagued the city more than the entire civil war; people went around listening to the words of intoxicated men and women, and noting down what was said in innocent jest: nothing was safe, and people had already stopped showing interest in the verdicts on the accused, for they were always the same.'

The legal system

If we approach imperial Rome with our minds full of the usual clichés about Roman law, we cannot help being surprised to find that conditions appear to have been just about the opposite of what we expect. What is known as Roman Law, *corpus juris civilis*, was only codified after the fall of the West Roman Empire in the 6th century A.D., and its influence has been greater on later centuries than it was before this. The Romans preferred to keep to custom and tradition rather than to laws, and they had, for instance, no written constitution; the State did not legislate on everything and, for instance, never passed any laws concerning marriage; as much as possible was left to the citizens themselves. Nevertheless, this reticence on the part of the State, which is admirable in principle, suffered from the weakness that the might of the strong in Rome was never really broken by the right. Among the most common clichés concerning the Romans there is one maintaining that it was law and justice, not power, conquest and riches, which were their real passion, at least at the time of the republic — but, at all events in the final years of the republic, it was the eagerness of the great to *assert and achieve their own right* which led to lawless conditions and cleared the ground for the principate. Even if the Emperor humbled the great, he did not exalt the humble; the little man could still only achieve his rights by being the client of one of the great. Inequality before the law and private initiative were and remained the characteristic of the Roman legal system.

Rome had no Public Prosecutor — but plenty of private ones. Not only could citizens bring cases on their own behalf, but they could do so, for instance, on behalf of the Emperor. If a prosecutor got a man convicted of insulting the Emperor he was rewarded; if the prosecution failed, he was punished. Thus there was a risk attached to it which ordinary citizens could not run, but there was so much to be earned that it became a profitable occupation to be a professional private prosecutor, the more so as the more powerful members of society could use these prosecutors, *delatores*, to get at their personal enemies.

It was the Senate which usually judged in these matters, and it was afraid of offending his Majesty if it did not convict people for lese-majesty, which was usually punishable by death. Of course, the Emperor himself was the supreme judge; under the republic every Roman citizen could appeal to the people; under the Empire he could (as the example of St. Paul shows) appeal to the Emperor: in theory the Emperor's authority as a tribune of the people made him into a kind of universal ombudsman; and indeed there are instances where the boss himself was more liberal than the Senate and the vice-regents who had the final say in the provinces — but Tiberius was not in the habit of showing mercy.

Civil law was the responsibility of two praetors who were elected each year: one was in charge of lawsuits between Roman citizens, the other looked after lawsuits for those who were under the jurisdiction of the Empire but did not have Roman citizenship. But the praetors had no authority to pronounce judgement: it was their task to listen to the two contending parties and to define the question at issue in a 'formula', with which the two parties went before the judge. They could choose their own judge, but if they could not agree, the praetor could appoint one or more of those on the annual list, for which the qualifications were wealth and station. Seneca explained his opposition to a suggestion that ingratitude should be made a criminal offence by arguing that only a wise man could judge on mental attitudes, and that it was not wisdom but a fortune which was demanded of a judge!

Nor did a judge need any legal training. The judiciary, i.e. the Emperor, the Senate, the City Prefect in Rome, the vice-regents and the private judges, could have the advice of judicial 'assessors', but theirs was a purely advisory capacity. Being a jurist was a hobby rather than a profession, but as the imperial bureaucracy grew and settled into a rut, a legal training became an excellent qualification for posts in the service of the State.

Lawyers were not more legally qualified than judges; they were trained speakers, orators, and under the Empire, when the popular assembly paled away and the Senate usually only said what the

83

Emperor wanted it to say, rhetorical talent could only be given free reign in the law courts. This was especially so in the *Basilica Julia* in the Forum, where the 'hundred men', the *centumviri* who in the course of time became 180, passed judgement in more spectacular matters. According to an ancient law, the *Lex Cincia*, it was forbidden to conduct law suits for money, and although a way around the prohibition had naturally been found, it does show that the legal profession was highly esteemed: members of the families of senators felt free to act as lawyers, and a career as an advocate in the courts was the surest way to the top for members of the 'new' families.

Seneca shows no particular respect for the legal profession in which he himself practised for a long time: 'What shameful lawsuits and what even more shameful lawyers do those thousands have who rush off to the Forum at dawn! This man lodges a suit against his father for arrangements which it would be far better if he respected; that man is in conflict with his mother, and a third is making accusations concerning a crime of which he is obviously guilty himself, and the judge is chosen to pronounce a verdict on what he himself has committed, and the public take the wrong side, led astray by the fair words of the defender.' The public played a considerable part in major trials, which were really a part of public entertainment; apart from the fashion of making accusations which came over imperial Rome at times, the city appears to have been constantly plagued by a fashion for lawsuits: just as orators could only let themselves go in law and not in politics, citizens, who had difficulty in gaining honour in politics, could at least assert their dignity and seek their rights in courts of law.

Vergil had seen it as the mission of the Romans to rule with justice and to give the law of peace. Occasionally Roman historians express horror at the terrible practices of the barbarians, which the Romans often forbade; in the provinces sentences of death had to be put before the vice-regent, as is evinced by the trial of Jesus. The Romans were, so to speak, conscious of their superior legal system, but they did not force their laws on to the people they had conquered. It was accepted without question that people must be treated differently, not only in the different societies, but within the same community. In Rome people had very different rights and duties according to whether they came of consuls' or senators' or equestrian families, whether they were freemen i.e. born free, or freedmen or slaves; the slaves had no rights at all, and in any legal examination of slaves, torture was obligatory. Nor were the same punishments meted out for the same crimes: ordinary people were condemned to forced labour or death in the arena (cf p146), while for the same crimes people of rank were banished — or given orders to commit suicide. — 'Is it lawful for you to scourge a man that is a Roman, and uncondemned?' asks St. Paul, whereby he frightens the military tribune who reveals that he himself has bought Roman citizenship for a large sum of money (something which was not legal, but which was possible under Claudius).

Roman citizenship gave certain rights which others did not have: non-Romans could be whipped, and they had no right of appeal to the Emperor. The law applying to citizens, *jus civile*, was a law of privilege and was completely distinct from *jus gentium*, which applied to all inhabitants of the Roman Empire and designated the customs accepted by the Romans, of which human sacrifices, for instance, was not one. While the law of the people, *jus gentium*, was thus narrower than the citizens' *jus civile*, its significance increased with the years, and by the 17th century it had become a designation of people's rights; but even Roman authors under the influence of Stoic philosophy occasionally use the term 'people's rights' of the 'law applying to all living beings' (*jus animantium*) — which was not exercised in any community, but which the Stoics had advocated in their writings.

In his earliest known work Seneca argues that: 'Fortune (*fortuna*) has distributed badly those things which are common to man and has allowed men born with equal rights to be subject to the dictates of others.' He moreover maintained that the essential thing is the moral attitude, not social position. But the ability to achieve one of the high-ranking posts, the honorary posts, *honores*, as they were called because they were unpaid and could thus only be undertaken by people of wealth, did not depend on the moral attitude, but precisely on the wealth and rank of the person concerned, and, in particular, on his 'friendships'. Perhaps it was due to philosophical scruples as much as to illness that Seneca was so long in entering the service of the State, which it was otherwise possible to do once you were 25 — Seneca was more than ten years older when he took the step. And the very fact that there was a limit to the influence attached to any grade meant that primarily ambition was satisfied — or not satisfied, for appointment to the lowest grade, that of quaestor, qualified you for the next ones, and that of praetor qualified you for a consulate; and it was felt almost as a humiliation if you did not reach the top of the ladder and, as consul, have a year named after you. On several occasions Seneca mentions this structure of state posts as an example of the vanity of human endeavours.

Meanwhile, his elder brother, Novatus, had had a successful career, in which he was doubtless helped by the fact that he was the adopted son of one senator Junius Gallio, who nevertheless brought down Tiberius' wrath on himself. But Seneca had other connections, especially his aunt, the widow of an imperial prefect: 'Even for my post as quaestor I am indebted to her, for she, who otherwise could not bring herself to speak or even to greet people in a loud voice, overcame her nervousness out of love for me... She became ambitious on my behalf.' — Ambitious is the right word in this context: *ambitiosus* means 'someone who goes the rounds' — and speaks well on behalf of himself or his protégé; thus the word gradually acquires the sense of striving for honour (ambitious in its modern sense) — and of an excessive desire to please.

Seneca's aunt pleased the right people, and Seneca became a quaestor (a financial administrator), and thus, when his period of office expired, also a senator. By then Caligula had succeeded Tiberius, and Rome had jumped from the frying pan into the fire.

IV THE TYRANT AND THE PHILOSOPHER

Caligula the god

When Caligula succeeded Tiberius, everyone breathed a sigh of relief. A couple of years after Caligula's accession the philosopher Philo was granted an audience by the Emperor in Rome as the spokesman for a deputation of Jews from Alexandria accused of refusing to worship him as a god. In his account of this most remarkable audience Philo tells that the Age of Gold, the Saturnine age, was no longer seen as a myth — 'because of the general affluence and well-being, the freedom from sorrow and fear, the joy and festive mood observed every day and every night in all people and all houses, and which persisted ceaselessly for the first seven months of his reign.'

The Age of Iron had once more turned into an Age of Gold. Even if Philo does not paint a reliable picture of the real state of the empire, he nevertheless gives an impression of the dominant mood, of the willingness of the many to worship the one. For a people without a share of power, the only way to a sense of power is to identify themselves with the powerful; but to satisfy this need for identification the ruler must either be a father figure commanding the respect of all, or else a promising young man. The unapproachable and unpredictable Tiberius, however, had not been a man with whom people had been able to identify themselves; on the contrary, they had taken all the more part in the misfortunes which had befallen Germanicus and his family. Now that Germanicus' last and youngest son, the 25-year-old Gajus, generally known by his pet name of Caligula, had assumed the imperial power, it was felt that justice was triumphant and a new age dawning. Caligula, still in the words of Philo, was considered a saviour and benefactor who would bestow an abundance of good deeds on the whole of Asia and Europe. All the greater was the dismay when after the first seven months of festivities the Emperor was taken seriously ill: 'Every part of the inhabited world was ill with his illness, indeed there was a sense of an illness more terrible than the one he was suffering from, for his illness was only physical, while the illness suffered by all people in all places attacked their spiritual strength, their peace, their hopes, their participation in and delight at all good things; for people began to remember how great and manifold are the evils springing from anarchy: famine and war, the destruction of forests, the devastation and conquest of land, the loss of property, abduction and the fear of slavery and death, evils which no doctor can cure and which knew of only one medicine: Gajus' recovery.'

General concern was, according to Suetonius, so great that some wanted to take up weapons in the fight for the Emperor's recovery, while others promised to sacrifice their lives for his — a promise which after his recovery Caligula demanded should be kept! We do not know the nature of Caligula's illness. Nor is it clear whether it provides a partial explanation of the peculiar behaviour which he subsequently exhibited; though even without an explanation of this kind his behaviour does not seem to be entirely inexplicable. He had grown up in his father's camp as the forces' favourite; even as a child he went dressed as a soldier and wore boots (caligæ) and so became known as Caligula; as a five-year-old he had taken part in his father's celebration of triumph after his victories in Germania, and as a seven-year-old he had taken part in his funeral procession, which at the same time had been a demonstration aimed at Tiberius, who was thought to have been implicated in his death. He had become accustomed to seeing himself as one destined to great things — and exposed to great dangers: he saw his mother exiled and heard of the deaths of his brothers while he himself was kept as a sort of prisoner in the imperial residence, first in Rome and later in Capri, and he could expect his turn to come. He witnessed Tiberius' distaste for the flattery which nevertheless was necessary in order to avoid his displeasure. He himself survived by dint of his obsequiousness and his ability to hide his desire for revenge; according to the orator Passienus Crispus he was the best of all slaves — and the worst of all emperors. As Emperor he took the consequence of his experiences in the imperial court and made himself the principal figure in a grotesque farce, an absurd drama, the tension and comedy of which depended on the fact that every single actor in the performance could lose his life at any moment. It is absurd that one man should have unlimited power over all others; such power is otherwise only fitting for gods, and so there was a certain logic in the fact that Caligula had himself — and, incidentally, also his sister

88

Drusilla, whom he married — deified: 'Just as those tending other animals, oxen, goats or sheep, are not themselves oxen or goats or lambs, but human beings whom fate has raised to a higher level, so I, as the guardian of the supreme flock of all, that of men, must be considered quite different from them, not of human, but of a superior, divine nature.'

Caligula received the Jews from Alexandria in a great park where he was inspecting buildings. They greeted him as Augustus, and he acknowledged their greetings; 'in such a gentle, human fashion that we felt that we had lost not only our cause but also our lives.' The Emperor said, 'Are you those haters of the gods who refuse to consider me a god; I who am recognised as such by all other nations, but not worthy of a mention for you.' The Jews answered that they had offered up great sacrifices when he came to the throne. 'Yes,' said the Emperor, 'it is true that you offered up great sacrifices, but you offered them up to another, even if it was in honour of me, so what is the use of that? You did not make your sacrifices to me.' Caligula went into another building, and the Jews had to follow him: 'Up and down, mocked and spurned by our opponents as though in a mime, for in reality it was all a mime, with the judge playing the accuser and the accusers a bad judge concerned only with his own antipathies and not with the truth.' And indeed the accusers formed part of the procession, loudly proclaiming their appreciation when Caligula remonstrated with the Jews. When he had a spare moment he asked a solemn and important question: 'Why do you not eat pork?' While their opponents shouted out in delight the Jews tried to explain that different people have different customs, and that there are also some who do not eat lamb. 'Quite right, too,' replied the Emperor, 'for it doesn't taste good.' And as they went on with their explanation he hurried into another room where he gave orders for translucent stones to be put into the windows. Then he noticed the Jews again and asked, 'What have you to say to it all?' — and as soon as they started to say something he went into another room and ordered some paintings to be hung up. But at last he was placated and said, 'These men appear to me to be not sinners but poor fools, since they refuse to believe that I am divine.'

Comfort in death – and death as a comfort

Philo is one of the two of Caligula's contemporaries to write an account of him. The other is Seneca. Seneca had become a greatly admired orator, but Caligula, who thought himself to be the greatest orator of all, was not taken with him, and using an architectural metaphor said that his buildings were all joints, and that there was no mortar in his sand. Gods are not keen on men who compete with them, and Caligula, of course, was a god: 'Seneca, who outshone his contemporaries and many others, too, in wisdom, was close to downfall without either doing anything wrong or giving the impression of doing so, simply because in the presence of the Emperor he conducted a lawsuit too well in the Senate. Gajus ordered his execution, but let him go free because he believed one of his friends who said that Seneca had advanced tuberculosis and would die in the near future in any case.' Perhaps this is the episode to which Seneca alludes in an epistle in which he talks of his illness and adds the somewhat ambiguous remark: 'For many illness has delayed death, and it was the saving of them that they looked as though they were close to death.' Under such insecure circumstances it might well be necessary to prepare yourself philosophically for death, and Seneca's first (extant) piece of writing is a letter of consolation to a woman called *Marcia* who could not get over the loss of a son — though his death had been from natural causes. In his lengthier philosophical manner Seneca says about the same as Hans Christian Andersen in 'The Story of a Mother': we do not know our fate beforehand; some are born to fortune, some to misfortune, and even a man who, like Marcia's son, has lived a happy life is not secure against the whims of chance: the very man who is most favourably placed might well have the very best reason to wish he were dead — a thought also expressed by Andersen when he let his Lucky Peter die at the height of his happiness. But these general truths are given a sharper point: 'For who can be found today whose circumstances are so secure and well-founded that he has nothing to fear of the future?' Seneca rejects myths concerning the realm of the dead and the torments encountered there and dwells instead on the exquisite torments which men inflict on men (though in principle 'only' on slaves): 'I see all the stakes before me, not all alike, but differently designed by the different designers: in some men are hanged with their heads downwards, on others they are impaled through the belly, on yet others they are crucified; I see the wooden collars, the whips and the machines specially made for individual limbs. But I also see death!' — What value would there be in a life under such a threat without the knowledge that it would have an end? We might love our lives *because* they will come to an end; there is only one way to ensure a full life: by living it to the full.

The letter of consolation, *consolatio*, was a genre much loved by ancient philosophers, whose philosophy of course had to prove itself even in the most difficult situations. Seneca follows an established pattern when he first looks at Marcia's situation and recognises that her sorrow is justified — only gradually to take the ground from under it, since sorrow cannot benefit the dead, but only harm the living. The evil thing is not the first involuntary emotion, for that is not subject to the will; but continuing, implacable sorrow can betoken a defiant will, and an unhappy person can actually seek solace and enjoyment in suffering. Moreover, in Rome professional mourners were obligatory in cases of death, and it was considered to be a token of respect to wear mourning, so — especially from a woman — convention demanded more tears than the loss itself. In this context, however, Seneca gives an example of the difference between convention and 'natural law': the sorrow of an animal is intense but short-lived, and if women are more inclined to tears than men, and barbarians more than civilised people, the explanation cannot be found in nature, for what is natural cannot be 'different'.

For Seneca *virtus* means particularly an individual's strength of resistance, and while the ancient Roman *virtus* was reserved for the man (*vir*), Seneca emphasises in accordance with Stoic tradition that there is no essential difference between man and woman: a woman's moral strength is just as great as that of a man. Among the examples which he finds worth following there are several Roman heroines, and Seneca can even go so far as to mention Marcia herself, who in unhappy circumstances had earned respect and recognised that death can be better than life. Her father Cremutius Cordus had written a history of the civil war, and during Sejanus' regime he had been accused of praising Brutus and calling Cassius the last Roman — a crime, writes Tacitus, which had hitherto been unknown and only recently invented. Cremutius voluntarily starved himself to death;

Marcia did not seek to prevent him, but saved his work for posterity. On the other hand, Caligula, who reacted against the literary taste of his predecessors and wanted to remove busts of Vergil and Livy, allowed the publication of Cremutius' work.

Among his consolatory arguments Seneca points out that myths do not allow even the gods themselves to escape sorrow — and that misfortune can also take its toll of emperors: 'so that they, too, can benefit mankind by showing that although they are supposed to be the offspring of gods and to have gods as their offspring, they have less power over their own fates than over the fates of others.' Previous emperors, the divine Caesar and his son Augustus, and Tiberius, are mentioned as examples of men who have been able to bear the loss of their closest relatives with composure; there is no reference to Caligula, but the silence tells its own story. In a later consolatory letter he is called, 'this man who could neither sorrow nor rejoice with dignity;' when his sister, the empress and goddess Drusilla, died he decreed national mourning and punished all those who did not look sorrowful, while he himself resorted to empty forms of diversion.

The right to rebel

The lack of a reference to Caligula in the letter of consolation to Marcia indicates that it was written and presumably also published before his death in A.D. 41. In the following works — especially those coming immediately afterwards — Caligula constantly forced himself on Seneca's attention as one of the worst examples he could think of: a man who not only could not control his own passions, but could even enjoy allowing others to suffer the consequences of them. He could use the proceeds of the tax from three provinces just to pay for a single meal, but he was not concerned with the supply of provisions in Rome; he could wish that the entire Roman people had only one neck, so that all their crimes could be dealt with at a single stroke, but as this was not the case, he struck off the heads one by one and achieved quite an impressive number. This 'sometimes so charming and forthcoming young man' could show such consideration for the closest relatives of those he had executed that on the very day of the execution he might invite them to dine at his table and make sure that they really enjoyed themselves. Or he might otherwise have them executed to free them from their sorrow. 'He had senators whipped and indeed went to such lengths that he had every reason to remark that this was the normal thing; he employed the most dreaded instruments of torture: the wooden collar, the iron boot, the wooden horse, fire and his own face.' Suetonius tells us that Caligula practised terrifying people out of their minds by his mere outward appearance, and rehearsed wild postures and facial expressions in front of the looking glass. In Seneca's opinion this was not at all necessary: he was sufficiently repulsive because of his sly looks, his pallor, his head (which, he says, was like that of an old woman with sparse hair), his thin legs and enormous feet. He hated being called either Caligula or Gajus, and he felt his imperial dignity insulted at the drop of a hat, but he loved to hit others where it hurt — something which rebounded on him at last: a certain tribune of the guard[1] by the name of Cassius Chaerea had a somewhat feminine voice, and Caligula suggested that his sex life was somewhat feminine, too, giving him watchwords such as Venus and Priapus (a pretty lecherous fertility god). Chaerea became the leader of the conspiracy which brought Caligula down: it was he who struck off the head of the Emperor. To the very end Caligula tried to fool his enemy, saying as he died, 'I am still alive'.

In his next two works, 'On anger' and 'On the steadfastness of the wise man', Seneca wrote of the folly of allowing oneself to be incited to anger or revenge and of the wise man's immunity to insults. Curiously enough, Chaerea receives a positive mention in this context, despite the fact that he allowed himself to be incited to anger and revenge and was susceptible to insults: 'It must be a consolation to us that, although in our compliance we have omitted to avenge ourselves, someone will surely come and demand the punishment of the man who has shamelessly and arrogantly subjected us to injustice, for evil qualities of this kind are not only directed against a single individual, nor do they result only in a single insult.' Apparently the compliance (facilitas) referred to here is not to be understood in a positive sense. The sensitive political question of whether it is wise in all circumstances to

---

1.   The praetorian guard consisted of ten cohorts of 1000 men, each under the command of a tribune. In the rest of the army there were six tribunes and sixty centurions to every legion (of 5-6000 men).

tolerate everything is not directly asked by Seneca, and he could hardly have done so in the circumstances. However, Cato appears not only as the model of a wise man who refuses to be insulted, but also as the model of a man of the opposition who refuses to submit to tyranny. Hercules was said to have opposed and overcome all kinds of terrors, and so he stood as the mythical exemplar of the wise man in the Stoic tradition; but what Hercules did in the myth, Cato did in reality: 'He did not pursue monsters with fire and sword, for he did not live in an age when men thought that the sky was supported on the shoulders of a giant: the old belief was dead, and his was a wiser age. What he fought against was ambition, which assumed so many distasteful guises, and that incredible yearning for power which not even a third of the world could satisfy... and freedom did not survive Cato any more than Cato survived freedom.' How was it possible to live up to this example under the rule of Caligula, whose yearning for power could not be satisfied by the *entire* world — 'this man who was born to make the customs of a free society give way to Persian tyranny'?

Seneca writes not that a nation *must* revolt against a tyrant, but that it *will* do when he has continued to harass it for long enough: 'The control of the passions and especially of this particularly vicious and unbridled passion (i.e. anger) is useful to slaves, but it is even more useful to rulers: everything is lost if by dint of their position men find it possible to give rein to their anger, and a power which is wielded to the detriment of the many cannot be long maintained; it is put at risk where all those who individually have something to complain of are united in a common fear. Therefore most tyrants have been brought down, sometimes by individuals, sometimes by the people when general dissatisfaction has forced them to combine their anger.' The more respectable figures in Seneca's tragedies (cf p288) say similar things to the tyrants, and the tyrants make roughly the same answer as, according to Dio Cassius, Caligula made to the Senate: this compliant assembly had first paid homage to and then scorned a Sejanus and a Tiberius — so how much importance could he, Gajus, attach to the homage that the Senate was now doing to *him*? Tiberius, said Caligula, had given him this advice: 'Spare none of them, for they all hate you and will murder you if they have an opportunity... Look exclusively to your own advantage and security, then you will not be molested, and you will manage best; you will also be honoured by them, whether they mean it or not. But if you adopt the opposite course it will not really benefit you: you may achieve a meaningless fame, but it will not do you any good, and you will be the victim of intrigues and meet a miserable end... Only as long as a man is afraid will he submit to the stronger man; otherwise he will wait for an opportunity to bring down the man who is weaker.'

The senators were horrified; they could not console themselves by saying that it was the unpredictable emperor's gentle jest, for he was calling unpleasant truths by their proper name: he was murdering in self-defence — and their only effective self-defence was to murder him. Perhaps there was a weak point in Caligula's logic of revenge: if it is the cruel ruler who constitutes the greatest danger to his subjects, it is also he — and not the gentle ruler — who is *in* the greatest danger. Later Seneca was to impress on Nero that gentleness is the ruler's best defence; but for Caligula there was no way back to the position of 'saviour and benefactor', and for his subjects there was no way forward which did not go over his dead body.

Agrippina and her accomplices

The purge in the imperial family meant that Caligula had no close relatives who could become rivals to him; only his three sisters had been spared, for they, of course, could not be emperors. At first Caligula's relations with them were good, and Suetonius maintains that they were also sexual. He had people swear by himself and his sisters, and he had the consuls begin their speeches by asking blessings on the same elevated personages. Later he only had them swear by the divinity of Drusilla, and it may be that the other two sisters, *Agrippina* and *Julia Livilla*, felt slighted, especially when during his illness Caligula made a will leaving all his possessions to Drusilla.

At that time Drusilla was still married to M. Æmilius Lepidus, who came from an ancient noble family and by dint of his marriage could reasonably hope to be next in line for the throne. Caligula cheated him by recovering and marrying Drusilla himself; but when Caligula made himself more and more impossible, Æmilius Lepidus tried to make the most of his possibilities. If Drusilla could not pave his way to the throne, perhaps Agrippina could.

95

In 28, when she was about 12 years old, Agrippina had been married to *Cn. Domitius Ahenobarbus* and on the 15th December 37 she had born him a son who came to be called Lucius Domitius Ahenobarbus, and who was subsequently given the name of Nero. According to legend it had been prophesied that Nero would become Emperor but murder his mother, to which Agrippina made the reply of a loving mother: 'Let him murder me, provided he becomes Emperor.' However, this scarcely sounds probable: Agrippina was not as unselfish as that. She certainly paved her son's way to the throne, but in doing so she paved her own as well; as a woman she could not achieve the highest pinnacle of power, so she needed the help of men; and she knew how to get it. Not only was she endowed with both intelligence and beauty, but doubtless also with an unfailing conviction of the right which by dint of her blood she had to the throne: she was the great-granddaughter of both Augustus and Livia (who had no children together). So, of course, was Caligula, but as he had disgraced the family by his eccentric behaviour, she was the obvious person to re-establish its honour and dignity. She herself did not shrink from the most immoral means of achieving her aims, but she nevertheless felt moral indignation when her distinguished relatives showed themselves incapable of preserving their dignity — at least on the surface.

Agrippina and Æmilius Lepidus came to an understanding — and to a sexual relationship. Tacitus is of the opinion that she surrendered herself to him less from a desire for sex than a desire for power; Agrippina always tried and usually managed to secure in the most efficient way the men of whom she made use.

In 39 Caligula, who after all was the son of Germanicus, went to war against the Germanic tribes. The expedition had no military objective or result; Suetonius tells that Caligula made some of his Germanic guards hide on the other side of the Rhine and then advanced on them and bravely lopped some branches off the trees. Meanwhile the Emperor had taken Æmilius Lepidus and both his sisters along with him, and this suggests that there was an objective after all, and that he behaved in such a strange way in order to fool his enemy. His enemy was not the Germanic tribes, but *Cornelius Lentulus Gætulicus* who had commanded the troops in Upper Germania for ten years, and whose position was so strong that he had been able to refute an accusation of having been in league with Sejanus. Now appearances seemed to

Gajus, known as Caligula (12–41 A.D.; Emperor from 37 A.D.). Ny Carlsberg Glyptotek, Copenhagen.

The praetorians. Restored relief from the time of Hadrian. Louvre, Paris.

indicate that he was in league with Lepidus and Agrippina, and Caligula had caught wind of it; the expedition ended with Lepidus and Gætulicus being beheaded and Agrippina and Julia Livilla banished: as a proof of their guilt their correspondence was made public.

Seneca makes a single reference to Gætulicus when praising the Lucilius to whom he wrote his epistles; he puts these words into his mouth: 'Gajus has not been able to make me betray my friendship with Gætulicus.' He also mentions Lepidus in one of his epistles and remembers, 23 years after the conspiracy, the name of the military tribune, Dexter, who beheaded him. It can be deduced that Seneca's close friend Lucilius was implicated, and we might suspect that so was Seneca himself. This is admittedly a guess which has not been made before, but neither has there before been any explanation of the otherwise most extraordinary fact that Seneca, who was not of a distinguished family, achieved a close relationship with Caligula's sisters — and his relationship with Julia Livilla was indeed so close that he was later accused of having an immoral relationship with her. The most likely explanation is that Agrippina sought allies in her attempt to bring down her brother — and sought them among his enemies: and Caligula had a particular dislike of the well-known orators. One of these was that Passienus Crispus who said of Caligula that he was the best of all slaves and the worst of all emperors — and whom Agrippina married after the death of her first husband.

As Caligula was carrying out an energetic purge of the intellectuals, it was in their interest to bring him down, an interest which it was possible to justify by means of Stoic philosophy. The traditional reason given for the execution of Gætulicus, who despite his military career was a poet and historian, is that Caligula feared him for his popularity with the soldiers and produced a conspiracy as an excuse to get rid of him; but it is more probable (as J.P.V.D. Balsdon, the champion of Caligula also believes) that he was at the centre of the conspiracy led by Agrippina and Lepidus, and that Caligula went to war in order to pre-empt a revolt, especially as he had replaced both the consuls just before his departure.

Anything strange about Seneca's finishing one of his pieces on the wisdom of being uninfluenced by insults with some consolatory words to the effect that surely someone will come and avenge us, becomes less strange when it is realised that Seneca could not directly defend the

97

murder of a tyrant, but only hint that there must be limits to our 'compliance'. Seneca sympathised with Chaerea and apparently more than sympathised with Gætucilus, Agrippina and Julia Livilla — and the consequences for him were to be fateful.

The author and his 'books'

Seneca's three books 'On anger' (*De ira*) are his first work of any size. They were quite obviously written under the impact of Caligula's régime: his presence makes itself so clearly felt that on one occasion Seneca has to remind himself that of course it is not Gajus' fury but anger as such that he is describing, even if Gajus' cruelty is very relevant indeed. The first book was presumably published in the actual year of Caligula's death, A.D. 41, but in fact we know nothing of when Seneca's works were published or how they were received, and we only know them from medieval manuscripts, the earliest of which was written down in the 8th century after the birth of Christ — which was the 8th century after the birth of Seneca.

Here, at the beginning of Seneca's career as a writer, it must be mentioned that a Roman could not make a financial career as an author. He had no copyright on his work; anyone could copy it and sell it, but usually the author sold it to a bookseller, who reproduced it in a very efficient manner: 'Twenty scribes, writing for several hours a day, could doubtless produce a thousand copies — which was considered to be a fair-sized edition — in a fraction of the time it now takes to publish even the most modest book' (H.V. Morton). The text was written down from dictation on papyrus sheets which were then glued together in a roll (*volumen*) which the reader unrolled as he read, and from which it was difficult to read aloud if the reader wanted to gesticulate, as the Romans usually did. It could also be difficult to unroll a quotation; this is why the Romans often quote imprecisely, from memory. Larger works were divided into 'books', which usually filled a roll each. As a rule, Seneca's 'books' are in the order of 30–40 pages.

The authors could also themselves publish their works by reading them aloud themselves. This could be done before a specially invited audience, who apparently considered it to be one of the duties and nuisances of social life to act the part of a literary public; or the less well-established poet could gesticulate and raise his voice anywhere where he could smell an audience, in the market place or in the baths: poetry was one of the commonest of street sounds in Rome. Seneca scarcely tried to make his works known in this way, but he, too, sometimes had to sit and hear people read aloud: 'The reader comes with a long screed, written very small, rolled very tight, and when he has read a long passage he says, "I will stop here if you like." The shout, "Read! Read!" is heard from them all, though they only wish he would be silent on the spot.'

'On Anger'

It is tempting to bring Seneca's *ira* up to date by translating it as aggression, all the more so as there is no better Latin word for aggression (though the word comes from *aggredi*, i.e. go over to, go for). Since Konrad Lorenz published 'On Agression' in 1963 there has been an argument as to whether aggression is natural to human beings and whether it serves some good purpose, as Lorenz believed. Aggressiveness, which is necessary for animals in their fight for survival, becomes over-developed in man and turns him against himself after he has overcome the other animals. War between human tribes must have resulted in an explosive growth of all so-called 'bellicose virtues' — in other words, of *virtus*! But in Lorenz's opinion the situation is not so simple that it is possible to abolish bellicose virtues and keep the others, and to the Romans *virtus* was not only the term for army morals, but for morals in general. 'Aggredi' — writes Lorenz — 'in its most original and widest sense of attacking a problem or concluding a task, would probably disappear from the lives of human beings if aggression disappeared.'

Strangely enough, Seneca makes a polemical attack on this view, though he ascribes it not to Konrad Lorenz but to Aristotle: 'He who does not know anger is a sluggish soul.' 'This is true,' replies Seneca, 'if there is nothing more powerful than anger in that soul. For it is not necessary to be either the attacker or the attacked, either sympathetic or cruel: one is too soft-hearted, the other too hard-hearted; the wise man must know the golden mean, and the strength of his actions must not be due to anger but to spiritual strength.' Anger cannot be used as a weapon in the service of the good, because unlike other weapons it cannot merely be laid aside. We only reluctantly entrust even ordinary weapons to agitated men: in gladiatorial combat and in war he fights best who maintains his reason and his ability to judge.

Here *ira* is nevertheless translated by anger. Perhaps aggression sounds more formidable and scientific, but anger sounds more human or, perhaps, more inhuman; it is a moral concept. And Seneca's psychology, like the psychology of the ancient world in general, is always inclined to express a moral judgement: its principal theme is the passions which disturb peace of mind — and which ought not to do so. The many portraits of historical personages with which Seneca illustrates his ideas are not psychological portraits, but moral sketches to frighten or (on rare occasions) to serve as an example. It is a virtue to understand, but only if the understanding leads to a more moral way of behaving. An 'objective' understanding of the reasons why a human being cannot act otherwise than he does was beyond what the philosophers of the ancient world could or would achieve. Seneca's *theoretical* understanding that there are inborn differences of psychology and not merely differences of class between human beings, so that the same cannot be expected, let alone demanded, of everyone, was limited to the doctrine of the four temperaments: since nature consists of four elements, earth, water, air and fire, men, too, must be made up of them, and according to whether the dry, the wet, the cold or the hot elements predominate, men become melancholy, phlegmatic, sanguine or choleric in nature. Since anger is the worst of the passions afflicting peace of mind, it is the choleric man who is most likely to lose *that* — and who thus constitutes the greatest danger to others.

Since at the same time anger is morally reprehensible it follows naturally that Seneca has to deny the existence of anger in animals, for of course they cannot act differently from what they do. By translating *ira* as aggression we would, then, end by denying the existence of aggression in animals; but that could probably be managed by distinguishing between *iracundia*, aggressiveness as an involuntary urge common to animals and men, and *ira* the aggression of which only human beings can be guilty — and which only human beings can control. And this is exactly the distinction made by Seneca: anger is not involuntary, but is the result of reflection and presupposes some sense of injustice; indeed Seneca actually defines it as the desire to avenge an insult. But to say that anger is only possible in human beings is not the same as saying that it is natural to human beings; human beings are distinguished from animals by dint of their reason, and while an animal reacts involuntarily and instinctively, men act wilfully and deliberately. That reason replaces instinct in human beings means that where reason is lacking there is no control of the passions, no — to use a modern expression — 'instinctive inhibition' towards one's fellow creatures. If man cannot control himself, and if such uncontrolled men rule, then society is 'a society of wild animals, apart from the fact that *they* behave acceptably towards each other and refrain from biting their fellows, while we feel satisfaction in tearing each other apart. We are distinct from dumb animals in that while they are docile towards those who provide them with food, our fury is also fed by those who feed us.'

Human beings can completely lose control of themselves not because they are partly reasonable and partly unreasonable but because they are either the one or the other; man is not by nature divided against himself. Plato and Aristotle had stressed the opposition and conflict between the noble and the less noble elements in the soul; the Stoics on the other hand emphasised the unity of the soul. This view is the epistemological precondition for the practical possibility of becoming wise, raised high above common worries, and it is also the explanation of how a man can become as devoid of reason as he in fact can. Reason and natural urges are not natural opposites: properly speaking and properly used, natural instincts or urges are reasonable: 'For the will does not occupy a special position so that from the outside it can observe the passions and try to prevent them from running wild, but it is itself changed into passion and can no longer recapture the useful and salutary strength which it has already discharged and deprived of its strength. Passion and reason have, as already stated, not different and distinct places, but they transform the will for the better or the worse.' The change for the worse is really the will's own fault: it results not from involuntary impulses but incorrect ideas; for instance — if the passion is that of anger — from the idea of an insult.

However, if you really have sustained an injustice, the idea of injustice is not wrong. Nor will Seneca deny that injustice occurs; he only argues that it is not wise to feel wronged. There is so much

101

enjoyment concerned with feeling wronged that the feeling must be suppressed before it grows too strong — the Romans, as far as can be judged, were quick to feel their dignity, *dignitas*, insulted, to feel wronged or to become indignant. Seneca does not distinguish between righteous and unrighteous indignation, between the sense of personal wrong and indignation at wrong as such, but he rejects both: 'If a wise man really ought to be as angry as is demanded by indignation, then he would not only have to be madly furious, but furiously mad.'

At the same time Seneca shows all signs of intense indignation, especially at the evil deeds of the great. The man who is forced to suffer insults in silence does not become so great a rogue as the man who can always take the liberty of following his impulses, and therefore anger is particularly common in 'the rich, the distinguished and the high-ranking, when all the vain and empty qualities in them have come to the top, just as they themselves have.' To them anger becomes so much a habit that no insult to their (imperial) self-esteem is necessary to bring it about; on the contrary, they provoke and imagine insults in order to have an excuse for fury — 'and they want to see people whipped and torn to pieces not in order to enjoy their revenge, but to enjoy themselves.' In this way anger, which as such is acute, has become chronic and thereby turned into cruelty. And since cruelty needs no insult it need not be an expression of indignation: 'Therefore they can laugh and rejoice and wallow in sensual pleasure and in general appear to be anything but angry: they can rage at their leisure.' This, of course, was the case with Caligula, although it is not he, but the traditional enemy of the Romans, Hannibal, who is named as an example at this place. The great are thus great examples of how anger ought to be contained before it becomes too great: others will oppose it if they do not do so themselves.

It is not wise to work up a fury over injustice, but neither is it wise to put up with injustice: it must be opposed, but without anger, without aggression, for with evil evil is not contained but magnified. And while it is true of a single individual that he gives cause for fresh injustice and fresh anger by taking his revenge, it is even more true of society and of those in authority. Just revenge is unjust: the object of punishment is not to satisfy the person punishing, but to improve the one being punished: 'We must not hurt a man because he has done wrong, but so that he shall not do wrong, and we must never punish with a view to the past, but with a view to the future, not in anger but in care.'

These words have been quoted before today; Alf Ross, the philosopher of law, writes that they have been quoted to an intolerable extent as words of wisdom, although the contrasts formulated by Seneca are 'nonsense which is only possible because it has not been understood that the conjunctions "because" and "so that" indicate completely different relations;' of course punishment is meted out *because* a fault has been committed and *so that* a person shall not do wrong: one is the cause and the other the object of the punishment. Logically this is quite right, but not entirely right if we look at the situation in the light of history and psychology, for a great deal of understanding is necessary before it is possible, like Alf Ross, to understand that it is a question of two completely different relations, and that there is therefore a difference between revenge and punishment. The Romans did not in their language make a clear distinction between revenge and punishment, between wrong and injustice, and had thus not achieved this understanding: they demanded that murderers should be thrown to murderers in the arena, not to frighten people from murder, but to satisfy their thirst for blood. Seneca was not content to observe that punishment is widespread where crimes are many, but he was clear-sighted enough to add that the opposite is also true. Those brutal punishments were the very ones he considered not to be frightening examples, but bad examples which 'rebound on those making them' — thus giving rise to yet more anger and more desire for revenge. 'When you judge the morals of one individual, think of those of the whole of society,' he wrote, thus emphasising that social conditions play their part in producing crime — and they are not improved through harsh punishments, which on the contrary have a brutalising effect on society. Seneca wrote in fact at greater length on the right to punish in his treatise on gentleness than in that on anger.

In speaking out against retribution and revenge — 'an inhuman concept which is nevertheless considered just' — Seneca was thinking not of different logical relations, but of different human relations. The evil chain of revenge and crime cannot be broken by revenge and punishment, but by forgiveness; if all sinners were to be punished, no one would go free, not even ourselves: Seneca, like St. Paul, says that we are all sinners — and like Jesus he exhorts men not to judge.

Considering that Seneca's entire way of looking at things is one of moral evaluation, it might seem that this is a contradiction, but Seneca himself says that in condemning the evil deed we need not condemn its perpetrator — in his place we might well have been guilty of the same thing.

The Stoics, who proclaimed that man *can* control his own circumstances, were the very people who exhorted people not to judge those who are at the mercy of their circumstances; there would be a basic contradiction in this if the suggestion were that we should begin by improving the others and not ourselves, or if it were not principally anger, the desire for revenge, which had to be combatted, in ourselves and in others. We cannot, however, free ourselves from the pressure of circumstances by being angry with them, and to become angry with others is the poorest imaginable way to teach them better. We do not become angry with a child because it does not know better, and yet: 'To be a human being is a better and more reasonable excuse than to be a child.'

However, just as anger can best be opposed before it is fully developed, the tendency to anger can best be combatted before a little human being is fully developed. A good upbringing must seek to inhibit aggressiveness — without inhibiting the natural temperament, something which might well present certain difficulties, especially if the temperament concerned is choleric by nature. So it is a question of finding the right middle way: the spirit is crushed beneath compulsion and flowers in freedom, but too compliant an upbringing creates irritable people; praise can give self-confidence, but applied thoughtlessly it can result in arrogance. Seneca's views on the upbringing of children can still be read as a contribution to discussion of the subject; admittedly, as a Roman he stresses that a child must be brought up to respect older people, but he adds that older people must also do their bit to deserve the respect of the child — and neither spoil nor humiliate it. He particularly emphasises that upbringing must prevent class arrogance, as a higher social station easily leads to a higher degree of anger; the child should not be allowed to win over his pedagogue, who belonged to the slave class, and it must enjoy the same conditions as those of its own age: 'He does not mind being compared with one who from the start has been placed equal to the many.'

For us adults the only thing we can do is to learn self-control. If we have not progressed so far that we can cope with any situation, we ought to avoid situations with which we cannot cope: jobs which are above us, exertions which are beyond us, bad company, painful subjects — everything which tires the body and soul and causes irritation. A large part of the third book consists of this kind of prescription for mental hygiene.

The wise man is he who can cope with any situation; only a man who has conquered human weakness has the right to judge it in others — and he is just the man who is unlikely to do so. It could be argued that the numbers achieving wisdom are so small that it might be doubted whether the Stoic man of wisdom is anything more than an ideal. Nevertheless, Seneca can still stress the paradox that wisdom is the easiest thing to practise, for it requires less effort to be in control of the forces within yourself than to be opposed by them. In a passage which is 30–40 years later than Seneca's treatise on anger, Jesus is quoted as having said, 'Narrow is the way, which leadeth unto life, and few there be that find it.' 700 years earlier Hesiod had said that the way to virtue is long and steep. Seneca, on the contrary, says: 'Nature, which has created us for what is right, comes to our aid if we will improve ourselves. Nor is it correct, as some have thought, that the way leading to the good is steep and narrow: it is the direct way. I will not purvey idle talk: the way leading to a happy life is easy, you can take it with good prospects and with the help of the gods themselves. It is much more difficult to do what you are doing. What is so reassuring as a peaceful spirit, what so troublesome as anger? What relaxes more than gentleness, what makes us more tense than cruelty? Chastity is always unemployed, lechery is extremely busy. It is easy to control all good qualities, but it is hard to be the slave of the bad ones. Anger should be banished (this is partially admitted by those who say that it should be reduced): it must be completely rejected, for it can benefit nothing. Without it crime can be opposed with greater ease and justice, and the guilty punished and brought to better ways. All the wise man has to do he does with kindness alone and without employing things difficult to control.'

The wise man and the human state

'On anger' is one of those works by Seneca which have been handed down under the name of 'dialogues'. They are not discussions like the philosophical dialogues of Plato and Cicero, or only in the sense that they are addressed to another person whom Seneca allows to produce objections, which he then goes on to refute. 'On anger' is addressed to Seneca's elder brother Novatus, and as he otherwise is praised as being free from vice it might seem surprising to find him in the role of an apologist for anger. In this case, however, it is reasonable to distinguish between Novatus as the man to whom the work is dedicated as a member of the family, and the fictitious interlocutor whom Seneca needs for the sake of his arguments.

The situation is different when we come to the 'dialogue' which further develops the ideas expressed in 'On anger'. 'On the steadfastness of the wise man' (*De constantia sapientis*) is addressed to a younger friend and relative of Seneca, Annæus Serenus, who was later appointed to a high post in Rome, and it is aimed at the objections to Stoicism which Serenus in fact had voiced — and which were fairly common.

The dialogue seems to result from a number of discussions between Seneca and Serenus, for we read that Serenus 'usually' says that the Stoic wise man has never existed. To which Seneca, of course, usually cites Cato as an example. But then Serenus cannot understand how Cato allowed himself to be insulted by the crowd in the Forum. He was not insulted, replies Seneca — it is not Cato we should be sorry for, but the State, the republic, which his opponents brought down: they could not harm Cato, for the wise man is raised above insults. Serenus, however, has heard too much of all this Stoic talk. You maintain, he says, that a wise man is never poor and never a slave, and that he is impervious to insults, but you must admit that sometimes he owns nothing, that he can be in the service of another and that he can be mocked and spat upon, tortured and tormented, condemned and killed. There may well be a difference between *being* insulted and feeling insulted — if you are insulted for long enough, you can become accustomed to it, but why should *that* be called wisdom? You promise miracles — and change nothing in things apart from their name. If you say that it is wise to put up with everything, then any fool can be wise, but if you say that the wise man is raised above injustice in the sense that no one dare do him any harm, then I will be a Stoic! says Serenus, who seems better at wisecracks than wisdom.

We do not maintain, replies Seneca, that a wise man can never be beaten or that he is never sensitive to anything, but that he is never beaten down and never shows his sensitivities. It takes greater strength not to be hurt than not to be hit, and it does not require much of a man to suffer something he cannot feel. The wise man is of flesh and blood, not of stone or iron; he does not live among wise men but among ordinary human beings; he cannot forbid them to do wrong, and the only way in which he can oppose wrong on their part is by not repaying it, and the only way he can improve them is by his own good example. Nor is it true that the Stoics change nothing in things but their name — they call things by their right names and can thus bring about a transformation in things instead of yielding as others do. Particularly the well-to-do and the spoiled give in, for they are sensitive to everything because they have nothing else to do, and they interpret everything in a bad sense because the only pride they possess is that which can be insulted. The wise man has an inner dignity, not an outside show of it — he is as disinclined to be mad with his fellow men as a doctor to be mad with a madman; he is like the doctor among the sick, like the adult among children. Most adults, who collect money and build stone houses which are a threat to their lives (as houses collapsed daily in Rome), have not advanced further than children who collect nuts and build sand castles on the shore and play at judges and high-ranking persons: the Field of Mars, the Forum and the Senate are in themselves a kind of playground. And those who strut around in toga and purple (officials had purple borders to their togas, the official dress for festivals and for denoting peace), only have a false appearance of strength; in the eyes of the wise men they are only weaklings who cannot even govern themselves.

Seneca's lack of respect for the authorities is so striking in this work that it requires an explanation (in the next chapter); otherwise he avoided making critical comments about the Senate. Less surprising is his lack of enthusiasm for the powerful men who distinguish themselves in 'the admirable art of ruining cities' and who have various tribes placed under them, a situation which only exists by dint of a mutual fear which forces them themselves to live in fortified mansions.

Only in the mind of the wise man is there peace, even in times of war; his little house has no doorkeeper, but is open to all — except *fortuna*. 'That there should be some who cannot be conquered and whom fortune cannot harm is in the interest of the human state.'

The human state (*res publica generis humani*) is Seneca's phrase for the *other* order which the Greek philosophers of nature sought in the natural order and upon which the Stoics founded human law. The conclusion of the treatise on the wise man emphasises that his cause is the cause of all, which coincides with Cicero's view of the state. The human state is not a utopia in the sense of a nowhere — it means those natural relationships between men which cannot come into their own in a society where passions dominate, i.e. where disunity dominates the whole: man seeks what is worthy of man; in passion one seeks one's own advantage.

The greatest glory (*gloria*) achievable is to transform anger into friendship, writes Seneca in 'On anger'. He continues: 'What would the Empire be today if a wise providence had not allowed the conquered to mix with the conquerors?' Seneca was not, like Vergil, only talking of the Roman race, but of the human race: the Roman Empire as the human state was the aim. But *that* was a utopia.

V. EXILE IS LONG BUT LIFE IS SHORT

Claudius, Messalina and Julia

Caligula's death was followed by relief — and confusion. The Romans had no written constitution, and the peculiarity of the Emperor's constitutional status emerged clearly when there suddenly was no Emperor. The first two emperors had, albeit with some difficulty, appointed their own successors; Caligula had not been so far-sighted. There were senators who wanted to grasp the opportunity and reconstitute the republic, but even if the Senate had agreed, it would only have been able to force through its will with the help of the praetorian guard which Sejanus had been far-sighted enough to station in Rome itself. And the praetorians acted more quickly than the senators.

It was an ordinary guardsman, Gratus, who discovered Caligula's successor when looking for his murderer. Claudius had hidden behind a curtain in the imperial residence, but his feet were sticking out, and when Gratus dragged him out Claudius thought that now it was his turn to be murdered. But the guardsmen took him to their camp and swore an oath of allegiance to him — thereby creating the precedent that an emperor first of all had to be recognised by the army. Claudius thanked the soldiers with gifts of money, and all subsequent emperors did likewise.

Although it seemed to be something of a coincidence that Claudius was dragged out in this critical situation, he was in fact the late Emperor's nearest male relative, and no other criterion existed. Although the brother of Germanicus and the uncle of Caligula, Claudius had so far not had the opportunity of distinguishing himself; he had been kept in the background, for he was no impressive figure: he stammered and was inclined to sway when standing; he had a nervous twitch in his head, and he was considered to be slightly weak-minded and therefore only suited to intellectual tasks: he became a learned man, studied the Etruscans and wrote historical treatises. Tiberius had treated him with scorn; but Caligula, who at one time considered making his horse a consul, graced his uncle with this title. Claudius maintained that in order to survive he had had to make himself appear more foolish than he really was, and although some people thought it impossible, he revealed both wisdom and a sense of judgement after becoming Emperor. Admittedly, he felt more in control of the situation when pronouncing legal judgements, something for which he had a mania, than when making governmental decisions; the timidity which had been knocked into him he took with him to the throne, and the fear of being murdered, which he had experienced in the first moments of his elevation, was something he continued to feel.

As Claudius had been kept out of political and social life he had had to find his own companions. Some of them were slaves, and a learned man had learned slaves (and the unlearned often had them in order to appear learned). It was common for the most able slaves to be freed — and to be entrusted with work of special responsibility for their former masters, who were now their 'patrons'. When Claudius became Emperor his emancipated slaves took over most of the administration of the State. In this way the timid Emperor could hide behind his former slaves and feel at home on the throne. However, he might also have had other reasons for this: the Senate was not an effective organ of administration, and it was beneath the dignity of free-born men to undertake office work. Consequently, without any constitutional basis, and simply in their role as the personal advisers to the Emperor, Claudius' freedmen became the most powerful men in Rome.

The most powerful of all were *Narcissus*, who was in charge of the imperial correspondence, and *Pallas*, who ran the Emperor's — and thereby to a large extent the State's — finances. (Pallas' brother Felix was made procurator in Judæa and appears as such in the Acts of the Apostles. Narcissus is mentioned in the Epistle of Paul to the Romans, 16.11, where a greeting is sent to those of his house which are in the Lord). *Polybius*, too, is worthy of mention. Apart from being secretary to Claudius, he had gained a reputation by translating Homer into Latin and Vergil into Greek prose; now he was appointed head of the department of applications. He often had the honour of walking with a consul on each side, says Suetonius disapprovingly, adding that, 'Under the rule of these men and his wives, (Claudius) really played the part of a servant rather than a ruler.'

110

On becoming Emperor, Claudius was almost fifty, three times as old as his (fourth) wife, *Messalina*. Like Caesar and Maecenas, Messalina is one of the relatively few historical personages whose reputations have been such that their names have come to stand for general concepts. She only had seven or eight years in which to make herself felt, but her position at court was a good starting point for a messalina, which means 'a shameless, immoral woman'. While Agrippina apparently only satisfied her desires in order to satisfy her desire for power, power for Messalina was a means to the satisfaction of her other desires. Messalina's mother, Domitia Lepida, was the sister of Agrippina's first husband, Domitius Ahenobarbus, and thus the aunt of Domitius (Nero), whom she looked after during the exile of Agrippina. So Messalina had been a sort of foster-sister to Nero, in whom she was later to see a rival to her own son, Britannicus. If blood ties with Augustus were the best qualification for the imperial throne, Agrippina's son had a better claim than Messalina's: Nero was a 'Julian', while Britannicus was only a 'Claudian'.

Apart from the fact that Claudius had Caligula's murderers executed so that they should not get the idea of murdering him as well, he proclaimed a general amnesty on ascending the throne; all exiles could return home, and amongst them were Agrippina and Julia Livilla. Claudius, who was notably fond of women, was very taken by his beautiful and gifted nieces, and Messalina felt a threat to her position. Dio Cassius writes: 'Messalina was furious with Julia because she never revered or flattered her; she was also jealous because Julia was extremely beautiful — and often alone with Claudius. And so she had her exiled by trumping up various charges against her, including one for immorality ... and she was the cause of her death soon afterwards.'

Agrippina avoided trouble because she was more cunning — and had succeeded in winning Pallas, the 'minister of finance'. The help of the ministers seems to have been necessary to achieve anything with the Emperor — and Messalina had allied herself to Narcissus. Seneca is among those who confirm this; he also quotes his friend Lucilius, the man whom he praised for not having betrayed his friendship with Gætulicus during the reign of Caligula, as saying: 'Nor have Messalina and Narcissus, who were enemies of society before becoming enemies of each other, been able to make me change my attitude towards a certain person with whom it was dangerous to be on good terms.' That person was Seneca himself. He and Julia Livilla were accused of having had an illicit relationship and were exiled to different islands. Seneca was sent to Corsica.

Augustus' laws on moral behaviour, which made various forms of extra-marital sexual relations a crime and were thus intended to raise the moral standard of society, were naturally a useful means of achieving private revenge; if you wanted to hurt two people, it was convenient to hurt them both at one fell swoop by asserting that they had sexual relations with each other. But no one would find a member of the imperial family and a distinguished male member of society guilty of immorality unless they were in disgrace for other reasons; Dio Cassius mentions that other accusations were indeed made against them, but he gives no indication of what they were, and the accusations were probably only pretexts for Messalina, who thus got another female of the imperial family exiled and put to death.

Seneca, who was married at this time, must have renewed his acquaintance with the fair Julia when she returned to Rome, and as he had been an accomplice of her and Agrippina, it was not difficult for those who wanted to do so to see something suspicious in this. It is noticeable that the historians, who are not usually particularly coy on that point, do not specifically say that they committed adultery, but only that they were accused of having done so. It is tempting to see Seneca's own version of the matter in these words: 'Imagine, too, how many kinds of insult are at the disposal of those who want to do us down: it can be done by means of a paid accuser or a false accusation or by making us hated by the powerful or by whatever other cunning tricks can be thought up in a peaceful society.'

These words are taken from the treatise on the steadfastness of the wise man, which was doubtless written in Corsica and can thus be read as Seneca's own attempt to be steadfast. So his younger friend Serenus was not only indignant on behalf of Cato, but also on behalf of Seneca. Among the trials which even a wise man can be subjected to Seneca mentions: 'the loss of honour or close relatives, unwanted divorce, an involuntary change of residence.' This last phrase was used by the Stoics as a euphemism for exile, and three weeks before his exile Seneca had lost a small son. In writing of the wise man's house which is open to all except fortune, he may have been thinking of his own more

112

Claudius (10 B.C. – 54 A.D.; Emperor from 41 A.D.). Ny Carlsberg
Glyptotek, Copenhagen.

Agrippina the Younger (15–59 A.D.), daughter of Germanicus, sister of Caligula, wife of Claudius, mother of Nero. Ny Carlsberg Glyptotek, Copenhagen.

Portrait of Nero as a child. Ny Carlsberg Glyptotek, Copenhagen.

modest surroundings in Corsica, for otherwise he did not live in small houses. And when he adds that the man who is armed against fortune does not allow himself to be laid low by those who are only the tools of fortune, it might be possible to see a hint of who the tool was: 'Some are foolish enough to believe that a woman can insult them. It matters not who that person is, how many bearers, how many heavy ear-rings, how elaborate a throne she possesses, she is a person without reason, and unless she has received some education or knowledge, she is incapable of controlling her wild instincts and her desires.' Seneca did not usually employ such harsh words of women — and he would scarcely have adopted this tone in speaking of Julia. It may well not matter who it was, but Seneca's contemporaries must have seen it as a reference to Messalina. If the treatise on the steadfastness of the wise man was published during Seneca's exile it showed that he had not allowed himself to be laid low by fortune — at least not by the first blow.

Seneca himself reveals that it was not Claudius who brought misfortune upon him; on the contrary, the Emperor broke his fall — and had him sent to Corsica: 'He spoke out for me in the Senate and not only did he give me life, but he begged for it.' The Senate, of which Seneca himself was a member, and which in 'On the steadfastness of the wise man' he compares with a playground, must have wanted to condemn him to death, despite the fact that immorality was not punishable by death, but only by exile and possibly the confiscation of half one's belongings. Only in political trials was the death penalty usually demanded for members of the higher strata of society.

Suetonius says that the accused were not given a chance to defend themselves. Tacitus has no information on the trial of Seneca (as his 'Annals' for the years 37-47 have been lost), but what he tells of another trial might throw some light on it. Messalina got the informer Suillius, who was later to play a part in Seneca's life, to accuse a man called Asiaticus, whose parks she wanted to take possession of. Suillius accused him of having been implicated in the murder of Caligula — and for immorality. Asiaticus had to do away with himself.

Informers, *delatores*, were also employed in the case of Seneca and Julia. An epigram which must date back to the exile in Corsica indicates that there were people in Rome who were making efforts to keep alive his unfortunate reputation; the poem alludes to those threats against grave-robbers, with which tombstones were often adorned; here the warning is directed against the person who profits by someone else's misfortune:

> Whoever you are (shall I obey my suffering and reveal
> your name?), enemy who even refuses to leave my
> ashes in peace. Not satisfied with knowing a life to be
> ruined you direct your mortal blows at a man who is
> dead. Believe my words: there are powers which
> nature itself gives to the dead; on the grave the shades
> stand guard. Hear, O worthless one, what the gods
> themselves will tell you, what the spirits of my
> forefathers themselves tell you, but hear: misfortune
> brings one struck by misfortune; touch not my fate:
> Break not the peace of the grave with importunate hand.

Can a man in all circumstances develop his abilities to the full? If he can, then he can certainly be said to have a potential for wisdom. Seneca thought it possible, and believed that freedom meant being raised above insults and finding in yourself the source of your happiness. He doggedly went on calling exile a change of surroundings, as though the surroundings did not mean anything, but otherwise made no effort to portray as better than they were the circumstances to which he was supposed to be immune:

> Wild and barbarous is Corsica: enclosed by its cliffs,
> desolately waste and inconsolate wherever the eye sees.
> The autumn knows no fruit, the summer no cornfield,
> and without Minerva's graces (i.e. olives) the winter is
> barren and grey. The spring has much rain but delights
> not a tender shoot, not a single blade of grass grows on
> ground deserted by the gods. Bread there is none, nor
> water, nor yet a spark to light thy funeral pyre, and
> here an exile finds nought but exile.

Seneca on Corsica

But even this barren island with its inhospitable position and its harsh climate has been the goal of one nation after another, something which

Seneca points out to show that his change of surroundings was not too bad. First came the Greeks, then the Ligurians, then the Spanish — Seneca could still see traces of this in the hair style and footwear of the Corsicans! And finally came Marius' and Sulla's Roman colonialists. Together with Sardinia, Corsica had become a Roman colony immediately after the first Punic War (in 238 B.C.), but the island as such had not become Roman; the Romans kept together in the large colonies of Aleria and Mariana on the east coast, and they were still regarded as foreigners by the natives. Seneca scarcely made life so uncomfortable for himself that he did not remain among his fellow countrymen on the east coast; it is true that he gives the impression of only hearing barbaric speech, and from ancient times a tower near Luri at the northern end of the island has been known as 'Seneca's Tower', but it does not date from such ancient times, and the area is difficult of access. And yet the way leading to wisdom also looks steep and winding from a distance; when you come close the inaccessible peak is seen to be made up of slopes and paths. This is the image with which Seneca begins his treatise on the steadfastness of the wise man, a work which seems to indicate steadfastness rather than wisdom and in particular gives the impression of being a programme piece. In his works from Corsica Seneca writes less about his external circumstances than about his efforts to free himself from them — and so we do not know whether Seneca ever got up to Seneca's Tower — but we can follow his path to wisdom, though, unfortunately, not to the very end.

After demonstrating his philosophical steadfastness to Serenus, Seneca gave his attention to more tender feelings in the letter of consolation to his mother, *Consolatio ad Helviam*, which has several times been quoted from above. Within very few months Helvia had lost her husband and two grandchildren in addition to Seneca's own son; and now, of course, she had in a way lost her son. Seneca exhorts her to rejoice all the more over those whose company she can still enjoy, her sister, her sons and her grandchildren, Novatilla and Marcus: 'May he survive us; may fate be content to rage at me!' exclaims Seneca, as though he had a presentiment that Marcus one day would meet the same fate as he.

But before Seneca reaches the more personal grounds for consolation, he examines the philosophical ones. Helvia had never looked to her sons for support, but had rather been willing to support them, and she had always found it more difficult to bear the misfortunes of those closest to her than her own. So Seneca has to try to convince his mother that he is not unhappy. He admits that he has waited so long with this letter because at first he had enough to do to console himself, and that only now does he feel strong enough to comfort others. Not that he has achieved wisdom — in that case he would not only not consider himself unhappy, but he would actually feel himself to be the happiest of all men. But in his weakness he has sought strength in the strong, and he exhorts his mother to do the same; it is in this connection he complains that his father had not thought that philosophy was suitable for a Roman and certainly not for a Roman woman.

Of course, the strong man does not allow himself to be influenced by his surroundings, but on this occasion Seneca emphasises that the weak man is particularly subject to bad influences in luxurious surroundings. Things in excess of the necessities of life do not limit our wants, but stimulate them *ad infinitum*. Seneca, who in *De ira* had attacked what was to be one of the seven deadly sins of Christianity, now strikes from his inhospitable rocks at three more of them: *avaritia*, *gula* and *luxuria*, i.e. avarice, greed and covetousness, and he formulates the well-known dictum on the high life of Rome: *vomunt ut edant, edunt ut vomant*: they vomit to eat and eat to vomit. And what they eat is not what tastes best, but what costs most. They destroy the forests in order to build ships to transport the expensive goods which their stomachs cannot contain; their purses are full and their souls empty. To do without all this is only a misfortune if those ancestors who founded the Empire lived a life of misfortune.

After listing his adversities one by one and overcoming them with his arguments Seneca lets his mother object that misfortunes, exile and poverty and disgrace have really all come at once. And in fact they are all overcome at once, replies Seneca — in accordance with the Stoic theory that man is not both passion and reason, but either one or the other. It may well be that the Stoics and Seneca are right in this, but that in itself does not make things any easier for someone who is not yet wise. A further look shows that Seneca writes that *the wise man* will not let himself be overcome by the misfortunes he encounters — but he does not say that he himself is wise.

116

Of the actual cause of the misfortune and dishonour which have overtaken him he has nothing to say except that no one is despicable who does not first despise himself. Other people's opinion of a man cannot change him: 'For the creator of the world, whether it be an almighty God or a reasoning spirit, powerful in its mighty works, or a divine spirit pervading the greatest and the smallest things, or fate and an unchanging chain of inter-related causes, has so arranged things that nothing is subject to an alien will, except the most insignificant of all. What is of real significance to man is beyond human power, and it can neither be given nor taken away.'

Here, as in the words of solace to Marcia, the sometimes slightly down-to-earth words of consolation finally give way to a vision of universal proportions. The world, nature, is arranged according to reason, and so is man by his nature: that is really why man need not be laid low by human power. Seneca took a broad view of philosophers' disagreements on the great questions: whether the world is ruled according to the teachings of the Aristotelians, the Stoics or the Epicureans, or by an almighty god, it *is* ruled, and the heavenly bodies are lofty witnesses to this. It was to them he raised his eyes when downcast, it is they in their unchanging course with which he compares his imperturbable wise man, and it is in the consideration and study of divine nature that he finds comfort in this otherwise comfortless island of Corsica. He tells his mother that he is studying the earth and its place in the universe, the seas with their ebb and flow, the space between heaven and earth, which contains countless terrors like lightning and thunder, wind and rain, hail and snow, and the heavens themselves: 'Remembering its own eternity, the soul progresses through everything which was and will be to all time.'

Seneca is here professing Plato's teaching of the pre-existence and immortality of the soul. In the letter of consolation to Marcia he shows her late son being received in heaven by his famous grandfather Cremutius — and lets Cremutius pronounce the supreme consolation: that souls do not die but return to the eternal regions from which they come. However, the world conflagration will put a limit on immortality, for in the end it will reduce everything to the first elements: this is the fate of all men and all things. Seneca uses the thought to comfort Marcia, and now in Corsica he actually derives consolation from it himself:

117

Greedily time seeks to devour all things and render
them desolate, to rob everything of its place, to let
nothing remain. Now rivers diminish and disappear,
now the ocean flees the coast, mountains crumble and
lofty peaks collapse and fall. But why talk of such
small things? The vault of this glorious heaven will of
itself suddenly burst into flame. Everything must die,
not as a punishment, but in obedience to a law: One
day our world will no longer exist.

Very conveniently, time has devoured the beginning of Seneca's third
and last letter of consolation, that to *Polybius*, the powerful minister
who occasionally enjoyed the honour of walking with a consul on each
side. Thanks to time, this epistle now begins with the idea that
everything will return to primeval darkness and chaos: And how can
we expect that fate will spare the individual when this is the common
fate of all things? Polybius had lost his younger brother, and Seneca
sought to console him with philosophical argument and historical
example — this latter being all the more appropriate in this case as
Polybius of course was secretary to the historian Claudius. Polybius
was probably less in need of consolation than the two mothers, Marcia
and Helvia; and the reason for the letter to him seems more artificial
and the tone less personal — but more private: Seneca's principal
object was scarcely to comfort the minister for applications — but to
remind him of his existence.

It cannot be surprising that the words appear somewhat artificial in
what is really a camouflaged application; for how is it possible, when
in reality you are applying for permission to exchange your 'little
house' for a bigger one, to suggest to a powerful man in the imperial
residence that he should take a broad view of the big world around
him. Nevertheless, Seneca flatters Polybius by saying that he is raised
above those things such as money and power and honour which men
envy each other. That he had them was common knowledge, but he
could not get enough of them. Seneca goes on to say that only the loss
of one other person could hurt Polybius more than the loss of his
brother, and that was the loss of the Emperor. That *he* is alive must be a
great consolation in this situation! Moreover, unique appointments
lead to unique duties: the great shall be the servants of the small, and

this is particularly applicable to Polybius: he is a man to whom all people turn in unhappy circumstances, and he cannot allow himself to be unhappy. But this applies even more to the Emperor, who through his clemency is healing the wounds inflicted on the Empire by his predecessor. The Emperor's *clementia* is something which Seneca himself is the first to extol, for it was the Emperor who pleaded for him in the Senate. Even the exile is safer under Claudius than the mightiest under Gajus, but Seneca nevertheless hopes that the Emperor will go even further in his mercy and look more closely at his case: 'For me the favour will be as great whether he recognises that I am innocent or wants to call me innocent.' Claudius has of course shown that the Empire is better ruled by kindness than by weapons — words which might have been a doubtful compliment to the not particularly energetic Emperor if Seneca had not at the same time emphasised that he did not flinch from using weapons: the campaign against Britain had just begun (in 43), and Claudius was on the point of leaving for the front in order to be able to return home triumphant and live up to the example of his father and his brother Germanicus. In such solemn moments rulers were traditionally inclined to be merciful, and Seneca had taken this into consideration: he probably sent a formal application to the Emperor and — in the knowledge that Claudius had difficulty in making his own decisions — supported it with this epistle to his colleague.

For in *Consolatio ad Polybium* it is a more famous writer singing the praises of a less famous one and exhorting him to arm himself against his sorrow with intellectual weapons, for literary monuments are the only ones not subject to decay. Polybius ought to write down his memories of his brother and preserve what he has instead of weeping for what he has lost; he ought to write of the deeds of the Emperor and use him as his model; perhaps he should also write fables in the style of Æsop, a genre which had not yet been attempted by Roman writers. (Either Seneca did not know Phaedrus or on this particular occasion preferred to ignore him). Thanks to his eloquence Polybius has the gift of making great things look small and small things great!

These last words might well look like hidden irony; in his praise for Polybius and Claudius Seneca at times verges so close on parody that he must have been aware of it himself; even if he could not play with all his heart and soul, at least he could pull out all the stops. It is also a

119

doubtful compliment to say that Polybius is probably the only person in the imperial court whose friendship people seek out of inclination rather than interest — an observation which in point of fact could scarcely be in Seneca's own interest, for Polybius was not the most influential man at court.

Was it critical insight which made Seneca conclude this letter of consolation and application with an apology for its mediocre quality — or was that also a tactical move? It is difficult to console others when you yourself are disconsolate, difficult to write decent Latin when your ears are filled with barbaric sounds, he admits, even though a wise man ought not to let himself be upset by external circumstances. But he had also to dissociate himself from the most inflexible forms of Stoicism: those who consider sorrow and pain to be beneath their dignity have never themselves been put to the test; not to feel misfortune is inhuman, but not to be able to bear it is unmanly.

Seneca was a human being, and not only a man, let alone a wise man. Like Ovid in Tomi he had made the discovery that intellectual life makes different demands to mere life: the urge to express yourself may well be an inner urge, but it is stimulated from outside — or else it is not stimulated at all. Seneca begged for his intellectual life — something with which some have reproached him; others have wanted to excuse him for, or even dissociate him from, the letter to Polybius, especially because its quality is inferior to that of Seneca's other works. There is no reason for either of these: where the intellect ails, so does the style. Seneca begged for his intellectual life, and his begging letter shows that there was every reason to do so. Seneca had been in Corsica for two years; in the long run it might be difficult to bear a misfortune to which no end can be seen, and no limit had been set on his exile.

But Seneca's démarche did not lead to the desired result, whether because Polybius would not or could not persuade the Emperor — there were limits to his influence, and only a few years later he himself was purged. Seneca was obliged to remain in Corsica for a further six years.

Seneca's epigrams

During this time Seneca does not appear to have produced any major works, but he probably wrote a number of minor ones. From the letter of consolation to Helvia we know that in addition to his nature studies he was engaged on 'some shorter works', and among these must be counted a collection of epigrams, three of which have been quoted above. Admittedly, only three of them have survived under Seneca's name, but they are included with 69 others in a manuscript closely related to Seneca and his time, in particular to the time he spent in Corsica. If Seneca did not write them, others have tried to write them as he would have done, and the second possibility seems less likely than the first, especially as we do not know any other poems by Seneca, who is said by Pliny to have written *versiculi* and by Quintilian to have composed *poemata*.

Two of the poems, nos. 26 and 27, say that monuments decay but poetry will last — a classical theme, the correctness of which is confirmed by the fact that these little poems are better preserved than the Forum Romanum, and one which was also touched on in the letter to Polybius. In the next epigrams (nos. 28—34) Claudius, now departed for Britain, is praised for having united the city (*urbs*) with the world (*orbis*) — such poems Seneca can only have written with an object in view, the same as in the letter to Polybius, which must be from the same time. This might indicate that the poems are arranged in chronological order; the more bitter poems warning against the friendship of the great and against making the most of others' misfortunes are indeed found in the beginning and the lighter ones towards the end, and so it is possible to see a progression from an initial expression of belief in the transience of all things to a final declaration of faith in the immortality of the soul. This last epigram, which has been called Seneca's epitaph, has been seen by some as a Christian falsification, but it expresses exactly the same dualism between the soul and the body as do the letters of consolation:

> Burdens, cares, honour dutifully acquired, flock
> henceforth to others, and leave me in peace!
> The god calls me hence. Accept my farewell, O
> hospitable earth, now that my earthly duty is
> done. Lay the body you claim for yourself in a
> burial mound: The bones I gladly give you —
> and to heaven my soul.

The collection also contains epitaphs on Pompejus, the traditional republican hero, Cato, the traditional Stoic hero, and Alexander the Great, Seneca's pet aversion, who is told that his conquest of the world has only led him to an early grave. The fact that another pet aversion, the Persian king Xerxes, is the subject of three of the epigrams has been used as an argument for Seneca's not having written them, but when Xerxes is said to have transformed the order of nature and to have reversed land and water, and when the solemn words of the great man culminate in an observation that 'the world is most certainly no longer ruled by Jupiter', it is difficult not to see it all as being ironical. In two epigrams the civil war is painted as a war between brothers: a soldier discovers that the enemy he has slain is his own brother and confesses that what used to be a heroic deed (*virtus*) has become a crime, and that by means of a moral effort (*virtus*) he must regain the sense of brotherhood (*pietas*) of which his (military) morals have deprived him. Thereupon he kills himself with the hand that slew his brother, and the poem ends with a prayer to fortune: always guide the civil war so that the conqueror cannot survive the conquered! Like the struggle between Æneas and Turnus in the Æneid (cf p56) this conflict between brothers has a symbolical significance: what has to be vanquished is not the alien warrior, who is not an alien but a brother, but the warrior mentality, and what must win is a different moral code than that of war.

Family intrigues in Rome

Among the more personal poems there are two written to *Passienus Crispus*, to whom reference has already been made. In one of them (no. 14) the poet says that not to have Crispus near him is in itself sufficient exile; the other (no. 52) is a moving poem written on his death, in which he is referred to as *præsidium meum*, my support. Seneca has obviously received both moral and political support from Crispus, who in 44 was consul for the second time; but Seneca's enemies were still stronger than his friends. The warm friendship with Crispus is typical of Seneca's own feelings of 'piety' towards those older than himself and his quite unusual ability to give unstinting praise to others; in one place he refers to Crispus as the most acute man he has known and quotes him as saying that he would prefer to be judged by an Augustus — and rewarded by a Claudius. This lack of confidence in Claudius' power of judgement is something which Seneca also expressed in his letter to Polybius when he said that it did not matter whether Claudius found him innocent or wanted to call him innocent.

Passienus Crispus is one of the few Romans about whom Roman writers only have good things to say. Not until 1939 was Ronald Syme able to say that he was: 'a great courtier, adept at hypocrisy, and the husband of princesses.' The last point is correct, and Syme, who also knew many other things which no one had known before, must have deduced Crispus' qualifications from it. Syme wrote a famous book on the Roman revolution and saw the entire history of Rome as the history of the families, in which tradition, patronage and connections meant more for social position than did personal qualities. This absolutely correct view made him entirely disregard the possibility that personal qualities were of any significance at all, and so it is quite consistent of him to regard all who achieved any position at all as necessarily being hypocrites. As a speaker in the court of the *centumviri*, Passienus Crispus had made such an impact that a statue was erected to him in the *Basilica Julia*; he (or possibly his father) had been adopted by Sallustius Crispus, who as one of the most important figures in Augustus' entourage had gained an impressive position — and a fortune to match. If Crispus himself could not impress the princesses, his riches could surely do so, for the princesses are said to have been very mercenary.

One of them was Domitia, the aunt of Nero and Messalina. One evil tongue said of her that she sold her shoes when she had worn them, and when it was said that this was unthinkable for such a rich woman, the evil tongue said that in fact the opposite was the case: she bought her shoes second-hand. Passienus Crispus conducted a lawsuit on an inheritance on her behalf against her brother, who was the husband of Agrippina and father of Nero. On that occasion he is said to have pointed out to them that they both already had everything the heart could desire, and to have concluded with the words: 'And there is nothing you have less need of than what you are fighting over.'

The other was Agrippina — who stole Crispus from Domitia. Her first husband, Nero's father, had died while she was living in exile, and when she returned to Rome there was no doubt that she needed male

123

and marital protection. It seems likely that she had once allied herself with Passienus Crispus and Seneca and other well-known orators and had brought suspicion on herself by striking up a relationship with Æmilius Lepidus, the pretender to the throne. Crispus did not have 'imperial' blood in his veins, but he obviously enjoyed the respect of Claudius, as he became a consul in 44. So he could be a good foster-father for Nero, at whom Messalina looked askance.

In 47 Claudius arranged a 'centennial festival', 800 years after the founding of the city, and 64 years after Augustus' centennial festival — Augustus had manipulated the figures in order to have the opportunity of celebrating the dawn of a new age. Part of the festivities were what were known as the Trojan Games, in which boys of the nobility could show off their prowess on horseback; among them was the Emperor's son Britannicus, who was six years old, and Agrippina's son, who was ten years old, and the latter received far more applause than the former. This, says Tacitus, was because Nero was still the last male descendent of Germanicus, and because the people were fond of Agrippina since Messalina hated her. And now, because the people were fond of them, she hated her and Nero all the more. She would also have pinned crimes on her and had her accused if she had not had other things to think about.

For she had got a man, C. Silius, on the brain, and as he is said to have been 'the most handsome young man in Rome', this is quite conceivable. It is on the other hand difficult to imagine that she entered into a marriage with him without hiding it from anyone, with the sole exception of Claudius. Perhaps Suetonius is right in thinking that Claudius knew perfectly well but that he allowed himself to be convinced that this marriage could well avert misfortune from him and land Silius with it instead. At any rate, this strange story of love and marriage resulted in the downfall of Messalina. After she had had Polybius liquidated, the other ministers began to fear for themselves, and it was Messalina's old ally, Narcissus, who hinted to Claudius that she was toying with the idea of putting C. Silius on the throne, something which was probably not true. Messalina was executed in 48.

At that time Passienus Crispus had just died, so conveniently that rumour would have it that Agrippina had helped him on the way, but rumour always likes that sort of thing. As Claudius now for the fifth time wanted to sample marital bliss and asked his advisers for advice,

Pallas advised him to marry Agrippina, who of course was of noble Julian blood and would bring a grandchild of Germanicus into the marriage. It was certainly not usual for Romans to marry their nieces, but Claudius allowed himself to be persuaded by the Senate to do what the situation and the people demanded.

'On the brevity of life'

Seneca had not written about the life of luxury in Rome like the sour-faced fox talking about grapes. When he again saw the city which at times he had found it so difficult to do without, all those things which he had found it easy to do without struck him all the more forcibly: the bickering in the Forum, where everyone appeared to accuse everyone else; the fight for official positions which you suffered from not having and then suffered from having; the desire to be considered as somebody by those who are somebody, and then to be considered as belonging to them by those who are not; resentment that they do not devote more of their time to you, while you devote even less to yourself, for you do not seek the company of others to do them a service, but to avoid your own company. When it comes to fortune and possessions, people are prepared to defend them with weapons, indeed with their lives — but if it is a matter of time, which *is* your life, then you ask others to attend to it. For time is not a material thing — and yet it is the only thing we really have and which we cannot get from others: no one can give us our years, and no one can give us back ourselves.

These busy people, men who do not own themselves but as it were are occupied (as the Latin word *occupati* implies), idle busybodies wasting time by not having time, and busy idlers who spend time killing time and life preparing life, are people Seneca writes about as gaily as one of Kierkegaard's aesthetes. There are those who would like to see time suspended until the next gladiatorial games, those who spend the whole day at the barber's and would rather see a revolution in the State than a revolution in their hair style, those who leave all work to their slaves — often trained for the most ridiculous jobs — those who have themselves carried from their bath to their chair and ask the slaves responsible for this important manoeuvre: 'Am I sitting now?' And the useless learning which once acquired makes men more knowledgeable about foolish things and thus more foolish in themselves, comes in for its share of criticism, as for instance consideration of who did what first. Is there any point in knowing that Pompejus was the first to let men fight against elephants and indeed be trampled underfoot by them, or does it not rather make other great men want to go a step further in inhumanity? For how benighted can men become from occupying high positions which never give them peace and quiet to think a reasonable thought? The higher you rise — the more sure you are of falling! One of the arguments in favour of seeking the company of philosophers is that they do not force you to die, but they teach you how to do so.

It was the 'existential' problem, the problem of being himself, of being his own master, which presented itself to Seneca now that his involuntary retirement was in danger of being replaced by the voluntary slavery which it was to put himself in the service of others, so that he had to do everything, even love and hate, on command. And just like the modern existentialist philosophers, Seneca also related this problem of *being* to the problem of *time*: you are only your own master if you are master of your own time — and Augustus, who was master of everything else, was certainly not that. In the dialogues from his exile Seneca wrote that the soul has a share in all time, both time past and time to come; now he says that the wise man has absorbed all the past into himself, and that 'to encompass all ages in a brief moment makes his life long.' Wisdom, of course, means being able to live in time, but raised above time, and: 'It is a sign of an easy, composed mind to be able to move freely in all the phases of your life.' Our past is the only thing which cannot be taken from us, and even that we do not make our own, for we can only do so by constantly answering to ourselves for our lives. 'But the man who has been too ambitious in his desires, arrogant in his scorn, unrestrained in victory, vicious in his intrigues, he must of necessity fear his own reminiscences.'

What Freud calls repression is in Seneca's language simply fear of one's own reminiscences, and with this formulation he emphasises that freedom in a psychological sense — to be able to move freely in all the phases of your life — is a moral phenomenon: life does not become a rounded whole unless you stand by the whole. A man whose life is divisible into parts has been alive but not really lived; life will be without fruit, joy or inner development for the man who forgets the

126

past, neglects the present, fears the future or lives only in the past or the present or the future. For a busy person who has acted without existing it can thus be a death sentence to be relieved of his post; thus the almost ninety-year-old *Turannius*, whom Caligula pensioned off from his post as prefect for corn supplies after he had held the job since the time of Augustus, took to his bed and had himself mourned as dead by all his household — until Caligula, who at least had a sense of the comical, allowed him to continue; he was still working under Claudius.

The work in which Seneca sets down these impressions after his return to Rome, 'On the brevity of life' (*De brevitate vitæ*), is addressed to Turannius' successor in the job as prefect of corn supplies, *Pompejus Paulinus*, who is expressly advised to retire from his very demanding life and take time to live while he still has time. There might be some point in reminding the prefect for corn supplies that man does not live by bread alone — and there might be something presumptuous in doing so. It has therefore been suggested that Seneca was helping Pompejus Paulinus to hide the fact that he was having to retire for political reasons. First and foremost, of course, the treatise must be read as a justification for Seneca's himself not wanting to be taken over completely; he could again take his seat in the Senate and risked becoming a praetor, but he preferred to remain free, and asked to be spared all this in a letter of supplication which admittedly was not addressed to anyone in authority, but to the god of the fine arts, Phoebus Apollo:

> Grant, O Phoebus, that I may complete what I began:
> tiny things not worthy of the envy of the common run.
> Free me from riches; let him be praetor who so wishes,
> make him whom it delights be popular. Give him a
> fleet of ships, and if he is wild about wild things, then
> make him happy in command of armies. Let him but
> terrify provinces with a dozen fasces[1]; Let him thrice
> be approved by the hand of the people[2]; and grant me
> leave to cultivate a little land and my harmless poetry,
> and let my daily companion be a brother. Give me a

1. Proconsuls in Africa and Asia had twelve *fasces* as a sign of their station.
2. i.e. Let him be quaestor, praetor and consul.

peaceful life without haste or reproval, with no room
in my being for fear or greed. Unknown and
unweakened, let me die of old age, let my brothers
attend to my last journey on earth.

Phoebus did not fulfil many of these wishes, not all of which perhaps
were intended to be taken particularly seriously. At any rate, with all
respect to his brothers, Seneca did not find their company sufficient,
but entered into what Dio Cassius describes as a brilliant marriage. His
first wife, who has not left many traces in his work, had meanwhile
disappeared from the story, perhaps because she had left this world, or
perhaps because the involuntary divorce had turned into a voluntary
one. It was very easy, also for women, to obtain a divorce, for
marriage was not 'sacred' to the Romans, and it was no concern of the
State; like adoption, it had from ancient times been a means of creating
an alliance between families, and during the republic divorces for
political reasons had been very common. Originally the woman, who
was considered to be of marriageable age at 12, was subject to the
authority either of her father or her husband in the marriage; in
Seneca's day she herself had the final say on whether to marry, and in
her marriage she kept her legal right to any fortune she might have.
Marriage was entered into in a private ceremony which J. Carcopino
has described and which in his opinion served as the model for the
Christian church wedding; a Roman marriage was admittedly not
made in heaven, but an auspex made sure that the auspices were good
and that the gods thus looked with favour upon the marriage. Seneca's
second wife was called Pompeja Paulina and was, judging by her
name, the daughter (or sister) of the prefect for corn supplies,
Pompejus Paulinus, to whom Seneca thus had yet another reason for
addressing himself.

Seneca and the erotic

Among the epigrams there is a collection of short love poems which
have no connection with what we otherwise know about or by Seneca.
However, they may perhaps be an expression of the elation he felt on
his return to Rome, which both the epistle to Pompejus and the poem

Battle in the amphitheatre in Pompeii between the Pompeiians and visitors from neighbouring Nuceria. Tacitus refers in his Annals to this event, which took place in 59 A.D. and led to the Roman Senate forbidding such combats for ten years. The amphitheatre in Pompeii was built about 70 B.C., and is the oldest in Italy. Its ruins have been excavated and correspond closely to this otherwise amateurish picture. In the foreground there is an open place with booths and tents; staircases outside the arena lead up to the gallery; at the top can be seen the awning over the spectators' seats. Fresco from private house in Pompeii. Museo Nazionale, Naples.

Aureus, *a golden coin, from December, 54 A.D., with Nero and Agrippina on the obverse and an oak wreath 'for the salvation of citizens' on the reverse, in the centre of which is the inscription EX S(enatus) C(onsulto), 'by order of the Senate'. The inscription on the obverse refers to Agrippina, Empress of the divine Claudius, mother of Nero. Nero's titles are relegated to the reverse.*

Aureus *from 62 A.D. with Nero on the obverse and the goddess* Roma *on the reverse, where the inscription tells us that Nero as* Pontifex Maximus *is the supreme priest, is a tribune for the eighth time, and has been consul four times.*

Sestertius, *a copper coin, showing Nero with a laurel wreath, graced with his full title: NERO CLAUD(ius) CAESAR AUG(ustus) GER(manicus) P(ontifex) M(aximus) TR(ibunicia) P(otestate) IMP(erator) P(ater) P(atriae). The reverse shows the harbour in Ostia, with mole and breakwaters. Above them are ships and a lighthouse with a statue; below is Neptune, the god of the sea.*

to Phoebus testify to. In this philosophical work, despite all his attacks on lecherousness, which 'is extremely busy', Seneca writes noticeably little about erotic feeling and seems neither to know Plato's enthusiasm for sensuous love nor St. Paul's fear of the flesh. He certainly wrote on marriage, *De matrimonio*, but what he said we only know from quotations in the Church Fathers. St. Jerome thus quotes him as saying that the wise man does not love with passion but with reason, and in one of his epistles Seneca makes a similar remark: erotic passion is like friendship insofar as it contains its purpose within itself, but as passion it is a sort of 'unhealthy friendship'. The Stoic aim of 'apathy' was not a lack of feeling, but freedom from passion (*pathos*); Seneca stresses that the Greek work *apatheia* cannot be translated by a single word. (Cicero had translated it as 'imperturbability'). Language indicates that passion is something suffered, something in which man is passive, despite his restlessness, but love is active, not bound and powerless, but free — and the only effective prescription for love, says Seneca, was formulated by the Stoic Hecaton: 'If you wish to be loved, then love!'

In his tragedy on Phaedra Seneca invented such glowing expressions for erotic passion that it is improbable that he himself did not know what it was. In the letter to Helvia he wrote that sensuous desire can be controlled with the consciousness, that its purpose is propagation and not merely enjoyment; but things are of course not so simple, and there is no reason to deny Seneca the authorship of the two or three more sensuous epigrams, one of which in the Greek manner is addressed to a boy:

> Oh, a divine countenance worthy of Apollo or Bacchus,
> which neither man nor woman can behold with
> impunity.

Such thoughts were not uncommon in Rome, particularly as the author implies he is willing (or unwilling) also to allow a woman to enjoy the charms of the boy. Seneca also thought up some beautiful expressions for male beauty in his tragedies, though he otherwise rejected 'Greek' love.

All Tacitus has to say of Seneca's love life is that he was accused of immorality. What he and Suetonius and Dio Cassius in the 60th book of his history of Rome see as accusations, is published as a fact by the same Dio Cassius in the 61st book — that is if it is the same Dio Cassius. Dio Cassius wrote his history of Rome at the beginning of the 3rd century, i.e. long after Seneca's time, and the 61st-63rd books, which deal with that time, have themselves been lost and are only known from an 11th century abridged edition by a monk called Xiphilinus from Constantinople. Xiphilinus has one or two nice things to tell about Seneca — that he had an illicit relationship with Agrippina and with boy prostitutes, and that he taught Nero the same art, facts which Tacitus and Suetonius would have taken great pleasure in passing on if they had known anything about them — and which we presumably owe to Xiphilinus' monkish fantasy.

Most of the erotic epigrams are written in the manner of Ovid and addressed to girls with charming fictitious names: Basilissa, Arethusa, Cosconia — and Delia.

> Talkative ear, what means this ringing in the night? If
> only I knew who was remembering me so audibly.
> 'Oh, so you ask who it is who makes your ears ring in
> the night, ring the night long? Delia is speaking of
> you.' Delia speaks of me, of course; more gently I hear
> that hum, murmuring lowly and sweet. Thus Delia
> used to break the silence of night, and with a voice at
> once gentle and urgent, with her arms fondly around
> my neck she caressed my ear with secret words — I
> am all ears! Yes, she is recognised! Now sounds more
> tenderly the music of the ear as a truer echo of a lively
> voice. Oh, let it go on resounding! But, ye gods, even
> while I say it, the sound fades and dies.

Basilissa, who likes playing hard to get, is told that with her ornaments and her make-up she is banishing beauty — and love, too, for love dislikes the over-ornate and seeks 'artless nature', which Seneca also in other contexts calls delightful.

Seneca did not as far as we know write any poems to Pompeja Paulina, at least not under her proper name, but in one of his last epistles, dating from the last years of his life, he writes that she lives for him and that for her sake he must look after the young person who lives on in him as an old man. For, although Seneca doubtless had taught her the fundamental principles of wisdom, Paulina had not learned to show bravery in her love; this was not surprising, for the life she came to lead with Seneca was not a particularly secure one. He was now at the beginning of his fifties, and was said to be intending to visit Athens, the city of philosophers, but instead he was given an important position in Rome, the city of the Emperor. Despite his prayer to Phoebus, he was made a praetor — and imperial tutor. In short, he was taken over, *occupatus*.

VI SENECA AND NERO

Seneca at court

After Agrippina became Empress, writes Tacitus, the city was as
though transformed. Everything was done according to this woman's
will, and she did not play with the State as did the loose-living
Messalina. Her rule was strict and decidedly manly. The manly
element in her rule sounds almost like a point in her favour to Tacitus.
A woman, who played a large part in social life, played no part at all in
political life and could really only make an impact if she actually
became Empress. This might explain part of Agrippina's ambition:
someone with gifts will undoubtedly feel an urge to make the most of
them, and Agrippina was without any doubt politically very gifted.

Agrippina did not see herself merely as the Emperor's wife, but as
his co-emperor; she had homage done to her along with him, drove in
his imperial coach, even in the Capitol, where others were obliged to
walk, and she gave her own audiences, which were announced in the
Official Gazette[1]. Partly with the help of Pallas, she got what she
wanted from Claudius. The year after the wedding the Emperor
adopted her son Lucius Domitius Ahenobarbus under the name of
Nero Claudius Drusus Germanicus Caesar and betrothed him to his
daughter Octavia. It was presumably on that occasion he was given his
own entourage and, as he was only twelve years old, a tutor.

There were several possible reasons why Agrippina wanted to
entrust Seneca with this task. Some sort of connection had existed
between them before, and it had probably been renewed and
strengthened by her marriage to Passienus Crispus. Despite, or perhaps
because of, his long exile, Seneca was a well-known and highly
respected writer, and he owed a debt of gratitude to Agrippina for
being back in Rome. For her part, Agrippina needed allies in her
struggle to ensure that Nero succeeded Claudius. And so she had the

---

1. *Acta publica diurna*: a daily publication which contained official announcements
    and society news.

two prefects of the praetorian guard dismissed and replaced by *Afranius Burrus*; he had distinguished himself as a military tribune and imperial procurator, though his appointment as prefect of the praetorian guard was a lightning promotion for which he could not help being grateful to Agrippina. Agrippina remembered the part played by the praetorians on Claudius' accession, and she knew how important it is to have the power of speech when you want to have power over others: Burrus, the prefect of the guards, and Seneca were, then, the right men to bring up Nero — to be Emperor.

Seneca could hardly refuse an appointment offered by an empress to whom he was indebted, and for philosophical reasons he could scarcely reject that involvement in public affairs which the classical Stoic writers had encouraged. It is a duty, he wrote subsequently, 'not only to think about what should be done, but sometimes also to take action and transform your thoughts into reality.' Now he had the possibility of influencing a young man who would have greater power over others than anyone else if Agrippina's policy succeeded — a policy in which she expected Seneca's support.

Even before this Seneca probably had a liking for Agrippina's son, who was Crispus' stepson and Julia's nephew — though admittedly also Caligula's nephew. Suetonius recounts that it was said that the night after being appointed tutor to the prince Seneca dreamt that it was Caligula he was to bring up. It was natural enough for that sort of story to be told; Caligula was in every respect the very opposite of what Seneca believed a ruler ought to be. Could this 'at times so charming and forthcoming young man' have been brought up to be a better ruler with a Seneca as his tutor? How much could the tutor to a prince accomplish in the dangerous court circles? At court they 'mythical' fratricidal conflict was still very much a part of real life. While Claudius had apparently not realised that by adopting Nero he had brushed his own son, Britannicus, aside, Britannicus himself had apparently realised it: he insisted on calling Nero Domitius, as though he had not been adopted, and Nero complained to his mother, and she complained to her husband, and he gave his son different teachers whose task it was to teach him something quite different.

Seneca's dream was soon fulfilled, says Suetonius: Nero was not long in showing the inhuman side of his nature. Suetonius certainly also points out that so far his upbringing had been neglected, and that while living with his aunt Domitia Lepida he had had a dancer and a barber as his tutors. This was during his mother's exile, and as Nero at that time was only 2 - 3 years old it can scarcely be argued that it was they who awoke in him his desire to play-act or his wish to show off. Since childhood Nero had enjoyed public affection simply because he was Germanicus' grandson, and he quickly accustomed himself to taking popular adulation completely for granted. Agrippina seized every opportunity to let Nero shine in front of the people, but at the same time she kept a 'strict and manly' grip on him and thereby presumably laid the foundations for his fundamental maladjustment. Seneca could have counteracted it if he had been able to put into practice the ideas on the upbringing of children discussed in 'On anger', but from the very start, of course, he was prevented from placing Nero 'equal to the many'. On the other hand he could reasonably well ensure that the pupil did not always win over his teacher; as is obvious from Nero's subsequent relationship with him, he succeeded in securing both his confidence and his respect.

Nero had many artistic gifts: 'He sculptured, painted, practised singing and trained as a charioteer, and the poems which he wrote now and then bore witness to his excellent schooling,' writes Tacitus. Suetonius adds: 'Even in his youth he had already cultivated all the sciences and arts. Philosophy was the only thing which his mother prevented him from studying, telling him that it would be a hindrance to a future ruler; Seneca, his teacher, kept him away from the older orators the better to retain his admiration for his own eloquence.' — Agrippina's harsh words about philosophy are probably from a somewhat later date, by when it had become clear that Seneca would not play the part intended for him; she had at least not prevented Nero from having a Stoic philosopher, Chaeremon of Alexandria, among his teachers. It was as an orator and not as a philosopher that Seneca qualified as tutor to the prince, and rhetoric was, of course, the main study for Romans. Seneca might well have had other motives than personal vanity for not saddling Nero with the declamations of the older orators. Nero was not to learn for the sake of the art but for the sake of life, and his words were going to count far more than those of the pupils in the schools of rhetoric, who had to think up speeches for imaginary situations. For the time being it was Seneca who wrote his public speeches. Previous emperors had been able to fashion their own sentences, writes Tacitus, without heeding the fact that they had not addressed the public at so tender an age. Nero was only sixteen when he made his first speech, in Greek, to the Senate, recommending that Ilium should be granted freedom from taxation — and he was successful in his plea; as Ilium in Asia Minor was thought to be identical with the Troy from which Æneas, the father of Rome and in particular of the Julian family, came, he was at the same time able to sing the praises of his own family. The 'ideological' reason for Agrippina's struggle for power on Nero's behalf was that in contrast to Britannicus he was a Julian.

Seneca was dragged into the court power struggle of which he had already once been a victim. He can hardly have had any reservations about taking the part of his own promising pupil against his old enemy Narcissus, who was soon in open conflict with Agrippina and now supporting Britannicus — whose mother he had had executed. Seneca had been disappointed in his hope that Claudius would allow gentleness to reign; as time passed Claudius, too, became more and more prone to the imperial unpredictability at which Caligula had excelled: he condemned, sometimes absent-mindedly, a great number of senators and equestrians to death; he wanted with his own eyes to see the old punishment for patricide — being sewn in a sack with a snake and other animals and thrown into a river — carried out; and he was an eager spectator at the mortal combats of the gladiators. Perhaps this was his way of getting his own back for the fact that Agrippina in reality had dethroned him — and his son. Nero had married his daughter and had acquired all the (formal) authority which Augustus had earlier given to his designated successors. Claudius is said to have expressed his regret at having married Agrippina and adopted Nero: and that is what is said to have made Agrippina act.

The death and apotheosis of Claudius

In October 54 Claudius died after eating some mushrooms. The old historians are all agreed that he had been poisoned by Agrippina and they betray such detailed knowledge of her methods that it must give rise to some scepticism. The rumour that he had been murdered would have arisen even if he had died a natural death, but on the other hand that is no proof of his not having been assassinated. At all events he died at a convenient moment: Narcissus was away taking the waters, and Agrippina could make the most of the situation to her son's and, as she thought, to her own advantage. Even before news of Claudius' death had leaked out, Nero was presented as his successor — to the praetorian guard, who did homage to him as imperator. The Senate followed suit, and the people were just as enthusiastic as when Caligula came to the throne.

It fell to Nero to deliver the funeral oration. He spoke in praise of the late Emperor's family, as was the custom on such occasions, and all listened respectfully to his account of his scientific achievements and of the peace which had marked his reign. However, no one could keep a straight face when Nero talked of Claudius' perspicacity and wisdom, even though, writes Tacitus with characteristic caution, the speech had been written by Seneca and was very skilful. 'For Seneca had a delightful talent which suited the taste of the age.' Talking of Claudius' wisdom was in itself asking for laughter, but it was far more provocative when the Senate decided to deify the late Emperor, an honour which hitherto had been reserved for Caesar and Augustus, and which Caligula had parodied by producing witnesses to the ascension into heaven of his sister Drusilla. Some witty character, possibly Seneca himself, actually wrote a vicious satire on the apotheosis of Claudius. Its title — *Apocolocyntosis* i.e. not deification, but pumpkinification — is admittedly only known from Dio Cassius, who writes that Seneca wrote a satire on Claudius. Nor is it quite certain that he is talking of the one we now know and which was not handed down together with other works by Seneca. The author does not actually talk of pumpkins, but says merely that Claudius has certain things in common with a spherical Stoic god (who, of course, was identical with the world) and that he is without head or brain. There is no doubt that the tone in this work is different from what we otherwise know in Seneca's writings, but the moral arguments supporting the view that he did not write it indicate a somewhat trite concept of Seneca's personality, a somewhat naive conviction that the man who sang the praises of Claudius in the letter of consolation to Polybius could not have dragged him in the dust after his death. That he had humiliated himself by making a vain appeal to Claudius' gentleness could have been ample reason for insulting the deified

136

Claudius who, like Tiberius and Caligula, had begun better than he had finished.

Although attempts have been made to relieve Seneca of responsibility for the epistle to Polybius on account of its inferior stylistic qualities, he cannot be relieved of responsibility for *Apocolocyntosis* for *that* reason. The satire in it is unsubtle, aimed not only at Claudius' divine status, but also at his human weaknesses, and it contains some rather light-hearted jokes, but stylistically it is of a high quality and is of special interest to literary historians as it is the only extant example of a roman *satura*, which does not originally mean a satire, but a conglomeration of different styles. The author goes from low comedy to elevated rhetoric, from vulgarity to subtlety, from verse to prose; the pedantry of historians is parodied, as is the pathos of the tragedians; the deeds of the heroes are accompanied by quotations in Greek; Clotho, the goddess of fate, swears 'by Hercules', and Hercules himself, who otherwise was the mythical hero of the Stoics, is portrayed more or less as a clown.

The plot is that Claudius, who throughout his life has put on a pretence of being alive, lands on Olympus after his death; the gods are astonished at this peculiar creature, but think he must be some sort of human being; Hercules, who is used to dealing with monsters, looks after him. Like some of Claudius' freedmen, the old god Diespiter now lives by selling citizenship (cf p85), and Hercules gets them to suggest that Claudius, whose wisdom of course is superior to everyone else's, should be incorporated into the ranks of the gods, and that this action should be added to Ovid's 'Metamorphoses'. But then Augustus, who otherwise has not said a word since being made a god, speaks out and asks whether this was why he re-established peace on land and sea: 'This man, senators, who looks as though he could not hurt a fly, threw down heads like dice from a shaker.' Augustus has to limit himself to naming his own relatives, and he mentions both Julia and Messalina, who were never given the opportunity to defend themselves, and finally suggests that Claudius, who for so long has hidden under the name of Augustus, should leave heaven within thirty days and Olympus within three. The divine senate accepts the suggestion, and Mercury accompanies Claudius to the underworld; on the way he sees his own funeral and understands that he has died, and down below he is received by Narcissus and Polybius and other old friends. He is placed

137

before Æacus' judgement seat and found guilty of the deaths of 35 senators, 221 noblemen and countless other Roman citizens — and is condemned to play dice in a shaker without a bottom. Caligula makes a bid to have him as his slave since he can prove that that was how he had treated him, but he cannot be bothered keeping him, and Claudius, who had been the slave of his freedmen, ends as court usher to Æacus' freedmen. Claudius had been as fanatically interested in pronouncing judgement as in playing dice.

Could a lampoon on a deified emperor be published during the reign of his adoptive son and successor — and by Seneca, his teacher? Seneca of course had attacked Caligula during the reign of *his* successor and hoped that Claudius would heal the wounds which his predecessor had inflicted on the Empire; now he hoped that Nero would dissociate himself from Claudius, but only twice does he mention Claudius in his later work, and then it is in a mildly critical tone. However, what he could not take the liberty of doing in his more serious writings, he could do in a *satura*. There was a Roman tradition for following something bombastic with something satirical: thus the triumphant leaders were mocked by their own soldiers in the triumphant procession, and in Emperor Vespasian's funeral procession there was a man who directly and openly parodied the late Emperor. It could not offend the Romans that a man who had spoken highly of Claudius in the funeral oration (which attempts have admittedly been made to deny of Seneca and ascribe to Nero himself) should speak disparagingly of him afterwards: in this way the balance was restored, and the truth about Claudius could be sought somewhere midway between the two.

But *Apocolocyntosis* was not merely written as a counterbalance or for fun. A closer examination shows that the question which Hercules puts to Claudius in the form of a quotation from Homer — 'Who are you? From what tribe? Of what parents?' — is the very question which Claudius *is* learned enough to answer with another quotation — 'Straight from Troy with the wind I came to the ocean city of the Cicons.' However, the next line from the Odyssey ('The city we plundered, the inhabitants we struck to the ground') would have been more suitable, says the narrator — for the suggestion that Claudius came from Troy, the home of Æneas, the progenitor of the Julian family, is the very thing being denied. The goddess of fever, who has accompanied Claudius to heaven, assures us that he comes from Lugdunum (Lyons), and Claudius is so angry that according to his custom he wants to have her executed. Lugdunum in Gaul, where Claudius was born, is called 'the city of Marcus (Antonius)': M. Antonius, who claimed to be descended from Hercules, Claudius' spokesman in the assembly of the gods, was Claudius' grandfather; Augustus' sister Octavia was certainly his grandmother — and so in his speech to the gods Augustus makes the otherwise ambiguous remark, 'Even if my sister does not understand Greek, I do, for the knee is closer than the calf.' This Greek proverb means: Nero is closer to me than Britannicus. As Diespiter justifies Claudius' candidature for the rank of god because of his relationship to Augustus, Augustus' words are decisive, for of course the gods understand a hint. Understood in this way *Apocolocyntosis* is 'a propaganda piece in a political struggle for which in the final analysis the throne was the prize.' (Konrad Kraft).

The propaganda for Nero is plain enough. The important thing, of course, was not what had happened in heaven: the writer says he has it all from the man who saw Drusilla ascend into heaven; so there are limits to the credibility of the story. What happened on earth everyone had witnessed: the day of Claudius' death was the birthday of a new era, and in their joy at this people could take a few liberties, especially as liberty could no longer be taken from them. While the Parces, the goddesses of fate, break the thread of Claudius' life, they spin that of his successor longer and longer; it is of gold as a token of the coming Age of Gold; Phoebus Apollo, who was Claudius' guardian deity, supervises the work himself:

> Continue, O ye Parces, then said Phoebus, for more than mortal span of life should be given to him who resembles me in countenance and beauty, and who can rival me in voice and in the art of singing. He will give a time of happiness to the weary and break the silence of the laws. As Lucifer pursues the fleeing stars from the heavens, or as Hesperus is radiant when they return, as the Sun (at dawn when Aurora, the herald of the day, blushingly dissolves the darkness) with radiant beam surveys the world and draws up the sun chariot which until now has been concealed in

readiness: thus is the Emperor here, whose dazzling
countenance radiates gentle warmth beneath the locks
which add their beauty to that of his neck.

The words were flattering to Nero, but they could also be an
expression of genuine admiration and a faith in better times. 'I would
rather hurt you with the truth than delight you with flattery,' Seneca
wrote to Nero in 'On gentleness', in which he added a warning word
to his flattery and not only made propaganda on behalf of his pupil but
also publicly sought to keep him to the promises he had made. The
rough jesting in *Apocolocyntosis* might also have concealed a more
serious educational purpose: the author might be asking the question
whether you make yourself worthy of being a god simply by being
Emperor — or only through your imperial actions. 'We do not believe
he is a god just because we are ordered to do so,' Seneca wrote of
Augustus, with an obvious allusion to the legal obligation to recognise
Claudius' divinity. Since the theological initiative of the Senate had
probably been taken with the connivance of Agrippina, who for her
part became the priestess of the new god, it can be imagined that Nero
derived more pleasure than she from the satire on the apotheosis of
Claudius.

Agrippina and Seneca: Nero's programme

Immediately after the death of Claudius Agrippina had arranged the
liquidation of Narcissus and an elderly member of the imperial family
whom some considered more suitable to rule than the scarcely 17-
year-old Nero; the first of the murders took place behind Nero's back,
the other against his wishes; but she would have gone on, says Tacitus,
if Seneca and Burrus had not got in her way. Burrus was a Gaul,
Seneca a Spaniard, and it had never before happened that two citizens
from the provinces had occupied such a high rank in court. There was a
contradiction in the fact that Agrippina had chosen her henchmen for
their moral qualifications: Burrus for the strict manner of life
associated with him, and Seneca for the charm and respect (*comitas
honesta*) with which he was surrounded: they were too powerful as

characters simply to be pawns in the court game. 'Moreover —
something which is extremely unusual when two share a position of
power — they acted in complete harmony with each other. . . They
supported each other and did their best to keep the Emperor, who was
at a dangerous age, to harmless pursuits even if he was not interested in
loftier subjects. They had to stand together in their battle with a
furious Agrippina who, fired by all the passions of a desire to rule, had
Pallas at her side.'

Tacitus did not count Nero's artistic interests as 'lofty', and by
'harmless pursuits' he was referring to erotic adventures. The first
object of Nero's affections had been a young lady at court, a freed slave
by the name of Acte, and this infuriated Agrippina, who thought it
beneath his dignity. But the discrepancy between the boy whose
mother would not allow him, and the Emperor who was the object of
everyone's adulation, had grown too big. The only thing Agrippina
achieved was to make Nero keep her at a greater distance and take
Seneca into his confidence, Seneca, of course, being wise enough not to
moralise. The indignation expressed by Tacitus and many later
historians at Nero's 'unfaithfulness' to his twelve-year-old Empress
Octavia was one which he did not share. He even gave Annæus
Serenus, to whom he had written 'On the steadfastness of the wise
man' and who had now become *præfectus vigilum*, the head of the corps
of night watchmen and firemen in Rome, the appearance of being
Acte's admirer and made him act as go-between between her and
Nero.

At first Agrippina always appeared at Nero's side, both on coins,
which were also a means of propaganda, and in reality. She had herself
carried in the same litter, something which could not fail to give rise to
rumours in Rome, for what on earth could they find to do in there? But
when at a reception for an Armenian delegation she made to take her
seat on the throne at the side of Nero, Seneca succeeded in putting her
in her place; he got Nero to go to receive his mother— and conduct
her out of the room. By a whim of fortune Seneca had succeeded his
old enemy Narcissus in the role of Agrippina's chief opponent. If
'gentleness were to reign' in society, Agrippina must *not* be allowed to
reign; Seneca could profit from Nero's personal urge to free himself
and from his popularity with the people, and he encouraged him in an
attitude which was not exactly that of Agrippina: 'He never neglected

an opportunity to display his gentleness, his generosity, even his kindness,' writes Suetonius, while Tacitus comments: 'He professed his gentleness in several speeches — which Seneca had the Emperor make in order to demonstrate his good influence or to spread his spirit abroad.'

The historians have less to say about Seneca's policy than about his role in the power struggle at court, but it is noticeable that they have only good things to say of the government during the five years when Nero looked to Seneca for support in his struggle with Agrippina. The Emperor Trajanus is quoted for a remark to the effect that all emperors were outdone by Nero's first five year period, and it is worth noting that St. Paul's often quoted words about the authorities being of God were written to the congregation in Rome during the first years of Nero's reign: 'For rulers are not a terror to good works, but to the evil. Wilt thou then not be afraid of the power? do that which is good, and thou shalt have praise of the same: For he is the minister of God to thee for good... For this cause pay ye tribute also: for they are God's ministers, attending continually upon this very thing. Render therefore to all their dues: tribute to whom tribute is due; custom to whom custom; fear to whom fear; honour to whom honour.' The Christian community was admittedly not of this world, but at this time it was not in declared opposition to the society of this world.

Nero had explained his programme in his accession speech to the Senate, the contents of which Tacitus sums up. By stressing that he was too young to have experienced civil war and internal strife, and that he did not bring hatred, insults or the desire for revenge to the throne, Nero showed himself as a good pupil of the author of 'On anger'. Tacitus comments that, 'In particular he dissociated himself from all those things which had given rise to such bitterness in recent times. He would not present himself as a judge of everything and would not permit accusers and accused to act in collusion with each other; nor would he permit anyone to be given an unreasonable amount of power. Under his roof no advantages were to be bought, and there was no prize for ambition. He was determined to keep court and state separate from each other. The Senate should be allowed to keep its former authority. Italy and the Senate provinces were to be the responsibility of the consuls, who were then to ensure that the Senate was informed. He himself would be responsible for the armies in his

142

charge.' Suetonius is content to say that the Emperor 'publicly proclaimed that he would rule according to the political precepts of Augustus.'

The essence of this was that the power which Claudius' personal advisers had wielded should go back to the Senate, whose independent initiatives under Nero's predecessors in particular had had the character of obsequious obedience to the Emperor's wishes. The Senate made a great show of its servility, but Nero felt that he was a little on the young side to be given the title of 'The Father of the Fatherland' and also rejected other expressions of homage on the ground that he had so far not shown himself worthy of them. Under Augustus the authority of the Senate had in fact been more formal than real, but Tacitus maintains that at the beginning of Nero's reign the Senate was able to make many independent decisions. In fact, of course, this was no guarantee of greater humanity: in principal the Senate could act as a counterbalance to a harsh ruler, but in reality it was only allowed to have a say in things by a gentle one.

An indication of the government's wish to increase the standing of the Senate is seen in the fact that the coins in 'Nero's five years', which were also Seneca's five years, often bear the inscription *Ex S(enatus) C(onsulto)*: 'By Order of the Senate'; the gold coin, *aureus*, and the silver coin, *denarius*, had on their obverse the oak wreath which was given to soldiers for having saved a Roman citizen — and to which Seneca in 'On gentleness' had ascribed a profounder significance: 'No decoration is fairer or more suited to the Emperor's position than this wreath for saving a fellow-citizen, more splendid than weapons wrought from a vanquished foe or chariots stained with the blood of barbarians or other spoils of war. True divine power consists in saving men in the interest of all; to kill at random and in great numbers is to exercise a power which is also possessed by fires and collapsing houses.' — Seneca started making propaganda for *his* policy on the coins from which Agrippina's portrait disappeared. Other coins from these five years portray the harbour in Ostia, which was completed under Nero, and the meat, fish and vegetable market in Rome, which was opened in 56.

The gladiatorial games

Agrippina had sought to secure control of the Senate by making it hold it meetings in the imperial residence — and being present herself behind a curtain. This did not prevent the Senate from passing a resolution to the effect that those appointed quaestor should not, as Claudius had decreed, be given the duty of arranging gladiatorial games. The reason was presumably that it was too great a financial burden for the quaestors. However, in an imperial edict from 57 Nero also prohibited provincial officials from arranging gladiatorial games, ostensibly because they could thereby bribe the people whose right it was to complain if the governor abused his office, and in these decrees it may perhaps be possible to see an attempt to limit this brutal form of public entertainment. Seneca is the first Roman known to have condemned the games, and it is quite obvious from an inscription in the gladiators' barracks in Pompeii that people were aware of this: 'Annæus Senecas the philosopher is the only Roman poet to condemn the brutal games.' Senecas is the Greek form of the name, and the gladiator concerned must be assumed to have been Greek.

It is at any given time difficult to imagine that everything or even something could be different. Since on so many points Seneca expressed views which have since become common, it is easy to forget that they were not so common in his own day — and to reproach him for not having put his ideas into practice, as though he was all-powerful in his office of advisor to the Emperor; though there is plenty of evidence to demonstrate that in contrast to most philosophers he really did do something. Seneca can scarcely have considered it possible to abolish the games, but it is probable that he sought to limit their brutality — and that in this he had a willing pupil in Nero, who was fanatically interested in the other great Roman entertainment of the races in the Circus, but not in the gladiatorial combats. Admittedly, he had a new wooden amphitheatre built to replace the older one (the more solidly constructed Colosseum was not built until after Nero's time), but at the opening games in 57, 'he had no gladiators killed, not even those who as criminals had been condemned to take part.'

This cannot have been popular — or it was only a very popular emperor who could take this liberty. The vast majority came to see

Zenon (c. 333 – c. 264 B.C.). Roman copy of Greek bust from the 260's B.C.. Ny Carlsberg Glyptotek, Copenhagen.

Seneca, the only portrait with an ancient inscription, part of the double herma of Seneca and Socrates. Copy from c. 240. Altes Museum, Berlin.

blood and wanted any gladiator who had not put on a good show killed, expressing this wish by means of shouts and roars. It was only in this extreme situation that 'the people' had any say, and the Emperor usually followed the wishes of the people when he pointed his thumb, on which all eyes were trained, up or down. It was in the gladiatorial games that the people had the opportunity of feeling an identity with the Emperor, and the Emperor stimulated this by distributing great numbers of gifts. What did the people feel when the Emperor did not follow their wishes? Could they also feel that true divine power consisted in saving men in the interest of all — and feel a part in *that* power?

Seneca made fun of those who wanted the time until the next gladiatorial games suspended, and although it would be going too far to say that the Romans lived for these massacres, there is no doubt that thay had a very important social, psychological and political function in the Rome of the emperors. The Romans had taken them over from the Etruscans, who originally sacrificed captured prisoners of war to their own fallen warriors (evidence of this custom is found both in the 'Iliad' and the 'Æneid') and they then combined the religious and entertainment elements by making the prisoners fight and kill each other. In Rome, too, the games were at first arranged in connection with the funerals of prominent men; in 105 B.C. the two consuls, the highest-ranking officials in the State, had for the first time the duty of arranging the games: it was the responsibility of the State to make harsh examples in order to combat the Greek effeminacy which was now spreading throughout Rome. In the final years of the republic it was especially the important military leaders who put on entertainments in order to celebrate themselves and to win the favour of the people. As is well known, Pompejus was the first to present elephants to the public; Julius Caesar also drew attention to himself in this field and arranged a whole battle with infantry, cavalry and elephants. In 65 he announced so many gladiatorial games that his opponents got the Senate to pass a law limiting the number of gladiators to 320.

Because of the popularity of the games, the emperors were interested in limiting the possibilities of private individuals to arrange them. According to a law of 22 B.C. the praetors (and subsequently the quaestors) were only allowed to arrange games twice a year with a maximum of 120 participants. Of course, this did not prevent the emperors themselves from doing so on particularly festive occasions; in his lapidary autobiography Augustus writes that he delighted the people with a naval battle in which about 3000 men took part, eight gladiatorial combats in which about 10,000 men fought, and combats with wild African animals in which about 3,500 were killed. Augustus and Caligula and Claudius enjoyed watching entertainments of this kind, while Tiberius, who has become renowned for his bloodthirstiness, disliked them intensely; from his day there is a law forbidding masters to condemn their slaves to the arena without a court verdict.

The gladiators were usually slaves, prisoners of war or criminals of the lower classes who could either be condemned to death in the arena or to be trained in the gladiator schools, of which there were three in Rome, and then to fight for three years — with a very slender chance of surviving. But free men who wanted to contract out of society could also sell themselves as gladiators and swear that they were ready to be burned, chained, whipped and killed with the sword. The gladiators were regarded with mixed feelings: they were the dregs of society, popular idols and the objects of superstitious fear. It is no coincidence that the last serious social revolt in the Roman Empire was started by gladiators who under the leadership of Spartacus broke out of the school in Capua and gained the support of thousands of slaves. In the gladiators, who were tortured and tormented, and who conquered and gloated, it was as though the people cultivated those things which were suppressed in themselves, their own degradation and their own desire for revenge. It is worth noting that the games were at their most popular under the *pax romana*, when the Empire was not threatened by enemies from outside and when it was difficult to keep (fighting) morale high and aggressiveness low; in the amphitheatre an outlet was found for aggressiveness, and it could be kept under control. How violent the unrest was under the surface is indicated by the fact that praetorian guards were stationed even at the more ordinary theatre performances; in the first year of his reign Nero abolished this military control to show confidence in the people and in order to let them keep order for themselves. The result was fights between the fans of the different actors and a fear of social unrest — and once more the military had to move in and restore law and order in the theatres.

If passions were thus raised even by the more peaceful plays, how much more likely was this to happen as a result of the warlike and large-scale spectacles! The performance, which lasted all day, began with the gladiators being driven in to the sound of fanfares, parading round the entire arena and greeting the Emperor with *Ave, imperator, morituri te salutant*: 'Hail, Caesar, those who are about to die salute thee!' After a few harmless and bloodless warming-up exercises the real gladiators got going, often dressed in different kinds of armour, some with swords and shields, others with nets and forks; connoisseurs were particularly fond of battles between different combinations of weapons rather than equally matched combats. During the midday interval, while most people went home for a meal, peaceful plays were sometimes put on, though sometimes the time was used to mow down the criminals who had not been considered worthy of becoming gladiators. Seneca witnessed a midday performance of this kind, presumably during the Saturnalia in 62, and he described the public reaction in his famous 7th Epistle:

Nothing is so destructive of one's moral strength as sitting idly at some kind of public entertainment. For then it is easy for vice to creep into us via our lust. How so? Well, when I go home I am more covetous, more ambitious, more desirous of amusement and for that reason more cruel and inhumane because I have been among human beings. I chanced to look in on a midday performance and expected to see something light and witty, a breathing space to allow human eyes to recover from the sight of human blood; but on the contrary. The combats so far had been the deeds of love — joking apart, this is nothing but murder! They have nothing behind which they can take refuge: exposed to blows with their entire bodies, they themselves never strike in vain. Most people prefer this to the more ordinary combats, and even the very popular duels. And why not? There are no helmets here, no shields to ward off blows from the swords: what is the point of armour and a knowledge of swordplay, for that sort of thing only puts off the moment of death. In the morning people are thrown to the lions and the bears, at midday to their audience. There is a demand for murderers to be thrown to murderers and the victor kept ready for a new bloodbath. All combats end in death, which is brought about by fire and sword. And so it goes on until the arena is empty. 'But he committed a highway robbery; he killed a man.' What of it? He has killed someone and deserves to suffer in this way, but what have you, you unfortunate man, done to deserve to see it? 'Kill him, whip him, burn him! Why does he run so timidly at the sword, why is he not bolder in killing, why is he not more willing to die? Whip them so that they are readier to strike and to receive each other's blows with willing naked breasts!' But now there is an interval. 'Then get a few throats cut so there is something going on all the time.'

Do you not then understand that bad examples rebound on those who give them? You can thank the immortal gods that you are teaching cruelty to a man who cannot learn it. The innocent soul who cannot make a firm enough stand for what is right must be kept away from the crowd: it is easy to be swept along by a mass of people.

The words about the man who cannot learn cruelty have often been thought of as implying Nero, though this cannot possibly be the case, as Nero *had* learned by this time, A.D. 62. They should rather be applied to Seneca himself or to any individual who does not become one of the many — as most did in the amphitheatre. St. Augustine tells of his young Christian friend who reluctantly allowed himself to be dragged in and sat with eyes closed until a roar of delight at a mortal blow made him open them — after which he followed the rest of the performance with wide-open eyes. Tertullian's treatise 'On the games' also shows that the Christians were so fascinated by them that counter-propaganda was necessary: even a pure Christian soul must be kept away from the masses which, as Seneca writes elsewhere, 'are a proof of the worst qualities.'

How was it possible to transform this mass of people into individuals — the individuals of which it consisted? There is not only evidence that this mass, this Roman mob, celebrated orgies of bestiality, but there are also plenty of indications of its enthusiasm for moral sententiousness in the theatre; Seneca tells of one Vedius Pollio who was generally hated for feeding his lampreys on slaves, and of the Roman nobleman who asserted his paternal rights and whipped his son to death — and whom the people then fell upon in the Forum. Cruelty did not lead to popularity in Rome; on the contrary, Tiberius and Caligula had made themselves impossible: was this not a hint? Individuals could not learn cruelty, but a crowd could. Could the

Emperor through his good example teach gentleness to the many? Surely an emperor who was so popular that he could even show mercy in the amphitheatre should be able to achieve something by the power of example — rather than merely through his power? In Seneca's epistle to Nero 'On gentleness' — or at least in those parts which are extant — there is no mention of gladiatorial combats, but there is a reference to Alexander (the Great) throwing men to the lions. However, 'the vice of killing, raging, delighting in the sound of chains and beheading people and allowing the blood to flow,' for which Seneca condemns tyrants, *was* the custom at the games in Rome, where it was the people who appeared in tyrannical guise, and it is against the background of the psychological state of society to which the mass murders bear witness that this humanist programme piece must be understood: 'Would our lives be much different if it were lions and bears reigning, if it were snakes and the most ferocious beasts of prey who had been given power over us?' But it should be remembered that, in contrast to human beings, animals do *not* delight in killing their fellows!

'On gentleness'

Seneca begins *De clementia*, 'On gentleness', which was written for the eighteen-year-old Nero, by confronting the Emperor with the general populace, which he calls ungovernable and even rebellious. These are harsh words to address to a ruler, and Seneca returns three times to the danger threatening a tyrant: a people who have been tyrannised long enough will inevitably rebel: the only defence against this danger is not weapons but gentleness, which is the truly princely virtue. It is not in the quantity of power but in the quality with which it is exercised that the difference between a tyrant and a king is to be found.

This would not have been acceptable in Augustus' time. The Stoics certainly used to contrast a monarch with a tyrant, but the Romans intensely disliked the word king, *rex*, and were inclined to consider themselves free, provided they were free from kings. The rumours that Julius Caesar intended to have himself made king were the cause of the conspiracy against him, and Augustus insisted that as princeps, 'the first man', he did not have more power, but only greater authority than others. Seneca makes Nero call the realities of power by their proper name: 'It is I who am master of people's lives and deaths.' He even puts words into his mouth which sound as though they were spoken by a tyrant in one of Seneca's tragedies: 'Which cities shall be destroyed and which shall arise is all subject to my judgement.' But neither does Seneca make any secret of the risks associated with such absolute power: 'Much was at stake for the Roman people when they still did not know the quality of your noble nature.' Was it within the capability of human nature to exercise such power — in a humane fashion? Seneca himself had experienced how Tiberius, Caligula and Claudius, who had all begun as 'kings', had ended as tyrants. Only Augustus had begun as a tyrant and ended as a 'king' — as Seneca made perfectly obvious. Was this sufficient to justify this kingdom or empire?

The power of the Emperor was obviously not open to discussion in this 'mirror for princes', as such guides to good behaviour for medieval rulers were called. (The expression may well date back to Seneca's words to the effect that he wants to show Nero himself as in a mirror). However, there is no need to doubt that Seneca meant what he said when he called the loss of the Emperor a 'catastrophe for the peace of Rome': it would mean the dissolution of the Empire. The bloodstained traces of the civil wars still instilled fear into people a hundred years after the murder of Julius Caesar.

It is striking that Seneca makes no mention at all of Caesar in *De clementia*, although Caesar's temple in Rome was dedicated to his *clementia*, and although in 'On anger' he had praised Caesar for having been so gentle after his victory in the civil war. There could perhaps be something ominous in presenting a man who in fact had been murdered as an example to be followed, and to use Caesar to show that gentleness always pays would have its drawbacks. In any case, Seneca did not have any particular love for either Caesar or Pompejus, both of whom fought to 'own' the State; but despite his admiration for Cato, who refused to survive freedom, neither did he have much sympathy for those who murdered Caesar, even if like Cato they professed Stoicism. In a slightly later work he says that Marcus Brutus 'might in other respects have been a great man, but on this point he seems to me to have made a serious mistake and not to have acted in accordance with Stoic teachings. Either he feared the title of a king, although

150

society is at its best under a just king, or else he hoped there would be room for freedom where there was such advantage in both ruling and serving, or else he thought that society could be brought back to its former condition, even if the old customs were no longer alive, or else that there would be equal rights for citizens and that the laws would come into their own where he himself had seen so many thousands of men in conflict — not about whether they should be slaves, but about which of the two they should be slaves to. . .'

Seneca did not believe that society could be recreated in its former condition, and he was in agreement with Stoic teachings in considering society to be most secure under a just king — and the murder of a tyrant to be justified. But of course, Caesar was not killed by a populace he tyrannised, but by friends whose 'insatiable hopes he had not fulfilled', and who all demanded what only one man could have.

Society needs one will: it was the conflict of many wills which led to the downfall of the republic. But if a ruler does not personify the will of the people, the people will oppose him — and quite rightly so, for he belongs to the state, not the state to him. Several times Seneca talks of society as a body with the Emperor as its head; the comparison was not simply taken out of the blue: the people undoubtedly felt a link between the condition of the Emperor and that of the state; they saw all strange signs as presages of what was to happen in the imperial house, and they gave the Emperor the honour for all the good things that happened — and the blame for all the bad ones. Even if the Roman historians can be criticised for having reduced the history of the imperial age to the history of the emperors and for having been more interested in the emperors' morals than in their policies, there is no denying that the emperors' moral character made its mark on Rome. In reality the Emperor's power was unlimited; it could only be limited through his self-control — and only be opposed by violence. The conspiracy against Caligula resulted from discontent with the Emperor, not with the imperial principle, and the military revolt against Nero was ascribed particularly to moral causes by M. Rostovtzeff, who wrote the social and economic history of Rome. Against this background Seneca's moral appeals and warnings to Nero take on more the appearance of *Realpolitik* than might at first seem to be the case.

The trouble is not that one man has power, for the people need one man at the centre, but that he uses it wrongly, as a tyrant rather than a king. 'Power need not corrupt if it is exercised in accordance with natural law.' That a monarchy is 'natural' can be illustrated by examples from the lives of animals and especially from the life of bees: the king bee (which the Romans unfortuntely did not know was a queen) is clearly distinguished from ordinary bees by its colour and its size — and by its lack of a sting! But even the ordinary bees leave their stings in the wound — just suppose the same were true of human beings, and 'their aggression would be broken along with their own weapons'! Seneca returns to the difference between animals and human beings which he had also dwelt on in 'On anger': human beings must make a moral effort in order to live in harmony with their human nature — and *that* is the major achievement of the prince: there is a limit to how much evil can be done by ordinary good citizens, but 'the raging of princes is war'. A king should also be better able than others to take a broad view of insults, even if in his case they are lese-majesty, for if insignificant people put up with offences, they risk being subjected to more and thus outraged, but the ruler will gain a better reputation by refraining from using the power which he already has: 'nothing is more majestic than to leave lese-majesty un-punished'...'although it is usually a more bitter pill than real injustice for persons of majesty to swallow.' Under earlier majesties, lese-majesty had been punished by death, although it is more princely to be more concerned with injustice to others than injustice to oneself.

Seneca defines gentleness as self-control in meting out punishment, cruelty as an insuperable urge to carry out punishment (rather as anger in 'On anger', where cruelty was defined as the desire to cause suffering). Both definitions are obviously aimed at high-ranking persons who have the right and often the reason to punish — and who would become tyrants if they punished as often as they have reason to do. Look at this city, writes Seneca, where throngs of people always fill the broadest streets and where three theatres (with about 70,000 places!) are filled at the same time — and then think how terribly empty and desolate it would be if only those men judged innocent by a strict judge were left at liberty! If it were desired to secure society against crimes by getting rid of the criminals, how much of society would be left? The object of (penal) law is to improve the criminal and society so that crime is avoided as far as possible: 'A lenient punishment is the best way of improving miscreants, for people are more careful of their lives when they have not been entirely humiliated... And the morals of society are best regulated by the sparing use of punishment, for people grow accustomed to crime when the number of criminals is great... and strictness, when it goes too far, loses its most desirable effect, that of creating respect.' The fewer the crimes, the fewer the criminals — as an example Seneca takes Claudius' strict line with patricide, which had not exactly reduced the number of patricides — and which according to Suetonius was due to his own desire to see the barbaric punishment carried out. When Seneca praises Nero for having brought law into the daylight again and for having regard to it, he is obviously thinking of Claudius: brutality and arbitrariness are now at an end — and even Suetonius confirms that Nero was very conscientious when sitting in judgement.

The moral of it all is that frightening examples do not frighten, but rather cause opposition, and that in all circumstances the Emperor's example is an example to be followed; so greater moral demands are made on him than on anyone else. Seneca compares the relationship between the Emperor and his subjects with that between a father and his children, a teacher and his pupils, a doctor and his patients: in other words (which are not Seneca's) Nero had been given the same task vis-à-vis the people as Seneca vis-à-vis Nero.

On one occasion Nero is allowed to raise an objection:

'But that is to be a slave, not a master!'

'Yes, but do you not see that being a master is for you a noble form of slavery?' replies Seneca. The idea of noble slavery went back to Zenon's pupil Antigonos Gonatas (in the 3rd century B.C.), and it was the formula for the Stoic idea of the ruler, which Jesus also formulated when he said that whosoever will be great among you, let him be your minister, and that whosoever will be chief among you, let him be your servant.

'How many things are impossible for you which thanks to you are possible for the rest of us?' continues Seneca: 'I can walk freely and fearlessly anywhere in the city, although I have no attendants and no sword in my home or at my side, but you must live armed in the peace which is your work... There are only few who note our movements: we are free to go out or withdraw or change direction without anyone bothering, but you can no more remain unobserved than the sun.'

153

Just because in any circumstances a prince will achieve a reputation, he ought to pay attention to it: cruel masters are detested, and the evil deeds of princes are never forgotten: 'How much better then would it be not to have been born than to be counted among those whose births have brought misfortune to the people.'

Could Seneca have a presentiment that he was writing this for — a Nero? Is it only because of Stoic dogmatics that this essay on — Nero's — gentleness talks just as much of cruelty — and also warns against compassion? The Stoic usually differentiated between gentleness or mercy as a strength and compassion (*misericordia*) as a weakness, the anxious preoccupation of the mind with the misery of others. In 'On anger' Seneca had mentioned compassion as being among the minor vices. But later he counted it a virtue, and it is not impossible that he had a special reason for warning his sensitive pupil, Nero, against both cruelty and compassion.

As has already been said, there was much at stake for the Roman people, as they still did not know when Nero's — volatile or noble[1] — nature would reveal itself. In the first years of his reign Nero had been gentle in word and deed; when Burrus gave him the first death warrant for signature, he exclaimed, 'If only I had never learned to write!' Seneca wanted as it were to testify to the general public and to Nero himself that he had made a good start, and to ensure that he continued to act and speak gently so that what now was a natural impulse could be fortified by reason.

It would be difficult to live up to the great expectations which he had created; 'if this goodness were not natural to you, but only a pretended thing, for no one can wear a mask in the long run. The artificial soon returns to what is natural, but what is founded on truth and, so to say, has its roots firmly fixed in the ground, will grow bigger and better with the years.'

The way in which this is formulated indicates that Seneca neither considered Nero's gentleness to be assumed nor too solidly established; for the time being it was mostly due to impulse — and was perhaps 'only' compassion? That Nero at eighteen was more impulsive than

---

1. *mobilis* or *nobilis*? The first gives more meaning in this context, the other is more flattering.

wise is not surprising, for no one is born wise, but much was at stake in this case because the Empire could not be ruled by impulses (as had been demonstrated by Caligula's example), but only by wisdom. And so Seneca wanted not only to show Nero what he was like 'as in a mirror', but also what he was to become. As a philosophical programme piece 'On gentleness' coincides with the speech to the Senate in which Nero had outlined his policy and declared that he would rule according to the political principles of Augustus: here, too, Augustus is presented as the model, as the prince of peace. Even if it may be true to say that Seneca had created 'this conventional Augustus, the type of the ideal prince, rather far from historical fact, which has had notable success throughout the Middle Ages and right up to our own time,' the objection must be made that Augustus himself had known how to create himself an image as a prince of peace, especially since he really had brought about peace, and that Seneca betrayed an excellent knowledge of Augustus' actual history. The point in making Augustus into an example from which to learn was that even though in his youth he had excelled in cruelty, he had later realised that he could achieve more with gentleness — something which was completely true. Seneca was reluctant to consider 'cruelty which has got tired' as true gentleness, but on the other hand, 'the will to proceed harshly must disappear before the reason for doing so.' The fact that conditions were more peaceful when Nero had taken over the Empire was an advantage rather than a merit — or at least the merit could be ascribed to Augustus rather than to Nero: Nero could begin where Augustus left off and transform the golden age which Augustus had prophesied and which his successors had turned into an age of iron, into reality, into 'the age of happiness and purity'.

Seneca was not the only man to express the hope that the innocence of the earliest times would return to this generation. Seven eclogues by one Calpurnius Siculus have survived, ascribing to the forest god Faunus the prophecy that a new Age of Gold, a new Saturnine age, a new era of peace like that of Numa will return, that gentleness will blunt raging swords, and that the youth whose features combine those of Apollo and Mars shall rule over the people like a god. Two young shepherds find Faunus' verses in the forest; they add to them and hope that Meliboeus, who has access to Phoebus himself, will prepare their way to the castle; as Meliboeus, the patron of the arts is said to have

155

insight into natural phenomena, to write poetry and to have received the gifts of Bacchus from the muse (and Bacchus, of course, was the god of tragedy) it is not difficult to see a portrait of Seneca in him.

The death of Britannicus

At the beginning of his reign Nero's gentleness had resulted in his dismissing Pallas — with honour. Pallas was the last of Claudius' powerful ministers, and in contrast to his colleagues he managed to descend from his high office with his life and even his fortune still intact. Agrippina, however, had lost her last support at court and felt cruelly slighted; like Claudius she challenged fate by reminding Nero that Britannicus was the rightful heir to the throne: she would recommend him to the praetorians, who usually proclaimed the Emperor. But of course, Burrus was their chief — 'So they could support the cause either of Germanicus' daughter or of Burrus the cripple and Seneca the exile, who pretended to guide mankind, one with his stumpy arm, the other with his school-teacher's tongue.' In these words, which Tacitus ascribes to Agrippina, there is an obvious stab at Seneca's humanism: he wants not only to guide the state but mankind as well; he himself, of course, had talked of the 'human state'. And it was he who wrote Nero's speeches for him, speeches which Agrippina criticised so sharply that Nero intimated that he would abdicate! It was probably about this time that Agrippina sought to make him understand that philosophy was nothing for an emperor.

However, it was still not certain whether Nero had paid more attention to the lessons of his mother or his teacher, and the question was put in the most terrible way at the imperial table one evening in February 55, in the presence of Agrippina but not Seneca. Under Agrippina's rule Britannicus had been out of favour at court, but he was now taking part in court banquets and meals. On this occasion the food disagreed with him; he vomited, but nevertheless stayed at table for five more hours. The historians are able to tell how during the actual meal Nero experimented with poisons intended to bring about immediate death; after the first unsuccessful attempt, the second succeeded five hours later: Britannicus was carried out; Nero said it was only one of his usual epileptic fits. The improbable story is perhaps not all that improbable; everyone believed the worst, and everyone except Agrippina and Octavia was prepared to put up with it: 'They thought of the ancient fratricidal conflicts and of the impossibility of two sharing the throne.'

What did Seneca do? Either he believed the official explanation of Britannicus' death — or he pretended to believe it. He could not both condemn the murder and maintain his influence — and was the first of these possibilities morally more defensible than the second in consideration of what might now be feared of Nero? The Roman historians, who otherwise never miss an opportunity to moralise, do not reproach Seneca on that point, but more modern historians have reproached him all the more, even going so far as to accuse him of complicity in the murder. But at all events Seneca's moral and political dilemma was more serious than that of his moral critics; several of his works indicate this, but 'On gentleness' does not. Therefore some have believed that it must have been written before the death of Britannicus, while others have seen unforgiveable hypocrisy in it. It is most probable that Seneca was — or wanted to be — in good faith.

'There are psychological impossibilities which are stronger than all the so-called direct evidence from authors who do not even write as contemporaries, let alone as eyewitnesses, and only base themselves on unreliable sources. The awkward young emperor who trembled before his mother's threats was scarcely the man to act in this way.' So writes one of those who have expressed doubt as to whether Nero murdered his brother. Nevertheless, it is in Nero's nervousness that we must seek the psychological explanation of such an action. He could not at one and the same time feel himself as the supreme authority in the world and as a boy under his mother's thumb without letting off steam in some way or other; because Agrippina exercised psychological power over him he ascribed to her greater real power than she had and went in irrational fear of her. His reaction on another occasion shows this. He had had Agrippina removed from the imperial residence and had deprived her of her guards; as she was obviously in disgrace everyone avoided her company, and some found it opportune to accuse her of wanting to marry one Rubellius Plautus (of an ancient noble family) and preparing his way to the throne. When Nero was told of this, naturally in the middle of the night, his immediate reaction was to have his mother and Plautus executed — and to dismiss Burrus

157

who, of course, owed his position to Agrippina. Seneca succeeded in calming the Emperor; Burrus kept his post, Agrippina was given the opportunity of defending herself and could very convincingly argue that her life more than anyone else's depended on Nero's: how many things had she not done for his sake — for which no one else would be able to forgive her ? Agrippina got off without any further prosecution; she withdrew to private life and wrote her memoirs — which unfortunately have been lost.

After that Pallas, too, was accused of wanting to put one Cornelius Sulla (of an ancient noble family) on the throne with the help of the guard; Pallas' freedmen were accused of complicity along with him, and his defence was based on the fact that he never discussed things with his freedmen; he gave orders only with movements of his head or his hands, or as written commands. He made such a bad impression that everyone wanted him to be found guilty, but he was acquitted; on the other hand those who had accused him and Agrippina were punished: it was no longer a good job to act as informer.

Politics, economics and morals

So far Nero was living up to the promises he had made in his speech from the throne. Until 62 — the year when Seneca retired from state service — his policy of maintaining a balance was carefully maintained. 'It was,' writes B. H. Warmington, one of Nero's most recent and sober biographers, 'as a result of the harmony between the Senate and Nero and his advisers that during much of his principate our sources find little to complain of except Nero's crimes and follies in private life; and it was the same harmony that enabled the Senate to overlook them.' Because of his authority as a tribune Nero could veto the Senate, but he only occasionally intervened, and then in order to prevent harsh punishments.

The economy of the Empire could be managed without Pallas. As late as 62 Nero could criticise his predecessors for having allowed the state expenditure to exceed income — and sing his own praises for annually having given the State a gift of 60 million sesterces. This he could do because the Emperor and the Senate each had their own accounts and each their own provinces from which to draw tax; under

158

Claudius the Senate accounts were taken care of by quaestors, but under Nero the responsibility was given to more experienced ex-praetors whom the Emperor appointed; in this way the promised distinction between court and state was not quite maintained in the economic sphere, but two completely distinct administrative apparatuses could scarcely keep a proper control of the economy of the Empire.

The tendency was for the imperial bureacracy to take over the entire administration of the State and the State the administration of the entire Empire, but the bureacratisation which was caused by and in its turn gave rise to a growing economic crisis in the Empire in the 3rd century A.D. did not make much mark on Rome in its time of greatness, which on the contrary was dependent on the State's not unnecessarily interfering in the affairs of the city authorities in Italy and the provinces. Outside Rome ordinary citizens only very rarely came in contact with the State; election propaganda daubed on the houses in Pompeii shows that the citizens there still made use of their right to vote, which the citizens of Rome had long since lost. Pompeii did not have a large, unemployed proletariat or the dangerous tenements which most of Rome's million inhabitants lived in, but it could also have its troubles: at a session of gladiatorial games in 59 the spectators also started fighting; those to suffer most were some visitors from the neighbouring city of Nuceria; several lost their lives, and the survivors complained to the Emperor, who passed on the case to the Senate, and the consuls forbade gladiatorial games in Pompeii for ten years. From this it can be assumed that the inscription by a gladiator from Pompeii quoted above is from Nero's first five years, though it is not certain that the prohibition was maintained for the entire ten years. This is one of the few examples from this period of state interference in local affairs — and in keeping with the policy which forbade provincial governors to arrange gladiatorial games.

Governors could be accused of abuse of power, which usually meant financial exploitation, but it was the Senate which passed judgement on the way in which senators discharged their office — and it was not happy to condemn a colleague. 'That provinces are exploited and a corrupt court supports one party after hearing both parties' bids is not surprising, since it is popular law (*jus gentium*) to sell what you have bought,' writes Seneca, who apparently was not blind to the problem, and the fact that twelve governors were accused and six found guilty in the period during which Seneca had influence scarcely indicates any widespread abuse of power, but rather a strong desire to limit it; after 62 the governors had Nero's blessing to exploit the provinces, and there are no reports of further trials.

As stated above (p62), Augustus had taken away from the private companies the responsibility for collecting direct taxes and given it to the city officials, but the indirect taxes, excise duties and customs dues were still collected by the *publicani*, the tax gatherers who were hated throughout the Empire. The constant complaints about the tax gatherers gave Nero the idea of making them completely superfluous — by abolishing indirect taxes. The Senate praised this magnanimous idea but raised the objection that in that case there would also be demands for the abolition of direct taxes from which Roman citizens were already exempt. So Nero issued an imperial edict removing numerous possibilities for abuse and giving guidelines on the authority of the tax gatherers and on how to treat complaints about them; as finance acts otherwise were passed by the Senate, Nero made it very plain from his edict who had the welfare of the people at heart — and deserved their gratitude.

Compared with the taxes previously levied from merchants in all city states, the Roman customs duty — of 2 or 2½ per cent — at provincial borders did not constitute a serious hindrance to trade, and the Roman Empire has been called 'the biggest free trade area ever'. As Nero founded and expanded ports, started work on canals and exempted corn importers from shipping tax, some have seen in the proposal to abolish customs dues a conscious effort on his part — and possibly on the part of Seneca — to stimulate trade and economic development; but in the opinion of Rostovtzeff there is 'not the slightest reason to assume the existence of any economic policy on the part of the Emperor in the first century'. It is more likely that Nero was honestly annoyed at the tax gatherers and wanted to make himself popular; and although Seneca's tasks as a statesman were not those of a philosopher, it is difficult to imagine how the man who in Corsica had asked what 'this trade, this destruction of the forests, this exportation of the oceans' was intended to achieve should now actually see it as his task to increase trade. A chorus in his tragedy 'Medea' speaks of the traffic which 'the first ship', the Argos, (the Thessalonian fir), had prepared the way for, but not in positive tones:

> The generations of our forefathers saw ages of brightness
> when deceipt was unthinkable on earth; each had
> enough on his native shore, where he grew old and felt
> rich though he owned but little and knew nought of
> the treasures hidden in the earth. All the world,
> happily divided into its separate parts, was brought
> together into one by the Thessalonian fir: it
> commanded the waves to speak the stroke of the oars,
> and alien oceans to fill us with fear... Now the seas
> have already done as commanded, and all obey the
> laws made by man,... Every pitiful bark sails the
> ocean's deep, borders are removed, and cities expand,
> city walls are rebuilt in foreign lands; nothing remains
> where it was on the open earth: the Indian drinks the
> chill waters of Araxes, and the Elbe and Rhine give
> water to the Persians.

These conservative opinions are ascribed to citizens from Corinth (which incidentally might have good historical reasons for doubting the blessings of this development, as Rome had seen a rival in Corinth and destroyed the city in the same year as it had destroyed Carthage). However, it is in accordance with Seneca's views: he scarcely imagined his 'human state' being realised as a free trade area! Like Plato in the Laws, he probably saw a 'world divided happily' into self-supporting areas — an idea with roots in the soil. To the Romans it was work with the soil, not industry and commerce, which was the source of all wealth, and their economic policy was especially aimed at helping agriculture. Under the *pax romana* the provinces blossomed; in North Africa vast areas which later lay bare for centuries were cultivated and densely populated. Reference has already been made (p. 42) to the fact that in the time of trade imperialism, when Carthage and Corinth were destroyed, the great landowners had cultivated wines and olives for export; now the provinces could supply themselves and even export as well, with the result that agriculture in Italy itself went into decline. As large quantities of cheap corn were imported from Egypt, Africa and Sicily, and as slaves in the peaceful age of the

161

emperors became a scarcer and more expensive commodity while 'free' labour became cheap, the landowners left their land in the hands of small tenant farmers, who once more mainly cultivated corn for their own needs.

From Nero's day there is a work in twelve books called 'On agriculture', *De re rustica*, by Columella, one of the many Spaniards to make a name for themselves in Latin literature. In the preface to the first book he recalls the good old days when the highest officials in the State themselves took part in the work in the fields, and bewails the fact that the Romans now hide themselves behind city walls and use their hands mainly at the circus (to clap!) and feel happy never to see a sunrise or sunset. The import of corn they arrange by inviting tenders at public auctions and they let the Saturnine lands of Latium go to waste. It is not the land which has become infertile (as was usually maintained, and as it was possible to read even in Lucretius' didactic poem 'On nature' from the first century B.C.), but it is the cultivation of it which has become unqualified: there are teachers in every conceivable and inconceivable subject, even in how to talk — but no teachers of agriculture. Yet from former times — from the time of the elder Cato — there was a great deal of Roman literature on agriculture, but nothing more recent: Columella wants to make up for what has been neglected, but practical experience is needed to make perfect. Therefore the landowner himself ought to take part in the running of the farm — the usual thing was for him neither to live on or for his land, but only off it. But to demonstrate the continued existence of fertile land and good agriculture in Italy Columella mentions the area around Nomentum (in the Sabines), which in his day was famous — 'especially the part which is owned by Seneca, a man of impressive insight and learning, on whose vineyards every *jugerum* is known often to have yielded eight sacks' (i.e. c. 2700 litres per acre). In his 'Natural history' (from the 70's) the elder Pliny mentions the famous estate which the grammarian Rhemmius Palæon had bought for 600,000 sesterces and sold ten years later for four times the price to Annæus Seneca, 'at that time the man whose learning and power were so vast that in the end his power grew too great and collapsed upon him'.

With power came riches: After the death of Britannicus Seneca had received his share of the Claudian possessions. Some, writes Tacitus, thought that eminent men had fallen upon the prey like robbers, while

162

others maintained that the Emperor had sought to ensure their support by forcing it on them. Seneca not only had estates in Italy, at Nomentum and Alba, but also in Spain, Egypt and Britain, and although in his epistles he could indicate a knowledge of the cultivation of vines and olives and could express joy that his income was based on the respectable occupation of the farmer (which Columella places above other occupations such as the army, trade and seafaring, and the activities of usurers and lawyers!) he had to admit that he had cultivated a greater acreage and had a more substantial income than his natural needs really demanded.

Pliny records that in Nero's day six landowners owned half of the African province and is of the opinion that 'large estates have ruined Italy and will soon have the same result in the provinces'; there is some doubt as to what he meant by these frequently quoted words, but perhaps he was simply implying the same as Columella: that people ought not to possess a greater acreage than they can use effectively and cultivate intensively. Seneca, who after all was said by Columella to be an honest exception, himself criticised the tendency to create larger and larger estates: 'A field big enough for a whole nation is now too small for a single master.' However, his point of view is moral rather than economic. Seneca had no more theoretical insight into economic development than other practical Romans; the Romans were content to increase their own wealth; or they were perhaps not content to do so and saw increasing affluence as a danger to — morals. Augustus had legislated against luxury, and 'limits' were set to it in Nero' first years, too. In one of his epistles Seneca, admittedly after taking leave of the court, toys with the idea that a proposal might be made on the 'abolition of wealth', so the Roman people can desire a return to the frugality which was the foundation of the Empire, recognising that they have acquired their wealth from vanquished foes. Seneca saw land and not work as the source of value, and despite his own work on the soil he appears simply not to have realised that new wealth can be created, but to have assumed that the sum of riches was constant: what you acquire, you take from others; if the few use more, there will be less for all. In artificial needs, in the craving for superfluous things, *luxuria*, he saw a departure from nature, not an economic driving force, and he would have been surprised to read in Hartvig Frisch's 'History of Civilisation': 'The level of a civilisation can be measured in *demand*:

the greater and more varied it becomes, the greater becomes production and thus turnover. Even with the greatest extravagance, a numerically small class of the population cannot make use of and thereby maintain a highly varied and highly specialised production. It is therefore a complete misunderstanding to argue that extravagance and prodigality caused the downfall of the Roman Empire. To judge from literary sources, inscriptions and monuments, wealth in the first century after Augustus was on the increase, mostly, of course, for the upper classes, but also for the lower classes of the population, and this age represents the supreme achievement of Roman culture in all respects; then poverty began to spread...'

Rostovtzeff also sees the first part of the imperial age as yielding good economic results: 'New sources of wealth were opened up. Countries which hitherto had been content with the simplest forms of trade were now opened up for planned exploitation.' But when civilisation was at its highest point he sees disturbing signs of the transition from intensive 'scientific' agriculture to more primitive methods and in the spread of small pockets of cottage industries at the expense of larger factories. What Rostovtzeff finds disturbing is thus the exact opposite of what Seneca worried about! This was because morality — or the lack of it — was in Roman eyes the driving force of history, while to modern historians it is economics which offer the explanation. They are in fact just as fatalistic as their earlier counterparts: for them the fatal thing is that that very economic upsurge did not materialise — which to Seneca was moral decline. So he was not the right man to carry out a deliberate economic policy. Even his contemporaries criticised him for not living in accordance with his philosophy, but from the point of view of Hartvig Frisch or Rostovtzeff it was precisely his moral philosophy and not his private initiative which was open to criticism.

The difference between the Roman view of history and that of modern times is also apparent in the fact that the Romans had no idea of a better world emerging from developments taking place. For the Romans utopia was in the past, and the one occasion on which Seneca, at the beginning of Nero's reign, expresses a hope for a better future, it is precisely the hope that the innocence of the earliest times will return. Politically it meant a return to Augustus' programme: the task was still to defend the status quo and to maintain world peace, something which in the long run could not create the same enthusiasm as at first. Thus it was not a bad thing for internal unity when in the first years of Nero's reign the Parthans attacked Armenia, which the Romans were accustomed to consider as a satellite state, so that Nero, too, was given the opportunity to bring about peace. The conduct of the war was left to Domitius Corbulo, who had achieved great distinction under Claudius, and this was seen as a good omen for the new regime: it indicated that 'the way was open to capable and deserving men'. At first the danger of war receded, and the news was greeted enthusiastically; then Corbulo mounted major expeditions in Armenia and in 58 captured the capital city of Artaxata, at which the Senate took the opportunity of erecting imperial statues and triumphal arches. It would also have proclaimed three new public holidays, but Senator Cassius Longinus objected that there simply were not sufficient days if the gods were to be thanked properly; the gods could also be honoured on ordinary days, in which case earthly tasks would not be neglected.

Nero, who preferred all other arts to the art of war, did not himself grasp the opportunity of gaining honour in the field. Augustus' recommendation that the Empire should not be extended but secured within its existing boundaries was one which he followed so meticulously that he even considered withdrawing the army from Britain, where subsequently, in 61, there was a revolt leading to much bloodshed. He did not show any particular interest in the army, 'which had been entrusted to him', and he never visited the imperial provinces. However, the wealth of the Empire permitted him to be more extravagant than his predecessors and to secure the army and people for himself by means of gifts: immediately after his accession he had rewarded the praetorians just as Claudius had done; a couple of years later the people received 400 sesterces each. ('An annual income of 24,000 sesterces seems to have been sufficient for a modest manner of life for one person in Rome'). In Rome some 200,000 people received cheap or free corn, an arrangement which played less part in reducing poverty than in reducing dissatisfaction — and increasing the Emperor's popularity. The best way of pre-empting rebelliousness in the people was to destroy corn in order to demonstrate that there was plenty of it. The post of prefect for corn supplies from which Seneca had advised his father-in-law (or brother-in-law) to resign had thus become one of great political significance; it was now undertaken 'in the most unselfish manner' by Fænius Rufus, who was, or came to be, a close associate of Seneca.

While the emperors made a great show of their distributions to the people by inscriptions on their coins, there are no coins recording their donations to the soldiers or the gladiatorial combats. This is indeed surprising — and might indicate that the emperors themselves were aware of the fatal significance of their dependence on the army and of the brutality lurking under the peaceful surface and demanding such bloody sacrifices.

Seneca accused. 'On the happy life'

In his speech of accession Nero had promised to prevent collusion between accusers and accused; he did it by a more strict enforcement of the old law, the *Lex Cincia*, which forbade the conducting of lawsuits for money. This also affected the infamous informers who had had a great time and a great income under his predecessors. Nero lived up to Seneca's argument that it is praiseworthy to leave lese-majesty unpunished; those who tried to derive financial benefit from comments which could be seen as critical of the Emperor failed to gain any convictions, but were themselves prosecuted and punished. There are some indications that it was Seneca who wanted to tidy up this unpleasant business, for when P. Suillius Rufus, who had been Messalina's henchman, was accused under the *Lex Cincia* he turned his defence speech into an indictment of Seneca.

According to Tacitus, Suillius said that Seneca was 'an enemy of Claudius' friends and had had to live in exile during his reign. At the same time, accustomed only to barren studies and ignorant youths, he was envious of those who placed their living and natural eloquence at the service of their fellow citizens. He himself had been Germanicus' quaestor, and Seneca had whored in his house: was one to be more severely condemned for receiving a voluntary gift for honest work from someone whose lawsuit one had conducted than for desecrating the bedrooms of princesses? What wisdom and philosophical doctrines had taught Seneca to scrape 300 million sesterces together during his four years of friendship with the Emperor? In Rome he netted the childless rich and their wills; Italy and the provinces were being bled

166

dry by his demands for vast rates of interest — while Suillius himself had a hard-won and modest fortune. He would rather expose himself to accusations and dangers than disgrace the good name which he had created for himself by deferring to an opportunist.'

It was a bold speech, for when it was made, in 58, not only was Seneca a powerful man, but it implicated the Emperor, too. Suillius was found guilty and exiled to the Balearics, where he lived a pleasant enough life, but when the accusers wanted to fish in troubled waters and also prosecute his family, Nero dismissed the case: it was wrong for the children to inherit the sins of the father — they were merely to inherit a good deal of his fortune. Although Suillius was generally hated and the verdict on him popular, the case was in the opinion of Tacitus, 'hardly without damaging consequences for Seneca.' And Tacitus was right: Dio Cassius' (or Xiphilinus', cf p130) harsh words on Seneca, which many others had embroidered upon, appear to go directly back to Suillius' accusations.

Although it is not wise to be put out by what others insinuate about you, Seneca felt hurt. Despite the criticism of luxury and his desire to become wise, he was in fact a man of the court and possessed of great wealth. A poor courtier was properly speaking even more unlikely than a rich wise man, and the fact than an imperial adviser who played his part in arranging the country's finances had his own affairs in order was scarcely compromising in itself. But perhaps it was compromising that he was a courtier at all, and thus a wealthy man. That there is such a great difference between good things and the Good that it can be difficult to see the Good for goods was, of course, one of the Stoic doctrines; could Seneca allow himself to throw the philosopher's stone when he himself did not live in 'the philosopher's little house' in which he at one time had established himself, but owned various magnificent villas outside the city?

He tried to take the matter with Stoic calm. So far his position had scarcely given him much peace to write anything but what his position demanded of him; in his treatise 'On the brevity of life' he had actually, before learning from bitter experience, written that important jobs do not leave a man enough peace and quiet to think a single sensible thought (something which might still partly explain a distinct lack of reason in high places). Now it was the job itself which needed defending. Apparently unruffled, he professed the Stoic doctrine which Suillius had used against him, and used the opportunity to write *his* treatise on the supreme good, about which all philosophers in the good old days had written something or other. If, in the top job he now occupied, he promised 'virtue' as the only Good, he could at least not be accused of merely making a virtue of necessity!

He gave the essay in which he justified himself the title of 'On the happy life' (*De vita beata*), and by happiness he did not mean chance happiness, the gifts of *fortuna*, purely external gifts which come our way; happiness dependent on good conditions is not unconditional and therefore cannot be the supreme good. Enjoyment and happiness in that sense may well in fact be something for which most people strive, but that does not mean that they are worth striving for. The easiest way of losing your real way is to follow others and do what they do instead of being yourself and becoming 'the artist of your own life'. Seneca writes of people in roughly the same way as Heidegger on 'das Man', which persuades us to believe what *people* believe, but Seneca stresses that by the 'crowd' he is not only thinking of the 'soldiers' but also of the 'officers': rank makes no difference. 'What does it matter whether they are slaves or free citizens, whether they are free by birth or have had their freedom bestowed on them?' As human beings they are all worth the same, and in a crowd they are completely undifferentiated.

'The crowd is a proof of the worst.' With these words Seneca rejects the morality of happiness which identifies the supreme good with what most people aim for and identifies happiness with enjoyment, as did the Epicureans — and subsequently John Stuart Mill. But while Stuart Mill's modern critics have particularly concentrated their attention on the 'naturalistic fallacy' which they claim it is to seek a psychological foundation for morality and to identify what is desirable with what is desired, Seneca on the contrary spoke of our 'natural desire' for the good; and he speaks of this moral objective in psychological terms just as he speaks of psychological matters in moral terms: 'The supreme good is the unyielding strength of the soul, foresight, sublime thoughts, healthiness, freedom, harmony and beauty.' 'The surpreme good is the harmony of the soul, for virtues must be where there is harmony and unity. Vices lead to disunity.'

Inward disharmony is thus for Seneca not only a painful, but a morally unacceptable state of mind: not to *want* to be yourself, not to want to accept your own nature, your fate. Fate, *fatum*, means — in contrast to chance, *fortuna* — the state of things resulting from the very arrangement of the universe and which it is not within our power to direct, but only to accept. We can spoil our fate by not accepting it, but we cannot avoid it, and it is foolish to have to be dragged along instead of going voluntarily. Fate, which Seneca also calls God, can no more do us harm than chance can make us good — thus the supreme good cannot lie in what befalls us, but in the manner in which we take it; freedom expresses itself in the ability to interpret the decrees of fate positively: 'to obey God is freedom'.

But the fact that wisdom and freedom reveal themselves in the will and ability to bear even a harsh fate and, if necessary, to accept suffering, is not the same as saying that life *must* include suffering in order to be — a happy life. In all circumstances to prefer the unpleasant to the pleasant is not necessarily wisdom, but may even be madness. The good things do not make us good — but they can make it easier to do good, which in itself demands wisdom, so that wealth after all is better placed in the hands of wise men than of fools.

So far, so good. But half way through Seneca changes his tone and loses something of his Stoic calm. 'On the happy life', like 'On anger', is dedicated to Seneca's elder brother Gallio, and as in 'On anger' Seneca is not in the long run addressing himself to his brother. As the treatise progresses it becomes more and more obviously aimed at Seneca's accusers, to whose accusations he makes direct reference: 'Why are you braver in your words than in your life? Why do you speak humbly to a superior and consider money as necessary for yourself? And why do you shed tears on hearing of the death of your wife or your friend or take heed of your reputation and allow yourself to be upset by malicious rumours? Why have you cultivated more fields than your natural needs require? Why do your meals not correspond to your precepts? Why are your appurtenances so splendid?... Why have you overseas possessions?' — To all this and more besides Seneca begins by replying that he himself is not a wise man, and there is no need to sing the praises of what is wrong just because you cannot live up to what is right; secondly, he argues that the wise man does not show his independence by owning nothing (in which case being wise would not demand a lot, but nothing at all), but by not being owned by anything.

169

Seneca maintains that he is not writing about himself, and that he is 'buried deep in all kinds of vices', but nevertheless he replies pretty directly to the direct accusations made against him by Suillius: possessions obtained 'without injustices having been committed against anyone and without any dirty profit' and which are used as honestly as they were acquired, are things to which a philosopher is entitled. And finally he accuses the accusers for accusing: they are not the right people to do that, they see the others' blisters and yet they themselves are infected with boils. Seneca's 'judge not' nevertheless acquired a slightly pharisaical ring here, for it must really be read as: 'Judge not me!' Seneca was undeniably in the difficult position, which was part and parcel of the position he occupied, that he could not speak directly of himself, and he was obviously not detached enough — or wise enough — to be able to speak indirectly about it. He had, so to speak, to defend himself in someone else's name and yet could not resist giving Socrates himself the last word and letting him reprove the accusers in Seneca's name — not indirectly and jovially as was Socrates' custom, but directly and indignantly.

Seneca also spoke with a good deal of bitterness about the lot of those who have distinguished themselves and are therefore more exposed to criticism: 'Do you see all those who praise your eloquence, run after your wealth, flatter you to obtain your favours, and praise your power? Either they are all your enemies or — which is the same thing — they can become such. The same mass of people who sing your praises may well also envy you. Why do I not seek something or other which is really good, something I can really feel, and not just something I can display?' Here it was perhaps really Seneca himself who was speaking, in recognition of the fact that life at court was not — a happy life!

Matricide

Since the death of Britannicus Nero had not been guilty of any real crimes, only of a certain amount of dissipation which was not worse than that of many another young man, but which nevertheless indicated that Nero had not accepted that a prince cannot take the same liberties as a subject. One of his hearty companions was M.

Salvius Otho, who later was proclaimed Emperor for a brief and meaningless remark, but was now one of those in Rome who knew how to enjoy their lives to the full and out-Neroed Nero in his manner of life. A remarkable young woman by the name of Poppæa Sabina, who according to Tacitus possessed everything but morals, had herself divorced in order to marry Otho who, of course, was a friend of the Emperor and could thus introduce her to him, which he did. But if Otho had aroused Nero's curiosity by painting her beauty and intelligence, she aroused his desire much more herself by playing hard to get and playing Otho off against him: Otho was a man who knew life and knew how to enjoy it, but Nero of course was a minor who obeyed the commands of others and not only lacked imperial power but also his freedom.

Naturally, Poppæa would rather be empress than mistress; this, however, presupposed that she should be divorced from Otho and that Nero in one way or another should get rid of Octavia. For the time being he got rid of Otho; it was — says Plutarch — thanks to Seneca's interference that his exile was turned into a promotion: he was appointed Governor of Lusitania (Portugal), where he revealed entirely different qualities from those seen in Rome and turned out to be a conscientious employee of the State.

Agrippina had lost her political power, but not her power over Nero, whom she tried to exploit with all the means at her disposal; the old historians are all agreed that she quite openly tried physically to seduce him; on one particular occasion Seneca is said to have avoided the worst catastrophe that could happen by allowing Acte to get in the way. Meanwhile, Poppæa was a more demanding opponent than Acte. Nero felt more and more humiliated by Agrippina's constant efforts to impose her will on him — and if it is true that the worst thing of all was about to happen on the occasion mentioned above, he must have found it very difficult indeed to escape her influence. And so, 'he decided on her death.' His sinister thoughts can be read in Tacitus, who is always well informed on the most dreadful events; his famous story of the shipwreck planned and carried out by a naval officer called Anicetus and intended to result in Agrippina's death is too good simply to be told in brief; suffice it to say that Agrippina got away with a few scratches and that Nero was appalled: could she not use the attempted murder, which she had naturally seen through, as a weapon against

171

him and get the soldiers on her side? Nero wailed like a naughty child whose naughtiness has been discovered, and who could help him against his mother — except Burrus and Seneca? He sent for them; Tacitus does not omit to point out that they apparently had not been initiated in the plan beforehand: 'Both stood silent for a long time because they did not wish to make a vain attempt to dissuade him from it. Perhaps they now believed that things had gone so far that Nero was finished if he did not strike before Agrippina. At last Seneca at least went so far that with a look at Burrus he asked if the soldiers could not be ordered to carry out the killing. He replied that the praetorians had sworn loyalty to the entire imperial household and that those who remembered Germanicus would not lay hands on his daughter. Anicetus himself must complete the task he had begun. He immediately asked to be given responsibility for the deed. This made Nero declare that not until that day had he achieved real imperial power, and that he could thank a freedman for this gift.'

Strictly speaking, Tacitus could not know what Nero, Burrus and Seneca had said when alone, for they would scarcely have revealed it. Seneca and Burrus were faced with a fact the accomplishment of which they accepted, and they could not have prevented it without losing their influence — and perhaps more besides. Nero had previously suspected Burrus of being in league with Agrippina, while Seneca had once been able to save her life; now he entered on the classical political compromise of putting up with a compromising situation in order to turn it to the best possible advantage. But his own position was undermined: he could no longer make such a strong stand on the principles which Nero had so brutally disregarded, and Nero no longer needed his support in his struggle with Agrippina.

Nero was not such a hard young man that he could have his mother murdered in cold blood; he was, both before and after the murder, plagued by all kinds of emotional states; he thought he was being pursued by the furies and did not dare return to Rome from the spa of Bajæ, where the murder took place, but neither did he dare stay in the place where the deed had been done, and so he fled to the Greek city of Neapolis. To the Senate he sent a letter justifying the execution on the grounds that Agrippina was planning to murder him, and he referred to her many attempts to achieve a share of power. Seneca was still thought to be the writer of the Emperor's communications, but if he was, it was no longer he who decided what was to go in them: 'Thus it was not only Nero, whose inhuman cruelty was beyond understanding, but also Seneca who fell into discredit, because such a letter was in fact a confession,' writes Tacitus, obviously in conflict with what he himself tells of the enthusiastic reception given to Nero by the Senate and the people when he finally returned to Rome — 'as the victor over a people of slaves.' It was this reception which finally convinced him that he could do anything he liked, and only now did he allow himself to give in to the disgraceful urges which Agrippina had so far prevented.

The Emperor at play

If we take a closer look at the disgraceful urges to which Nero capitulated, we discover that at first they consisted especially of the desire to drive a chariot and 'the no less shameful desire to sing like an actor to the accompaniment of a cither.' This might nowadays appear so harmless that the indignation of the Roman historians might appear slightly amusing, though it is amusing to note that this has not prevented the vast majority of modern historians from sharing it! If there was any reason at all in Nero's public appearances — in the circus and on the stage — the ancient historians at least were not able to see it; and so it is probably an idea to distinguish the facts which they record from the scandalised manner in which they record them, especially as they maintain that Nero made himself more and more impossible by his behaviour — and bewail the fact that he made himself more and more popular, something which Tacitus explains by arguing that 'the mob of course loves amusement and is delighted when the Emperor moves in the same direction.'

Suetonius tells an anecdote indicating that even as a schoolboy Nero had been keen on horses: in the middle of a lesson he once started whispering about a charioteer who had been 'dragged', and when the teacher asked to be spared irrelevant remarks he assured him that it was Hector he was talking about. He went to all the races he could manage; but for the time being he had to satisfy his urge to drive a chariot himself by playing with counters on a board. The races between the white and the red, the green and the blue were the only form of popular entertainment which could compete in popularity with the more bloodthirsty games; at the beginning of Nero's reign the stables exploited the situation and made such enormous wage demands that the praetor who arranged the games in the *Circus maximus* wanted to replace the horses with dogs, but Nero gave in to the demands of the stables — and of the people — and paid the bill himself. He increased the number of races to 50, so that they lasted all day like the gladiatorial games, and he himself presided over them. And now that his mother could no longer forbid it, he insisted on driving himself; Seneca and Burrus found it wisest to let him have his way, says Tacitus, as though it were still they who decided things; he was allowed to practise in a private circus which Caligula had constructed on the Vatican Heights, but when he had practised for long enough he moved over into the *Circus maximus* and 'invited the entire Roman people' to watch.

The no less shameful art — of singing to the cither — was one in which he had taken lessons from the virtuoso cither player Terpnus since the very beginning of his reign. So far he had only played for an intimate circle, but now he wanted to extend that circle and, still in the year of Agrippina's death, 59, he invited men and women from the higher strata of society to take part in some — not yet public — games, the *Juvenalia*, and to rehearse parts in Greek and Latin plays; Nero himself performed on the last day of the festival; Seneca's brother Gallio was his herald, and Seneca and Burrus his prompts! The following year he went a step further and in the Greek manner started public competitions in horsemanship, athletics and music, which also included poetry and oratory; the games were to be repeated every fifth year and to be called *Neronia*. Nero's spirit was felt throughout, though he did not appear either as a competitor or a judge; former consuls were the judges, Seneca's nephew Lucanus, 'little Marcus' as Seneca had once called him, won the poetry prize for a poem in honour of Nero.

Tacitus sums up the points of view for and against this new departure. Some preferred the old games organised by a praetor; as Roman citizens were under no obligation to take part in them. Others thought it quite a good thing that the State should take over the games so that the praetors need not use fortunes on them. Some believed that Roman customs suffered from these Greek fashions, for now distinguished Romans had to degrade themselves as actors; all that was needed now was for them to put on fencing gloves and for games of this kind to replace military service. And would justice be more likely to be done if the judges had an ear trained to appreciate tremolo tones and charming voices? But most were in favour of the 'licentiousness' of the games, though they found a more pleasant-sounding name for it — and even if Tacitus himself believes that the games accelerated the decline in morals, he nevertheless has to admit that there was nothing particularly indecorous in the way in which they were organised.

It was particularly Greek athletics which scandalised the conservative Romans, who tended to associate them with Greek sexual habits. Nero no longer hid his Greek sympathies but exhibited them openly in his dress and his hair style, though the fashion never caught on. But he pressed on, year after year, by not only opening the first public baths of the imperial age, but also a 'gymnasium' (from the Greek word gymnazein: to fight naked) in which Romans could become accomplished in the Greek sport, and he presented senators and noblemen with the oil to rub themselves in. Since senators and noblemen might be expected to be able to afford the oil themselves, this imperial generosity could only be seen as a gentle encouragement to follow the Greek line.

The Neronic Games did not include gladiatorial combats, though they did take place in the new amphitheatre. Nevertheless, although they differ in detail, all sources agree that Nero did make men and woman of high society take part, not only in the peaceful plays, but also in gladiatorial combat and battles with animals. There is no indication that any of the distinguished members of society lost their lives on such occasions, and so we can take it that they managed to save their lives, though perhaps not always their honour. They were obviously quite harmless games. Was it Nero's intention to *make* the games harmless, turn them into a sort of parody — for that is what they must have been with such gladiators — or did he want to humiliate the great? The way in which Tacitus puts it, that the ancient games, i.e. the gladiatorial combats, were preferable to the new ones, in which Roman citizens took part, could indicate a feeling that the new games were intended to replace the old ones which the quaestors as mentioned above were no longer compelled to arrange. It was the State that arranged the new ones, and it was former consuls (and not

175

mere praetors) who presided over them: Nero had no need for all this merely as an excuse to appear in public himself — especially as he did not himself take part in public until 65 — and a less prejudiced eye than that of the historians might be more inclined to see them as quite a reasonable new departure in cultural policy, as a conscious attempt to limit the brutality of public entertainment by replacing it with something else. It is not surprising that the historians could not see any point in this kind of entertainment: the bloodthirsty games which the consuls had arranged in 105 B.C. deliberately to counter Greek effeminacy still represented for them the good old Roman warrior spirit.

What role did Seneca play in this imperial pageant, apart from the part of prompt which Dio Cassius ascribes to him? As Dio Cassius also says that Seneca kept away from the imperial receptions, he is presumably implying that Seneca could have kept away from the games if he had had anything against them. Seneca makes use of the race track as a metaphor for the course of life on one occasion, but otherwise he betrays no particular sympathy or antipathy for the races in the Circus, and he probably thought it wise to try to stem Nero's urge for showing off in that sphere — which really only became completely uninhibited after Seneca's retirement. On the other hand there is no reason to believe that Seneca, who himself wrote tragedies in the Greek manner, was unsympathetic to Nero's more artistic efforts; in *Apocolocyntosis* he had allowed Phoebus to praise his singing, and in Seneca's tragedy on 'Furious Hercules' the hero is scolded by the villain for not being a hero because his done-up hair is running with nardus oil and because his famous hands move to the unmanly sound of the tambourine. This description of Hercules is so unusual that it is tempting to see a reference to — and thereby a defence of — Nero in it, all the more so as Nero had his hair done up with buckles like a charioteer.

Seneca's enemies maintained (says Tacitus) that he wrote far more poems than previously now that Nero himself was taking more interest in writing poetry; this does not necessarily mean, as was said, that he was trying to outdo the Emperor, but it might rather indicate that he was encouraging him in his poetic ambitions. As Nero's teacher, Seneca must of course have stimulated and perhaps even awakened his interest in the Greek and Latin poets. He introduced his poetically gifted nephew Lucanus at court, where other poets and philosophers were also frequently met; it was some time before Nero's 'artistic jealousy' made it dangerous to excel in the same arts as the Emperor. For the time being Seneca could have a reasonable hope that the Greek dramas in which Nero appeared could play their part in avoiding much worse forms of drama; besides, Augustus had already introduced Greek games, not only in Actium and Neapolis, but also in Rome where, however, they had not survived him — and in this respect, too, Nero and Seneca could maintain that they were continuing the policy of Augustus.

The *Neronia* were the only large-scale innovation in the year after Agrippina's death; they indicated no break with Seneca's policy, but were rather an expression of it. The regime did not immediately change character; Nero was gentle enough to recall Agrippina's exiled victims. Admittedly Rubellius Plautus whom she had once been accused of wanting to put on the throne was exiled instead, but that was because a comet in the year 60 was seen as a warning of coming changes at the top; and as Plautus by dint of his relationship with the imperial family was closest to the throne if it should become vacant, Nero encouraged him to pre-empt the rumours and retire to his estates in Asia. On that occasion Seneca is said to have argued that Nero would not achieve anything through harshness, for however many he killed, he would not be able to kill his successor — but it was probably not on that particular occasion that he said it. The murder of Agrippina was still the gruesome exception to the rule that Seneca had prescribed for him in 'On gentleness'; it was Nero's 'Greek' effeminacy which scandalised the more conservative Romans, and at this point his regime was generally thought to be too soft rather than too hard.

The slaves

In 61 the city prefect in Rome was murdered by one of his slaves. In a case such as this all the slaves owned by the murdered man were subject to the death penalty. In the Senate there were those who thought that this old law should be abolished.

Slavery was common in all ancient societies; the idea that people were born unequal was generally accepted — also by the philosophers:

Aristotle believed that some are born to rule, others to be ruled. Only the Stoics saw slavery as an arbitrary social institution and not as a natural state. 'Although everything is permitted towards slaves,' wrote Seneca in 'On gentleness', 'there is nevertheless something which the law applicable to all living creatures forbids us to subject any human being to.' The law said to be applicable to all human beings did not exactly have a legal status, but in the imperial age the scarcity and the price of slaves made their masters more interested in taking care of them. Slaves could, and in many cases did, earn their freedom, and the growing social and economic significance of freedmen indicates that the position of slaves was no longer completely hopeless. The conservative senators observed this development with anxiety; as long ago as 56 the Senate had debated a proposal that masters should be able to punish freedmen who turned out not to be worthy of the confidence shown in them. There was a majority for this in the Senate, but the consuls put the proposal before the Emperor, whose advisers were disagreed. Seneca's view, which he subsequently defended at length in his treatise 'On good deeds' was that society cannot judge on mental attitudes, and that ingratitude therefore cannot be made a criminal offence. This view prevailed in the Emperor's council and in the Senate.

During the imperial age slight improvements had been made in the legal status of slaves. Under Tiberius masters had been forbidden arbitrarily to condemn their slaves to the arena; under Claudius it was decided that slaves who were dismissed because of illness should be free, and that masters who killed slaves in order to economise should be punished. Seneca refers to a rule which was probably due to his initiative and which the historians characteristically have not considered worthy of mention: slaves were given the right of complaint to an official, probably the city prefect — 'who must keep a check on brutality, lasciviousness and meanness in the distribution of the necessities of life.'

Now, in 61, after the murder of the city prefect, the highly esteemed lawyer Cassius Longinus made use of the opportunity to make a speech on the entire principle in the Senate. He had allowed through several new laws, although he preferred the laws of his forefathers, but now the time had come to say stop. The important thing was not that the slave concerned had scarcely had sole responsibility for the crime, but that a suitably frightening example must be made, for how could the few feel safe among the many when not even a city prefect was safe in the care of 400 slaves! 'Our forefathers,' said Cassius, 'had no confidence in the attitudes of their slaves even if they were born on their land and in their house and from childhood had grown up with affection for their master. In our slave population we have many whose customs are different from ours and who have an alien religion or no religion at all. It is only possible to control such a motley crowd by fear.'

Cassius Longinus was descended from the Cassius who had murdered Caesar, and he represented the ancient Roman ideals; as governor in Syria he had overworked his soldiers 'as though the enemy were at the door,' and he was opposed both to an exaggerated adulation of the Emperor and to Seneca's humanism — which in this case met with a decisive defeat. Cassius' views won the day in the Senate, where the suggestion was even made that the freedmen of the murdered man should be punished. This was prevented by the Emperor, but the four hundred slaves were executed according to the barbaric old law. This mass murder has given rise to far less historical scandal than the murder of Agrippina as, of course, it only concerned slaves and not a former empress, and since it was not Nero but the Roman Senate which perpetrated it. No one has bothered to indicate Seneca's reaction, but it is not difficult to guess what it was.

In his treatise 'On good deeds', which stems from this time, Seneca rejects the view that a slave can do his master no good, since he is his property: 'Anyone denying that a slave can do his master any good knows nothing of human law (*jus humanum*); what is important is the position he adopts, not the position he occupies. The good is not closed to anyone, but is open to all and gives access and invites everyone, free-born or freedman or slave, or king or exile; the elegance of the house or the size of the fortune is no criterion; man in his nakedness is sufficient. . . We all have the same beginning, the same origin; one man is thus no more distinguished than another unless he is more honest by nature and better suited to do good.'

The elegance of the house and the size of the fortune — these were the very criteria governing the inequality which reigned everywhere, and which were not in accordance with human law; they are due to the whims of chance and not the will of fate, to social and not to natural order. The transition from a privileged society to one based on law was for Seneca a condition for the continuation of society, and for Cassius Longinus it was the path leading to its destruction. In his famous 47th epistle, however, Seneca believes he must avoid the misunderstanding that: 'I am tempting slaves with the bonnet of freedom and casting down their masters from their lofty pinnacles because I have said that they ought rather to honour than fear their masters. "Oh," you ask, "are they to honour them like clients paying an early morning visit?" Anyone making this objection forgets that what is sufficient for a god cannot be too little for a master. A man who is honoured is also loved; love cannot exist along with fear.'

This can be read as a reply to Cassius Longinus' speech in the Senate, and it is highly likely that it was written under the impression of the ghastly affair. What Seneca here says of the relationship between masters and slaves corresponds to what he has said elsewhere of the relationship between a ruler and a subject: crime leads to crime, cruelty produces opposition, something which there was plenty of reason to emphasise now, for the death sentence on the city prefect's slaves scandalised people so much that the praetorians had to clear the way for the condemned on their way to the place of execution.

So far Nero had in the name of freedom omitted to interfere in the decisions of the Senate, and he adopted his usual practice in this case; by following his 'political principles' he was able to disregard more humane considerations. Seneca's humanism had suffered a defeat, and it was presumably in that same year, 61, that in a treatise called *De otio* Seneca recommended his friend Serenus, who as *præfectus vigilum* also had a high position, to retire from state service.

Only a year of two earlier it is worth noting that Seneca had addressed another work to Serenus in which he had considered 'what one ought to do at a time when it is useless to try to influence the state', but nevertheless had encouraged him to hold on. Seneca has often been reproached for not living in accordance with his thinking, and it is probable that this was more difficult for him than for his critics, who on the one hand did not think quite so much and on the other did not have to rule Rome. Seneca was not at liberty to retire from the court, and even if he did come to assume a share of the responsibility for decisions with which he could not sympathise but could not prevent, there were still a large number of things which he — and perhaps he alone — could prevent. At least it can be said that Nero's regime only changed its fundamental character *after* Seneca's retirement.

'On peace of mind' – and retirement

Seneca had written to Annæus Serenus on steadfastness at a time when he himself was in need of it; it was to him he now wrote 'On peace of mind' (*De tranquillitate animi*), in a humoristic tone which indicates that he himself was taking it easy, as though it were not *his* problem, but also with such deep insight into Serenus' problem that it is not going too far to assume that he knew it from his own experience. The problem is that Serenus both prefers a frugal life to a luxurious one, and a luxurious life to a frugal one; that he prefers a contemplative life to an active one, and an active life to a contemplative one; that he prefers to work for his fellow-citizens and most of all for his fellow human beings, and that he would also prefer to exist solely for himself. That is in short the existential problem which Seneca places before Serenus, and as is well known, it consists in the argument that in everything we do we have to come to terms with ourselves; it only disappears when we wholeheartedly commit ourselves to everything we do, when, in Seneca's terminology, we are wise and not merely desirous of becoming wise. Serenus asks Seneca for a medicine to cure his illness, which is not a real illness, for he is not really on the wrong road, though neither is he on the right one. He does not allow himself to be tossed helplessly about as by a storm at sea, but neither does he act according to his own will: he is suffering from spiritual seasickness, nausea — the same word which Sartre used as a term for existential nausea in the novel 'La Nausée'.

For internal poverty to go hand in hand with external wealth is not a new phenomenon, and it is well known that the more you 'are', the more difficult it is to be yourself. If you look beyond yourself for what you can find only in yourself, you must constantly be searching for something new; — and you will constantly be disappointed and end in the frustration resulting from having wanted in vain, *frustra voluisse*, for if you finally achieve the goal of your wishes, it will turn out not to be what you wanted after all. Seneca's description of the unpleasant sides of civilisation, of boredom and officiousness in those who have enough

181

but cannot get enough, is strikingly modern — or else the phenomenon is. He also comes close to giving a psychoanalytical explanation of it: it results from unhappy desires which we neither have the strength to control nor the courage to satisfy, so that they turn inwards and 'are shut up in a narrow room without an exit and suffocate themselves.' But in Seneca psychological explanations give way to moral considerations of purpose: by nature man is inclined to the good; properly speaking there is only one thing for him to do, and if he does not act in harmony with himself in everything he does, he will be in opposition to himself, and everything he undertakes will be an attempt to flee from the true task.

Peace of mind is present when 'the soul can move easily in the same rhythm and be favourably disposed towards itself,' and of course, it cannot do this if it must constantly live up or down to demands from outside or undertake dubious tasks. The great contrast is to be found between 'unaffected naturalness' and the 'external role': it is demanding always to live in a mask (*persona*, as it is called in Latin), but it is also dangerous to be natural and straightforward, for then you lay yourself open to the scorn of others. Yet it is better to be scorned for naturalness than to suffer external dissimulation, and it is just as unfortunate to shun others as it is to seek the company of others out of fear of your own. Certainly a man can only do good to others if he is himself, but to be yourself is to do good to others; man is born for the good of all. Therefore it was a Stoic principle that the wise man more than anyone else should take part in public life.

However, society does not honour naturalness, and on the contrary, it is difficult to combine it with high offices — *honores* — and so it is easy to doubt the suitability of playing an active part in society, all the more so since Stoic authorities are not in complete agreement on this point. Serenus, who has otherwise become more Stoic since Seneca taught him about the steadfastness of the wise man, has not entirely learned not to make wisecracks about the wise man: 'With the willingness of the beginner I follow Zenon, Cleanthes, Chrysippos, of whom practically speaking none took part in political life — and none of them failed to exhort others to do so.' In reply Seneca quotes a later Stoic, Athenodorus from Tarsus, who wrote on the question at greater length: he said that the ideal thing is to place yourself in the midst of public life — but as circumstances are not ideal, then you should keep away from the Forum. That is what Athenodorus said at the time of Augustus; what does Seneca say now, in Nero's day? 'I myself,' he says, 'believe that Athenodorus was too quick to submit to circumstances and to take to flight. No more than he will I deny that in certain circumstances it is best to retire, but only step by step'. . . . 'If fortune has denied you a place among the leading figures in the State, then nevertheless stand firm and help with your cries, and if they silence you, then stand firm and help with your silence.' You should neither retire from an influential position simply because it does not give sufficient influence and because you cannot decide everything for yourself — nor cling to the privileges which the position might give you. What chance has placed in your hands, it can also deprive you of; in that case it is wise to say, 'Thank you for what I have had and owned. . . If you want me still to keep anything of yours, I will look after it; if not, then here you have my silver and my money, my house and my household, and so it is yours again.' It was the gifts of fortune which Seneca had had to justify in 'On the happy life' and which he subsequently declared himself ready to renounce, and the address to fortune sounds a little like a summary of the speech which according to Tacitus he made to Nero, the tool of *fortuna*, in 62.

'On peace of mind' is the first of the works from Nero's reign in which Seneca takes the liberty of voicing criticism of circumstances, as he had been able to do before he himself became partly responsible for them. The unpredictable Caligula appears here again, as an example of man at the mercy of his surroundings. Seneca goes so far as to say: 'At times one becomes fired with hatred for the entire human race and struck by the happy outcome of so many shameful deeds'; strangely enough, 'hatred for the entire human race' (*odium generis humani*) was exactly what the Christians were accused of and executed for after the Fire of Rome in 64. What is now left of the 'age of happiness and purity' which Seneca had proclaimed in the early years of Nero's reign? What is left of Nero's innocence, which he had praised: 'when one considers how rare naturalness is, and how innocence is unknown and honesty scarcely to be found where it does not pay'?

Serenus, who as imperial prefect worked directly under Nero, obviously no longer felt happy in his job. Seneca consoled him with the argument that his position was still easier than those of people 'who are tied to a glorious position and groan under a ponderous title and who, from ambition rather than will, allow themselves to be determined by a public role.' But he also admits that it can be difficult to withdraw from the role: 'There are indeed many who cannot of their own free will relinquish their high posts, from which they can only descend by falling; but they would be wise not to hide the fact that having to place burdens on others is the greatest of burdens for them, that they have not raised themselves up, but have been raised up as on a cross.' According to the Stoics it was a duty to take part in political life, and that duty he was now comparing to a punishment.

'On peace of mind' was without doubt written after 'On the happy life' from 58 and before 'On retirement', for in this Seneca goes a step further and unreservedly recommends retirement, which does not mean an inactive life, but a life without political activity. In principle Seneca has not changed his mind: by nature men have an urge both to contemplation and activity; the ideal is to combine one with the other, and in the ideal state there is no contrast between benefitting yourself and benefitting others. But if the state is so corrupt that it cannot be helped, it is not wise to exert yourself to no avail and to sacrifice yourself for nothing; then it is wiser to reflect that a man is a citizen in two states, one which has boundaries and one which has none. A man has a responsibility towards his fellow citizens, but especially towards his fellow men, and also towards the man which he is himself: if a man does not achieve his rights in the state, he must fight for human rights. Think of Athens where Socrates was condemned to death and whence Aristotle had to flee; think of Carthage, which was not only cruel to its enemies, but inimical towards its own people. Seneca does not say, 'Think of Rome,' but he says, 'if I look at all states, I do not find one which can tolerate the wise man and which the wise man can tolerate.' 'But if there is no such state, then retirement (otium) begins to be necessary for all.' In short, Seneca is now inciting people to 'the great refusal'.

Now it is Serenus who has to remind Seneca of Zenon's and Chrysippos' exhortation to political activity. Seneca replies first that the person who always obeys a single authority is more at home in a clique than in the Senate — and there is a significance in these words, for what state was the Senate now in? And secondly he asserts that Zenon and Chrysippos did not work for a single state at all, but for the whole of mankind; they achieved far more than if they had

184

commanded armies, been appointed to high posts or proposed laws. No one can be reproached for spending his whole life studying the mysteries of nature, and the man who has become too old for his post has every conceivable right to dedicate the remainder of his life to it. A large part of the extant fragment of 'On retirement' touches on the great questions of nature, which had occupied Seneca in Corsica and which he had not had time to bother with while 'in office': he had obviously not only negative political reasons, but also positive philosophical grounds for wanting to retire.

Serenus died in office shortly afterwards, presumably in 61. From the omniscient Pliny we know that he and several officers in the watch corps died from mushroom poisoning. It is a significant aspect of the character of Seneca the Stoic, who in his letters to his friends warmly praises friendship but seldom indicates his own feelings, that he 'wept unrestrainedly' over the death of Serenus, something which he himself admits and condemns in an epistle: it caught him completely unawares that Serenus, who was so much younger than he, could die before he himself did, 'as though mortal fate took heed of people's ages.'

Seneca's departure

Serenus was succeeded as prefect by Ofonius Tigellinus, who as a stable-owner and horse-breeder had common interests with the Emperor. The following year Burrus died — 'it is not certain whether from illness or poison' — but as he, too, was succeeded by Tigellinus it is not an unreasonable hypothesis to suppose that he made his own way forward in both cases. From now onwards Tigellinus was the strong man at court; admittedly, as a symbol of the power struggle at the top he was given a colleague in the praetorian prefect Fænius Rufus who as præfectus annonæ had made himself the darling of the people and still listened to Seneca. But Nero listened all the more to Tigellinus and Poppæa, and they maintained that Seneca was trying to curry favour with the ordinary citizens and that with his wealth, his parks and country mansions and as a poet and orator he was trying to outshine the Emperor: since Nero had begun writing poetry Seneca was indeed writing much more than before! How long was Seneca to have so much say in the affairs of the State? Nero was no longer a child, and it was time he got rid of his guardian! Seneca had had his time, or at least the time had come when he could put into effect the thoughts which he had formulated and possibly also published in 'On retirement'. Tacitus writes:

Seneca was not unaware of the slanders, but was informed of them by those who still had any moral integrity, and when the Emperor more and more obviously shunned his company, he asked for and was granted an audience, and began thus: 'Now, Caesar, it is fourteen years since your path met with mine when you were a promising child and eight since you assumed power: in the intervening years you have lavished upon me such great honour and wealth that my happiness lacks nothing, except perhaps moderation. I will refer to great examples, not of my station, but of yours. Your great-grandfather Augustus allowed Marcus Agrippa to retire to Mytilene and Gajus Mæcenas to live almost as a foreigner, without the duties of a citizen, in the capital city itself; one of them had been his comrade in arms, the other had carried out various great duties in Rome, and both had received great rewards, corresponding to their deserts. But what have I been able to do to make myself worthy of your generosity, apart from my philosophical efforts which as it were throve in the shade and were only lent lustre because it seemed I supported you in the studies of your youth — a task which was its own rich reward. Yet you have endowed me with such influence and such vast riches that I often have to ask myself: Am I, born into an equestrian family in the provinces, to be counted as one of the most distinguished members of society? I, an upstart, have bathed in the sunshine of noblemen who can boast of a long line of ancestors! Where is the undemanding spirit of frugality? Is that what has designed all these parks and spread over all these estates and all these expanses of land and blossomed in investments far and wide? In my defence I can only produce one argument: that I have been unable to refuse the tokens of your favour.

But the measure is now filled for us both: you have shown how much an emperor can give to a friend, how much a friend can accept from an emperor — what is beyond that carries within itself the seeds of envy. That cannot of course reach you who are raised high above all the more wretched attributes of man, but it weighs heavy on me, and I need relief. Just as, weary in the field of battle or at the roadside, I would ask for support, so must I, an old man unable to live up to even the slightest tasks, seek help on my way through life; I am no longer capable of carrying the burden of my riches. Let my estates be administered by your procurators; let them be yours! I shall not in this way be reduced to poverty: when I have renounced everything which can dazzle me, I can use on my own spirit the time now put aside for attending to my parks and mansions. You have an abundance of strength and the experience of several years in exercising the highest authority: now we, your friends from ancient times, can ask to be relieved of our duties. This, too, will serve your honour: that those men whom you have brought to the supreme positions can also manage for themselves on a more modest level.'

Then Nero replied in this way: 'That I can stand here and give an immediate reply to your prepared speech is the first thing for which I can thank you, who have taught me not merely to formulate the thoughts which I have had, but also those I have at the moment. My great-grandfather Augustus allowed Agrippa and Mæcenas to enjoy their retirement after their work on his behalf, but only at an age when his prestige was sufficient to justify his treatment of them, and yet he did not take back from them the rewards he had given them. They had shown themselves deserving of them in war and danger, and such were conditions when Augustus was young. Nor would I have looked in vain for your weapons and your support if I had grown up in times of war; but what I needed in my situation, you gave me, and you gave to me in my childhood and youth the benefit of your reason, your advice and your precepts. And what you have given me will last as long as I live; what you have received of me — parks and riches and mansions — are subject to changing fortunes. It may look like a great deal, but many men who are far less qualified than you have received far more. I am embarrassed to mention the freedmen who exhibit greater wealth, and I must blush with shame that you, who are closest to me, do not exceed the others in power and riches. For surely you do not consider youself inferior to Vitellius, who was consul three times, or me to be less than Claudius. Or do you find it reasonable that Volusius[1] in a long

---

[1] L. Vitellius, who was consul under Tiberius and Claudius, was the father of the later Emperor Vitellius. L. Volusius Saturninus was city prefect — and 95 years old when he died in 56.

life has been able to accumulate more than my generosity can give you?

The truth is that you still have the strength to accept the tasks and their reward, while I as Emperor have only taken my first steps. If I am in danger of stumbling in my youthful impetuosity, is it not you who the more firmly should correct and guide me and support those manly qualities in me which serve my reputation? If you leave your Emperor, it is not your quiet life but my greed, the fear of my cruelty, which will be on everyone's lips. And although your modesty will be praised loudly, it is not right of a philosopher to reap honour for something which brings dishonour to his friend.'

Then he embraced and kissed him; such was his nature, and it had become his habit to hide his hatred under false gestures of flattery. Seneca thanked him — that is the end of every conversation with a ruler, of course — but he ceased to live the life of a great man, asked to be excused from great receptions, avoided large retinues, seldom showed himself in the city and stayed at home under the pretext of bad health and philosophical studies.'

It is clear that Nero had learned to fashion his own speeches; it is most likely that he wanted witnesses to the audience he gave to Seneca, and so the speeches as recorded by Tacitus can be assumed to be more or less authentic.

Only after Seneca's retirement did Nero dare to reject and exile Octavia. However, this awoke the anger of the people, and Nero was sufficiently concerned to bring her back. That made the people rejoice and overturn the statues of Poppæa, and that naturally awoke Poppæa's anger. The prefect of the fleet, Anicetus, the man who in his day had helped Agrippina to her death, was now engaged to witness to the fact that Octavia had seduced him in order to ensure the support of the navy in her rebellious plans. Octavia was again exiled and subsequently put to death — and Nero married Poppæa.

The stages on Nero's path to 'freedom' are illustrated by those named as pretenders to the throne. Cornelius Sulla and Rubellius Plautus in 55 escaped prosecution, in 58 and 59 they were exiled, and in 62 murdered; Pallas, too, who had been given an honourable dismissal, was according to rumour helped to his death so that the Emperor could have the benefit of his large fortune. Only now did Nero's regime lose all signs of conscience; Tigellinus acted as his bloodhound, just as Sejanus had been Tiberius'. The other praetorian prefect, Fænius Rufus, who was indebted to Seneca for his post, had for that reason alone not a particularly strong position.

As for Seneca, he had not put himself out of danger by keeping away from court. Tigellinus spoke of 'the presumptuous Stoic sect which makes the people restless and rebellious;' he hardly knew Stoicism from personal study, but only from those who professed it, and among those was not only Seneca but also Senator Thrasea Pætus, who drew attention to himself during the first trial for lese-majesty in Nero's reign. A practor had written a poem satirising the Emperor, and he was accused of lese-majesty by Tigellinus' son-in-law, who had become a senator thanks to his connections. According to law this was punishable by death, but Thrasea Pætus said that under a good emperor the Senate was not bound to condemn a criminal to the prescribed punishment; it would be sufficient punishment to him to be exiled and allowed to continue his miserable life, and it would bear witness to the humanity of the Roman State. Most of the senators still had courage enough to support this view, but the consuls dared not implement the resolution without hearing the Emperor's opinion. He replied that when the Senate had judged a man guilty of a serious crime, it ought to leave it to the Emperor to temper justice with mercy, but that it could do as it liked. The Senate maintained its resolution, and from that time onwards Nero became more and more antagonistic towards it, although he had less and less reason to be so as time went on and it lost the courage to make independent decisions.

Thrasea was not received by the Emperor when the Senate went to congratulate him on the birth of a daughter to Poppæa; later Nero is said to have told Seneca, perhaps feignedly, that he had become reconciled with Thrasea, something on which Seneca congratulated him. 'This led to celebrity and insidious danger to outstanding men,' writes Tacitus, who also has a slightly cryptic remark to the effect that Seneca came under suspicion as a friend of Calpurnius Piso: 'This gave Piso reason to be on his guard and led to the great but unsuccessful conspiracy against Nero.'

VII POSITIONS, ATTITUDES AND DEEDS

The Epistles to Lucilius: Training in Wisdom

Seneca was in disfavour and therefore in danger of his life. This made him all the more eager to finish his work while he still had time. There were many things which had piled up while his official duties had taken all his time. In the last three years of his life not only did he finish the seven books on nature, but also seven books 'On good deeds', the first of which were probably written in the good days before 59. In addition he was working on a major piece of moral philosophy of which only a few quotations have survived, and he set about demonstrating that the universe is governed by a providence which is concerned with man; however, he only succeeded in completing a quite short essay entitled 'On providence'. Some of Seneca's tragedies were probably also written during this period, and in addition there was a large number of philosophical letters: 124 *epistulæ* to Lucilius are extant. Understandably enough, Seneca was compelled to burn the midnight oil: it was now a case of making up for lost time and showing others the right course which he himself had only found after becoming tired of wandering aimlessly; now he had to admit to himself that his life had been spent in vain and empty pursuits.

Considering that Seneca had always warned against vain and empty pursuits and tried to show others the right course to take, this is an amazing admission. But Seneca takes it very seriously in his Epistles which unlike the earlier writings are not only concerned with a single philosophical theme; they are about two men, the teacher and his pupil, the author and his reader, Seneca and Lucilius, and their common philosophical aims. The Epistles to Lucilius are Seneca's most thorough attempt to fashion the mind and the spirit: they are a gradual introduction to Stoic thought; but because they take the form of replies to the pupil's questions and objections, they emphasise that Stoicism is not merely a matter of understanding correctly, but also of acting correctly and in particular adopting the correct attitude — something made difficult by a position of authority. Especially the first Epistles,

190

from the autumn of 62, indicate the enormous sense of relief Seneca felt on being released from the service of the State; in several of them he encourages Lucilius, who was imperial procurator in Sicily and also a philosopher and poet (possibly the author of an extant hexametre poem on Etna), to do the same. The 82nd Epistle appears to indicate that he did so.

As he had done with Serenus, Seneca put his own case to Lucilius, but this time he could do so wholeheartedly, for now he was wholeheartedly committed to his cause. When previously he had defended himself against Suillius' accusations that he did not live according to his teachings, he could quite rightly maintain that a man is under no obligation to praise what is wrong just because he himself is not living in the right way; it is possible to understand what is good without being able to live up to it, and this is both a good and a bad thing, of course, for not only can understanding what is right lead us in the right direction, but it can actually get in our way. Seneca, of course, criticised Roman education for concentrating on words, for fashioning the understanding but not the soul.

That 'virtue is knowledge' and that virtue can be learned was quite clear to Socrates and Plato. But although Seneca drew no distinction between wisdom and virtue either, he nevertheless had to distinguish between a wisdom which expresses itself in deeds, and a knowledge which does not, and so he was forced to place greater emphasis on the will, *voluntas* (for which the Greeks did not have a specific word): wisdom is 'always to want the same thing and always not to want the same thing.' But in this way only the wise man can will: you cannot attain to wisdom purely via the intellect, and certainly not through reading, and neither can you simply will it; to will the right thing is necessary before progress can be made, and in its way is a piece of progress in itself, but the very idea of willing the right thing implies that either for personal reasons or because of external circumstances it is not possible to achieve it: there is still a long way between a good intention and achieving the good, and the gap can only be closed when your entire personality is in harmony with itself and cannot do anything but — the good. To do good requires no great exertion, but to become good demands a great effort.

The difficulty of making the transition sought by the Epistles is seen from the fact that Seneca can write to Lucilius both that what he needs in order to become 'good' is to will, and elsewhere that 'you cannot learn to will'. What you can learn, if not on your own, at least with the help of a teacher, is to get rid of wrong ideas and overcome external obstacles and thus free your natural urge to achieve the good. Before a human being can possibly learn to use his reason he has already received many wrong ideas: 'Many things take us in the wrong direction, parents as well as slaves.' Vices are forced upon us, we are not born with them. Philosophy is really nature's own resistance and liberation movement combatting social pressure.

Seneca sees a confirmation of man's urge to do good in the fact that those who perpetrate evil are never happy. Admittedly, in 'On anger' and 'On gentleness' he had written about tyrants 'raging with sensual pleasure'; but how does it come about that even those who have completely chosen to disregard all human considerations try to pretend that their vicious actions are good actions, and that 'the man who is responsible for terrible and bloody punishments wants to be praised for gentleness and goodness?' If it is only a gesture to public opinion, how is it then that even the great mass of people thinks so highly of the good? Seneca does not say, as La Rochefoucauld was to say later, that vice's homage to virtue is hypocrisy, and neither does he believe with Machiavelli that only tactics make a prince embellish his evil deeds; on the contrary, he says that the good is so naturally strong that in their heart of hearts even evil men must approve of what is better. There is no criminal who would not prefer to achieve the object of his crime without committing the crime: no one can do wrong with a good conscience. On the other hand, it has to be admitted that there is no one with a really good conscience, as can be seen from the fact that we hide ourselves behind so many doors and doorkeepers; the higher we rise, the more we take refuge behind; we do not want to be seen unawares by others, for that is like being caught red-handed. Society as a whole is constructed like a defence against the good for which all have a natural longing and an unhappy affection. Unless, that is, they free themselves from the established norm, the madness which otherwise reigns supreme — and find their own standards.

This is what philosophy teaches us to do: it demands that 'every man shall live according to his own law'. 'Assert your right to yourself!' writes Seneca at the very beginning of his first Epistle to Lucilius, and he uses the word *vindicare* which from ancient times (cf p39) had meant to assert your right (to vengeance) out of consideration for your honour (*gloria*) and your wounded dignity. For Seneca, on the other hand, a person's dignity was seen in his not allowing himself to be insulted; while it was in the bloody field of honour that the ancient Roman virtue was put to its supreme test, in Seneca's opinion man deserves the greatest honour for victory not over external foes, but over internal enemies such as the passions. Seneca degrades the ancient *gloria* to meaning simply public estimation, while for true honour, which is independent of the opinion of others and therefore the only thing worthy of praise, he uses the new word *claritas*. 'The development which had started long before, replacing the ancient state-oriented Roman ethics with a new, individualistic element had taken place in Seneca, too,' writes Max Pohlenz. But this moral individualism does not only break with the 'ethics', giving the State a superior right to that of the individual and judging the individual according to his position in society, but also with that individualism which ancient ethics had led to in the years before the dissolution of the republic, and which allowed the strong individual to achieve his own aims at the expense of the whole. What you can only enjoy at the expense of others is not — the good; Seneca knows that Lucilius' well-intentioned parents have wished for him plenty of what there is not plenty of for all; he himself wishes for Lucilius what he wishes for all: complete command of himself. The good is open to all, and what is reserved for the few, i.e. wealth and high office, are not even a means to attaining the objective, but are obstacles in its way. Not only does Seneca stress that every man has his own law, but he also emphasises 'the common feeling... which unites human beings with other human beings and makes it clear to us that there is a common human right.' His individualism sprang from a profounder awareness of community with his fellow men than the ancient sense of community.

The good example: Demetrius

Only now did Seneca feel that he could follow his own law and be in command of himself: 'I realise, Lucilius, that I am not only being improved, but transformed,' he writes in his 6th Epistle. And as Lucilius has obviously complained that his letters are carelessly

193

conceived, Seneca replies that he would rather express himself forcefully than simply formulate words: the important thing is to say what you mean and mean what you say; everyone can do that, irrespective of intelligence, and nothing is more disgraceful than a philosopher who seeks approval and admiration. It may well be that one needs a teacher and master in this art, which does not demand genius and is the easiest art of all, but it demands the whole man and can thus be the most difficult art of all. But then one ought to choose a man whom one can admire more after having seen him — than simply after hearing him.

Seneca's friendship with Lucilius was already well-established: even in 41, when Seneca was exiled, Lucilius had shown his loyalty. Now he, too, was an elderly man, but in his youth he had been a good deal younger than Seneca and presumably even then Seneca's pupil in philosophy. In one place Seneca calls him *his* work and promises him a share of his own reputation — a literary mannerism which was not exactly natural to Seneca, though he turned out to be right. He wants to show Lucilius the right road while he himself hopes to profit from his attention, for the (inner) dialogue with a friend whom he can accept as a witness to his life is one way of keeping himself on the right road; nevertheless, Seneca does not present himself as an example. Nor is he any longer content to refer to older philosophers like Socrates and Cato; now, in A.D. 62, he cannot even help wondering whether Cato did the right thing in entering into politics: the problem when he did so was no longer one of freedom, but of whether Caesar or Pompejus should own the state. No, wisdom was to be seen as large as life on the streets of Rome in the shape of Demetrius, whom Seneca mentions for the first time in 'On the happy life' and praises in all his later works. To him Demetrius seems to have been sent by providence, so that this age should not be without its critic and example any more than any other age; but Demetrius, whom not even this age has been able to corrupt, has nevertheless been unable to reform this corrupt age. He is really a wise man, although he himself denies it, calling himself not a man acquainted with virtue but only with poverty. In his poverty he is not like a man who despises everything which others possess, but rather one who himself owns everything — and has given it to others. Caligula, of course, had a certain respect for odd behaviour, and he once offered Demetrius 200,000 sesterces; Demetrius' comment was:

'If he had really wanted to tempt me, he ought to have tried offering me the whole Empire.'

Demetrius was a Cynic. The early Stoics had learned a good deal from Cynic philosophy, and Stoicism had subsequently absorbed it. But in Rome Cynicism again went its own way and as a token of contracting out of society became more and more common in the imperial age; in the age of Marcus Aurelius 'dogs' were to be found everywhere. Until the fashion changed under the bearded Emperor Hadrian it was not considered fitting to be unshaven after, at the age of about 23, solemnly having sacrificed your first beard to the gods until, in your sixties, you entered upon old age — but the Cynics let their hair and beard grow wild and hurled insults at the well-shaven and well-groomed citizens who did not live in harmony with nature. Seneca found it contrary to nature to neglect the simple duties of cleanliness, and believed that the man whose love of wisdom distinguished him from the others should not differ outwardly, and that a good example should not be repulsive. He also doubted the value of speaking too freely to people who did not wish to listen, for too many words undermine the weight of words, and you weaken your own authority by speaking to deaf ears. But with Demetrius it was another matter: he wrote nothing, but he put his wisdom into practice with eloquence and Socratic irony; he had no need to search for words, for they came with the power of inspiration: 'I listen quite differently to our friend Demetrius after seeing him run around half naked. . . he is not only a teacher of the truth, but a witness to the truth.'

It seems that in his old age Seneca sought the company of Demetrius, who helped him to get rid of wrong opinions and superfluous desires. His moral criticism of wrong attitudes turns rather into a criticism of the faults of the social order; it is at this time he toys with the idea of abolishing wealth, for: 'When men began to ascribe value to money, the real value of things was diminished.' The worst thing is not that people place material things above spiritual values, but that they furthermore make the material world into a fictive world. In his essay 'On good deeds' we find this criticism of the capitalist mystification given as a quotation from Demetrius:

'I see iron being extracted from the same darkness as gold and silver, so that there shall be no lack of tools either for mutual slaughter or for rewards for it. And yet all this has a sort of material reality; it is after

195

all something tangible which the deluded gaze can let the soul seek. But I see all these patents and bills of exchange and shares — empty symbols of possession, shadows cast by a greed which concentrates its efforts on finding something with which to beguile the soul so that it happily believes in something which does not exist. For what are all these things, interest and instruments of debt and profits, except just as many names for human greed, which is contrary to nature. I can certainly reproach nature for not hiding its gold and silver deeper down and placing such a weight over it that it cannot be extracted, but then what are these bills and estimates and payment dates and excruciating rates of interest apart from torments which we have created for ourselves, products of our own social order, things which cannot be seen with the eyes or grasped by the hands, fantasies of meaningless greed. How miserable to take pleasure in a huge ledger listing your fortune and your vast possessions which have to be cultivated by forced labour, and herds of cattle so great that they need provinces and empires for grazing, and a body of slaves bigger than nations at war, and private mansions which are more extensive than vast cities.'

The man who wrote — and presumably not merely quoted — this was or had been one of the richest men in the Empire and knew better than most about the false world of money. Before this he had maintained that it was possible to be both wise and rich, but now he realised that it is as difficult for the rich man to *become* wise as it is for a camel to go through a needle's eye, although he did not exactly use that image. Seneca did not stop at the one attempt to get Nero to take over his estates, and when after Seneca's departure the finances of the Empire and the Emperor went into rapid decline, he got a good deal of what he wanted. The great fire of Rome in 64 also cleared a space for Nero's golden house, *Domus aurea*, which was certainly as extensive as a vast city and for the first time allowed Nero to 'live like a human being'; the result was that the Emperor sent official desecrators out into the provinces to gather riches for him. Seneca did not want to be suspected of having any part in this desecration and asked permission to leave Rome; it was refused him, so he excused himself on the grounds of ill health and stayed at home. It is clear from the letters to Lucilius that Seneca was a sick man, especially liable to attacks of asthma, but his illness was presumably seen in high places merely as an excuse — which, of course, it also was.

196

Preparation for death

That summer, together with his friend Cæsonius Maximus and a few slaves, Seneca undertook a journey in a quite ordinary farm wagon, without any provisions other than figs and without any other bedclothes than the cushioning in the wagon. Dried figs were a common New Year greeting, and Seneca writes to Lucilius that every day is like a new year which will give him happiness because of his happy frame of mind; for the mind is 'never more generous than when it has discarded all external things and achieved peace by fearing nothing and riches by desiring nothing.'

But apart from social position and superfluous things there is something else that prevents the right attitude: the opinion of other people. Seneca still has difficulty in thinking of the primitive means of conveyance as his own; when he meets company properly equipped to travel, and that often means an entire regiment, he is ashamed of what he has: 'I have not yet made much progress, I am not yet brave enough openly to acknowledge my frugality, and I am still concerned about what those whom I pass by are thinking of me. I ought instead to speak out against what the rest of the world is thinking. . .' And then follow some words of reproach which perhaps are reminiscent of what Demetrius had said; Seneca had all along been able to write such things, but he could still not express them with the same authority as Demetrius.

Seneca also encourages Lucilius to practise frugality, that is to say the 'askesis' of the Cynics. It might look like a whim for rich men to pretend they are poor, but it was a serious game: Seneca knew his life was in danger and therefore also the lives of his friends; it was important to be prepared, to make himself independent of those things which chance had bestowed on him, and if necessary of his own life. If the letters to Lucilius, digressive as they are, have one main theme, it is death, death which is part of life, for we die every moment, and we only stop when we stop living. The more richly we live, the closer is death, and a life without consciousness of death is unconscious.

Lucilius has an enemy who wants to do him down, and like Seneca himself he suffers from periodic illness. Seneca does not say that he has nothing to fear, but that he must try to anticipate the worst thing that can happen — and recognise that either it will be tolerable or soon past. What we fear does not last long, but our fear of it can last all our lives, and *that* is what is so terrifying. We often suffer far more from our own imaginations than from real things; we fear misfortunes which never happen, and we allow ourselves to be surprised by real misfortunes, as though what can befall anyone at all could never befall us. We are afraid of uncertainty, but the only certain thing in life is death, which puts an end to all sufferings and which we are at liberty to seek.

'The exit is open.' To give up in the face of physical pain is a defeat, but if you are faced with the prospect of physical pain for the rest of your days, preventing you from living an active life, then it is possible to put an end to your life while it is still worth living. It is just as pitiable to seek death from fear of life or death as it is to keep yourself alive at any price: in itself death is not more evil than life in itself is good, only the good life is good. However, we do not only have duties towards ourselves, but also towards those others who are part of our lives; in his youth Seneca himself had had his aged father to take into consideration, and now in his old age he had his still young wife Paulina: if you can sacrifice your life for the sake of others, you can also sacrifice your death — and live for their sake.

The real intention behind all these reflections on death emerges clearly in the 70th Epistle: 'Someone is coming to kill you; wait a moment! Why do you want to anticipate him? Why do you make yourself into a tool for someone else's cruelty? Is it because you envy your executioner, or do you wish to spare him? Socrates could have refrained from eating and died of hunger instead of poison; nevertheless, he spent thirty days in prison in expectation of death, not in the expectation of a miracle. No, he wanted to give to his friends a Socrates from whose companionship they could derive benefit and pleasure to the very end.' Tacitus writes that Nero had ordered one of Seneca's own freedmen, Cleonicus, to poison him, but that the attempt failed, either because Cleonicus revealed it or because Seneca had a suspicion and refused to eat anything but wild fruits or drink anything but water from the spring. His exercise in frugality was not only a whim.

'On providence' – and fortuna

For Seneca the great contrasts were not life and death, but *fatum* and *fortuna*, fate or the natural course of things (for: 'Fate is nothing but the series of mutually related causes; it is the first cause, from which all others follow') and chance. Celestial harmony indicates that chance had no part in the creation of the world, but the closer you move towards the earth, the greater the scope apparently available to it. A chorus in the tragedy 'Phædra' addressed to fate or nature says:

> Why, if such power is in thy hand
> To balance by an ordered plan
> The mass of things, why dost thou stand
> So far from the affairs of Man?
> Thou dost not care to help the good
> Nor punish men of evil mind.
> Men live — by chance, to Fate[1] subdued,
> And evil thrives, for Fate[1] is blind.

Tragedies, p. 136f.

Lucilius had met the same problem and asked Seneca how, if the world is ruled by providence, it can be that so many good men suffer evil. Since Leibniz this has become known as the theodicy problem, theodicy meaning the justification of God, and in his essay 'On providence', *De providentia*, Seneca undertakes: 'to plead the cause of the gods'.

Seneca's reply was very simple and logical: the good things would be good if they only fell to those who were good, and evils would be evil if they only struck those who are evil — and if, for instance, a man could only become blind if he deserved to lose his sight. As this is not the case, the decisive thing cannot be what a person must endure, but the way in which he endures it. If only good things befell the good, they would have no occasion to show their moral qualifications; that very thing which appears to be meaningless, the evil which befalls the good person, points to the moral significance of existence.

Socrates himself had stressed that no evil can befall a good man —

---

1. i.e. *Fortuna.*

and thus opposed the primitive tendency to see the pleasant and the unpleasant things befalling a man as rewards or punishments. The great disavowal of this mentality in world literature is the Book of Job, the author of which was contemporary with the great Greek philosophers. Job's friends want his illness to be seen as a punishment, for there must be a meaning to it, but Job firmly maintains that there is no meaning to it, and of course it is not Jehovah who is punishing Job, but Satan who is testing him.

It has appropriately been said by J. Ferguson that *fortuna* in Seneca corresponds to Satan in the Book of Job. It is not a mere chance that *fortuna* does not only mean chance and luck and lucky chance, but that as time goes on it develops the sense of rank and station and wealth: just like Satan, *fortuna* tempts man with power and riches and tests him with suffering, and just as Satan can do nothing against the will of God, so *fortuna* can do nothing contrary to the decision of fate. Seneca never really has a good word to say of *fortuna*, but he does say in one place that *natura, fatum, fortuna* are simply different names for God's different ways of working; however, it is worth noting that it is especially by means of *bad* fortune, *mala fortuna*, that God achieves the good. If an immediate connection between current values and moral values is no longer accepted, it is easy to see a contrast between them: for it is those who oppose evil who suffer most evil: 'A great example presupposes misfortune.' In misfortune no consolation is to be derived from the thought that misfortune is a punishment; on the other hand thinking of those who have suffered evil for the sake of the good can reconcile us to our own fate: they have suffered: 'in order to teach others to suffer, they are born to be examples.'

In 'On the happy life' Seneca had certainly made the distinction between good and evil on the one hand and the pleasant and unpleasant on the other, which according to Stoic thinking were morally indifferent, *indifferentia*, but nevertheless in his real life he had preferred pleasantness to unpleasantness. Now he is inclined to see a stark contrast between a pleasant life and a happy one, and to consider the suffering caused by the unpleasant aspects of life as a moral qualification. In 'On gentleness' he had expressed the hope that the Emperor's good example would affect the entire Empire and a new age dawn. Now Seneca selected his great examples from among those who had opposed the powerful; they could teach others to do the same thing, even though they themselves could not improve things; Cato is also an example of this, for his death was of great moral significance, but without political significance. A man cannot of himself change anything but his own attitude; the very awareness that he cannot be hurt by anything that is not determined by fate can help him to bear his fate. If nothing can happen unless the gods will it, it is their will to test the man who suffers a hard fate, and the test, *exercitatio*, is a mark of distinction rather than a punishment — if the man concerned passes it.

'The more we endure, the more the gods are pleased with us. Just as we Romans take puerile pleasure in seeing men battling with wild animals, the gods enjoy the sight of a great man fighting against evil fortune;' a strange metaphor considering Seneca's condemnation of the battles in the arena! Seneca cannot give the gods more than this spectators' role in the world of man; they themselves are subject to the fate which is their own will; they have commanded once and for all, and after that must obey, and we must do as they.

Although in this connection Seneca does not touch on the greater cosmic perspective, it must be remembered for the sake of completeness that according to Stoic thinking the world was irrevocably moving towards its own destruction: Seneca's description of the end of the world in his essay on nature is from about the same time as 'On providence'. Within this cosmological framework it was logically difficult to ascribe any historical significance to the good deed. But it was tempting to place in a superior world which will not be destroyed the elevated moral code to which the best bear witness in the midst of moral decline. In one of his epistles Seneca expresses the view that: 'This body is not a home but an inn in which we only stay for a short time.' In this feeling he believes he can find: 'the strongest evidence that the soul comes from a higher place.' The belief in the immortality of the soul was based on the Pythagorean-Platonic-Stoic tradition; however, the Stoics found it difficult to let immortality last longer than to the next world conflagration which reduces everything to its prime elements. And so Seneca's attitude to the idea of immortality is unresolved and inconsistent; he refers to the idea that he himself 'should step into unmeasurable time and enter into possession of all eternity' as something which great men have promised rather than proved, a great hope and a beautiful dream.

But Seneca does not let this hope and dream affect his essay on providence and relax its strict logic; in it he finally allows none less than God to certify that men can surpass the gods by enduring evils which the gods themselves are raised above — and to console men by saying that they are free to escape misfortune if it is more than they can bear: the exit is open. That a brave death might lead to a better life is something which not even God seems to know. The good deed is not done for the sake of the reward, but it bears its reward within itself, and this is true even if it consists in sacrificing life: if life is hard, death is a release.

This Stoic theodicy praising the ability to endure suffering could appeal to a suffering humanity no longer firmly tied to the primitive interpretation of life which was part and parcel of a tiny community. According to a primitive conception nothing is coincidental, but in contrast the Romans, as the elder Pliny put it, were so much at the mercy of chance that they had made chance into their god. Nevertheless, Stoicism still contains a primitive core insofar as it subordinates chance to fate and finds meaning in the meaningless; and the Stoic hero, the only effect of whose sufferings is to teach others to suffer, is still related to the *mythical hero*.

The mythical hero and the suffering god

While the typical fairy-tale hero has luck, *fortuna*, on his side and wins the princess and half the kingdom and lives happily ever after (though the fairy tale is not concerned with that), the mythical hero represents man's actual conflict with all the terrors of existence, ultimately with death, and he does not only take on responsibility for his own fate but that of mankind in general. Historically the mythical hero derives from the 'divine king' whom some tribes sacrificed at the end of his time so that his strength could be absorbed into the new cycle and contribute towards the regeneration of nature and society. It emerges from the legends on the death of Romulus that the Romans, too, had a vague recollection of this divine king and his fate: Livy leaves it vague as to whether he rose into heaven during a thunderstorm, or whether he was killed by 'the fathers'. It is also possible to see a connection between the divine king being sacrificed for society and the Stoic 'king' who is the slave of the lowliest; the sense of advent which was expressed under Augustus and on the accession of Caligula and Nero also appears to have grown up from this mythical subsoil.

But although Seneca still compared society with the body of the king, a large community could no longer feel an identity with its king in the same way as a small one can; despite the Saturnalia, the annual cleansing and renewal had no longer any social or psychological reality. The official religion was a sort of insurance against the fear linked to existence, but it brought no relief from it. On the other hand the mysteries did, and they spread together with the Roman Empire. The central feature in them was the individual's personal experience of the suffering. death, burial and resurrection of the god, and this mystical cycle was often felt as identical to the cycle of nature, for instance in the Eleusinian mysteries and in the cult of Dionysos/Bacchus. The rulers of Rome, who in principle were hospitable towards foreign gods and in 205 B.C. had imported the Great Mother, Cybele, from Greece, had their reservations on this ecstatic form of worship and in 186 B.C. tried to limit the worst excesses of the Bacchus cult; it is significant that the Latin word *superstitio*, which is related to the Greek *ekstasis*, is given the sense of exaggerated behaviour and superstition. Mention has already been made of the fact that in Seneca's youth attempts were made to expel the foreign cults, but under Caligula the Egyptian Isis was given her temple in Rome, under Claudius the Attis cult was given a Roman high priest, and the Syrian goddess Atargatis was given a temple during the reign of Nero; it was said that she was 'the only divinity whom Nero, this man who denied all others gods, found worthy of homage.' In all these cults the goddess, the Great Mother, appears in connection with a man, Cybele with Attis, Isis with Osiris, Atargatis with Thammuz, who is either her child or lover or both, and who suffers and dies and is reunited with the mother goddess. While the divine king was sacrificed for the renewal of society, the death and resurrection of the god had no significance for society but, at most, for the congregation; in the final analysis it was only the individual who was redeemed and received a share in the immortality of the god.

Seneca's Stoic hero is, as it were, a secularised version of the mythical hero. Seneca himself compares Cato, who fought against the lust for power, with Hercules, who fought against monsters: Cato is the Hercules of his day; Tiberius, too, in his memorial speech on

Augustus had compared *his* achievements with the twelve labours of Hercules. Among Seneca's tragedies there is, in addition to a 'Furious Hercules' also a 'Hercules on Oeta', which is scarcely by Seneca but still written in the Stoic-Senecan tradition. Hercules, who through his labours has pacified the earth, thinks he deserves immortality, but it is only through a painful death that he, the half-son of Jupiter, can qualify for heaven. His jealous wife has attempted to tie him to herself by a magic garment which his vanquished enemy Nessus has left behind, but the Nessus shirt turns out to be impregnated with a poison which eats Hercules up. In this way his sufferings have no really valid cause, and they have no other purpose than to give him the opportunity of suffering intolerably and dying like a man — or like a god. This Hercules Oetaeus is interesting as a Roman version of the suffering god and redeemer of the world who has brought peace to earth and by men is enjoined always to keep watch over them from his heaven; meanwhile Hercules himself has more in common with a bragging, irritable though determined gladiator than a Stoic wise man — or a Christian martyr.

However, the idea of suffering as a moral qualification is not so far from that of vicarious suffering that a Roman could not have conceived it — though he would have seen it as an impossibility. In the first half of the sixties Seneca's nephew Lucanus wrote his great epic on the civil war, in which Caesar is the villain; it is not Pompejus, however, who is the hero, but of course Cato, the only man fighting for freedom, while the others are fighting for power. He expresses a wish for the gods of heaven and the underworld to let him be punished for all and to let his blood redeem (*redimere*, really: 'to buy the freedom of') the people and wash away the guilt caused by Roman customs. So this Cato is not satisfied simply to be an 'example' teaching others to suffer, but he wants to achieve something practical with his sufferings, change the course of history, deflect fate — something which a human being, of course, cannot do. In contrast to Hercules Oetaeus, Cato is not thinking of his own immortality, but of the redemption of the people. At the time of the early emperors, it should be noted, the belief in immortality among Romans is less in evidence than a sense of transitoriness, for which there is even a formula on gravestones: NF F NS NC: *non fui, fui, non sum, non curo*: I did not exist, I did exist, I am not, I do not care. The Romans were so deeply concerned with history and society that redemption for them meant the redemption of society rather than of the individual. Perhaps this partly explains why it was Christianity and not the other religions promising redemption which gradually conquered Rome and took over the Kingdom of the Earth, for Christianity differed from the other religions by letting the son of the god intervene in the course taken by the world and proclaim a new world.

Nero and Christ. Seneca and Christianity

While in their times of tribulation the Romans feared the end of the world and in good times hoped for a golden age, the Christians at one and the same time looked for the end of the sinful world and the glory of the world to come. On Nero's accession Seneca had been hoping for an age of purity, but at the beginning of the sixties, in his great work on nature he wrote an inspired piece on the end of the world, and his tragedy 'Thyestes' was presumably also written at this time.

> And are we chosen out of all earth's children
> To perish in the last catastrophe
> Of a disjointed universe? Are we
> To see the world's end come?
> A cruel fate[1] brought us to birth, if we
> Have lived to lose the Sun, or if our sins
> Have driven him away.
> But we must not complain, nor fear;
> Too fond of life is he who would not die
> When all the world dies with him.
>
> *Tragedies p. 83*

In St. Matthew's gospel, chapter 24, Jesus prophesies that the sun 'shall be darkened, and the moon shall not give her light, and the stars shall fall from heaven, and the powers of the heavens shall be shaken'. And these tribulations are said to be at hand: 'This generation shall not pass, till all these things be fulfilled' and: 'He that shall endure unto the end,

1. i.e. *Fortuna*.

the same shall be saved.' 'And they shall see the Son of man coming in the clouds of heaven with power and great glory.'

By his death on the cross Jesus, who had proclaimed the kingdom of God on earth, shared the same fate as the suffering deity in the myths and the mysteries: Christ's death and resurrection became the central tenets of Christianity; however, the mythical cycle in Christianity was not only to have a cultic significance but a significance for the history of the world: by assuming all the sins of the world the god put an end to the old sinful world. The letter to the Hebrews, which was perhaps written at the time of Nero, contains some direct polemics against the heathen belief in fate and the belief in the irrevocable and unending cycle: Christ would not 'offer himself often, as the high priest entereth into the holy place every year with blood of others; For then must he often have suffered since the foundation of the world: but now once in the end of the world hath he appeared to put away sin by the sacrifice of himself. And as it is appointed unto men once to die, but after this the judgement, so Christ was once offered to bear the sins of many; and unto them that look for him shall he appear the second time without sin unto salvation.'

On the 18th June 64 a fire broke out in Rome and raged for six days; then it started again after apparently being put out; three of the city's 14 regions were destroyed, and only four were untouched. According to the mythical way in which that time experienced all phenomena, a misfortune of those dimensions could not be a coincidence, and it was compared with the destruction of the city by the Gauls in 388 B.C., which was also thought of as the end of time: people complained, writes Dio Cassius, 'no longer over personal losses but over the universal catastrophe.' But the Christians must have seen the universal catastrophe as a confirmation of what had been promised to them and they can scarcely have hidden their expectations — and there were probably those who noticed this and were scandalised. The rumours which arose (and which are still hawked around) that Nero himself had had the city set alight lack any reasonable foundation at all, but the Romans felt a very close affinity between society and the Emperor and made the Emperor responsible for everything that happened. Therefore the catastrophe was catastrophic for Nero, who loved to feel loved, and he did what he could to limit its harmful effect. But, writes Tacitus: 'Neither humane measures nor imperial distributions nor propitiatary sacrifices to the gods could lay the terrible rumour that the fire had broken out on command. In order to put an end to it Nero bestowed the blame and the most excruciating torments on those whom people called Christians and to whom they felt repugnance for their outrageous behaviour. The man who gave the movement its name, Christ, had under Tiberius been put to death by the procurator Pontius Pilatus; in this way this pernicious superstition had been suppressed for a time, but it broke out again, not only in Judaea, where it had originated, but in Rome itself, where all disgusting and disgraceful customs congregate and find support. Those who proclaimed themselves Christians were therefore arrested first and then, on the basis of information derived from them, a large number of people who were found guilty not exactly of incendiarism, but at least of hatred for the human race. Not only were they doomed, but they were treated with derision as they died: clothed in the skins of wild animals they were torn to pieces by dogs, or they were crucified and as darkness fell set alight as illuminations. Nero had placed his own parks at the disposal of the city for this pageant, and he himself organised a show in the circus — dressed as a charioteer he mixed with the crowd and drove his own chariot. Therefore, although they were guilty and deserving of the most severe punishment, they awoke public sympathy, as they appeared not to be sacrificed for the common good, but as the victims of one man's cruelty.'

The Christians, who looked for the end of the world and might be suspected of trying to hasten it forward themselves, were sacrificed in order to pacify the people and the powers; they endured their sufferings as heroically as any Stoic hero: just as Christ had suffered for men, his disciples now suffered for Christ and made themselves worthy of following him into his kingdom.

It is noticeable that Seneca, who in his 91st Epistle writes of the fire of Lugdunum (Lyons), makes no mention of that in Rome. However, what he writes in the late summer of 64 in his 95th Epistle could have been written under the impression of the slaughter of the Christians, which was the first of Nero's brutal orgies: 'Cruel deeds are carried out on the decisions of the Senate and the people, and what is forbidden for private individuals is commanded in public. What would cost a life if it were carried out in secret is praised when done by men in uniform... Man, who ought to be sacred for men, is now killed for amusement and entertainment, and while it used to be a disgrace to teach men to give and receive wounds, they are now dragged out naked and unarmed; and you have seen sufficient of a man when you have seen him die.'

Otherwise Seneca never indicates any acquaintance with the Christians; through his brother Gallio, to whom he was close throughout his life, he could theoretically have heard about St. Paul (cf p76), but in view of the slight significance which Gallio as governor of Achaea attached to the internal quarrels of the Jews, it is unlikely. However, many of Seneca's expressions are reminiscent of Christ's words in the gospels, and in his letters to Lucilius he expresses more personal religious sentiments than the more impersonal belief in fate: 'God is near you, with you, in you'.... 'Believe me, I am laying bare my innermost feelings: in all adverse and harsh circumstances I have made up my mind not only to obey, but to approve of the decision of God; I follow him with my whole heart, not just because it is necessary.' He stresses that in relationship to the gods the important thing is the right and pious will, and he wrote an essay 'On superstition', *De superstitione*, which is only known from quotations used by the Church Fathers as arguments against heathen superstitions. St. Augustine admittedly felt compelled to criticise him for respecting official religious practices (something he did as a social custom) despite his devotion to God, but otherwise the earliest Christian writers were inclined to make use of him. 'Seneca, who is often of our opinion,' writes Tertullian, who also refers to Seneca in his famous dictum that there are 'souls who by nature are Christian'. Lactantius calls Seneca 'the most acute of the Stoics' and writes: 'What could be said with greater truth by one who knew God than what has been said by this man who did not know the true faith? He could have been a true man of God if anyone had shown him the way.'

How tempting then it must have been for men of good will to imagine that someone had shown him the way. In the Epistle to the Philippians St. Paul wrote: 'All the saints salute you, chiefly they that are of Caesar's household.' And was Seneca not of Caesar's household? Perhaps it is this passage which gave rise to the imaginary correspondence between St. Paul and Seneca which was written some time before 300 and thought to be genuine throughout the Middle Ages. It was probably written as an 'exercise' in a school of rhetoric

208

and is fairly untalented, but it is interesting in that it relates Nero to Christ: if Christ is the innocent who bears the sins of the world, Nero is the lecher who must pay for them: 'Just as the best of all gave his head for the many, so shall he be condemned to burn in fire for all.'

Since Christ had been 'once offered to bear the sins of many', it was strictly speaking unnecessary for Nero also to be burned for all. But naturally enough, as time passed the attitudes of the Christians were affected by the fact that the glory of the world to come took its time in coming and that in the meantime they were subjected to persecution. The Stoic ideal of steadfastness also became a Christian virtue, but there was still the difference between suffering for the Stoics and suffering for the Christians that in the one case it was chiefly a moral qualification, whereas in the other it was also a qualification for the world to come. And the idea that good will be rewarded leads automatically to the idea that evil will be punished; the Christians looked not only for relief from their sufferings in this sinful world, but also sought an outlet for their anger. Nero's name could in Hebrew also be interpreted as 666, the number of the beast in the Apocalypse, and they not only imagined that he, the first to persecute them, should burn on behalf of them all, but also that he should punish them. Just as the body of Christ had disappeared from the grave, so Nero's grave had disappeared from the face of the earth, and thus arose the superstition — says Lactantius — 'that Nero was taken up from the earth and kept alive in order not only to be the first but also the last persecutor of the Christians and to proclaim the kingdom of the Anti-Christ.' And when Christ returns to enter into his divine and eternal kingdom, people believe, says Lactantius, adding that it is only a superstition: 'that Nero, too, will return as the precursor and herald of the Devil when he is about to appear to destroy the world and exterminate mankind.' This is how Nero, the prince of this world, the pupil whom Seneca had tried to bring up to be the servant of the lowliest, entered into the popular imagination in the Christian world!

It was Christianity, not Stoicism, which became popular, and its popularity was due to the primitive dualism which placed the Anti-Christ in opposition to Christ and clearly distinguished between the natural and the supernatural, the human and the divine, the evil and the good. Lactantius, who acknowledged that Seneca had expressed many things better than the Christians, also wrote a criticism of him which clearly draws the distinction between Stoicism and Christianity. His objections are:

> that the natural is not the good,
> that knowledge of the good (wisdom) is not itself the good,
> that suicide is not allowed, and
> that compassion is not a weakness.

If we ignore the last point, the other three can be summed up as saying that according to Stoicism man through his nature and his reason can liberate himself, from life if from nothing else, while the Christian view is that he can only be redeemed by grace.

But the Christian realisation that we are all sinners did not make the Christians more tolerant towards those sinners who were not saved by the grace of God, but condemned by his anger. It is noticeable that in 'De spectaculis', written about 200, Tertullian condemns the gladiatorial games even more passionately than Seneca, but at the same time he comforts the Christians, who had difficulty in avoiding taking part in these sinful entertainments, by telling them that they will be provided with a far more bloodthirsty spectacle on the promised day, which also came to be known as the Day of Wrath, *dies iræ*. What Tertullian condemned on earth, he accepted in heaven, and the wrath which was suppressed on the surface lived on beneath the surface and was given a divine format; even Thomas Aquinas could promise that the blessed should be witnesses to the torments of the damned, so that their bliss might be the greater. Wrath, the urge to mete out punishment, which for Seneca was the most repugnant of all vices, made its mark on Christianity because Christianity had arisen under persecution — and because it later gained power and the kingdom. Jesus had said: 'Forgive them, for they know not what they do,' and Seneca had written: 'Forgive them, for they are all out of their minds.' It was not this evangelical and Stoic spirit that won the day in the Church; that spirit had to be satisfied with a limited moral victory.

Lactantius' final objection to Seneca, that compassion is not a weakness, had really already been countered in 'On gentleness', where Seneca had written that everything that can be expected of a man who feels compassion is done by the man of wisdom, 'but with a quiet mind'. In the Stoic view compassion was com-passion, a suffering together with someone, that is to say a suffering, a passion, and a man who acts in passion does not act freely. However, it is worth noting that whereas in 'On anger' Seneca had counted compassion among the 'minor weaknesses', in one place in his essay 'On good deeds' he talks of 'humanity or compassion' and elsewhere mentions compassion together with magnanimity and gentleness. If he had not changed his views, he had at least changed his use of words and put dogmatics aside; it is only in 'On gentleness' that he views compassion as 'psychological weakness', and that was aimed at Nero (cf p155). The point is that you have to be yourself if you really want to be something for others, something which is also implied by the Christian command: 'Love thy neighbour as thyself.'

'On good deeds'

In 'On the steadfastness of the wise man' Seneca had, as it were, produced a negative definition of the wise man as one who is immune to insults. But the opposite of insults, *injuriæ*, is good deeds, *beneficia*, and in his main work of moral philosophy, *De beneficiis*, he considers the wise man from his positive aspects and stresses that wisdom is practical wisdom and is to the benefit of one's fellow men. In his own name Seneca writes to Lucilius that he would reject any wisdom granted him on condition that he should keep it to himself: 'There is no good thing which we can rejoice in possessing without someone to share it with.' That the wise man in unhappy circumstances has sufficient in himself is not the same as saying that under all circumstances he has enough in himself; he *may* be without friends, but this rarely happens, because he does not need friends for support but friends with whom to share what he has. As already said, 'friendship' was an ancient designation for mutual interest; 'business connections' is what Seneca calls this, stressing mutual liking and common aims as being of the essence of friendship.

However, this philosophical friendship presupposes not only inner freedom, but also financial independence — or at least the ability to feel independent of financial dependence. Apart from the distribution of corn there were no social services in Rome; the system of clients was a sort of institutionalised private social service: every morning the

211

clients waited on their patrons and in return received a small sum (the size of which was finally fixed by tariff!). 'It was incredible how patrons and clients competed with each other in doing favours to each other,' writes Dionysius of Halicarnassus in the time of Augustus, while a modern Danish scholar, Per Krarup, comments: 'The entire Roman pattern of behaviour was determined by a constant exchange of such services. The superior party, the patron, does favours, *beneficia*, to his clients, and it is an unwritten law that anyone receiving such *beneficia* is morally bound to repay then in *officia*... Gratitude was the supreme virtue. A man who has done many favours can expect gratitude from a host of people, and he thereby gains great power and influence. In this way the word *gratia* (gratitude) acquired the meaning of "favour, popularity, position and influence".'

Later *gratia* also acquired the Christian sense of 'divine grace', a concept which Seneca does not know but is looking for at the end of 'On gentleness' where he stresses that the Emperor's gentleness is richer than simple forgiveness. By meaning both the favour granted and the favour enjoyed, *gratia* came to denote the bond, the spirit which links the giver and the receiver to each other, and according to Seneca this is the very spirit which creates a true human society. For a good deed has both a material and a spiritual aspect, and it is the latter that interests Seneca: in 'De beneficiis' he has little to say about the relationship between patrons and clients, but all the more on the relationship between human beings.

'On good deeds' is addressed to a certain Liberalis, i.e. a Mr. Generous, who could be seen as the symbolical receiver of Seneca's *beneficium* if he had not in Epistle 91 been mentioned in connection with the fire of Lugdunum, where he was born. Seneca has noticed in Liberalis a certain reluctance to be outdone in the favours of friendship and far too great an eagerness to reciprocate them. Unlike other debts, debts of gratitude are not a heavy burden which you should hurry to get rid of: given in the right spirit a gift bears its reward in itself, and received in the right spirit it has already been repaid. Certainly, some find it so difficult to owe anyone anything that they wish evil in those who have done them good — in order to have an opportunity of paying back! 'It has become a very hazardous business to show favours to others. As it is considered a disgrace to repay them, people simply curse the very existence of the man who has done the favour.' Roman aggressiveness and 'sense of honour' are clearly discernible in the furious battle to do favours to each other, and gratitude, the supreme virtue of all, appears often to have been akin to a desire for revenge.

The difference in social status which was the mainstay of Roman society got in the way of that human equality which is implicit in true *gratia*. The common view was that the right to do good was reserved for superiors, while the inferiors were expected to do their duty. But Seneca stresses that the superior particularly needs the services of friends who will tell him the truth! A son might outdo his father in good deeds, even if he owes him his life, for the good is not life but the good life, and that is something which you do not receive ready made from your father. Slaves can do good to their masters, something of which Seneca produces historical examples and for which he produces human arguments, and he asks why a person's social position: 'is more inclined to debase the action than the action to do honour to the person.' On the other hand, if the man who does good boasts of his superior position, he thereby humiliates the man whom he intends to help, and his good deed will therefore be the product of a good position rather than a good attitude.

The formula according to which Seneca tries to revise ancient Roman values is that good and evil should no longer be judged on the basis of rank, but on moral qualities. In all cases the attitude of mind is decisive, and it is impossible to judge on attitudes of mind: every man has his own judge in his own conscience. If you have public opinion against you, it is enough to have a good conscience; if you have not sufficient means for doing good, then it is enough to have a good will. Seneca is the first man to assign to good will and good conscience the fundamental importance which these concepts were later given by Christianity.

So Seneca views the will in the same way as Immanuel Kant, the great moral philosopher of the 18th century who would not recognise anything as good except a good will. Seneca, too, stressed that a deed can only be called good if it is done in the right spirit, but while Kant denied that there was any moral value in actions resulting from liking or pleasure and not exclusively from duty, Seneca on the other hand would refuse to consider good any actions not performed out of consideration for one's fellow human beings. To do good is certainly to be disinterested in the sense of not doing good in order to achieve

213

something good for yourself ('The man who does good is copying the gods; the man who demands payment for it is copying the usurers'), but the man who does good wants to do what is in the interest of the other — though not necessarily what he wants. Moreover, Seneca specifically refuses to consider what under any circumstances can be called good (which is what Kant was talking about). 'For,' he says, 'nothing is intrinsically moral for everyone; the important thing is who is acting towards whom, when, why and where and all the other circumstances without which the value of the action cannot be ascertained.'

It is difficult to produce one single formula for such a richly nuanced view of what is moral, a formula like Kant's 'categorical imperative' which commands: 'You must act in such a way that the maxim for your will at any time can also be accepted as the principle for general laws.' But when Kant expresses the 'practical' imperative in concrete terms: 'You must act so that you always have regard to the human factor both in yourself and the other person as the object and never merely as the means', he is only saying the same as Seneca when in simpler terms he referred to the human considerations which forbid us to be cruel and arrogant towards a fellow human being. It is an attitude which seeks to be positive to all in word and deed and sentiment, which does not consider irrelevant any evil befalling someone else and in particular considers as good the good which befalls you yourself because someone else can derive benefit from it. And the same attitude is implicit when Seneca speaks of the gentleness which spares the blood of others as though it were one's own, and which recognises that it is not humane to abuse human beings. The *humanitas* which to Cicero means man's work to civilise himself is not until Seneca given the sense of a feeling for one's fellow human beings; in stressing the importance of his fellow men Seneca is more in agreement with the message of Jesus than with much later Christian ethical thought, which places a man's relationship to his fellow men second to his relationship to God. Even in Kant's very protestant ethics his fellow man, who must not be used as a means, is in reality an abstract concept, the mere reason for the moral action which is an object in itself.

St. Paul wrote that there is neither Jew nor Greek, bond nor free, there is neither male nor female: for ye are all one in Christ Jesus; Seneca wrote that *nature* has commanded man to do good to man,

214

whether he is a slave or a free man. But nature is another name for God who has 'given man two things, reason and a sense of community, which can turn the weakest into the strongest.' The aim of Seneca's work on good deeds is, he writes, 'to give a definition of what binds human society (*societas generis humani*) most together, to give a law for our life,' — which, it should be noted, is not the same thing as legislating for the way in which society is to be organised. If it is *gratia*, gratitude, mutual liking, which holds a community together, ingratitude on the other hand is the wages of the world in which everything is done for the sake of the reward and where one man's meat is another man's poison — or in the words of Seneca (which might remind us of Herman Broch's description of the 'autonomous value systems which emerge in a society without common values'): 'Who derives no benefit from the suffering of his fellow human beings? The soldier wants war if he wants honour (*gloria*); as corn prices rise, so does the farmer; the price of eloquence increases with the numbers of lawsuits; bad years are an advantage to the doctor; those who sell luxury articles make a profit on the depravity of youth; if gales and fires leave houses untouched, those in the building trade will face ruin. What any individual wants if likely to be the same as what all the others want.'

It appears to be the lack of a social sense that maintains the business-based society, in which human community has difficulty in asserting itself. There is a clear relationship between Seneca's two states — and those of St. Augustine. After Alaric's conquest of Rome in 410 Augustine defined the difference between earthly society, *civitas terrena*, which is doomed to destruction, and divine society, *civitas Dei*, which shall include the saved and which already exists in Heaven. The lack of an eschatological perspective makes the relationship between Seneca's two states more complicated; despite his belief in fate he never went so far as St. Augustine in believing that some were predestined to salvation and some to eternal damnation — ('according to God's hidden but righteous judgement'. For it is written that: 'All God's ways are mercy and truth,' and his grace cannot be unjust or his justice cruel').

Although Seneca could not say that his human state was of another world, he could scarcely say that it was of this world, the good things of which actually tend to get in the way of the good: 'All those things

215

to which you attach importance, and which make you believe yourself rich and powerful as long as you possess them, have despicable labels attached to them as long as they are called houses, slaves, money — but to give them away is a good deed.' However, the transformation of passively good things into active goodness was only possible through kindness, and Seneca denied that he wanted to bring down the mighty from their seats because he had said that slaves ought rather to honour than fear their masters.

Seneca had certainly also said that he whom many fear must also fear many. When he wrote to Nero on gentleness, he had believed in the good example of the Emperor, but he had also warned him against being a bad example. He had scarcely changed his mind about the Emperor as an institution, but certainly about this particular Emperor as a person, and the last section of the last book on good deeds is formed as an answer to the sad conclusion which not only the servant of princes can reach: *perdidi beneficium*, the good I did was to no avail. It is striking that as an example of a person who has become angry with the one to whom he has done good he mentions a *prince* who has become the enemy of his own country. Of his attitude towards a 'friend' such as this Seneca writes that even if his moral wickedness 'has not turned him into my enemy, it has made him detestable to me, and I have greater and more powerful reasons for attending to my duty towards my fellow men than towards a single person.' Not only can death be a relief, but murder can also be a good deed if it is a tyrant who is sacrificed for the general good of mankind: on this point Seneca would not exclude armed conflict between the two states.

What is true of the relationship between slaves and their masters and between citizens and their ruler, that 'you cannot love the person whom you fear', is also true of men's relationship to the gods, but with the essential difference that the gods never give cause for fear. As God and nature were one for the Stoics, Seneca can in this context also refer to the glory and might of nature: See what the gods achieve every day without demanding anything in return; should we, then, demand recompense for our small deeds? If in 'On providence' Seneca had to defend the gods for apparently allowing good men to suffer, he now has to defend them for doing good to the evil: 'If, you object, you follow the example of the gods, you must also do good to the ungrateful, for the sun also shines on the unrighteous, and the ocean is open to pirates.' Yes, replies Seneca, let us follow the example of the gods: 'It is not magnanimous to give and lose, but to lose — and give.'

It is after all not very far from this Stoic humanism to Jesus' command that we should love one another: 'Love your enemies, bless them that curse you, do good to them that hate you, and pray for them which despitefully use you, and persecute you; that ye may be the children of your Father which is in heaven: for he maketh his sun to rise on the evil and on the good, and sendeth rain on the just and on the unjust. For if ye love them which love you, what reward have ye? Do not even the publicans the same?'

Only Seneca excluded the enemy of the people from this golden rule.

VIII: NATURE

'Natural questions'

'I live in harmony with nature if I completely surrender myself to it as its admirer and worshipper. Nature, meanwhile, requires me to do both, to be both active and contemplative, and I am both since activity is impossible without contemplation.'

Thus writes Seneca in 'On retirement', *De otio*, from which it can be deduced that one of his reasons for wanting to retire from active life was his desire to complete the consideration of nature which he had begun in Corsica. And even if he had to admit that a whole life was not long enough to solve the problems of nature, he nevertheless only needed a short time to write his *Quæstiones naturales*; these admittedly do not treat all questions concerned with nature, but they still contain eight books on clouds (IVb), winds (V), earthquakes (VI), comets (VII), light phenomena in the heavens (I), thunder and lightning (II), the waters of the earth (III) and the Nile (IVa). (The books have survived in two groups which in the course of time have been transposed so that the first has become the second and the second the first; moreover, two of them which are only partly extant have been combined, those on clouds and the Nile).

From the introduction to the book on the Nile, which must surely have been the last to be written, it emerges that Lucilius, to whom this work, too, is dedicated, is still procurator in Sicily, which he is not in Epistle 82 from the early summer of 64; so the entire work must have been finished before this date. Likewise it must have been begun before Seneca's farewell audience with Nero, as the earthquake in Pompeii in February 62 is mentioned in Book VI as though it was a recent event. Nero, who is not specifically named in the other writings from the last years, but who often seems to be referred to indirectly, receives favourable references on one or two occasions in 'Natural questions'. Seneca quotes and writes admiringly of one of his verses; the comet which appeared in 60 (cf p177) is said to have put an end to the bad reputation which comets generally had, (for Nero was *not* dethroned);

218

he refers to two centuries whom 'Nero in his love of truth as of other virtues had sent out to explore the source of the Nile'. An avid desire for knowledge is something which must be ascribed to Nero just as much as his avid desire for other things; the expedition to the Nile, which penetrated further south than any expedition for another 1800 years, was something, however, which Seneca himself probably had a hand in planning.

At first Seneca did not want his retirement to be seen as a breach with Nero. However, he changes his tune in the later books. In Book II there is a reference to the Etruscans' belief that Jupiter does not discharge his fatal flashes of lightning without first conferring with other gods, and this makes Seneca argue that of course they did not *believe* in this myth, but that they maintained it for moral reasons which Seneca then makes his own: 'If only those who have achieved great power among human beings would learn not to discharge lightning without consultation! If only they would listen to and consider the advice of others and show moderation and remember that not even Jupiter considers his own judgement to be sufficient!' But Nero was no longer prepared to listen to well-meaning advice, and the tone of the next Book is sterner: 'Ruling nations have in the past collapsed at the height of their power... Even now, even at this moment, God is raising up some and humiliating others; he will not let them fall gently from their heights, but will leave nothing of them behind.'

In the foreword to this Book (III) Seneca emphasises how much better it is to study what always *is* (nature) and what *ought to be* (ethics) that to study what *has been* (history): 'How much more excellent it is to praise the deeds of the gods than to glorify the vicious expeditions of a Philip or an Alexander or the deeds of those other men who have won fame by destroying nations.' In his later years Nero had plans for following in Alexander's heroic footsteps and adding military triumphs to his achievements in the fields of art and sport. But Seneca ridicules all the borders arbitrarily fixed by mortals — it is best to keep to natural borders! Seen from the heavens, armies on the march would only look like columns of ants: 'That earth on which you sail, wage war, found your empires — which are minute even if the ocean washes them on both sides — is but a tiny dot. Above is boundless space which the soul is privileged to take into its possession if it disengages itself as far as possible from the body and cleanses itself of all filth, and buoyant and free and content to possess only what is strictly necessary, soars aloft.' In this way Seneca dissociates himself from the political sphere to which he had been tied in his active years; nature was the true place of refuge for the man who had lived contrary to nature.

'Its own necessity'

How despicable is a human being who does not rise above the human, writes Seneca the humanist now, bluntly and directly. Those human and physical attributes above which a man must raise himself in order to gain insight into what is 'its own necessity' are of course the passions which make man a prey to chance. But even it if takes less to conquer cities than to conquer oneself, the opponent is still not particularly impressive: gaining freedom *from* what is human in a narrow sense only takes on meaning when it gives man his freedom to be able to participate in what is more than man and yet what man himself is, since man is a part of nature and, as nature is divine, of God.

'God is near you, with you, in you,' writes Seneca in almost Christian terms in his 41st Epistle, but he continues in a pagan spirit by recalling the sense of the divine caused by the mysterious atmosphere of some grove, by a deep elaborate grotto not fashioned by human hands, or the eternal surge of great rivers. But while Seneca was thus able to feel the spirit in nature, he found no spirits behind natural phenomena. He mocks the official priesthood in the Greek city of Kleonai which had the task of predicting hail: 'When they had predicted a hailstorm, what do you think happened? Did people rush home for their raincoats and leather garments? No, they made sacrifices each according to his ability, this man a lamb, that man a hen. And as soon as the clouds had tasted a little blood they veered off in another direction. You laugh? Then I will give you something else to laugh at. If a man had neither a lamb nor a hen, then he turned his hand against himself and — without doing lasting harm to himself — cut his thumb, and in case you should think the clouds greedy or cruel, let me assure you that this blood sacrifice was indeed sufficient.' And if it did not suffice, the blame was laid at the door of those who had neglected their duties. And Seneca reminds his reader that even in ancient Rome, according to the laws of the twelve tables, people were punished for ruining other men's harvests by casting spells on them, and that in ancient times people had believed that they could produce or avert rain by means of magical incantations.

Seneca could not know that he himself was living in ancient times, but he could not ignore the fact that there was still a primitive tendency to see expressions of some will in natural phenomena. The earthquake which destroyed Pompeii in 62 (and which must not be confused with the volcanic eruption which buried the city some seventeen years later) gave him the opportunity to stress that natural catastrophes are not caused by the anger of the gods: they have their natural causes. The same is true of death: it is not a punishment; you can fall and kill yourself without thunder in the skies and without the presence of earthquakes. What we fear is not reality, but our misconceptions of it: 'As the cause of our fear is ignorance, is it not worth achieving knowledge so that we can be freed from our fear?'

To free ourselves from fear of the gods was also the declared aim of Lucretius, Epicurean philosophy of nature as he formulated it in his great poem 'On nature'. But while the Epicureans conceived of the world as the product of chance, of the movements of atoms, and thus relieved the gods of the responsibility for an imperfect world, the Stoics still honoured them for creating a perfect world (apart from the fact that in talking of 'gods' they were talking figuratively, for there is only one god, who is identical with the world). The idea that the gods refrain from interfering in an imperfect world is in fact less uplifting than the idea that they *cannot* interfere because it is already divine. That the world is divine is the same as saying that it cannot be otherwise, that everything is in its eternal order, preordained by fate. Epicure himself had written that it would be better to believe in the myths about the gods than to become a slave of the fate of the philosophers, for in the first instance there is still the hope of placating the gods by honouring them, while in the latter case we are at the mercy of an inevitability which knows of no placation. 'Necessity is an evil, but it is not out of necessity that men allow themselves to be ruled by necessity,' says Epicure. The Epicureans believed in free will and justified this through the 'free' movement of atoms — in many ways a weak argument, since strictly speaking anything can happen when something can happen without a cause; the Stoic idea that nothing *can* happen which does not *have to* happen seems to be an easier way to peace of mind.

221

While the Epicureans rejected the *divination*, the prediction of things to come, of the will of the gods, which was a public institution in Rome, the Stoics had in principle to accept it, for if everything which happens is the necessary consequence of everything that has happened in the past, it must be predictable on the basis of the past — or, rather, on the basis of a sufficient understanding of it. But Seneca stresses that the gods do not guide the birds in their flight for the auguries to prophesy from them, or arrange the entrails of animals so that the haruspices can interpret them: this is no work for gods. Nor do they issue flashes of lightning in order to annul other prophecies — which were less reliable than lightning. Seneca makes the objection that predictions must necessarily predict the same thing, and if the different ways of making predictions do not lead to the same result, it only indicates our imperfect knowledge; moreover, when it is only the flight of *certain* birds and only the position of *certain* stars which can act as signs, it is because we do not understand the whole. As Seneca otherwise showed no interest in prophecies, it is doubtful whether he accorded any significance to predictions based on single phenomena, to which the specialists had to limit themselves. Of course he had to deny that men could avert fate by means of sacrifices; on the other hand he would not deny the efficacy of prayers or placation ceremonies, for they, too, have their place in the course of fate if man is not to be made entirely passive: if we can thank fate for recovery from an illness, we can also thank the doctor who is the instrument of that fate; in this way the sacrificial priests are the servants of fate.

Seneca intended to return to this aspect of the matter and to show that fate does not exclude free will, but he never managed it. However, although it might be difficult to see the logic in the Stoic's definition of freedom as an acceptance of necessity, it is not difficult to understand the psychology behind it: the man who in a psychological sense is free knows no conflict of the will and has no choice; he, the wise man, does the one thing needed of him; like nature, he is 'his own necessity'. Therefore Seneca can write that: 'It is actually the easiest thing in the world to live in harmony with nature; it is only the madness which we so commonly see around us that makes this difficult...' This makes it the task of the individual to free himself from the many and to live — not according to accepted norms, but according to the law of nature.

222

And although it is difficult to see the logic in accepting that a fall from nature is possible, since nothing can happen contrary to the will of fate, it is nevertheless clear enough that it is not because of their freedom but because of a lack of freedom that men act contrary to nature, to fate, and allow chance to gain power over them. *Fortuna* rules human life 'completely without order', but it is not itself of the natural order.

The fall from nature

In his works on the philosophy of nature Seneca wrote about the natural order; on the fall from nature he wrote at greater length elsewhere, though presumably at about the same time.

In his tragedy on *Phaedra* who has been overcome by an all-consuming desire for her stepson Hippolytus, her nurse tries to persuade him to do Phaedra's will. She tells him to rejoice at life while he is still young, and by life on this occasion she means little more than sex life: without Venus there would be no life at all, and as the goddess of love is worshipped more thoroughly in the towns than in the country, the nurse ends by saying: 'Follow nature, go to the town, seek company.' This is a challenge to Hippolytus who is a devotee not of Venus but of the chaste Diana, the goddess of the hunt. He detests life in the town, where people take refuge behind a thousand columns and jump at the slightest sound, and where they spill the blood of a hundred oxen over the altars of their gods; in nature people only have to defend themselves against wild animals; there you can seek shelter among old trees, the branches of which tremble in the wind but have nothing to hide and nothing to tremble at; there you drink not out of golden goblets but out of your bare hand, and you satisfy your hunger with fruits and berries. This is how Hippolytus claims people in the beginning of time lived together with the gods; they did not know the blind yearning for gold, they did not send credulous ships out into foreign seas, but kept to their own shores; they did not fortify cities with mounds and towers and wield terrible weapons with murderous hands; they did not catapult boulders at city gates; the earth was not at the mercy of men's ploughing oxen, but its fertile soil provided undemanding generations with food, while the forests gave them their treasures and afforded them shelter. But the pact was broken by a shameful lust for profit and mindless aggression and the desires of the flesh; a bloodthirsty greed for power turned the weaker members of society into the prey of the great, and might was right. Mars, the god of war, invented new arts and a thousand ways of dying, and blood flowed over the lands and coloured the oceans red. Crime made its entry into the home: there was no crime which was not committed: brother fell to brother, fathers to sons, spouses to spouses, and mothers killed their own children.

It is Hesiod's ancient myth of the golden age which Hippolytus is taking over; and that Seneca had also taken it over is evident from his 90th Epistle, where he writes in similar vein: 'What generation has been happier than these (first) men? Together they enjoyed the gifts of nature: like a mother, nature saw to the needs of all, and it vouchsafed careless possession of a common property... Then greed made its entry into this happiest possible world order... it made all strangers to each other and replaced the vastness of common possession with the narrow limits of private property. Avarice produced poverty, and in its unrestrained greed for more it lost everything. However much man strives to make up for the loss of ancient things, however much he adds field to field, drives his neighbour from his house and farm with force or rising prices, however much he expands his estates to encompass entire provinces and only thinks of land to which a long journey is necessary as his true possessions: no expansion of our lands and estates, however vast, will bring us back to our point of departure.'

The fall from nature which Seneca here seeks to explain, the change which had taken place between the earliest times and his own day, can be compared with the Fall which occupies a central position in Christian thinking. Carnal desire, which in Christianity is the original sin, is admittedly one mentioned by Hippolytus, but this is because it is particularly repulsive to *him* (as the object of his stepmother's desires); in his philosophical work Seneca never gives it the same significance as the other two vices of greed and the lust for power.

In addition to desire the myth of the Fall shows the knowledge of good and evil causing the first human beings to lose their natural innocence and the earth to be cursed. Corresponding to this Seneca writes that the first men were better than those of his day because they did not know evil, but there is a great difference between not knowing sin and not being able to sin, for the latter requires wisdom. And man is not wise by nature; it goes without saying that man would be an animal if he were what he is by nature — and did not have to become himself by dint of his freedom and his reason. While the Christian interpretation of the myth of the Fall shows man as falling because he is free, for Seneca he falls because he is not free: man is still potentially free (to be wise), while the Christian view is that he is left to the mercy of God; thus Lactantius made the objection to Seneca (p191) that knowing what is good is not good in itself.

The contradiction which Christian thinkers have found difficulty in explaining away, that men sin of their own free will, and that they *all* do so, can in the final analysis only be resolved by confessing that man *is* depraved by nature. For Seneca the aberration is due to lack of understanding not only in the first innocent men, but also in those of his own day, who were likewise not born wise and whose aberrations increase with the greater aberrations of their age. Under prevailing conditions: 'The good is difficult to find, for it needs instruction and guidance, but evil is learned without a teacher.' Seneca had to admit of course that he had only found the right way late in life, apparently with the help of Demetrius, whose 'Cynical' views appear to have made their mark on Seneca's strikingly pessimistic view of culture.

Rightly speaking, it is amazing that when Roman civilisation was at its highest point Seneca did not express any feeling that the Romans had achieved great things. He could be optimistic all right on behalf of science, and he could predict that: 'Our successors will be surprised that we have known nothing about such obvious things'; but it never occurred to him that this research could be translated into technical progress; on the other hand he had a vague presentiment that knowledge can have harmful consequences, and in this spirit he quoted Demetrius: 'It will not do you any particular harm to ignore what it is not possible or beneficial to discover. Truth lies in the depths and is covered by a veil. And we cannot complain that nature is mean, for it is not difficult to discover things, except those things which have no other reward than the discovery itself; it has placed everything that will make us better and happier within our reach and before our eyes.' On the one hand Seneca expresses support for 'basic research' into how things happen and rejects 'applied research' into what they can be used for; on the other hand he rejects useless learning, for the essential thing is not that we should become more knowledgeable, but that we should become better; however, the one is determined by the other, for the soul is strengthened by considering nature. For Seneca the practical effect of an understanding of nature is its effect on the soul: there must be something beneficial or even redemptive, *salutare*, in everything we do and say.

And Seneca acts on this principle: all his reflections on nature are given a moral application which is sometimes pretty narrow in outlook, as when the 'reflection' of sunlight in the rainbow leads him to complain of the way in which men abuse looking-glasses in the service of vanity and obscenity, or when he disapproves of snow and ice (in Rome with all its heat!) being misused to cool drinks — Nero himself had invented a famous *decocta*: boiled iced water with various flavourings!

But he gives a broader perspective to his criticism when he asks what is the point of all this inventiveness and replies that it is to turn water, which nature has freely placed at the disposal of man and beast, into something saleable. By nature all men are placed equal, but the rich have turned natural good things into things to be bought and sold, and now nothing is considered good if it be not expensive; so it is a shame that air and sunshine cannot also be bought for money! God provided us with winds: 'to maintain healthy conditions in the air and on earth, to summon or suppress the waters of the rain, to give nourishment to the newly sown seed in the fields or the fruit on the trees', but we human beings have learned to misuse them in order to propel our war fleets and to conquer from our fellow men what should be common to all. And we make greater efforts to gain such objectives than we ever would for the sake of peace. As time goes on, the things in nature which are beneficial and even necessary to life scarcely make up for 'what man in his madness invents for his own destruction,' said Seneca, thinking not of atomic power, but of wind power!

It is worth noting that it is not reason, *ratio*, but greed, *luxuria*, that brings men to contrive new things, and madness, *dementia*, which leads to inventions! Here Seneca disagrees with the earlier Stoic philosopher of nature Poseidonios who c. 100 B.C. had maintained that practical skills had been invented by wise men who had then left them in the hands of lesser men. No, says Seneca, all the skills and arts which flourish in the cities and fill them with noise were invented by those who had an interest in them, which wise men do not have; much has only been invented in our own time, window panes (of mica) and hot water pipes in the walls, and stenography, all of them luxuries which are not due to philosophy, but to the lowest of slaves.

Seneca's scornful remarks on slaves are of course to be taken figuratively, referring to those men who in contrast to philosophers are slaves *of their own greed*. In Rome as in Greece it was admittedly common to look down on city occupations as 'the work of slaves', whether the work was carried out by slaves or by free craftsmen. But those who looked down on production were the capitalist minority who consumed the products and owned or had shares in the various concerns. As was said on p163 there was not a large market for mass-produced consumer goods, but a small and affluent public wanting to buy luxury articles, which for that reason had to be 'invented' with greater and greater ingenuity. Reading the description in Petronius' novel 'Satyricon' of Trimalchio's sumptuous repast (at which the narrator, incidentally, for the first time sees powdered mica used as a floor decoration!), we have to agree with Seneca that it was greed, *luxuria*, that contrived new things. As a freedman Trimalchio was admittedly an upstart, but in their enjoyment of life the Romans were and remained upstarts in general and never learned to place quality above quantity. To judge from the stories told by the historians, things were no more decorous at the Emperor's banquets than at Trimalchio's. Tacitus expressly emphasises that in contrast to other wealthy Romans Nero's 'judge of taste' (*arbiter elegantiæ*) was 'a master in enjoyment'. He was presumably the self-same Petronius who wrote 'Satyricon'.

Seneca's semi-mythical explanation of the fall from nature was not contrary to historical fact: it was quite literally the private encroachment on 'the vast common property' of *ager publicus* (cf. p. 43) that started the process of making the rich richer and the poor more numerous, and which created the enormous unemployed proletariat, the great problem in Roman domestic politics. Even those who understood the problem could not see any different solution to it than that suggested by the Gracchus brothers; but to found colonies was no longer a solution, because the import of cheap corn was making small farming unprofitable, and the distribution of cheap corn and the other necessities of life to those without possessions kept both them and the problem alive. It was simply impossible to find work for them in the cities, because the large middle class which could consume a larger production did not exist, and because the great houses with their slaves, freedmen and clients were still self-supporting to some extent. The Roman authors could see the fatal character of this development, which in their eyes was like a moral decline, a fall from nature, and for that very reason they could not see a way forward, but only a way back — to 'nature'.

The transition from a primitive society to a slave society was described by Friedrich Engels in terms similar to Seneca's description of the transition from the golden age to the iron age: 'It is the lowest interests — common greed and a brutal desire for enjoyment, despicable avarice, the selfish appropriation of common property — which gives rise to the new, civilised society, the class society.' In 'The foundations of Marxism-Leninism' he is quoted and commented upon as follows: 'Nevertheless, the slave society meant a great step forward in the progress of man. A further development took place in the social distribution of work — between agriculture and the urban trades and between the various kinds of trade... The use of the labour of the slave masses makes it possible to construct dams and irrigation systems, roads and ships, water pipes and large buildings in the cities. And as some members of society, thanks to the exploitation of the slaves, were exempted from taking a direct part in production, the conditions were created for the development of science and art.'

Seneca only knew humane criteria for progress — on the odd occasion when he uses the word it is in connection with the 'progress of the soul'; in his eyes a development which was determined by and in its turn determined 'the lowest interests' was an evil thing. So not even on behalf of art and science would he have been able to share the optimistic view of progress of Marxism-Leninism. In his old age he even considered painting and sculpture to be a luxury — and in a way rightly so, as the art industry was one of the most lucrative — and specialised — in Rome, where artistic decorations were much more common than in any modern city. Those arts which ultimately are aimed at earning money, he saw as far removed from philosophy, which alone can make man free and alone know the difference between good and evil; in his view the study of nature only did justice to its object when it was carried out for enlightenment and not profit.

In Seneca's rejection of useless knowledge and the ridiculous inventions of greed, we can sense a fear of the alliance between 'disinterested' science and financial interests, which became the driving force in the modern capitalist development, but which was not established in Rome. Carcopino (p73) believed that the Romans were too interested in things making a profit to be willing to carry out disinterested research; Paul-Louis has emphasised that the Romans, who from the start had conquered rather than created riches, and who had taken over the technical methods of the nations they had subjugated, thereby lost 'every motive to make any methodical efforts'. Both explanations are already to be found in Pliny's 'Natural History' (from the 70s): Modest circumstances, he says, encourage people to give, luxurious circumstances to take; an abundance of things blunts the spirit; more people are sailing out into the world than before, but 'for the sake of gain, not knowledge'.

The Romans and science

The Romans were rational enough when it came to solving practical — administrative and also technical — problems, but in their theories they were not particularly rational, and they had not much to add to what the Greeks knew about science. In his work on nature Seneca quotes over thirty Greeks but only one Roman; admittedly in this context he omits to mention Lucretius, perhaps because his poem 'On nature' was Epicurean in its tendency — and thus also Greek-inspired. In the first canto of his poem Lucretius emphasises that things are not created from nothing: if that were the case, everything could come into being anywhere and at any time; men could be born from the sea and birds from the clouds, and the same trees could bear different fruits. Lucretius would naturally have no reason to emphasise how unreasonable that kind of idea was if the Romans saw them as completely unreasonable; most Romans lived as far as can be seen in a world where strictly speaking anything could happen. The historians never omit to write about the strange occurrences which took place when anything special was about to happen (especially in the imperial household): women gave birth to animals, comets were seen, the earth trembled, lightning struck, doors sprang open, statues burst into laughter, horses shed tears and so on. Dio Cassius writes that Nero's attempt to dig a way through the Corinthian isthmus made the earth bleed and groan, thereby indicating something of the fear of tampering with nature which was common before the scientific attitude won the day — and which prevented it from winning the day.

In his 'Natural History' Pliny wants to appear as a representative of an enlightened view and so, for instance, he rejects the idea of the immortality of the soul, but at the same time he uncritically accepts other people's accounts of strange creatures in foreign countries, while in the section on medicine he considers it to be entirely a matter of fact that everything can have an influence on everything else. The idea of natural causality was simply not a matter-of-course to the Romans, and the idea of examining nature by means of experiments and systematic observations never struck them. Examples of the theories which Pliny could formulate on the basis of his own (typically Roman) observations are the suggestion that laughter must be seated in the diaphragm because gladiators laugh when they are pierced there, and that there must be a connection between the eye and the stomach because men vomit when they have an eye put out. His assertion that dolphins can live to the age of thirty, as has been demonstrated by 'experimentally' chopping the tail off one, is the exception which proves the rule. The examples he lists scarcely suggest that it was humanitarian considerations which prevented the Romans from seeking knowledge through experiments on animals and human beings. A remarkable instance of how even educated Romans could just as well believe one thing as another is the belief of Lucretius and Pliny that if a barrel of wine is struck by lightning the wine will run out even if the barrel does not break up, while in Seneca's opinion the wine will coagulate and remain in the barrel even if it is broken.

This kind of observation is otherwise rare in Seneca, who was less interested in causal relationships between individual phenomena than in the general pattern of things. Like Lucretius he realised that something cannot come from nothing, but he accepted in principle that anything can come from everything, in accordance with the Stoic view that the four basic elements — water, earth, air and fire — are in a constant process of being changed into each other. He certainly looked for the natural causes, but his object was still a moral one, and a satisfactory solution to him was a solution which gave him peace of mind. In this he was not different from other philosophers of the ancient world; even Democritus, who in his theory of atoms (which Epicure and Lucretius took over from him) went furthest in an impersonal, materialist view of the world, wrote that 'peace of mind' was the object of understanding. We are inclined to believe that the men of the ancient world, who never achieved a real scientific understanding, failed to achieve a real relationship to nature, but the opposite is the case: they had too primitive a relationship to nature to be able to achieve a scientific understanding.

Originally man certainly felt a need to interpret phenomena, but not to explain the intrinsic, objective relationship between things. The reason why science only established itself after the emergence of Christianity was probably that Christianity, with its distinction between sacred and profane, supernatural and natural, purged nature of its spirits and opened it to unprejudiced research. Though it was not all that unprejudiced at first, for by the Renaissance the medieval scholastic interpretation of the world had so limited independent efforts at understanding it that thinkers had to seek a criterion for truth outside revelation. The Greek philosophers of nature were not so tied by an authorised faith that their deviation from a primitive superstition was given such a heretical character. According to the Stoics, evil is due to a fall from nature, but the Christian concept of the Fall, which makes nature evil, indicates a sharper conflict between 'spirit' and 'flesh', between intellect and feeling; it is this which gives rise to an intellectual need to find an explanation to phenomena instead of the original need to find a meaning in them. In Christendom an understanding of nature was distinctly not *salutaris*, salutory for the soul; the soul had to find nourishment elsewhere; there arose a gulf between (objective) knowledge and (subjective) spirituality, while they were one and the same thing to the Stoics.

The dualism, between spirit and matter, soul and body, which was finally accomplished in Christianity was already potential in Plato and Aristotle, who also played their part in fashioning the medieval view of the world. The Stoics rejected Platonic idealism and dualism; theoretically, of course, Stoic calm depended on man's not by nature being at odds with himself, not a battleground for superior and inferior forces, and not being a citizen in two worlds, a superior and an inferior. To the Stoics everything was matter, even reason which was

231

the creative force of matter and thus identical with the deity. So not only must the Stoics reject an idealism which localised the creative principle outside the world, but also the materialism of Democritus and Epicure, according to which the world consisted of atoms in empty space. To the Stoics it was presumptuous to accept that the well-ordered universe owed its origins to the chance movements of atoms. Seneca writes indignantly about the philosophers who believe that they themselves have a soul which can foresee and act consciously, but that all the orderly universe is devoid of reason, directed by blind chance or by a nature which does not know what it is doing. If things only consisted of corpuscles they would fall apart; reason, which pervades everything and gives all things their energy and strength, does not allow of the existence of empty space in the world, but only outside it. The argument between the Stoics and the Epicureans on the nature of matter is a kind of primitive pre-echo of the modern discussion on whether light undulates or is corpuscular in nature.

The biologist Jacques Monod has written a book appropriately called 'Chance and necessity', and there he maintains that our primitive urge to feel ourselves secure and to believe that things are determined by a superior principle prevents us from determining things scientifically. Objectively we have to admit that there is no intrinsic meaning in things, that they and ultimately we ourselves are products of chance, but our innate need for a meaning makes us demand: 'that we ourselves are necessary, inevitable, predestined from all time'. Jacques Monod believes that some need of this kind is implicit in all religions, most philosophies and some aspects of science, but his words are particularly apt when applied to Stoicism, which worshipped necessity as a god and gave chance, *fortuna*, responsibility for all evil. While the belief in necessity for Monod is irrational and 'animistic' and the acknowledgement of chance is rational and scientific, more or less the opposite was true of Seneca: it is because of his reason that man is in harmony with nature, which is 'its own necessity', and it is because of his passions that he deviates from it and gives chance power over him.

Reason, *ratio*, has obviously changed its meaning since ancient times: in Stoic usage reason is applied to the entire man, in modern usage only to the rational or intellectual aspect as opposed to the irrational or emotional. In modern scientific civilisation the conflict between these

232

two aspects has according to Jacques Monod become an 'illness in the soul', an illness which Seneca apparently tried to prevent with his rejection of any knowledge which does not lead to wisdom and of 'the ridiculous inventions of greed'.

Seneca's universe

Historically speaking, Seneca occupies a middle position between an animistic attitude, which personifies nature, and a scientific one, which impersonalises it. We have already seen that he rejected the tendency of 'the ancients' to see spirits and expressions of a will in natural phenomena, but he still spoke of 'the will of nature' and of 'the life spirit' or 'the life force', which permeates all things. He even drew a contrast between natural causality and primitive teleology and in so doing rejected Etruscan thinking: 'We think that *because* clouds collide a flash of lightning is discharged; they believe that clouds collide *in order to* discharge a flash of lightning, for as they refer everything back to the deity they believe not that phenomena indicate that something is happening, but that they happen in order to indicate something.' But he firmly maintained that things indicate something in happening, because there *is* a meaning in all creation. He rejected the belief of the older Stoics that everything was created for the sake of man: 'We are not the reason why nature lets winter follow summer: these phenomena have their laws, to which the divine world order conforms. We think too highly of ourselves if we consider ourselves worthy of having all this set in motion for our sake.' But he maintained that all this is to the benefit of men, that there is a providence ruling our lives — and not interfering in them, because it itself has predetermined them and takes part in them.

With his theory that reality consists of invisible atoms Democritus had made the distinction between things as they seem to be and things as they are, thereby taking the first step towards a scientific picture of the world which does not merely reflect nature as we experience it. He himself formulated this contradiction between reason and the senses: '*Reason*: apparently coloured, sweet and bitter, but in reality is only atoms and empty space. — *The senses*: Intellect, we pity you — you take your arguments from us and seek to overcome us with them.

Your victory is your defeat!'

How unnatural it was even for philosophers of nature to abstract from the immediate evidence of the senses is apparent from the fact that both Heraclitus and Epicure believed the sun to be about the size of a foot. Epicure took over Democritus' teachings on atoms, but it was *in order to* remove the necessity of awe-inspiring gods to explain the origin of things, and when, in contrast to Democritus, he assumed that the movements of atoms were not strictly determined, but sometimes 'chance', that was *in order to* find a basis on which to explain free will; he was not driven along by an urge to discover what fundamentally keeps the world together but by an urge to keep the soul together. With the epistemological conflict which Democritus had formulated so precisely, the *theoretical* foundation had been laid for the psychological conflict which was to become the 'illness in the soul' in the scientific Christian world. Even if Epicureanism and Stoicism cannot be seen as a conscious effort to prevent it, they nevertheless arose — in the 'Hellenistic' age when everything was disintegrating — as attempts to keep everything together, and as the harmony of the soul was their goal, a natural limit had thus been set to their understanding of nature: only the truth which was uplifting was truth for them — but that was decidedly not the same, objective, truth!

Seneca also seeks to mediate in the theoretical conflict between the senses and reason. For him it was just as wrong to think that things are what they appear to be as to imagine that the essence of things escapes the senses. He often stresses that appearances are deceptive: it looks as though the rainbow exists in the heavens, as though the haloes, the tiny rings visible round some celestial bodies, are attached to them, as though shooting stars are stars; but in reality a rainbow is a reflection of the sun in the clouds and the haloes only exist in the eyes, and shooting stars originate in the air: so great are their numbers that if they really were falling stars there would not be any stars left in the heavens. If lightning were in the clouds there would be lightning all the time; if it were melting snow that made the Nile rise, then like the Danube it would rise in the spring and not in the summer; if the wind — as Democritus believed — arises when there are a large number of atoms in an empty space, then it would be windy when it is foggy. Thus it was often with the help of logic that Seneca repudiated the theories of others — including the atom theory: if the world consisted

234

of atoms in an empty space, then it could not survive!

Meanwhile logic and reason are just as prejudiced as sight, for they are determined by their premises. For Seneca it was a fundamental tenet that the ultimate components of the universe are not atoms devoid of quality, but the four basic qualities, the dry, the damp, the warm and the cold, which make up the four elements: earth, water, fire, air. But the Stoics maintained their monism right down to the most minute details: the elements are not so different that — through concentration and dilution — they cannot be changed into each other: everything comes from everything, and everything is one and the same. For Zenon as for Heraclitus the fundamental element was fire, which Zenon called the 'artistically creative fire' — the cosmic cycle is in no way like a mechanical process, but is a constant process of creation. As death occurs when the heat leaves the body, it was natural to see the warm element as the life-giving principal, but it was necessary to distinguish between the pure element and the warm spirit of life or the soul, *pneuma*, which consists of fire and air. Originally *pneuma* meant the air breathed in; *spiritus* means both air and breath and spirit, which indicates that the original concept of the spiritual was material, a view which the Stoics maintained. For Seneca it is the spirit, *spiritus*, which as it were keeps the spirits up in things and gives them their strength; there is air or spirit or life or reason in everything: the material is spiritual and the spiritual material.

As it was on this basis that Seneca looked for the 'natural' causes, there was a limit to what he could find. When everything comes from everything it is easy to explain that rain and lightning come from the clouds, and rivers and winds from the earth. But the fact that it was ultimately in the elements that Seneca found the reasons for natural phenomena did not prevent him from looking for more specific causes: it is the collision of clouds which causes lightning (the ancient world had, of course, not the slightest idea of electricity); it is the greater or lesser heat and purity in the atmosphere that decides whether the water in the air turns to rain or snow or hail; it is under the influence of the sun that the currents of air turn into winds. In the book on earthquakes Seneca correctly sums up a theory which he ascribes to Anaximenes on their terrestrial causes: according to this it is movements in the layers of the earth and especially their different ages which are the cause. But he nevertheless maintains that 'the principle cause of earthquakes is the air (*spiritus*) which is volatile by nature and is constantly changing its position.'

Seneca is not entirely happy comparing the air in the earth with the air in the stomach, which can also take the form of wind; however, although it is not quite the same thing there is still a certain similarity between what happens in the earth and what happens inside ourselves; just as we tremble and quake with fever, earthquakes and other natural catastrophes resemble illnesses to some extent; the currents of air and water in the earth are also reminiscent of airpipes and veins in the body. As there is life in the universe and the universe consists of the four elements, there must also be life in the elements — logic says this so convincingly that in contrast to everyday experience Seneca has to maintain that it is 'not probable, but true' that life can arise from fire. That there is something conducive to life in water can be seen from the moss that forms on it, but in that case there must also be life in the air, and the earth is both a 'component of the world', i.e. an element, and its *materia*; the word comes from *mater*, mother, and thus the mythical concept of Mother Earth lives on in the cosmology of the Stoics. The earth contains the nourishment which all living creatures live on; animals and plants — and the stars! Even the sun, which is so many times bigger than the earth, receives its nourishment from it, and this is of course only possible because the earth has the spirit of life, *anima*, within it, and because the 'nourishment' or life energy streams back to the earth again. If nature only takes up the nourishment necessary there is enough for the world to exist to all eternity: just as there is enough nourishment in an egg to bring about the entire development of the individual, so the world from the beginning of time has contained within itself the seeds of its own entire development.

But where there is life there is both birth and death, and the same is true of the universe. In death living things are dissolved into elements, but the elements, which are as it were the materials of the deity, cannot themselves be destroyed but only changed. And the cosmic cycle begins precisely with the primeval element being transformed into the other elements, which thus are held in balance with each other, until the 'unity of opposites', the harmony of disharmonies, which the world is, is disturbed and the process is reversed. Zenon adopted Heraclitus' idea that fire was the prime element and that the world would be purified in a vast conflagration, while Chrysippos took over Thales' idea of water as the beginning of all things; Seneca writes in the book on the waters of the earth that 'fire is the end of the world, and water its beginning', which, however, does not prevent him from finishing the same book with a grandiose and detailed description of the end of the world as a great flood. It begins with the oceans rising 'at the behest not of the tide, but of fate, for the tide is the servant of fate': behind the 'natural' reasons there is, then, still the will of fate or nature or God. The catastrophe arises 'when God thinks the time has come to start on something better and to put an end to the old order', and that the human race should be renewed.

The process of destruction is accompanied by and — as a chorus in 'Thyestes' indicates — perhaps also caused by a moral decline which reveals itself in man's deviating from nature, from fate, and surrendering himself to chance, *fortuna*, and 'believing in the constancy of those good things which are the gift of *fortuna*.' When good things are counted as more than good, the world will stand no longer — 'a single day will bury the human race; everything that *fortuna* for so long has favoured and allowed to develop and raised above all other things, all magnificence and splendour and empires of great peoples, will be destroyed in the flood.' And the last men will flee up to the highest mountain peaks, without hope, and at last without fear, 'unhappy beyond the sense of unhappiness.' But once the human race and the wild animals whose customs it had taken over have been destroyed, the earth will emerge again from the water and force it back to its old boundaries: 'The old order will be re-established. All creation will arise again and mankind will be given back to the earth, without any knowledge of evil, born under the best auspices. But neither shall their innocence persist; it will last only as long as they are new on the earth. Soon vices will creep in. The good is difficult to find; it needs a leader and guide; evil is learned even without a teacher.'

The thought of the eternal repetition of the world cycle is the logical way of expressing that opposition to the new which was so common in ancient times — a way of abolishing time for all time, for what is happening is always *the same*. For if reason has created a world once, it is obvious that it will create it in exactly the same way on the second, third, fourth occasions etc.. Nietzsche, who in 1881 thought of the same old idea, saw in it the supreme expression of the love of fate, *amor fati*. Seneca did not examine the idea in greater detail.

In his theory of colour Goethe describes Seneca as a scientist and especially praises him for his 'really magnificent descriptions', for instance of the Nile, of floods and of earthquakes. But it is in his description of the end of the world that Seneca's art reaches its highest point, which indicates that this kind of nature study is closer to poetry than what we now understand by natural science. Goethe certainly believed that there is 'something very clever in Seneca's opinions and convictions', but he had to deny him a real relationship to nature, 'for it is not nature that interests him, but the events in it. By events we mean the sudden and complex happenings which shock even the most primitive men,' i.e. earthquakes, lightning and thunder, comets and so on.

What Goethe thus criticises in Seneca is, however, exactly the same as Seneca complains of in his contemporaries: that they are not interested in ordinary things, but only in unusual phenomena: 'No one looks at the sun unless it is in eclipse.' For Seneca it was a natural thing to make the most of those 'events' which interested his public the most, especially as it was his declared intention to remove the mystique from them: earthquakes are not due to the anger of the gods, but caused by air in the earth; lightning is not despatched by Jupiter, but is 'not without reason', and comets are not signs lit up for the occasion in the clouds and soon vanishing again: they are planets which simply disappear beyond our horizon.

It is in his book on comets that Seneca is at his most scientific. In order to form a correct theory on them it was obviously necessary to acquire a knowledge of all the comets which had ever been seen, but observations of them had only begun 'recently' i.e. a couple of hundred years earlier, in Greece. However, Seneca concludes that comets follow fixed paths like the planets: 'For the two in our own time did so'. These were the one which was seen before the death of Claudius and the one discovered during Nero's reign and observed in a regular course for about six months. These two observations made Seneca so sure of himself that he rejects the theories of others, even of the great Stoics, with the warmth of conviction and something of the glow of indignation. Zenon believed that comets do not have an independent existence but are seen when the light from two planets meets; Poseidonios believed that comets exist, but only for a short time, as they only result from a concentration of air. Even Aristotle did not think that comets are different in principle from other light phenomena in the atmosphere; there was also a man called Artimodoros who believed that the vault of heaven was a massive roof and that above it there is a fire which sends out its flames into space; this is an 'unashamed lie', is Seneca's comment, and to refute this theory is only to 'fight with the air', as athletes did in training. Seneca was not the first to think of comets as planets; the Pythagoreans had done so previously, but on this point Seneca used his reason to defend what his eyes told him in face of the great authorities such as Aristotle and Poseidonios. Ptolemy, whose view was current until Newton, did the opposite a hundred years after Seneca, who moreover also asked whether the universe revolves around the earth or whether it is the earth that goes up and down. But he dared not answer the question.

However, as Goethe says, Seneca is 'extremely charming in his confidence in later generations'. In the most scientific of all his books on natural philosophy he reveals a remarkable belief in progress and research: a man will come one day and explain the nature of comets, he prophesies: 'A time will come when our successors will be surprised that we knew nothing of such obvious things.' And about the same time he writes in his 64th Epistle: 'There is still much to be done and there always will be, and no one, even if he is born a thousand generations after us, will be precluded from adding to it.'

This optimistic view of research hardly appears to harmonise with the pessimistic view of culture and the sense of doom which are also very obvious in Seneca's later works. If there are still a thousand generations to be added, the end of the world cannot be an immediate prospect. Myth and fantasy are one thing, history and science another. But for Seneca the difference was not so great, and when, doubtless basing himself on his own historical reading, he prophesied mythical doom and at the same time, basing himself on his urge to understand, foresaw infinite scientific progress, both views were equally well founded: the empire of the great Roman people — and that meant almost the entire world — did in fact collapse — before someone came and explained the paths of comets!

IX: THE TRAGEDIES

Self-control and ecstasy

The Stoic wanted to live in harmony with nature, but is it natural to be a Stoic? The critics of Stoicism have seen Stoic calm as a neurotic means of protecting oneself against social reality and have translated 'apathy' as a lack of feeling, not as freedom from passion. Even the ancients discussed whether the Stoic wise man had ever existed in reality, but the Stoics themselves maintained that he alone behaved naturally — thereby saying something fairly critical of the societies in which being wise was not exactly an everyday occurrence. It has not become more common since then, but there is a surprising similarity between Seneca's portrait of the wise man and the portrayal of the normal man which can be read in Arthur Janov's 'The primal cry' — the latest in modern psychology — and of course there is a corresponding similarity between the neurotic whose strength is turned against him and who has tensions instead of feelings, and the fool of whom the Stoics spoke. Just as Janov insists that men are either neurotic or normal and that there is no intermediate stage, the Stoics insisted that men were either wise or foolish; admittedly the fool can strive for wisdom, in which case he is not completely foolish, but as long as his calm has to be fought for, it is artificial and not natural. It is difficult to become wise, but it is not difficult to be wise — it is, as Seneca said to the fools, much more difficult to do what they are doing! The fool, the neurotic, lacks something inside himself and can therefore never have enough; he is constantly preoccupied with himself because he is not himself; the wise man has enough — and therefore has something to give to others; he does not suffer on his own account and can therefore feel for others.

But in a society which is not so wisely organised that what is psychologically normal is in accordance with the reigning norms, the man who behaves naturally is particularly exposed and has a special need of the psychological defence which, when it establishes itself as a defence mechanism, makes the soul neurotic. At the end of his essay

'On tranquility of mind' Seneca writes of the tension within us when: 'we feel we are being judged every time we are observed', and of the risk of being despised: 'if we are completely open to everybody, for there are many who despise those things to which there is easy access.' However, it is nevertheless 'better to be despised for being natural than to endure constant dissimulation'. And because it is not easy to be yourself, a 'Stoic' approach to life and view of life are necessary to attain the balance — between sociability and loneliness, activity and contemplation, stress and relaxation. In 'On tranquility of mind' Seneca tries to show Serenus how to achieve such a balance, and as a counterbalance to the more traditional Stoic precepts he writes in the last section on man's natural predilection for games and betting. Even Cato had (by Julius Caesar!) been accused of being fond of drinking; this should not lower Cato in people's estimation, but rather make them look more favourably on drinking. Of course we must be careful not to give our souls bad habits, but occasionally they must be allowed to have some fun and to put aside dullness and sobriety for a time. The god of wine is called *Liber*, i.e. 'free', for he liberates and enlivens the soul. And Seneca persists in quoting the Greek poet's words to the effect that 'at times it is delightful to go out of your mind', and as though speaking from his own poetical experience he adds that: 'Only a spirit which is deeply moved can speak in elevated style and in words raised above the ordinary... No one who does not stand outside himself can reach the loftiest peaks and most inaccessible pinnacles.'

Although Seneca writes this with a particular eye to the poet, there might be a general truth in suggesting that men sometimes must be placed outside themselves in order to be themselves. Mircea Eliade (p12) wrote of the people of the tribal society that they were really only themselves when placed outside themselves, when they stepped out of 'profane' into 'mythical' time and 'in the moments of ritual and significant actions' repeated prescribed patterns of action and as it were played a role on behalf of everyone. Here, in the cultic ritual, we must look for the origins of drama: when the actor puts on his mask and costume and buskins he puts himself outside the limitations of time into what is valid at all times and he performs vicarious acts and accepts vicarious suffering; intellectually, but no longer physically, the public takes part in the drama; what inspired the poet when he was placed outside himself is passed on to the spectators by the players. The whole

241

tribe could take an active part in the cultic drama, and even in the Dionysos Theatre in Athens the entire population could be gathered together around a drama.

In Rome it was more difficult to gather the entire population of a million together and impossible to gather them around an entertainment of an intellectual nature. In this strictly stratified society, divided into classes and tasks, 'artless naturalness' has difficulty in triumphing over the 'external role'; the individual is not really himself in his social role, but is more inclined to be himself when he steps out of his social role — as in the Saturnalia, though they were more like a carnival and a diversion than a cultic act bringing the people together.

However, both the individual need for ecstasy and the social need for unity are bound to make themselves felt in a larger society where they are more difficult to satisfy. The state religion was a systematised awe of the gods and authorities and contained no ecstatic potential; individuals looked to the mysteries, the crowd to the public games, *ludi*, the numbers of which were still growing so that in Nero's day there were as many holidays as working days. The very number of these festivals gives an indication of how empty they were of real content and clearly shows the conscious efforts being made by those in power to keep the people under control. Every happy occasion in the imperial household or in the field created an excuse for new festivals. Many of the old ones had a 'mythical' core, but it was the wilder forms of entertainment which appealed to the masses. To the Romans ecstasy meant licentiousness, not identifying with mythical heroes but with charioteers, gladiators, pantomime dancers and, perhaps on a higher level, with the Emperor. As spectators at the games the people had the honour of being in the company of the Emperor who lacked serious enemies abroad against whom the people could unite and so had to gather the people around himself as his 'clients'; the absence of a cult which could satisfy more deep-seated needs made the cult of the Emperor a political necessity, and in fact Nero might well have had political motives for his wish to appear as a hero before the people so that its feeling of identity with him could be stronger.

The Roman theatre

In addition to the amphitheatre with its gladiatorial games and the circus with its races, the theatres with their more peaceful dramas could gather a large audience; Seneca writes that the three theatres were filled at one and the same time, but although they had room for 70,000 people this was (according to Carcopino's calculations) not more than a fifth of the capacity of the circus. There were no evening performances as in modern cities; shows began in the mornings in connection with some of the public *ludi*, that is to say only on certain days of the year. The officials responsible for the arrangements were also responsible for any losses, and the theatre directors whom they engaged and who chose the plays only had the authors' fees refunded if the plays were a success. This did not encourage experiments, but it reinforced the deep-seated tendency to prefer the old to the new.

In Rome drama had not grown out of an ancient cult; if Titus Livy is to be believed, it had been imported from Etruria, certainly with a religious object in view, as a means of deflecting the anger of the gods which in 364 B.C. had expressed itself in an epidemic of the plague. It was, writes Livy, something completely new for the warlike Roman people who so far had only known the performances in the circus. The first plays consisted only of dancing to the music of flutes, and they failed either to liberate the body of the plague or the mind of fear, but Livy believes that he ought to remind people that the beginnings of the present theatre madness were very healthy indeed. Only many years later did Livius Andronicus, a Greek who also translated Homer into Latin, dare to introduce an action into the play, writes Livy, who thus tries to give an organic, 'native' explanation of the emergence of Latin drama; but it is likely that the first tragedies and comedies which Livius Andronicus staged and performed in were translated from Greek, and that their performance was part of a conscious cultural policy in Rome after the First Punic War (241 B.C.) when Sicily and thereby a large Greek population had been incorporated into the Empire; throughout the period of expansion there was a distinct tendency to profit at home from what was encountered abroad and to place the Romans on the same cultural level as the Greeks, and it was at this time Roman drama was at its peak. It was and remained Greek-inspired, but it developed from a primitive start with performances on improvised wooden stages, to lavishly mounted plays which only came into their own when the larger stone-built theatres were constructed at the end of the republic and the beginning of the principate. But drama depended on public favour in order to survive, and so it died — the last known performance of a new tragedy took place in the reign of Augustus; comedy was displaced by mime, tragedy by pantomime.

Mime had its origins in the popular performances of jugglers and acrobats; it demanded little equipment and could be performed anywhere, but even before 200 B.C. it was included in one of the great *ludi*, after which it spread to the others as well. It was rather like a naturalistic and satirical farce in which the actors appeared without masks and without buskins, as was necessary for the tragic gait, and in which female roles were played by women who often appeared in daring erotic intrigues. In a way Seneca defends the realism of the mime, which others found offensive, by stressing that the writers of mime ignored things which were more offensive than those they invented, a comment which implies a criticism of the customs of the day rather than a defence of the morality of mime. On the other hand Seneca sets great store by the vast amounts of applause which the moralising maxims in the mimes inevitably produced in the public at large, and he several times quotes the mime poet Publilius Syrus (by whom a large number of maxims is extant) and considers there is more ardour in him than in all the authors of comedies and tragedies.

Roman tragedy had developed into a sort of opera; the leader of the chorus declaimed to the accompaniment of music and the actors shone with their solo arias, *cantica*, and were in fact even called *cantores*, singers. At the time of Augustus two dancers took the consequence of the fact that the spoken word had difficulty in reaching the multilingual audience in the huge open-air theatres, and they created the pantomime, a sort of one man ballet in which the dancer, who was also called the pantomime, played all the parts in a dramatic action based on the heroic myths or often on the Greek tragedies. Sometimes his movements would be accompanied by a chorus and an orchestra or by drummers beating time, but in more moving places they were silent and let his acting speak for itself. Demetrius, the wise man mentioned in Chapter VII, did not have a high opinion of pantomime, but when he had seen the pantomime Paris perform the divine adultery of Venus and Mars and portray all the reactions of the gods he changed his mind

244

and said, 'I not only see, I hear what you do, for you can speak with your hands.' It was better business for the poets to write libretti for pantomimes than to write tragedies; Ovid remarks that his poems were often danced before an audience, and Marcus Lucanus wrote a lot of libretti. But the aggressiveness of the Roman public showed itself here, too, in their enthusiasm for the pantomimes: it was so great that Seneca could call the young people of the nobility the slaves of the pantomime; when in 56 Nero had decreed that a military presence was no longer necessary at theatre performances, fights broke out among spectators taking the sides of different dancers — who were then exiled in order to prevent 'divisions within the people'.

This was the state of the theatre when Seneca wrote his tragedies in the Greek manner. The well-known Greek tragedies had been performed at the Dionysos festivals in Athens; in Latin Dionysos came to be called Liber, and Seneca believed that Liber could still help people to get rid of their dullness and sobriety; but Seneca was thinking of individual rapture and not collective enthusiasm and excitement. There is disagreement as to whether Seneca's tragedies were intended for performance, but it can certainly be said that they were not intended for performance at official religious festivals. The difference in application between Greek and Roman tragedy is reflected in their contents: even if they are rulers, the Greek tragic heroes are representatives of mankind, but Seneca's heroes really are rulers by profession, tyrants; and while the tragic element in Greek tragedy (according to Aristotle) is undeserved suffering resulting from man's fate itself, the sufferings of the Roman heroes are very much brought on by themselves. Since then the individual has come to power and has achieved greater responsibility and incurred greater guilt. Just as Tacitus made the emperors into the principal personages in his historical 'Annals' because only the emperors were free in a subjugated society, so Seneca makes rulers his principal characters; however, the freedom they enjoy is not a natural manner of behaviour, but licentiousnes: the tyrant is tyranised by his passions.

Greek tragedy: fate and guilt

The background to Greek tragedy is the moral crisis in the period in the 7th and 6th centuries B.C. when 'tyrants' in most of the small Greek states allied themselves with the people and dethroned the ruling noble families. It is in the transitional phase from aristocracy to democracy, from a society based on farmers and nobles to one founded on citizenship and trade, that men become ethically conscious and realise that there is a difference between goods and the good, that riches are not a token of the favour of the gods, that there is a difference between financial and moral deserts. But at the same time doubt is cast on the justice of the gods as they do not reward the good and punish the evil. As long as the individual was secondary to the tribe things came out right if it was assumed that the children were punished for the sins of their fathers, but when society took the enforcement of justice from the tribe and made the individual responsible for his own actions, the question arose of reward and punishment after death. The liberation of the individual from the tribe and the resultant breakdown of the tribal community made it difficult for the ruling tyrants to gather a divided people around a common cult. The tyrant of Athens, Peisistratos, started the Pan-Athenean festival and from 566 B.C. tried to make Homer popular by arranging competitions between rhapsodes singing Homer, but Homer's gods were of course aristocratic and amoral. The cult of Demeter, the Great Mother, and Dionysos, mystery gods who appealed to the individual regardless of prestige or social position, and the cult of Apollo in Delfi, who was the only god with the power to cleanse people of the guilt, which the individual now, in the society based on law, was thought to be infected with, indicate the twofold religious need of devotion and forgiveness in order to break through the barriers of individuality and to have the individual confirmed within his own limitations. Both tendencies are present in tragedy, which was related to the Dionysos cult, and which according to Aristotle purged the spirits of the spectators by bringing about *catharsis* in them; *catharsis* also means the cleansing of guilt, which Apollo of Delfi could bring about.

Tragedy did not 'of its own accord' result from the Dionysos cult; the Dionysos festival in Athens was started by Peisistratos in 535 B.C. as part of his cultural policy, which sought to give people something around which to unite other than the aristocratic Homeric gods; the tragedy which was performed on that occasion was written by Thespis and its contents had nothing to do with Dionysos; the central figures were heroes not gods, and it was their fates which — to use the words of Aristotle — awoke terror and pity in people. In 510 B.C., the year when the last tyrant was overthrown, mention is made of a competition between writers of tragedies; Aischylos is known to have taken part for the first time in 500 B.C.. It was in the Athens of Cleisthenes and Pericles, when the development into a 'democratic' state was complete, that Greek drama really flourished, and it took the great questions of the just ordering of the world and the responsibility of man as its main theme.

A comparison between Agamemnon as represented by Homer and Aischylos will throw some light on the changed attitudes in this epoch. In the 'Iliad' Agamemnon lives without any idea of moral good and evil, and in his world there is no distinction between goods and the good, the unpleasant and the evil. The good things are the rewards of the gods, and the gods complain when they feel their authority threatened; in Homer's world both gods and men are very quick to feel unjustly treated, but they have no concept whatever of justice. An Agamemnon might well regret actions which have unpleasant consequences and thus turn out to have been unwise, but he never has a bad conscience about them. It was Agamemnon who as supreme Greek commander in the Trojan War insulted Achilles, the hero whose anger gave the Greeks so much trouble. Called to account, Agamemnon declares:

> Often have the Achaeans spoken to me of the matter
> and upbraided me, but it was not that I did it: Jove,
> and Fate, and Erinys that walks in darkness struck me
> mad... All things are in the hand of heaven, and Folly,
> eldest of Jove's daughters, shuts men's eyes to their
> destruction...
> I was blind, and Jove robbed me of my reason; I will now
> make atonement, and will add much treasure by way of
> amends.[1]

1. Samuel Butler's translation. In 'Great Books of the Western World', *Encyclopaedia Britannica*, (1952)

As the difference between gods and men was one of degree rather than essence, it was up to men to know their limitations; this is what is meant when Apollo of Delfi says, 'Know thyself', and it is implicit in the belief in Nemesis: a man who rises too high will be brought down, too great a happiness leads to unhappiness. The chorus in Aischylos' 'Agamemnon' opposes this belief and asserts on the contrary that evil begets evil, while good leads to good:

> I alone have not the faith of the others:
> A sinful deed, whether open or hidden,
> Will bring forth a stronger offspring
> Who will be fully like his father;
> But happiness ever blesses
> the dwelling of justice with fair sons.

But the happiness which brings good in its train and does not challenge the gods is based on the Good, not merely on good things. It is indeed stressed in a later strophe spoken by the Chorus that Justice prefers humble cottages to lofty halls, and it is hinted that it is the 'falsely praised power of riches' which leads to evil, not because it produces envy on the part of the gods, but because it gives rise to bad qualities in men. But the tragic heroes are all at home in the lofty halls; all belong to distinguished families — *that* is where the sinful deed can beget a stronger offspring.

Aischylos demonstrates this in his three tragedies on the descendents of the warring brothers Atreus and Thyestes: in 'Agamemnon', Agamemnon, the son of Atreus, is murdered by his wife Clytemnestra and Thyestes' son Aigisthos; in 'The Choephoroi' (the women bearing propitiary sacrifices) Clytemnestra is murdered by Orestes, the son of Agamemnon and herself; in 'The Eumenides' Orestes is pursued by the Furies and seeks help from Apollo, who virtually commanded him to avenge his father although he was incurring further guilt by killing his mother. Apollo refers the matter to the court in Athens, where the goddess Athene herself conducts the case and has Orestes acquitted. With this the Furies have lost their function and have henceforth a status as 'Eumenides', the benevolent spirits to whom men can pray for good weather. Through the mediation of the just gods society has taken the maintenance of justice away from the tribe.

When Clytemnestra is visited by the avenging Orestes she excuses herself — like Homer's Agamemnon — by saying that 'fate bears the guilt', and Orestes replies that in that case fate is also responsible for her death. For Aischylos, too, it is obvious that man can do nothing against the will of fate, but that does not prevent man from deserving his fate. Aischylos got no further than the paradox that: 'God burdens the children of men with guilt when he wants to destroy their houses.' These words from a lost tragedy are known from Plato, who quotes them in order to refute them, for: 'If a just order is to be maintained in society, people must be strictly forbidden to suggest that God, who is good, can be guilty of evil towards anyone.' Their use of ancient myths was one of the things which made poets unwanted in Plato's state.

Naturally Seneca found it as difficult as Plato to resign himself to the thought that God, who is good, can be guilty of evil towards anyone. But as Seneca identified God with fate, and as man in his Stoic opinion could not achieve anything contrary to the will of fate either, the question of guilt became all the more urgent. Seneca's revisions of the Greek fate tragedies are so many attempts to answer it.

'Agamemnon' – fate tragedy or court tragedy

Aischylos' 'Agamemnon' was performed in Athens in 458 B.C. and tells of the hero's return from Troy. Before Agamemnon could leave for Troy at all he had to sacrifice his own daughter Iphegenia in order to placate the goddess Artemis, who had commanded all the winds to drop so that the fleet could not put to sea. In Aischylos' tragedy the chorus describes this terrible event and stresses that Agamemnon incurred guilt when he did as the goddess commanded: 'Through the heart an urge to heavy deeds, unholy, unblessed, unfitting broke'; but he would also have done wrong if he had not obeyed 'God's law'. Clytemnestra professes joy at her husband's return, but murders him once he has arrived and thus avenges the death of her daughter. Meanwhile, she has been living together with Aigisthos; as he is the son of Thyestes and Agamemnon the son of Atreus, he, too, has a good old-fashioned motive for avenging the murder. The chorus of old men remonstrates with the murderers, Aigisthos also wants to murder the old men, but Clytemnestra, who knows no regret and rejects the

249

complaints of the chorus, has had enough: 'Their deaths are now useless; what we did had to happen'; the evil spirit of revenge has been satisfied, and now it can look elsewhere. However, the chorus prophesies that it will bring Orestes to this place.

The chorus has more than anyone else to say in Aischylos' tragedy, for the important thing is not the plot, which everyone knew, but the meaning, which could be difficult to understand; on the one hand it deprecates the evil law that people are murdered for murder, but on the other hand accepts that: 'Die if you kill' is the law of God: a divine justice reveals itself — or hides itself — in the guilt-laden deeds of the world. On this basis the murderers of course can justify themselves, but the chorus at one and the same time condemns the murderers and refers to the law of God, which not only says, 'Die if you kill', but also, 'Suffer and learn': suffering is not only a punishment, but also a way to an understanding and a sense of sin. And the chorus can express its faith that: 'God loves us indeed, though sternly seated on his throne divine'.

To Seneca there was no divine law behind the evil law that revenge begets revenge. When his Ægisthus boasts of having been born at the behest of Phoebus, Clytaemnestra replies: 'Why bring gods into this shameful thing?' Those words could be spoken by Seneca himself.

The chorus of wise old men in Aischylos' tragedy who reflect on the meaning of life and reason with the characters in the play, has in Seneca's version been replaced by two choruses, one of Greeks and one of captured Trojan women. In Seneca's tragedies the chorus rarely enters into a dialogue with the characters, whose dialogues thus fill all the more; the four choruses are usually complete in themselves and thus divide the tragedies into five parts, which were later called acts; the first 'act' is usually a monologue in which the theme is struck; here it is Thyestes who, as the personification of the irresistible urge for revenge in the Tantalus family appears from the underworld and foretells of terrors to come. The Greek women sing in two choruses of the gods and of Hercules, but the songs are superficial catalogues of the deeds of the gods and the heroes, without any other connection with the drama. On the other hand their first chorus, which is addressed to *fortuna*, contains the moral of the play. In his drama Aischylos accepts the mystery that even evil happens in accordance with God's plan; Seneca maintained his faith in fate but could not make it responsible for evil, and as has already been shown he tried to solve the problem by distinguishing between fate and chance, *fatum* and *fortuna*. While Aischylos says that the gods bring guilt upon the families whom they wish to punish, Seneca says in the first chorus that everything that *fortuna* has raised up shall be brought down: the castles of the great are destroyed by mutual crime, *scelus alternum*; even without opposition from outside greatness sinks beneath its own weight, and *fortuna* falls on account of its own burden. Thus *fortuna* represents superficial happiness which challenges the gods and tempts men.

Consequently Seneca is more interested in the psychological motives of his characters than is Aischylos. While in the Greek tragedy Aigisthos justifies himself by saying that there is a divine justice in his revenge, Seneca's Ægisthus justifies the murder of Agamemnon with the suggestion that everything is allowed at court; Clytaemnestra cannot reckon on Agamemnon's forgiveness, and it is a case of getting in her blow first. While there is no discussion of the murder in Aischylos' play before it has been committed, and while his Clytemnestra feels no scruples, Seneca's Clytaemnestra can formulate Stoic maxims to the effect that it ought to be easy for a man to forgive who himself needs forgiveness. She regrets that together with Ægisthus she strayed on to the wrong path, but she also knows that moderation in crime is foolish. Typically of those who are both unsure and self-certain, she is inclined to say the opposite to those who contradict her. As Ægisthus encourages her in her murderous intent, she becomes morally indignant and wants to get rid of him instead of Agamemnon, and then to take her own life; only when Ægisthus declares himself ready to die does Clytaemnestra declare herself ready to murder.

The title hero, Agamemnon, does not get many words in edgeways in this drama on Clytaemnestra; he only appears in a short characteristic duel of words with his prisoner, the prophetic Cassandra: 'No danger threatens you' — 'Great danger threatens you' — 'What has a victor to fear?' — 'That which he does not fear.' Not only does Cassandra foresee Agamemnon's death, she also 'sees' it, even though the murder takes place off-stage. By way of contrast to her Greek predecessor Clytaemnestra is as implacable as ever after the murder; she has not had her urge for revenge satisfied, but she is seen in an embittered dialogue with her daughter Electra, whom she also wants Ægisthus to kill, but whom he will 'only' have immured. The

251

drama ends with Cassandra's desire for revenge and her prophecy that Orestes will come to take his revenge and will finally be struck with madness.

There are no consoling words to the effect that God loves man even if he is stern. The most consolatory thing is the chorus of the women of Troy, who sing the praises of death the liberator, a peaceful gate to eternal rest; he who has overcome 'the horrible love of life' need not fear impotent *fortuna* and the unreasonable god of thunder — who quite reasonably does not stand so high in the esteem of the imprisoned Trojan women as he does in that of the victorious Greek women. *Fortuna* has no power over those who have lost everything — *fortuna*, chance, gains power over the man who — from a desire for power or other passions — loses power over himself. Clytaemnestra describes the condition:

> My marrow and my heart are being consumed by the
> flames; pain sharpens the sting of fear, jealousy beats in
> my breast, and evil desire has laid its yoke immovably
> on my soul. And amidst this fire in my tormented mind
> my shame awakes, though weary and in chains and
> bowed deep down... I have given all my power away;
> wherever anger, pain or hope leads me I must go, and
> my ship is at the mercy of the waves: the soul which
> errs is best led by chance.

Clytaemnestra is well acquainted with evil; Seneca's characters have a greater moral consciousness than the Greeks and so a worse conscience and so a greater measure of cynicism; in them it seems that understanding rather leads to pain and crime than pain and crime to understanding — and in Seneca's 'Oedipus' there are signs of the tragedy of a man who cannot live with his *knowledge* of himself.

The absurd drama of Oedipus

The characters in Greek tragedy have lost their Homeric innocence — even if they want to, they cannot blame fate, but must accept that they are responsible for their fate; only with this realisation did the individual as such come into being. But at the same time as man loses his innocence, so do the gods; they heap guilt on men in order to punish them. Seneca might well be able to explain why the gods let the good suffer, but he had difficulty in accepting that they could also let them *commit* evil, and his 'Oedipus' shows the difficulty he has in coping with the Greek fate tragedy — of which Sophocles' 'Oidipus' is the prototype.

Apollo has predicted that Oidipus will murder his father and beget children with his mother. Oidipus hears of the prophecy and leaves his country in order to prevent its being fulfilled; he comes to Thebes, whose king, Laios, has recently died, and he qualifies to become his successor by solving the riddle of the Sphinx. He marries Laios' widow, Jocasta, and has four children by her before Thebes is visited by the plague. The citizens appeal to King Oidipus, who once saved the city from the pestilence of the Sphinx and now promises to do everything he can to remove the curse which the plague represents (for disease was of course seen as a punishment). Oidipus has sent his brother-in-law Creon to the oracle of Apollo in Delfi, and he comes home with the decree of the gods: the land must be cleansed of guilt if the entire population is not to die: King Laios was murdered, and his murderer must be punished. Oidipus promises to avenge Laios 'as though he were my father', and he curses his murderer. The soothsayer Teiresias knows who the murderer is and under threats is forced to betray his secret: it is Oidipus himself! Oidipus can naturally only see this accusation as absurd and suspects a conspiracy between Teiresias and Creon, who of course is nearest the throne. Jocasta tries to calm him: no credence should be given to soothsaying: it was prophesied to her and Laios that their son would murder him, and for that reason the son was exposed, and Laios was murdered by unknown assailants. Oidipus now hears that what has been foretold for him has also been foretold for the son of Laios and Jocasta — and remembers that on the way to Thebes he himself had actually murdered an old man who got in his way. In this tense situation he receives a message saying that his father has died a natural death, but nevertheless he dare not return home and assume the kingdom of his fathers, for the worst part of the prophecy still threatens him. The messenger reassures him with the news that he is not the real son of his parents: they took in a child that had been exposed, because they themselves were childless. Oidipus confronts the person who long ago received the child with the person who exposed it: he recognises his fate and, having lived unseeing, puts out his own eyes: his wife, who is also his mother, hangs herself. Oidipus leaves his country to purge himself of guilt — and the chorus voices the moral: Oidipus, who was wiser than others and happier than others, was overcome by greater torments than others, and therefore no one must be called happy until he has died without torment.

From the very start Seneca's Oedipus is more distrustful of himself than Sophocles' Oidipus, and he suspects that it is he who is responsible for the plague which has visited the people. He knows that according to the prophecy of the god he is predisposed to dreadful crimes, and it is not possible to create a viable kingdom on the basis of such crimes — of which he feels guilty even before he knows he has committed them. He knows that he must leave the kingdom to save both it and himself, for regal power challenges *fortuna*.

Seneca thus stresses that it is Oedipus' misfortune that he is king; it demands qualities in him which he does not have, thanks to his unfortunate predispositions. When Oedipus learns that it is the murder of his predecessor, King Laius, which must be expiated, he recognises that he himself ought to have seen to that: it is the king who must think of the well-being of kings, for those who have feared him while he was alive are indifferent towards the king when he is dead — he does not doubt that fear is the bulwark of a kingdom; he is a greater tyrant than his Greek namesake. And when he is confirmed in his evil suspicions by the powers of heaven and the underworld, he hangs on to his own power and his own knowledge with all the more determination: he knows that he is innocent of the murder of King Laius, and he knows himself better than the gods do.

The channels used by Oedipus to communicate with the powers are different in Seneca's work to those in Sophocles'. Tiresia is not a soothsayer who has a knowledge of hidden things; his blood is, as he himself says, not so young and warm that he can receive the god in his breast: he must in Roman fashion seek illumination in the entrails of a sacrificial animal, and he does it according to all the rules of the game; as he is blind, it is his daughter Manto who has to report the dreadful signs which Tiresia is able to interpret, but as he wants to know for certain who the sinner is, he conjures up the dead Laius who — admittedly only in Creon's version — leaves him in no doubt that it is

Oedipus who is the sinner. It is not the gods' long-standing anger, but a crime which has brought destruction on Thebes, and the country will be saved when the criminal leaves it. This was what Oedipus suspected; now that he has it confirmed he prefers in desperate self-defence to suspect a conspiracy to put him off the throne.

Sophocles' Oidipus did the same thing; nevertheless, after learning the truth he was reconciled to Creon, the object of his suspicions. For Sophocles the unveiling of the past is a long and painful process and leads Oidipus to accept his fate, so that at last he stands bereft of everything but transfigured in the light of the truth; in Seneca it is short and brutal, and it is with a certain triumphant sense of having been unjustly treated that Oedipus achieves certainty of what he suspected. As though he was already acquainted with newspaper headlines he calls himself 'the crime of the century' and is not far from boasting of his fate. He is unreceptive to the logic of Iocasta, and when she argues: 'This is the fault of fate, no one is guilty of his own fate,' he cuts her short: 'Spare your words, dear mother, and spare my ears.' Sophocles' Oidipus does not address his wife as his mother; Seneca's characters dwell on the absurd element in the family relationship they have got themselves into. In Seneca Iocasta kills herself with Oedipus' sword and thus has the opportunity to point out that with this sword her husband was killed — 'Yet why not call him by the proper name: my father-in-law!'

In a later (unfinished or only partly extant) tragedy called 'The Phoenician Women' Oedipus presents himself as a new riddle of the Sphinx: 'The son-in-law of his grandfather and the rival of his father, the brother of his children and the father of his brothers.' That is Oedipus, the great tragic hero of the greatest of Greek tragedies; what is tragic to Sophocles has become absurd to Seneca; with his sense of the grotesque within himself and his irritable insistence on his own misery his Oedipus is already something of hero à la Beckett. Nothing is so bad that Oedipus' scornful words cannot make it worse; in 'The Phoenician Women' he is seen in the company of his daughter (and sister) Antigona, who can call on more tender expressions in his furious torrent of words, but an Oedipus cannot have the luxury of human feelings — there is no knowing what that might lead to! When he is asked to make peace between his sons Eteocles and Polynices, who are struggling for power in Thebes and are prepared to destroy it in order

255

to conquer it, he instead calls down destruction on both his family and his city:

> Act, dear sons, and show your noble birth in deeds.
> You should transcend my honour and my fame and do
> things so a father might know that his life bore fruit.
> That you will do; you were born to it; this noble blood
> can commit more than simple, everyday crimes.

As Oedipus declares himself to be incapable, Iocasta (who in this version has not taken her own life) must place herself between the warring brothers; she has been worried that one of her sons has been driven out by the other, and she has sought advice from the god, who scornfully told her that she would not cease to fear for her son until she herself came to fear him. That she now does; now the struggle is beginning; she tries to bring them to their senses, saying that it was a mistake which made us guilty against our will; it was *Fortuna* who treated us shamefully — this is the first crime to be committed consciously!

In the ancient Greek epic on Oidipus on which Sophocles had based his tragedy it had not been prophesied by the god that Oidipus would commit a crime, and in fact it was more or less a coincidence that he did so. In Sophocles, too, Jocasta tries to explain away Oidipus' tragedy by giving chance, *tyche*, the responsibility, until the fate pattern becomes clear — and it is obvious that Oidipus *is* guilty of the fate which he has based all his life on trying to avoid. It is in this fateful situation that Seneca's Iocasta presumes to remonstrate at the way in which the world is ordered and insists that no one is guilty of his fate, and although Oedipus rejects this, he cannot like his Greek predecessor reconcile himself both with his fate and himself. And clearly Seneca also had difficulty in accepting *this* fate. For him it was obvious that the moral value of our actions is not dependent on their result but on the attitude of mind behind them, and it did not accord with his Stoic thinking that man can commit a crime against his will but according to the decision of the gods and of fate. On this basis Oedipus can only be said to be responsible for the actions which he has tried to avoid if he fundamentally has had a murderous or sexual desire to commit them because of the 'Oedipus complex' which Freud discovered. Seneca did

256

not get so far in his psychological interpretation of the Oedipus myth, but he did try to find a reason for Oedipus' fate in his own attitude: Oedipus *has* challenged fate and assumed regal power in the kingdom he chanced to reach, even though he knew his own inclinations!

According to Stoic thinking evil cannot befall a good man, and so in order to introduce some moral balance into Oedipus' accounts Seneca had either to make him into an evil man being punished for his crimes or else write in defiance of the belief in a fate which treats human beings so badly. But firstly, as Aristotle had pointed out, it is not tragic but right for a man to be punished for his sins, and secondly, it was a Stoic dogma that men cannot be treated badly by fate but only by *fortuna*; but the man who allows himself to be led by chance is 'an erring soul'. When Iocasta in 'The Phoenician Women' no longer (as in 'Oedipus') can blame fate but only *fortuna*, she thereby also ascribes some responsibility, though a far smaller portion, to man; this is not a crime determined by fate and the god and *therefore* a sacrilege — it is a 'mistake'. In the same way Oedipus himself talks of the crimes which he has innocently committed, and his daughter Antigona says expressly that contrary to the wishes of the gods he is innocent and that the guilt has not reached his heart.

But it has — and Oedipus replies: 'I fear myself, I fear my own heart which is conscious of all crimes.' Oedipus' crime cannot be distinguished from his own bad conscience, which is not so much a consequence of the crimes as the reason for them: it is in his conflict with himself that Oedipus 'makes a mistake'; all his life he has been fleeing from himself and has therefore become the prey of *fortuna*.

Meanwhile, Latin has the same word for 'conscience' as for 'consciousness', *conscientia*, knowledge of yourself, and when Iocasta says to her sons that all the crimes have hitherto been mistakes made against their will, but that they are about to be the first to commit a crime of which they are conscious, she is voicing a more humane sense of justice; it corresponds to Seneca's own view that you can only commit a crime consciously. However, the words can be understood as a realisation that consciousness and guilt go together and that a man who is conscious of himself thus makes a break with the old primitive order.

The last chorus in 'Oedipus' sings of fate and presents it as an irrevocable series of causes with which not even the gods can interfere, but it is added that many have fulfilled their fate precisely by fearing it. Would they perhaps have avoided it if they had *not* been afraid of the evil but had assumed their fates with Homeric innocence? In this chorus there is an indication that it is consciousness that makes man uncertain, and that is what Oedipus himself indicates in the monologue introducing his tragedy and the most original part of it: the god's prediction of the crime has turned Oedipus' consciousness of innate evil tendencies, into a bad conscience. Understood in this way Oedipus is the man, the individual, who has broken out of the mythical community and who has to fashion both himself and society; and seen in this way there is also some sense in the fact that the hero, the individual, can only free himself with violence from his primitive infantile state of mind — by murdering his father, and that in his civilised rootlessness he flees back to his mother's lap.

The drama of Hercules the ruler

Seneca's characters often dissociate themselves from the gods and sometimes even express doubts as to their existence. There is a curious imbalance in his tragedies between the mythological framework which he took over from his Greek predecessors, and the more critical Roman awareness of his characters. But this kind of tension is already discernible in Euripides, the third of the three great Greek dramatists, who was not much younger than the other two but nevertheless represented a different era. While Aischylos found a divine purpose in existence and Sophocles presupposed one, Euripides sought one; but he had difficulty in reconciling himself to gods who were amoral by nature and was inclined to drag them into (what has since become called) the limelight. In 'Furious Herakles' (from 421 B.C.) it is the jealous Hera who persecutes Herakles, her divine spouse Zeus' son with a mortal woman, and dispatches the demon of madness on to the stage to make him mad, something which the demon is slightly reluctant to do. When in his madness Herakles has killed his wife and children and is about to punish himself with death, he is consoled with the knowledge that it is Hera's fault and that the gods themselves are guilty of many things and still live unashamedly on Olympus. But although Herakles himself blames Hera, he refuses to believe in the reprobate actions of the gods and sees them as the unworthy inventions of poets. In this way he leaves it unclear whether it is the gods of this kind or gods in general that Herakles, the son of a god, does not believe in — and with him Euripides, who often uses gods and demons in his tragedies, but only as *dei ex machina*: where men are ruled by their passions the gods appear, as it were, as the external manifestations of the irrational elements in man, as a means of visualising internal states on the stage. It is not often that the gods actually bring about the good; they rather gain power over the man who does not have power over himself, and really represent what Seneca called *fortuna*; the corresponding Greek *tyche* interestingly enough also plays a greater part in Euripides than in his predecessors.

Thus Seneca stood closer to Euripides, and he used Euripides' tragedies as the basis for most of his own. 'Furious Herakles' inspired him to a more Stoic treatment of the question which was asked in the Oedipus tragedy: how can man sin against his will, something which was all the more appropriate as Herakles was traditionally seen as the prototype of the Stoic hero.

In the myth Herakles carries out twelve tasks which have been assigned to him as a punishment for his killing his wife and children; Euripides' approach is profounder, and he makes the murders come after the heroic deeds, something in which Seneca follows him. The twelve labours of Herakles, which consist mainly in killing wicked monsters, he portrays in 'Furious Hercules', *Hercules furens*, as deeds beneficial to mankind. When the drama begins, Hercules has carried out eleven of them and is now engaged in fetching Cerberus, the hound of hell, up from the underworld. Hercules' earthly father Amphitrion describes conditions on earth during his absence in this way:

> The earth has felt the absence of the bringer of peace:
> here every successful evil deed is called a virtue, and
> here the good must obey the guilty; right depends on
> power of arms; the law is broken down by fear.

In this way Seneca makes a political point out of the Hercules myth and can freely draw on the criticism of contemporary society he made in 'On the brevity of life' as a major element in the first chorus in the play; it is a morning hymn depicting the beginning of the day's work

259

and contrasting the calm of country life with the nervousness of city life, which is described more as though it were modern Rome than ancient Thebes in which Hercules is to be seen.

Hercules is in the underworld and is thought by most people to have been killed, and meanwhile Lycus has taken control of Thebes and had the former king, Hercules' father-in-law, and his sons murdered. Lycus denies that he is an illegal ruler: he can thank himself, not his forefathers, for his kingship and is proud of being a self-made man; a man who boasts of his descent is singing the praises of others. Nor would it be true to say that the old king was fighting for his right and Lycus only for power: the decisive thing is the result of the struggle, not the motive for it. Lycus naturally knows that the first art required of a ruler is that of tolerating hatred, but he also knows that it is easier to rule if the people do not hate you; he, too, wants to break the evil chain of revenge — in Euripides by getting rid of Herakles' family so that they cannot avenge their father, and in Seneca by marrying Hercules' wife, Megara, the daughter of the old king:

> If mortals nurse their hatred to all time and tend their
> fury when awakened, if fortune's friend keeps his
> weapons and fortune's opponent resorts to his, then
> war will spare nothing, and the fields are grey and
> desolate, and ash from burnt down cities covers their
> peoples. For the victor it is best to conclude peace, and
> for the others a necessity.

Lycus is Seneca's most 'Machiavellian' character: he wants to turn the situation to his best advantage and would like to maintain the appearance of being a good man; only when Megara refuses to marry him does he comdemn her and her children to death. By allowing Lycus, who only plays a minor role in Euripides, to have the main say, Seneca turns his drama on Hercules into a drama about a ruler, in which Hercules and Lycus illustrate the old Stoic contrast between the king and the tyrant. Hercules appears from the underworld at the right moment and kills Lycus and his followers. In Euripides the chorus rejoices that justice has been done, and Amphitrion confirms that it is right to love your friend and hate your enemy. In Seneca it is not directly said that you should love your enemy, but there is a hint of some connection between Hercules' righteous anger and his attacks of fury. Amphitrion exhorts him to purge himself of his guilt and to ask his divine father to spare him more trials; Hercules would like to use his enemy's blood as a propitiatory sacrifice, for no larger or fatter beast can be slaughtered to Jupiter than an unjust king; but he thinks again and tries to fashion his words into a prayer worthy both of Jupiter and himself: may harmony reign in heaven and on the sea and on earth, may deep peace nourish the peoples so that iron can be used to cultivate peaceful farm land and the sword can remain in its sheath: no longer shall there be cruel tyrants, and if the earth is to beget more evil, let it happen without delay so that Hercules can straightway put an end to it: it is clear that Hercules finds it difficult to escape from his urge to fight and take revenge; that is what develops into the fury which makes him kill his own family, whom he killed Lycus for wanting to kill. In this way Seneca, who moreover lets Hercules' madness come upon him on the stage, while Euripides only reports it, gives a psychological reason for the madness which in Euripides is caused by the demon of madness.

In Seneca's play Juno certainly is behind the developments, but she is kept out of the action and only appears in a prologue where she rightly admits that as Hercules has no enemy equal to him, he must become his own enemy — or as Seneca has it elsewhere: many have conquered cities, but few have conquered themselves. Juno is in fact not only annoyed on her own behalf, but worried on behalf of the gods: Hercules has conquered the world and the underworld and has carried the heavens on his shoulders — is there not reason to fear that he will usurp power from the gods and make himself master of a masterless world?

And that is exactly what Hercules does want in his madness. The earth has no room for a Hercules, and if the gods will not give him access to heaven, he will find a way of doing it himself: he will liberate Saturnus, whom Jupiter once employed to force them from power, and he will ally himself with the Titans and the giants, whom Hercules himself once helped the gods to overcome. It is madness, and yet there is method in it: Saturnus reigned when there was a golden age on earth and the gods moved among men and did not hector them as Juno hectors Hercules, and it was of a new Age of Gold Hercules spoke in his prayer to Jupiter. Man has come to moral awareness, and he cannot

261

recognise amoral gods, but a man who cannot recognise gods has difficulty in knowing his own limitations. If we keep Juno out of the picture, as Seneca does in the actual plot, Hercules' madness is akin to that of the emperors: he is the Roman who rules the world, has conquered all his enemies and become an enemy of himself, and has become a tyrant by killing the tyrant. Hercules recovers from his madness in the understanding that there is no forgiveness for him who has not himself forgiven, and that he carried out his Herculean tasks on orders; only this evil deed was his own, despite Juno. The greatest labour of Hercules is left: to live like Hercules after this.

Seneca's 'Hercules' is thus even more than Euripides' the tragedy of a ruler, and the political and moral perspective is broader. The hero Theseus, whom Hercules has freed from imprisonment in the underworld, tells of his impressions; he adds to Sisyfos and Tantalus, the classical villains who are being tormented down there, the tyrants whose backs are being lashed by plebeians, and then he formulates the moral of the play:

> He who is gentle in his power and who, though master
> of life, keeps clean his hands of blood and lets
> gentleness reign in his land and spares the soul, will,
> when he has had many rich years of life, see heaven or
> will blissfully see the happy groves of Elysium as judge.
> Refrain from spilling blood, you who rule men, for
> every evil deed is measured with a greater measure.

This recommendation is somewhat reminiscent of Seneca's warnings to Nero in 'On gentleness'. It has already been mentioned (p176) that Hercules is accused of being effeminate because he has nardus oil in his hair and plays the tambourine — and that it is not difficult in this to see an allusion to Nero, all the more since the emperors were traditionally compared with Hercules. If this was flattering to Nero, then Hercules' Caesarian madness must be taken all the more seriously as a reminder to him. 'Furious Hercules' can be dated with greater certainty than Seneca's other tragedies — to the beginning of Nero's reign.

It has already been mentioned, (p204) that among Seneca's extant works there is another tragedy on Hercules, 'Hercules on Oeta', though it is completely lacking in the moral perspective which is the original element in 'Furious Hercules'. As it moreover differs in essential respects from the other tragedies, not only in length (it is almost twice as long), but also in style, and possesses neither the rigorous composition nor the tautness of language, the pithy sayings or the duels with words which otherwise are characteristic of Seneca, it can be asserted that it was not written by him: it is the work of a minor dramatist writing in his manner, and this puts Seneca's tragedies into relief.

Phaedra and the tyranny of passion

Like Homer's Agamemnon, Euripides' Herakles is struck down by a mighty goddess of madness, but he cannot so easily escape the responsibility himself. Like Sophocles' Oidipus he murders his closest relatives against his will, but while the god, Apollo, merely predicts Oidipus' crime, the goddess Hera is directly instrumental in that of Herakles. The gods appear to become crueller as time passes, but that is also true of others in power when they are losing their power. To anyone with a sense of the humane the gods must appear to have very few humane characteristics, and wherever the gods appear in Euripides there is trouble afoot.

His tragedy 'Hippolytos' starts with a prologue by Aphrodite, who is angry with Hippolytos, the son of Theseus, because he prefers to lavish his affections on Artemis, the chaste goddess of the hunt. While Theseus is in the underworld, she ensures that his wife Faidra is filled with an all-consuming desire for her stepson Hippolytos. Her nurse tries to persuade him to do as Faidra wishes, but she fails; Faidra takes her own life but leaves a note on which Theseus on his return can read that Hippolytos has ravished her; Hippolytos has promised to be silent and cannot speak openly with his father. Theseus exiles him and appeals to his father, Poseidon, the god of the sea, who makes a bull arise from the sea and rid him of Hippolytos. All this is predicted in Aphrodite's prologue: all goes as the goddess wishes, and like marionettes human beings can play the parts allotted to them. But the gods are not entirely agreed: it was of course Hippolytos' relationship to Artemis that angered Aphrodite — and Artemis appears before the dying Hippolytos and consoles him by promising to take her revenge on Aphrodite; she also consoles the guilt-ridden Theseus: 'He who is tempted by a god *must* fall. He has no responsibility for his sin. Hear my advice, Hippolytos, and forgive your father. Bear no grudge. It was your fate. You *had* to die.'

The 'Hippolytos' we know is an adaptation of the tragedy which was performed in 428 and incensed the Athenians. To make erotic passion into the central theme in a tragedy and to let a woman actually try to seduce her stepson on the stage, as Faidra did in the first version, was a bold experiment. Seneca, who had no need to fear giving offence to the Romans, followed the first version of Euripides' tragedy in his 'Phaedra'. In his play there is a scene between Phaedra and Hippolytus, in which she gradually reveals to him the state of her feelings. When he benevolently and naively believes it to be 'pure' love for the absent Theseus, she replies: 'Yes, for Theseus when he was your age' — and she extolls his beauty, which the chorus soon sings in praise of as well: Hippolytus is obviously handsome enough to waken a woman's desire without Aphrodite having to act as intermediary.

The chorus admittedly also sings the praises of the god Cupid, whose fire devours gods and men and animals. Seneca did not pay much attention to erotic passion in his philosophical works, but he did not lack words for its fire, and while in 'On anger' he wrote that anger can conquer the most intense love, here he says that anger, even when firmly established, will yield to the fire of Cupid which — as its crowning achievement — can even overcome cruel stepmothers! The words he utters in praise of Cupid hint at a psychological explanation for Phaedra's conflict: she has obviously (like Juno) been somewhat unkind towards her stepson until she became fired by love for him — elsewhere there is also an indication that Hippolytus' hatred of all the female sex is the result of his hatred for his stepmother.

When Hippolytus has finally understood he draws his sword in horror to plunge it into Phaedra — who says that now he is fulfilling her wish, with the result that he throws the tainted sword down. Although he was conscious of many things, Seneca was scarcely aware of the powerful sexual symbolism in this. It is the sword and not merely a note which incriminates Hippolytus: he has threatened her with his sword and ravished her, says Phaedra; Theseus believes her and condemns his son on the spot, ordering his punishment without listening to him. When Hippolytus' body is carried off the stage,

Phaedra in anguish confesses her action and takes her own life; now it is Theseus' turn to regret: Seneca's drama is more brutal, but also more logical in its action than 'Hippolytos'; it does not end with a sentimental reconciliation between Theseus and his dying son, but with an attempt, which the chorus describes in gruesome detail, to assemble Hippolytus' mangled corpse. There is no goddess here to give comfort, and Theseus cannot console himself with the thought that the bull which arises from the ocean, and which Seneca's messenger describes with almost scientific accuracy, is the responsibility of the god of the ocean, for it was sent at his own request. Now he wishes the earth would swallow him up, but this time the gods turn a deaf ear to his appeal. If he were asking for crimes to be committed, they would listen to him, he believes.

Thus Seneca could not avoid the intervention of the god of the ocean, though he accompanies it with this bitter comment; otherwise, however, he excluded the gods from his drama. Phaedra is the only character to blame the god of love for her passion; her nurse knows that passion can be controlled at first and that it grows in strength if it is cultivated, as is often the case in lofty halls where people have nothing better to do:

That love is god
is the vile fiction of unbridled lust
Which, for its licence, gives to lawless passion
The name of an imagined deity.
Venus from Eryx, we are to believe,
Sends her son wandering over all the earth,
And he, skyborne, shoots out his wicked darts
From one small hand — the littlest of the gods
Endowed with such almighty power! Vain fancies
Conceived by crazy minds, they are all false!
Venus' divinity and Cupid's arrows!
Too much contentment and prosperity,
And self-indulgence, lead to new desires;
Then lust comes in, good fortune's fatal friend;
Everyday fare no longer satisfied,
Plain houses and cheap ware are not enough.
Why, tell me, does this sickness seldom taint

A humble home but strikes where life is soft?
Why is pure love found under lowly roofs,
And why do common people generally
Have wholesome appetites where modest means
Teach self-control — while wealth, propped up by power,
Always asks more than its fair share of things?

Tragedies, p. 106

And why do the tragedies always deal with the great and never the lowly members of society? Humble people are only seen in the tragedies in the shape of servants and nurses who nevertheless often speak with the voice of reason to their passion-ridden masters. It is quite obvious in this case that the nurse is used as a mouthpiece for Seneca, who was himself a sort of nurse in *his* court. In Seneca's work there is no implication that the more powerful members of society as such are more magnanimous than the lesser ones; on the contrary, he constantly stresses how fatal it is if the mighty do not have power over themselves — and demonstrates that anger is particularly noticeable in 'the rich and distinguished, when all empty and vain things have risen to the top as they themselves have done.'

The nurse, however, is not only the author's mouthpiece, she is also a sort of human being who has to find her way around at court, and as she achieves nothing by her reason she gives her mistress her full support. She does so not only for tactical reasons: her feelings are 'healthy' and she is capable of the sympathetic understanding which eludes the great; the fact that the humble achieve nothing by fair words, but have to join forces against the great is not the least — though perhaps the least conspicuous — tragic element in the tragedies of the great.

The nurse tries to persuade Hippolytus to follow Venus and nature and make his way to the city and seek the company of the citizens. Hippolytus, who in a charming hunting song has shown himself to be a well-qualified lover of nature, replies in a long speech (cf p223) on the degenerate life of the town in contrast to the 'real' life in harmony with nature, thus producing a kind of cultural and historical explanation of the power exerted over civilised human beings, i.e. those living in the big cities, by passions such as the desire for power, revenge, possession and sensual love. But this is exactly what Seneca calls *fortuna* which, as it is put in the final chorus, leaves cottages in peace but rumbles like thunder in royal palaces, *fortuna* which fashions the lives of men 'without order or arrangement'. *Fortuna* means a deviation from the natural order of things, not what cannot be but what could be different. While the tragic element in Greek tragedy was according to Aristotle undeserved suffering resulting from man's fate and serving a scarcely understood purpose in the divine plan, tragedy for Seneca is more associated with unnecessary and pointless suffering. In his 'Phaedra' the innocent Hippolytus falls a victim to the passions of his parents, in Euripides' tragedy as a victim to Aphrodite. In Euripides Theseus is consoled by Artemis; in Seneca he recognises his guilt. Seneca's tragedy contains no reconciliation, no catharsis, but to a modern mind it is scarcely more uplifting to know that it is gods rather than men who cause men suffering.

Medea and the affront to nature

Hippolytus lists various examples of the fall from nature: brother kills brother, fathers are laid low by their sons, wives kill their husbands and mothers their children (not to speak of stepmothers); if we exclude 'The Trojan Women', these stand as a summary of Seneca's tragedies, at least if we add to them the husband who murders his wife and the father his son. In Seneca's tragedy on Medea, the mother who kills her children, a chorus also hints at an 'historical' explanation of the power which passions exert on man. Jason was given the task of fetching the Golden Fleece from Colchis; he fitted out a ship, the Argos, which achieved a mythical status as the first ship; with it began those seafaring exploits which turned a world otherwise peacefully divided into natural components into one great market and thus betokened a break with the natural state of things. And the reward appropriately earned by the first ship was a golden fleece — and Medea!

Not for nothing does the pessimistic view of culture expressed by the chorus culminate in a prophesy of epoch-making discoveries: 'Centuries will come when Oceanus frees the world from its fetters,

1.   Oceanus was the term both for a sea god and for the Atlantic; Thetis was his wife. Thule, the country furthest to the north, was localised to Shetland or Norway.

267

and a great land will emerge and Thetis will loosen worlds from her embrace, and the furthermost land will no longer be Thule.'[1] According to legend the golden fleece was so well guarded by the king in Colchis that Jason could only secure it with the help of the king's daughter Medea, who was skilled in magic. Medea killed her brother and committed a series of crimes for the sake of Jason, who in return married her. They were given asylum in Corinth, where Jason repudiated Medea, who meanwhile had born him two sons, in favour of the king's daughter Creusa — and in favour of himself, for through his new marriage he became the heir to the throne in Corinth. Medea was exiled, but before leaving she sent her children to the bride with gifts intended to kill her, after which she murdered them in order to wound their father, the unfaithful Jason. Medea was the granddaughter of the sun god and with his help she escaped on a chariot drawn by dragons.

Apart from this celestial helping hand, which shows that even the sun god puts family considerations above morals, the gods play no part in Euripides' tragedy on Medea. Medea is not the victim of a god, but is let down by a man, and there is no god to absolve her from guilt, as Artemis does for Theseus in 'Hippolytos'. On the other hand the chorus of the women of Corinth shows a remarkable sense of solidarity with another woman: 'Just is your demand for vengeance, Medea', they assure her. In Euripides' version the tragedy of Medea becomes the tragedy of the woman who must do everything, even commit crimes, for the sake of a man who does nothing for her; as Medea in addition is a barbarian woman and Jason a great Greek hero who thinks that he has deserved the gratitude of Medea for taking her away from her barbaric fatherland, Euripides' defence of Medea must have been extremely offensive to his Greek public; he found himself in the third and last place in the drama competition in the year 431, when his 'Medea' was performed for the first time.

Naturally, Seneca could not help being interested in Medea, for she is an obvious illustration of his argument that anger will overcome even the most ardent love. But precisely because Euripides' tragedy shows her at the mercy of her passions and not of fate or a god, he was not forced to alter it as much as he had been in the tragedies on Herakles and Faidra. His departures from Euripides are partly dramatic improvements: in Seneca's play Medea has her children taken

268

from her, which gives her a better motive for murdering them, and Jason at least *says* that he has acted under pressure and done the will of the King of Corinth in order to save the lives of Medea and the children — in this way his conflict becomes more serious, and he has a somewhat less sorry role to play. To Seneca, whose public was not so discriminating as that of Euripides, the conflict between a barbarian woman who allows herself to be led by her feelings and the Greek hero who is looking to his own advantage is less important than the conflict in Medea herself. But that means that Medea, too, becomes more concerned with herself than with Jason and the children. Euripides' Medea finds such moving words for her love of her sons that her prayer to her own 'anger' (*thymos*) to spare them is charged with all her suffering; for Seneca's Medea the children are pawns in a game of vengeance, and so she can regret not having given birth to as many children as Niobe (i.e. fourteen) so that her vengeance could be the greater. Euripides' Medea is undivided in her feelings and does not have room for both love and hatred, while Seneca's Medea is divided between love and anger, but yet sufficiently in control of herself to give a precise description of her state in an exemplary *suasoria* (cf. p. 70). Like all Seneca's characters, she can formulate striking sayings; to the king who exiles her for the crimes she has committed on behalf of Jason she says: 'A man who judges before the other party has been heard is unjust even if his judgement is right.' She also knows that love has no room for fear, so that Jason's fear testifies against his love. But between her considerations of principle she finds more moving expressions for the injustice which has been done to her: 'But if he yielded and acquiesced under pressure he could yet have come to me and spoken to me for a last time. In his arrogance he had not the courage to do so. To extend the time allotted before I had to flee so cruelly must surely have been possible for a king's son-in-law.'

It may be that Medea has difficulty in moving people's hearts, but on the other hand she can move heaven and earth. She is not a barbarian woman who is versed in magic: she is a magician by profession. The fourth act of the drama shows her at work: her nurse describes how she mixes her deadly poison; in solo arias Medea calls upon the powers of darkness and causes the world to tremble before she sends her children off with the bewitched bridal gifts. When in Seneca's tragedy Medea furthermore murders her children on the stage and throws the bodies down on to Jason's head before she rises into heaven, it contains all the elements of theatrical blood and thunder.

The chorus asks that Jason may be spared the misfortunes which have befallen the other argonauts. The immediate cause of the misfortune that befalls Jason is that he has broken his promise to Medea, but as Medea is said to be the argonauts' reward for breaking 'the sacred laws of the world', she, the witch who can turn the power of nature against men, must be seen as a representative of affronted nature. However much Seneca aims at a psychological interpretation of the Greek myths and legends, his tragedies are never only psychological dramas, but always contain a greater perspective — but in 'Medea' the greater, cosmic perspective is not commensurate with the lesser, the psychological perspective.

In Seneca's other dramas of revenge the ruler cannot rule over himself; it is those at the top who run wild. Medea is the only one of the title figures who is rejected, let down by *fortuna* and by all men. But although he lets her ask the king a question typical of one who has been wronged: 'Why do you make a distinction?', Seneca was nevertheless more interested in the terrible effects of her anger than in any extenuating circumstances: Medea is less a human being in need than a self-possessed witch who wants to 'attack the gods'; the murder of her children appears to be less the desperate act of a woman carried along by passion than the triumphant act of someone sensing sensation.

The need for vengeance and the end of the world: 'Thyestes' and 'The Trojan Women'

While the fall from nature forms the background to the tragedies of 'Phaedra' and 'Medea', there is in 'Thyestes' no question of a happy natural state from which society has deviated; on the contrary, 'Thyestes' shows the necessity — and impossibility — of overcoming a barbarian past. The development of civilisation is, as has been shown already, an ambiguous or dialectical process, an alienation from nature, a more human adaptation of natural instincts. The ancient writers were not sufficiently dialectical to see both developments under one heading, but placed them as it were each in its own drama; that Seneca was particularly concerned with the fall from nature is natural enough, as his society could not show any great progress on the human level. In the great age of Athens Aischylos (cf p 249) had used the myths centred on the urge to seek revenge associated with the Tantalus family in order to illustrate the transition from the law of vengeance to a law based on civil rights and duties. Seneca went back to an even earlier stage in the family history, to the fratricidal conflict between Atreus and Thyestes, which appears to have been a favourite theme among Roman tragedians.

Atreus and Thyestes were the grandsons of that Tantalus who suffered the torments of Tantalus in the underworld for killing his son and serving him as a banquet for the Olympic gods. Myths often provide unconvincing rational explanations of their own irrationality, and here we are given to understand that Tantalus wanted to experiment to see whether the gods were omniscient enough to notice what they were eating. Strictly speaking, however, Tantalus scarcely needed to use his own son in an experiment of this kind. Remembering father Abraham and his willingness to sacrifice his son it is reasonable to assume that Tantalus wanted to find favour with the gods by sacrificing his own son, although the gods did not (any longer) demand it of him. Like the myth of Abraham and Isaac the Tantalus myth reminds us of the development in civilisation which turns human sacrifice into a crime. The great villains undergoing punishment in the underworld must be seen as ancient gods and heroes who were displaced by the Olympic gods; while Tantalus represents the tribal society in which the king or a male child was sacrificed for the renewal of society, Atreus and Thyestes represent the more developed agricultural community's ruling family — but in Seneca's drama they also represent the human family, mankind. Just as mankind, having won the battle against the wild animals, turns its weapons against itself, so the ruling family comes into conflict with itself.

Atreus and Thyestes were rivals competing both for Aerope, who was married to Atreus but in love with Thyestes, and for the throne in Mycenae which Thyestes through the help and cunning of Aerope succeeded in winning but failed to keep. Atreus has exiled his brother but called him back and offered to share his power with him. Together with his three sons Thyestes is now on his way to the palace in Mycenae, but he is not in a hurry: he is perfectly aware that Atreus is not interested in giving up any of his power, but is more likely to want to take his revenge on him.

We, the spectators of this drama between brothers, already know what Thyestes suspects; we have seen Atreus' furious outburst of self-criticism: 'You are weak, spineless, decadent, you are (the most degrading thing of all for an almighty tyrant) unavenged! Atreus also believes that Thyestes intends evil, so it is a matter of getting in the first blow, and crimes are only avenged by greater crimes. Atreus' servant tries the well-tried human arguments, Seneca's own, but he soon gives in, out of fear and loyalty, mostly out of loyalty according to him, but probably mainly out of fear. He suggests that Thyestes should be killed by the sword, to which Atreus replies: 'You talk of the effect of vengeance, I of vengeance itself.' In a kind of inspired moment he has the idea of the crime of all crimes, which not only will give him his revenge, but transcend human limitations — just as Nero is said to have done, Atreus discovers the terrible delight that there are no limits to what a king can do.

When Thyestes wants to turn back, his son — who is called Tantalus after his tormented grandfather — opposes him. A child does not talk of trust and brotherly love, which are too abstract for it; but lacking in experience as he is, he has not quite the same grounds for suspicion as his father and uncle. Whether or not there is any justification for talking of men's innate aggressive tendencies, it is probably true to say that a human child which for so long is dependent on parents and nurses is by nature inclined to trust his fellow human beings and only learns to distrust from experience. What Tantalus' trusting eyes see is the advantage which a reconciliation will bring to his father and himself: a far more comfortable life — and royal power, which is handed down from father to son. Tantalus does not quite understand the implication of his father's words to the effect that the kingdom has not room for two; for him it looks as though his father is still intent on being unhappy, though he has no longer any reason to be.

While exiled and unhappy, however, Thyestes has been forced to adopt an ascetic view of life which he now proclaims to his son:

> Take it from me, my son, great prizes tempt us
> By their false aspects, and our fear of hardship
> Is likewise a delusion. While I stood
> Among the great, I stood in daily terror;

272

The very sword I wore at my own side
I feared. It is the height of happiness
To stand in no man's way, to eat at ease
Reclining on the ground. At humble tables
Food can be eaten without fear; assassins
Will not be found in poor men's cottages;
The poisoned drink is served in cups of gold,
I speak as one who knows, and make my choice
The life of hardship, not prosperity.
Mine is no lofty dwelling-place built high
Upon a mountain top to overawe
The common folk below.

My house is undefended, but secure.
Great is my peace, as my estate is small:
Kingdom unlimited, without a kingdom!

Tragedies 64–65 & 66

But Thyestes' Stoicism is constrained: he has not sufficient power over himself, for he allows himself to be persuaded by Tantalus — or by his own ambition.

Then follows the act of reconciliation, beautiful and slightly sentimental on the surface but cynical and pitiful in its real content: Thyestes will not accept royal power from such a good brother to whom he declares he is indebted; Atreus asks — more or less as Nero asked Seneca in his farewell audience — whether Thyestes thereby wants to prevent him from gaining honour on that account? Royal power is the gift of chance; to give it to someone else is a moral victory. This is Atreus' formulation, and it is as good as Seneca's own in 'On good deeds'. Thyestes agrees to be king in name, but declares that he will serve Atreus. And that calls for a celebration!

Would anyone believe it possible? exclaims the chorus of citizens: cruel Atreus changed his manner and attitude when he saw his brother again; it is indeed true that nothing can achieve more than the true bonds of kinship. The chorus' first song was about *scelus alternum*, the alternation of crime and vengeance which is the plague of the Tantalus family, here representing the family of man, and about the vicious circle of vengeance which means that successive generations find ever

273

greater pleasure in ever growing crimes: divine justice no longer applies, nor does common injustice. The second chorus was about royal power: a king is not a man who has power over others, but one who has power over himself; the man who is known by all but dies without knowing himself is to be pitied. Now, however, on its third appearance, the chorus speaks in praise of the miraculous peace now reigning after the long civil war in which brother has slain brother — a good old theme from the days of Augustus. Admittedly, all the good and beautiful things said in this tragedy are uttered on a false basis: in their understanding of the cruelty afoot readers or audiences are constantly one step ahead of the characters, whose pious words and desires immediately stand as — theatrical illusions. Nevertheless, this sudden change for the better reminds the chorus how unstable is the state of man: no one should rely too much on his own happiness, and certainly not if he is in a position of power.

> You — to whom the ruler of earth and ocean
> Gives the dread power of life and death — be humble;
> That overweening face does not become you.
> No threat of yours that makes your subjects tremble
> Is greater than that your master holds above you.
> Kings of the earth must bow to a higher kingdom.
> Some, whom the rising sun sees high exalted,
> The same sun may see fallen at its departing.
>
> *Tragedies, p. 71*

Then the citizens must listen with horror to the messenger's detailed account of how Atreus, suitably observing all the sacred prescripts, sacrificed and dismembered his nephews on the altar of his house after using their entrails to take auguries, and then with his own hand prepared a banquet of them for their unsuspecting father — or does he perhaps suspect something? Now the chorus starts on a new theme: the peace which prevailed in all the world has given way to the cataclysm which will destroy it. The connection between events in the households of the great and cosmic phenomena was still a real one to the Romans. But while in 'Medea' it was the witch who brought disorder into nature because of the wrong that had been done to her, here it is nature itself which protests, by letting the sun sink in the wrong direction and encircling the sinful earth in darkness.

Atreus cries out in triumph as the gods flee from him: he feels competent to dismiss them. He represents a fully-developed and chronic form of the Caesarian madness which Hercules was a momentary victim of, and like another god he notes that everything is good, very good. But the best is yet to come: in delight he watches Thyestes vainly trying to enjoy himself after the great banquet — see, now he is going to sing, already slightly under the influence of the wine made from the children's blood. And in a solo aria, which we must imagine sung loudly to a raucous accompaniment, Thyestes tries to live up to the happy situation and praises himself for having borne misfortune so bravely and now bravely taking the burden of government upon himself — but he cannot quite manage it; tears love the channels to which they are accustomed — or is it great happiness which seeks an outlet in tears? A sense of dread stirs within him — he is digesting his sons — and he asks Atreus to bring his children to him. Through a series of devilish ambiguities Atreus gradually reveals their fate: his sons are closer to him than ever before, and they shall never be taken away from him. Thyestes feels ill, and the wine runs from his mouth; Atreus shows him the heads of his sons and tells him that he has all that remains of them as well as all that does not remain — Atreus is well schooled in rhetoric. Thyestes' grief and self-reproach and his prayer, not for redemption and forgiveness but for punishment and destruction, only make Atreus remark that he is upset that it was not he himself, Thyestes, who had the idea first; indeed Atreus works himself up into a state of moral indignation at the thought that Thyestes could have done it *to him*! In his desolation Thyestes can only leave Atreus to the gods whose existence he himself had previously doubted; with somewhat greater conviction Atreus can leave Thyestes to his own children.

But it is in this tragedy, the most godless of them all, that nature, fate, god, expresses divine displeasure with an obvious theatrical effect. Fate willed that Oedipus should commit his crime, but in the case of Atreus he wills it himself, and while in 'Oedipus' it is the gods who strike the earth with pestilence, in 'Thyestes' it is Atreus' misdeeds which introduce disharmony into cosmos. Even if disorder in the lives of man is not the same as disorder in nature, there is ultimately a unity of fate between heaven and earth: there are limits to the

275

amount of unnatural deviation and dissipation nature can tolerate — whether the moral decline is the symptom of a cosmic process of destruction or, as the chorus suggests, the reason for it:

'Heavy is the lot to which we were born: to lose the light of the sun or to drive it away.'

Even if it is not the will of fate determining the history of the Tantalus family, that history nevertheless is an irrevocable train of events which has to be played out; the progenitor of the family and the original cause of its shame, Tantalus himself appears in the prologue and is told by one of the furies, the goddesses of vengeance, what is about to happen in his house, with the result that he only wants to return to the torments of Tantalus in the underworld. Thyestes comes in rags and tatters to the palace in Argos and says fair words about preferring humble surrounding to luxurious ones, but nevertheless he changes his rags for royal garments in order to play the part allotted to him.

Seneca had no Greek model for this extremely Roman tragedy, but a couple of hundred years before *Accius* had written an 'Atreus' which is only known from a few quotations. On various occasions Seneca quotes the famous imperial saying: 'Let them hate me, provided they fear me'; and a couple of quotations in one of the epistles might well indicate that he himself had seen the play. There is a man crossing the stage and arrogantly proclaiming: 'Behold, I rule over Argos!' — he is a slave earning five denars a month. And the other, who says: 'Be still, Menelaos, you shall die by this hand!' — he has a pile of rags for a bed. The same can be said of all those pampered people who sway in their litters high above the common run of men — their fortune is a mask: tear it off, and you will despise them!

Perhaps in this interpretation of 'Atreus' we can find part of the inspiration for 'Thyestes'. If life is a play, how can the play be anything but a parody of life, i.e. of court life. There is something almost ridiculous in the construction of 'Thyestes', in the prior knowledge which the audience has of cruelty which is only gradually revealed to the characters in the play, in the pedantic description of the monstrous acts; 'Thyestes' has very rightly been called a marionette tragedy. These powerful men who in untrammelled freedom act from a neurotic determination to avenge wrongs by repeating them, are not

276

tragic figures but blown-up clowns, slaves of their desires, pipes for fortune's finger. It would be comical — if it were not the children who had to pay for the sins of their fathers.

The Atreus-Thyestes myth, like the sacrifice of the sons of Tantalus, points the way back to the cultic human sacrifice which Atreus so blasphemically parodies in Seneca's tragedy; there may be even a historical, cannibalistic basis for the Thyestes banquet. What was once a sacred act is already criminal in this myth: it expresses a warning against and a rejection of an ancient pattern, to which the omnipotent ruler, who feels himself raised above all more modern norms, is most liable to revert. Seneca's Roman updating of the myth is also a secularisation of it: man has liberated himself and put himself in the place of the gods — but human sacrifice does not become more humane when men are no longer sacrificed to gods but on behalf of other human beings.

'What custom is this? When was a human being used as a grave offering to a man?' asks Agamemnon in 'The Trojan Women', *Troades* — placing special emphasis on *man*, for he has himself sacrificed his daughter for the homeland when Artemis prevented the Greek fleet from coming to Troy. Now things have gone wrong again; the Greeks have won, but once more it is impossible to get a wind in their sails, and this is again thought to be because of the late Achilles; even while alive he was easily upset, and now, after his death, he still feels insulted and is demanding his share of the spoils, more specifically Polyxena, the daughter of King Priamus. Achilles' son Pyrrhus appears to plead his father's case to Agamemnon, who appears as the gentle ruler. He may well, he insists, have desired the defeat of Troy, but he would have preferred to prevent its destruction — however the desire for revenge could not be controlled; victory brings arrogance in its train, but it ought also to lead to caution, for where the victor now stands the vanquished once stood. In Agamemnon's reflections on victory there are probably reminiscences of another victor's, Scipio's, misgivings after the destruction of Carthage: 'I fear and foresee that one day someone else will tell the same news about our fatherland,' he is said to have remarked to Polybius in the hour of victory.

Now there must be an end to the slaughters, says Agamemnon, for he who has the power to command and does not prevent misdeeds, himself commands them. He will not tolerate the murder of a virgin,

277

which is justified as a sacrifice and glossed over as a 'wedding', for it is said that Polyxena is to be Achilles' 'bride': in politics men have always had the skill of giving fair names to foul deeds. But however wise his words, Agamemnon does not speak with real moral authority. The two warriors have both so many tender spots that it is easy for them to hurt each other. In the heat of battle Pyrrhus chances to praise his father for having given kings their lives — but of course it was Pyrrhus himself who killed King Priamus of Troy. Why did he do so? Because it is often more merciful to take away life than to give it. And then the argument starts:

> — And now in mercy would you have a maiden
> slaughtered upon a tomb?
> — Since when have you thought it a crime to sacrifice a
> maiden?
> — A king must put his country above his children.
> — No law forbids a prisoner's punishment.
> — Where law does not forbid, shame may forbid.
> — The victor has the right to please himself.
> — Who has most right, should least indulge his pleasure.
>
> *Tragedies, pp. 168–69*

But this wordy battle is only a battle of words; the soothsayer Calchas is given the last word and in the name of fate demands that Hector's young son Astyanax should be sacrificed as well as Polyxena. But fate, which demands such cruel sacrifices in so many Greek tragedies, is in this Roman version quite obviously merely political necessity being glossed over as the will of the gods; in Rome political manipulation of religion was part of the order of the day. Wise Ulixes (Odysseus) does not hide the fact that, apart from Calchas' interpretation of fate, there are plenty of political reasons for killing Hector's son: it is unwise to allow a potential avenger to grow up. But when Andromacha pleads for her son's life Ulixes is humane enough to swear that it is not he but Calchas and the gods who are demanding it.

While Seneca's heroes and heroines in general suffer from (what the chorus in 'Agamemnon' calls) a 'horrible love of life', even when they want to take their own lives, Andromacha after the death of Hector is finished with life; she is paralysed and numbed — she uses the word

278

stupor of her condition, a term which has become a technical expression for reaction-less passivity. Hector, who is still the master of her mind, has commanded her to be prepared; he has appeared to her in a dream, not as a hero but in a pitiable condition — yet he was still fair to behold! — and commanded her to hide her son, but there is not so much of Troy left that a child can be hidden in it. Finally she has managed to hide him in Hector's burial mound, confident that the Greeks will not commit sacrilege — and declares that Astyanax is no longer among the living. When Ulixes replies that that is fortunate for her, as he would otherwise have been cast down from a tower, she is naturally terrified, and Ulixes asks what she is afraid of, for her son *is* dead. When he threatens to level Hector's burial mound she has to admit what she has done and to hand over Astyanax; when, as his weeping mother takes her leave of him and Ulixes is waiting impatiently, he realises what fate awaits him, he begs his *mother* to spare his life, *Miserere mater* — one of the passages in Seneca reminding us that he was a predecessor of Shakespeare.

In the next episode another unhappy woman appears, fair Helena (as she used to be), for whom Greeks and Trojans have fought for years, a woman equally hated by victors and vanquished; she is entirely alone in her sorrow, while they at least can share their happiness and misery with each other. As an indirect commentary on her fate the Trojan women sing of the comfort of having another with whom to share sorrow:

> All are content to bear what all are bearing.
> If none were happy, none would believe himself
> Unfortunate, however great his troubles.
> Take away wealth, and gold, and thriving lands
> With droves of oxen at the plough — how then
> The spirits of the down-pressed poor would rise!
> What is misfortune but comparison?
>
> *Tragedies p. 198*

The tragedy begins and ends with Hecuba, Priamus' queen, who is also finished with life, but whom death in its cruelty refuses to claim. She sees the last members of the royal family being taken to their deaths, while in the lottery to divide the spoils of war she falls to Ulixes.

Finally we are told how Polyxena and Astyanax met their deaths, scorning death with Stoic calm, lamented by both Trojans and Greeks. Hecuba's words are bitterly ironic: Sail home in safety, you men of Greece; the girl and boy are dead, the war is ended. In high spirits the Greek messenger hurries the captured Trojan women along: now there is wind in the sails, and the fleet can put to sea!

Hecuba touches on the main theme in Seneca's tragedies in the very first lines:

> The man who puts his trust in kingly power,
> The potentate wielding authority
> In his high court, having no fear of gods
> And their capricious will, the man who takes
> His happy state for granted — let that man
> Look upon me, and upon thee, O Troy.
> Here is the proof, the strongest ever given
> By Fate,[1] to show on what uncertain ground
> The pomp of power stands.

Tragedies, p. 155

But 'The Trojan Women' differs from the other tragedies in being more — tragic, if by tragedy we mean undeserved suffering. This time fate has not been challenged by presumptuous rulers; the destruction of Troy does not have the character of a punishment, but is rather the end of the world which has been ordained. Hecuba and Andromacha are only the first ladies among the nameless Trojan women after whom the tragedy is named and whose common experience of pain purges and enriches it; their choruses are among the most beautiful Seneca wrote. But if 'The Trojan Women' is less 'negative' than the other tragedies, almost all of which end on a note of grinding disharmony, it is because death is presented in a positive light. 'Call no one happy before he is dead,' was the wise old Greek saying with which Sophocles' 'Oidipus' ended; the Trojan women call Priamus happy *because* he is dead. And although they believe him to be in Elysium, they place their hopes not on a life after death, but a death after life:

---

1. i.e. Fortune.

Racing in the Circus Maximus in Rome. The race, in which at most twelve chariots could take part, was run around the 'spine' spina, which can be seen in the centre of the picture, and which was equipped with a lap counter and so much decoration that the spectators had difficulty in seeing everything. At each end of the spina stood three conical columns, metae, which had to be passed seven times. The winning chariot has just passed the post; an official is waving the palm of victory. According to tradition, the Circus Maximus was built at the time of the kings; it was rebuilt by Julius Caesar and, according to Pliny, at the time of the Emperors it could hold a quarter of a million spectators; only the official organisers are seen on the picture. Relief on side of sarcophagus, 3rd century A.D.. Museo Civico, Foligno.

The Circus Maximus was almost 600 metres long. The walls facing the street were lined with shops, in one of which the fire broke out in the summer of 64 A.D.. The chariots started in starting bays under the buildings in the northern end (foreground). The obelisk in the centre of the spina was erected under Augustus and now stands on the Piazza del Popolo. Detail of a reconstruction of Rome in the 4th century A.D.. Museo communale di Roma.

Floods in the Nile delta. A victory (?) is being celebrated in the pergola covered with vines and in the summerhouse in the foreground. In front of the summerhouse are a bowl and drinking horn for the Roman soldiers. In the wickerwork hut the sacrificial animals are being tended; on its roof there

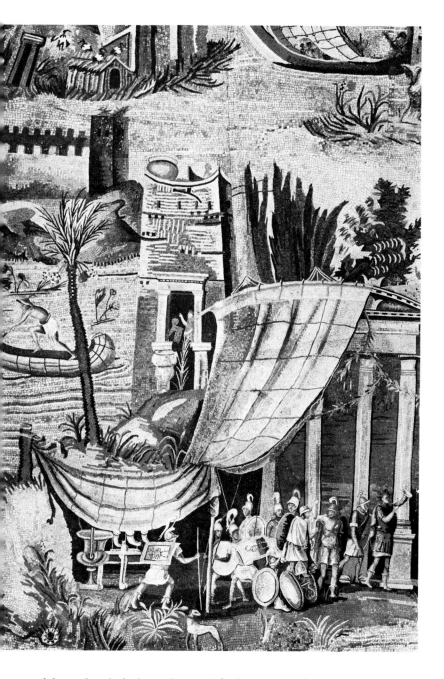

are sacred ibis, and in the background a temple for them; on the left an
Egyptian temple. Detail of mosaic from Palestrina (Præneste), 2nd
century A.D.. Palazzo Barberini, Palestrina.

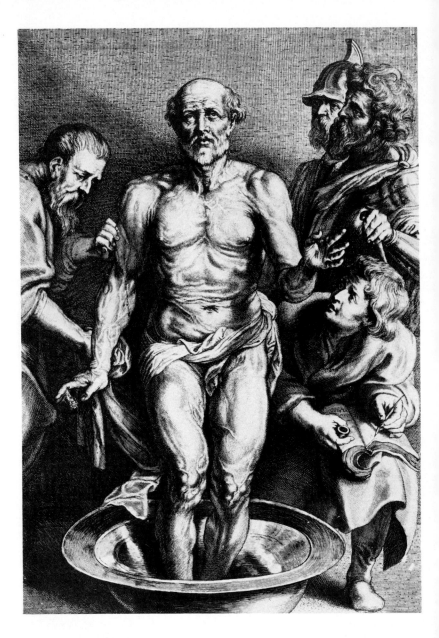

The death of Seneca. The picture is inspired by Tacitus' account, but is scarcely historically accurate. The artist has clad his figures in the garments of his own day; the hair and beards are also in the fashions he knew, while Seneca's bath tub is a little on the small side. Print after painting by Rubens. Rubens Museum, Antwerp.

Is it the truth, or but an idle tale
To give false comfort to our fears,
That the soul lives on when the body is laid to rest,
When the wife has sealed the husband's eyes,
When the last sun has set,
When the ashes are shut into the solemn urn?
Do we in vain give up our life to death?
Has the poor mortal still more time to live?
Or do we wholly die?

Tragedies, p. 170

It is not so terrible, is the reply: death is a 'whole' and strikes at the soul as well as the body; the realm of the dead is only an unpleasant dream, and if you want to know where you are to be after your death, then ask where they are who are still unborn.

'Thyestes' and 'The Trojan Women' are dramas about destruction, one desperate and wild, the other serene and gentle in its sense of doom; these are the masterpieces of Seneca's dramatic writings and his most original works; 'The Trojan Women' has no more than the general framework in common with Euripides' tragedy by the same name.

The chronology of the tragedies

Nothing is known of when the tragedies were written, or in what order; they are neither mentioned by contemporary writers nor by Seneca himself. So scholars have been completely free to make up their own minds on this point and they are in such disagreement that it is impossible to say what 'scholarly opinion' on them is. A favourite method has been to find contemporary references and then to conclude that the tragedies are contemporary with the events concerned; and as life at court had a good deal in common with the ancient myths, almost everything can be seen as a reference to something or other. So in the vengeful Medea it is possible for those who want to see a portrait of the vengeful Agrippina, who admittedly was not a witch, but nevertheless was allied to one. It is more reasonable to see allusions to Nero in 'Furious Hercules' and thus to date that to the beginning of Nero's reign.

Another method has been to compare passages in the tragedies with related passages in the philosophical work. In his work on Seneca (which is more voluminous than informative) Léon Herrmann has made a detailed comparison and has for instance reached the conclusion that links between 'Thyestes' and the epistles are very numerous indeed, but strangely enough he then places 'Thyestes' among Seneca's earliest tragedies, and it can be difficult to understand the point in an analysis of this mind. Admittedly, one cannot take it completely for granted that related passages are from the same time, for Seneca did not change his opinions even if his mood changed as time went on. For instance, Medea says that a man without hope knows no fear either; in the 5th Epistle this saying is ascribed to the philosopher Hecaton. Meanwhile, it is not necessary to be a Hecaton or a Medea or a Seneca to get that idea — it is more surprising that Andromacha in 'The Trojan Women' says that the worst is to be feared when no hope is left — and that can obviously not be found in the philosophical work. On the other hand Phaedra's nurse says roughly the same as Epicure said: that a criminal might well be able to live in safety, but not in security, and as Seneca formulates this idea in Epistles 97 and 105, and as Hippolytus' pessimistic view of culture as expressed in the monologue in 'Phaedra' corresponds exactly to Seneca's own view of history as put in Epistle 90, and as the chorus on *fatum* and *fortuna* corresponds to the ideas in 'On providence', there is some likelihood that 'Phaedra' was written during Seneca's retirement.

A couple of younger contemporary writers give some clues on chronology. Quintillian, the professor of rhetoric, who was born c. 35, tells that in his youth he heard introductions 'in which the propriety of a phrase for a tragedy was discussed between Seneca and Pomponius Secundus'; — presumably he is referring to some introductory discussion preceding the reading of one of the tragedies. Pomponius was also a dramatist, and a play by him had resulted in violence in 47; in his official capacity he was in Germania from 50 to 51, and Seneca was in exile until 49; so the discussion must have taken place towards the end of Claudius' reign; and if the Miliboeus (p155) who among other things is praised as a tragic poet in Calpurnius Siculus' bucolic poems, is alluding to Seneca (as seems likely), he must have been known as the writer of tragedies at the beginning of Nero's reign. In 62 Tacitus mentions the accusations made against Seneca for writing more *carmina* now that Nero himself was writing them; *carmen* (*tragicum*) was a common word for tragedy. This confirms that Seneca was writing tragedies in the sixties, and it is reasonable to date 'Phaedra', 'Thyestes' and 'The Trojan Women' to this period, at least if it is reasonable to think of Seneca's more 'mature' works as being later than the less mature ones.

Other writers have also considered 'Oedipus' and 'Agamemnon' to be less original. They differ from the other tragedies in that they contain 'polymetrical' choruses, that is to say choruses in which the metre is constantly changing, an external decoration that is more likely in a less experienced writer than a more experienced one. Then there are some technically clumsy aspects: two choruses in 'Oedipus' end with stage directions: 'What it this? A door is opening, one of the king's slaves approaches, hand on forehead. Tell us the news.' In other tragedies the chorus goes over to ordinary iambic verse when it describes what is happening on the stage, and in 'Medea', 'Thyestes' and 'The Trojan Women' these pieces of stage information are completely absent. On the whole it looks as if the later the tragedies the better they are, but the same applies to this argument as to all others leading to completely different results, that it justifies a feeling rather than proves anything. The dating of the tragedies is in any case not terribly important, but there might be a connection between when and why they were written.

Intention and effect

What was Seneca aiming at in his tragedies? Until a few years ago scholars were fairly definite that they were not intended for performance but only for reading aloud. Plays were written in Rome in order to earn money, and it is 'incredible that Seneca, one of the richest men in Rome and a man who openly admits his distaste for close contact with the common people or their amusements, should have composed plays intended to win the favour of the general public.' In Seneca's day there were no longer regular performances of tragedy and comedy in Rome; along with the gladiatorial games and the races, it was the mimes which enjoyed public favour. Seneca certainly disliked most of these forms of entertainment, but on various occasions stressed the enormous effect which the moral sayings of the mimes could have, adding: 'How much more true this is when a philosopher utters such words, when his verses are permeated with moral precepts, for they are far more effective in putting over his teachings to uneducated spectators!' Seneca believed thoughts have a far profounder effect when expressed in verse, and so it seems likely that he was seeking to attract the interest of a larger audience with his verse; his dislike of the entertainments preferred by the ordinary people might make him want to replace them with others. The strange thing, that a humane person like Seneca should wallow in blood in his tragedies is less strange if we think that he wrote them for a Roman public which was used to stronger stuff. Seneca's tragedies are more pointedly dramatic than their Greek counterparts, and the terrifying effects are aimed as much at the eye as at the ear — it is an unreasonable hypothesis to suppose that Seneca only intended them for reading aloud in one-man-shows. These theatrical heroes, loudly declaiming their own prowess, must be imagined complete with masks and buskins, and the melodramatic style which a modern reader might find it difficult to take (and which indeed can seem empty when the Latin verse is translated into modern prose), requires all the available trappings: flutes, drums and thunder machines, if it is to make its full impact. But it is one thing that Seneca with all his popped-up terror effects did what he could to catch the imagination of a larger audience, and like any other dramatist wanted to see his characters brought to life on a stage — and a completely different one whether his tragedies were in fact performed during his lifetime.

Public performances of tragedies by Seneca would in fact have been such notable occasions, especially while he was one of the most powerful men in the Empire, that there would have been rumours and reports of them. But it was quite common for rich private individuals to have private troupes of actors, and in particular the Emperors usually did. It is true that Seneca did not need to write tragedies to earn money, but on the other hand he had the means of having them performed — or at least Nero had. In his edition of the tragedies Theodor Thomann has tried to show their stage qualities and has argued that they were intended for 'Nero's court theatre'; Nero always pursued his interests in narrower private circles before he did so publicly, and it is reasonable to suppose that both Greek and Roman tragedies were performed at court. Even the accusations levelled at Seneca for wanting to out-do the emperor as a poet indicate that Seneca encouraged Nero in his artistic interests, which are even indirectly defended in 'Furious Hercules'. But as also appears from the case of Lucanus, Nero, who long delighted in surrounding himself with poets and philosophers, at one time became professionally jealous of all other poets, and what until then might have been a form of cooperation could not be so any longer. Seneca's last tragedies could not be performed at court, but some of the earlier ones might well have been — and on Seneca's part they may well have been intended as a contribution to the 'Greek' cultural policy which Nero's artistic activities signified.

It is quite easy to produce historical evidence proving that the tragedies are suitable for performance. Soon after appearing for the first time in book form, in Ferrara in 1484, 'Phaedra' was performed in the Forum in Rome; in 1551—52 'The Trojan Women' was staged in Trinity College, Cambridge, and Seneca's tragedies were the principal literary inspiration for English Renaissance drama; Shakespeare, who knew 'little Latin and less Greek', nevertheless appears to have read Seneca in Latin, and in one of his first tragedies, 'Titus Andronicus', he tried to out-do 'Thyestes' in horror. As a tragedian, Seneca has had his second renaissance in our time; 'Thyestes' was staged in Italy in 1967, and 'Medea' in France in the same year. In 1968 followed Peter Brook's version of 'Oedipus'. It has even been said that Seneca, who depicts the individual's unhappy struggle against merciless powers, could very well be the dramatist of our time — however worrying this might be.

Perhaps our age can recognise in these terrifying nightmares something of the self-aggrandizement of the modern emancipated individual, deprived of all norms and standing on the brink of catastrophe. What more harmonious ages have dismissed as theatrical and unrealistic might in these days appear more original — even 'primal'. It is not for nothing that various of the myths employed by Seneca tell of exposed children crying for their parents and cursing their gods. Seneca interprets the latent pathology of the myths in the Roman spirit; there is more 'neurotic' tension in his tragedies than in the Greek dramas; they are no longer ritual and not yet realistic dramas, but a sort of psychical drama, humane in intent but brutal in inspiration. What Antonin Artaud wrote in the 1930's on 'the theatre of cruelty' can be applied to Seneca's drama better than to that of anyone else: 'The theatre will not... become a real means of creating illusion until it feeds its audience on realistic precipitations of dreams, in which its criminal sense, its erotic obsessions, its wildness, its chimeras, its utopian view of life and things, indeed even its cannibalism is catered for, not on a falsified and illusory level, but inside it.'

Seneca's own court tragedy, 'Octavia'

Seneca's 'bloodthirsty' tragedies have actually been used as an argument against his professed humanism. But it is naive to believe that a philosopher who so passionately encouraged the control of the passions had himself no passions to control. In one of his first epistles he writes of the enjoyment of artistic creation, and it is probable that he himself enjoyed 'going out of his mind' and 'putting aside dullness and sobriety for a time'.

The most amazing place in his prose writings is in his essay 'On providence'. In it Seneca refers to the foolhardy youth Phaeton, who insisted on driving the chariot of his father, the sun god, and had an accident which almost set the world ablaze; he calls him 'this generous adolescent' and speaks highly of him for having said that the trip appealed to him and that the journey was worth a fall. For it is the lowly and weak soul which always seeks the safe way, the lofty soul seeks what is lofty. This admittedly stands in contrast to the many wise choruses about seeking the safe middle road. Had Seneca for a time had enough of the wise man, and had he after all a foible for youth and its daring? Phaeton's flight into the heavens and to his death was, it is interesting to note, depicted on murals in Nero's *Domus aurea*.

Of course Seneca must have viewed Nero's licentiousness with horror. But when in 'On good deeds' he defended the murder of a tyrant, had he completely lost the sympathy he used to have for his beloved pupil? And even if he could tell himself and thus indirectly tell the public that he had done what lay in his power, could he avoid a sense of responsibility? In the tragedies which (we imagine) he wrote in his retirement, in the desperation of 'Thyestes', in the resignation of

'The Trojan Women' it is tempting to see a profound and personal addition to the portrait of Seneca contained in the Epistles to Lucilius. In many of the epistles Seneca speaks philosophically and in principle about suicide; Oedipus' monologues in the unfinished 'Phoenician Women' are as it were filled with a suicide urge. In Epistle 104 Seneca writes that it is his duty to live for Pompeja Paulina, who lives for him, and in 'The Phoenician Women' Oedipus declares himself ready to suffer all conceivable torments and still live for the sake of Antigona. Oedipus, the once wise ruler, who is now exhorted to exercise his influence on his vicious sons; Agamemnon who preaches gentleness to the deaf ears of Pyrrhus; Thyestes who when exiled from court sings the praise of frugality but allows himself to be tempted back to the deadly court life — all these figures express so much of Seneca himself that his tragedies can also be read as evidence of Seneca's own court tragedy.

Suetonius writes of Nero that: 'Proud and arrogant because of his successful atrocities, he said that no one before him had known how much a prince can allow himself.' After *his* successful atrocities Seneca's Atreus says something similar and feels competent to dismiss the gods. A Roman audience would not see Seneca's court tragedies as historical dramas; the mythical terrors did not belong to the past for those living in court circles in Rome, where the original crime of fratricide was almost the custom: those with the strongest claim to the throne were by definition also close relatives. Tacitus says that Augustus 'never went so far in brutality as to have a member of his family killed', but immediately after his accession his successor Tiberius had his adoptive brother, Augustus' grandchild Agrippa Postumus, put to death. Caligula ordered Tiberius' grandson and *his* adoptive brother Tiberius to commit suicide — it was unfitting for anyone to lay hands on a member of the imperial family, and the neglected young man who had not received a suitable training in the use of weapons had in his last moments to ask to be shown how best to take his own life. On his accession Claudius had no brother whom he needed to kill, but Nero let Claudius' son and his own adoptive brother Britannicus drink poison 'in cups of gold'. All this did not cause any great stir amongst the Emperor's subjects: 'They thought of the old fratricidal conflicts and of the impossibility of two men sharing the throne,' says Tacitus.

Myth, the myth of Romulus and Remus, Eteocles and Polynices, Atreus and Thyestes could thus actually be used as a sort of motivation for a certain brand of *Realpolitik*. For different reasons of *Realpolitik* there was all the more cause for Seneca to attack the myth. If the myth expresses the desires which man has but the law forbids (and Freud's discovery of the Oedipus complex seems to indicate this), will the man who is not bound by the law but can allow himself to follow his desires not to live up to — or down to — the mythical patterns? The ancient barbarity still made itself felt in high places, in those who as it were stood above society, up there where the law places no constraints on — the man who is the supreme guarantor of the law. But if it is right that men go wild when they are not kept in check, the tyrant is right in arguing that people must be kept down by force and violence if they are to be prevented from behaving violently against other men. The opposite point of view, the humane conception, is that it is compulsion which makes men go wild and power which corrupts, and the power struggle is at its most brutal on the pinnacles of society. In Seneca's tragedies the two viewpoints are placed face to face as the expression of a basic conflict between brutality and humanity:

Minister:	Let the king want what's right, who will oppose him?
Atreus:	The king who binds himself to want what's right sits on a shaky throne.
Minister:	No throne can stand where there is neither shame nor law nor trust nor care for sanctity or piety.

Tragedies p.54

Oedipus:	No king can rule who is afraid of hatred. Fear is the sovereign's shield.
Creon:	But when men fear, then must imperious sovereignty fear them. Fear must recoil upon its author's head.

p.236

Eteocles:	It the king will be loved, he rules with the hand of a weakling.

288

Iocasta:	If the king's power is hated, it lasts but a short while.
Nero:	Am I forbidden to do what all may do?
Seneca:	From high rank high example is expected.
Nero:	Fine government, when subjects rule their masters!
Seneca:	Their rage has cause if all their prayers are fruitless.

p.279

These last lines are from the tragedy 'Octavia' which has come down to us among Seneca's tragedies, though it cannot have been written by him as he appears in it. 'Octavia' is the only extant Roman tragedy with a theme that is Roman and historical rather than Greek and mythical, and it shows that it is not *there* the difference lies. Here it is not Tantalus or Thyestes but Agrippina who, as the personification of the evil genius of the family turns up from the underworld; here it is not Hippolytus but Seneca who casts longing glances back to the golden age, and it is also he who, like the chorus in 'Thyestes', fears that this is the end of time, for crime reigns supreme, lawlessness rages and evil desires are triumphant.

The tragedy takes place in 62; Nero wants to have Plautus and Sulla executed and to dismiss Octavia in favour of Poppæa; Seneca seeks to dissuade him. The author betrays a close knowledge of Seneca's works and makes him use his own words in the great dialogue with Nero, but Nero does not lack arguments either, and he produces the obvious objection to the idea that gentleness is the tyrant's best defence: it cost Julius Caesar his life.

The author of this Roman drama has taken one of the most dramatic situations in the early imperial age, one of the few moves towards a popular rebellion — characteristically enough caused by the repudiation of Octavia. But all the people achieve is to make the Emperor furious; when Octavia's nurse comforts her by saying that 'the people's power is great', her reply is short and incontrovertible: 'But the Emperor's is greater.' And indeed, Nero can make light of Seneca's warnings; here Seneca has to play the same part as the nurse or the servant in his own tragedies. However, in contrast to them he does not give way but insists on his point of view until finally the Emperor has to command him to be silent: You are too difficult for me; I can take liberties of which Seneca disapproves.

Since 'Octavia' was written by a contemporary (possibly a certain Curiatus Maternus) it shows how at least some men of his day saw Seneca's 'role' at court. This court tragedy leaves no doubt that it is not the supreme and independent ruler but the philosopher who is supreme and independent. Only there is nothing more he can do than utter words of wisdom. 'Octavia' is not by Seneca, but it is his personal tragedy.

X: NERO AND SENECA

Nero's mythical history

About A.D. 200 Philostrates wrote an account of the Greek philosopher Apollonius of Tyana, a contemporary of Jesus and Seneca; in it Nero's Rome is portrayed as a police state with spies on every street corner. On his way to the city, accompanied by 35 disciples, Apollonius is warned against Nero, who publicly takes part in the races, sings in the Roman theatres, consorts with gladiators, indeed even appears as a gladiator himself and cuts the throats of people in the arena.

'Dear friend,' replies the philosopher, 'Can you imagine a more interesting sight in the eyes of intelligent men than an emperor who is so shameless? Plato says that man is the plaything of the gods, but an emperor who has become the plaything of men and can show off so shamefully to the rabble — that indeed is an interesting subject for philosophers to discuss.'

'But Nero can have eaten you all raw before you have the opportunity of seeing him perform,' is the reply. And when Apollonius walked into Rome, only eight disciples followed him.

Even Greek writers share the Roman indignation at the Greek-minded Emperor's Greek pastimes — and add the non-Greek ones as well in order to make the story better, for there is no reliable historical evidence to confirm that Nero actually performed as a gladiator or indulged in cannibalism. Nero continued to prefer peaceful competitions to the bloody ones and would rather be seen on the race-track than in the battle field, where he never put in an appearance; it rebounded on him, but the fatal flaw was not his interest in sport and art as such but the fact that he lost interest in the Empire at the same time as personally taking over control of it. His 'own' period of rule is marked by grandiose initiatives in the fields which enjoyed his personal interest, especially the rebuilding of Rome after the fire, his own 'golden house', which architecturally speaking was a pioneer work, the canals through the Corinthian Isthmus from the Avernus Lake in the Campagna through the mountains to the mouth of the Tiber — though none of the

291

projects was completed. In his final years Nero had plans for an expedition to the Caucasus, perhaps because he wanted to blaze new trade routes to the East, perhaps because he wanted to crown his Greek triumphs by following in the footsteps of Alexander the Great. Until now he had admittedly not started any wars, but been content to suppress attempts at breakaway or rebellion, in Armenia, Britain and, from 66, also in Judaea, but now he raised a legion of particularly tall Italics (over 1.80 metres) which was to be called the Alexander the Great Phalanx.

Nero's own special legion had so far been the five thousand 'augustians' of the equestrian class, who saw to the artificial applause when Nero performed, and his greatest triumphal procession was a tour of Greece from September 66 to the beginning of 68; in order to be able to take part in all the Greek games he had got the 211th Olympic Games postponed from 65 to 67; for the first and last time in the history of the Games he also managed to have included a competition in music and drama; and the Emperor won both this and that and much more besides, and his trophies filled several waggons. He did not visit Sparta, where the strict discipline probably did not appeal to him, nor did he go to Athens, according to rumour because he was afraid of the Furies there which had tormented the matricide Orestes. In Corinth he proclaimed Greek 'freedom' on the 28th November 67, a word which sounded sweet to Greek ears, but in reality meant little more than exemption from tax; an inscription of the proclamation is still extant and gives a good impression of Nero's imperial style: he was now writing his own speeches:

'Unexpected, O men of Greece, is the gift I give to you, although perhaps everything can be expected of my generosity, and so great is it that you could not have asked for it. All Greeks who live in Achaja and the country until now called Peloponnes are hereby given freedom and exemption from taxes, something which you did not all enjoy in your happiest days, for you were all the subjects of foreigners or of each other. I would wish I had been able to give this gift when Hellas stood in full flower, so that more could have profitted by it, and I must remonstrate with time which came before me. Yet it is not from sympathy but from kindness I act thus kindly to you, and as a thanksgiving to your gods whose benevolent providence I have always felt on land and sea, and which has given me the opportunity to perform so great a beneficial deed, for other rulers have given freedom to cities, but Nero alone to a whole province.'

Another highlight of Nero's foreign policy was the reception of the Armenian king Tiridates, who was to receive the royal crown from the hand of Nero — he already had the kingdom. The war against the Parthans, which had gone on intermittently throughout Nero's reign, had finally ended with an agreement that both parties should leave Armenia, the king of which was the half-brother of the Parthan king: he was to be recognised and formally installed by Rome. The journey was paid for by Rome; it cost 800,000 sesterces a day and lasted for nine months. Nero received his vassal in Naples and conducted him to Rome, where Rome turned up in its entirety, and Nero in his triumphal robes gave a fresh sample of his rhetoric:

'You have done right to come in your own personage to enjoy my gracious favour. For what your father did not give you as an inheritance and your brothers could not give and ensure you, I will give you: I hereby make you King of Armenia, so that both you and they may know that I have the power to take and to give kingdoms.'

Nero's urge for self-aggrandizement, which these speeches indicate, and his predilection for the grandiose, which marks all his undertakings, is also obvious in the colossal statue he had erected of himself about where the Colosseum (which was called after it) now stands. All these colossal projects demanded colossal sums of money, and Nero has the honour of having introduced one of the first known devaluations in history, a reduction in the value of gold and silver coins, which gave the state or imperial coffers a large once-and-for all profit; but it was not sufficient. In his youth Nero had wanted to abolish all indirect taxes for the sake of the people, but now he had to resort to more traditional methods by increasing taxation and confiscating the estates of rich men, possibly after first condemning them to death. It was the custom for the distinguished to show their distinction and gratitude by leaving part of their fortune to the Emperor — in particular those who were in disgrace, hoping thereby to prevent the Emperor's anger from being inherited by their children. The provincial officials were given orders to extract as much as possible from the provinces, and no further lawsuits were carried out against governors who exceeded their powers. An inscription from Egypt, which of course was the Emperor's 'own' province, tells, soon after the death of Nero, of various forms of abuse which the new government promises to abolish.

All sources are agreed on dividing Nero's principate into a 'good' time (Nero's first 'five-year period') and a 'bad' time, and both Tacitus and Dio Cassius date the good time to the period when Seneca and Burrus had influence. 'They took the entire government into their own hands and administered matters as well and justly as they could and won the applause of all,' writes Dio, who admittedly says that they gave up after the death of Britannicus, while Tacitus lets Nero's fury start with the death of Agrippina. But a distinct change in Nero's attitude and the policy of his government is only demonstrable in 62 when Seneca retired and Nero sought support from Tigellinus: his brutal acts, which so far had only been 'private', now became general and public.

Did Nero change, or did he, as he freed himself from his mother and Seneca, merely show himself in his true colours — and as he had been all along? Busts and portraits of Nero on coins show that his originally handsome head changed both its expression and its size and finally appeared as grandiose as his speeches to Tiridates and the men of Greece. The expression in his eyes, which metal and marble admittedly do not easily capture, appears to become more and more sombre; his mouth shrank into his fat cheeks and was pushed further and further up towards his nose by his chin, which protruded more and more. But these physiognomical changes and the grand gestures need not necessarily be symptoms of deeper psychotic processes. Nero's cruelty expressed itself originally in panic actions; the mere suspicion of danger made him lose his head, as is especially shown by his reaction to the first (false) accusation against Agrippina (p158), and it was only the great and unsuccessful conspiracy in 65 which made him see danger lurking everywhere and made his brutality chronic. Nero was afraid of his mother and of the other members of the imperial family, and exterminated them more to get rid of his fear than because of real threats. But his fear was justified in a way, and Nero suffered not from any ordinary kind of madness, but from 'Caesarian madness', a kind of maladjustment which an emperor had to be more than normally normal to avoid. It demanded rationality and a strength of character which Augustus and Tiberius and in his way even Claudius, peculiar as he was, had, but which the imaginative and volatile Nero did not have. Who could continue to see himself as an ordinary person when others paid homage to him as a superman and even as a god? The Romans admittedly looked askance at the adulation of the Emperor as a god which was common in the East; perhaps it was for that reason Nero planned his Alexander expedition to the East and wanted to visit Egypt, where he was accounted the saviour and benefactor of the world, and otherwise preferred the Greeks who hailed him as Zeus the Liberator, as Hercules Augustus, the New Sun and the New Apollo. But even in Rome he went further than his predecessors and after 65 appeared on a coin as Apollo Citharoedus.

Apparently Nero wanted to believe in his own divinity and like other 'divinely inspired' artists had difficulty in distinguishing between the applause of the public and the favour of the gods. For he had a passionate need for applause, writes Suetonius, and he was zealous in his opposition to others who sought public favour in the theatre or the circus. As for the other gods, he does not appear to have been particularly devoted to them; the Syrian goddess Atargatis was the only one whom for a short time he found it worth worshipping, but he let down this goddess of love in favour of a little statuette of a girl which he thought protected him against conspiracies, something which tells us a thing or two about Nero's 'faith': he often resorted to magic to overcome his fear, and according to Pliny he tried all kinds of it. He wanted to be able to command the gods, for 'the deepest vices of the soul gave him greater pleasure than the music of the cither and the singing in tragedies'. Pliny also believes it would have been better if the powers of evil had given him their help than that he should have had to use prostitutes and mistresses as his spies! But Nero did not think the magic worked, and magicians maintained that freckled people could not establish contact with the powers. To this Pliny objects that Nero was not freckled! On the contrary, he says, he was extremely good looking (though somewhat fat as the years went by), and if he did not learn to apply the magical punishments which Tiridates had taught him during his visit to Rome, it was probably because they were humbug — thought Pliny.

It is doubtful whether Nero really was fonder of the black arts than the arts, but he obviously came to the conclusion that all virtues are insufficient to make a man perfect. To the old saying of Terence, which Seneca was fond of quoting: I am a human being, nothing human shall be unknown to me, he added: nor anything inhuman! He is said to have asserted that all men are lecherous, but that most manage to hide it, and is also supposed to have said that no prince before him had shown what liberties a prince can allow himself, 'for he considered it one of the duties of the Emperor not to be second to anyone, not even in the very worst of vices' (Dio). It is to be assumed that as he realised what liberties he could take Nero discovered with amazement how many splendid vices he had.

Was Nero a particularly depraved person — or was he simply particularly favoured by *Fortuna*, to whom he built a temple in his golden house? 'I will never strictly speaking advise anyone to be confident that he has strength enough not to become a Nero,' writes Kierkegaard's Judge Wilhelm (whose analysis of Nero is otherwise without any historical foundation). This was also Seneca's opinion, if we are to judge by his words of praise and warning in 'On gentleness' and by the view often expressed elsewhere and especially in the 42nd Epistle that: 'It is only their unfortunate position which prevents many people from rivalling the most depraved in brutality, ambition and dissipation.' Powerlessness makes vice powerless, power makes it powerful.

This is one principal theme in Seneca's tragedies. Many people have been surprised and many have made the objection that Seneca, who pleaded for humanity in his moral writings, delighted in brutality in his blood-dripping tragedies. But there would be no reason to plead for humanity, no cause for humanism, if the inhuman were completely outside the bounds of human possibility. Writers need not be particularly complex just because they have a particular understanding of the complex: Even the elder Seneca had asked: 'Do you perhaps believe poets write what they themselves advocate?' (p72) To turn brutality into myth and poetry is also a way of controlling it; to anticipate in the imagination is to prevent in reality. But for Nero, who found it easy to turn his imagination into reality, it was a different matter. According to Dio Cassius the roles he liked best were:

> Oedipus, who murdered his father and got his mother with child,
> Orestes, who murdered his mother, who had already murdered his father,
> Thyestes, who had his brother put to death,
> Hercules, who in madness killed his wife and children,
> Alcmeon, who killed his mother, by whom he felt betrayed, and
> Canace, who committed incest with her brother.

Apart from the fact that Nero had no brothers and sisters with whom to commit incest, and that his daughter died a natural death, he committed, if the accounts of the historians are to be believed, in reality all the crimes, the perpetrators of which he depicted on the stage. It is told of Nero that:

> If not the perpetrator, he was at least a participant in the murder of his stepfather, Claudius (and that once when he heard someone praising mushrooms as a celestial repast he said that his father had certainly become a god after eating some).
>
> He had a sexual relationship with his mother; though historians are not agreed as to whether he seduced her or vice versa. In any case Nero had amongst his mistresses one who bore a striking similarity to Agrippina.
>
> He had his stepbrother Britannicus murdered after sexually assaulting him several times during the days before the murder.
>
> He had his first wife Octavia murdered after having tried several times to strangle her.
>
> When his second wife Poppæa reproached him for coming home late from the races, he kicked her so hard she died of it.
>
> He had her son, his stepson, killed 'because he played at being Emperor'.

Either the historians have turned Nero's life into a myth, or he did so himself, or else it was a bit of both. That he consciously tried to make his private life 'mythical' is obvious from the fact that when he appeared on stage he had the heroes' and the gods' and goddesses' and heroines' masks drawn with his own features and those of his mistresses and lovers. The last time he appeared he is said to have spoken an Oedipus monologue ending with the words: 'Now my wife, my mother and my father demand that I should die.'

Suetonius has a curious remark to the effect that Nero did not usually dream, and although it cannot be true it is reasonable enough that Nero should have discounted dreams, as he could experience everything in reality which others could only dream of. But he was not only a man who could allow himself everything: it was not for nothing that he preferred to play suffering heroes and also died in that role. And although the Romans were jubilant at his death they soon began to miss him; they did not exactly imagine that he, like other suffering heroes, would arise from the dead, but at least they imagined him still to be alive: 'There were all kinds of rumour current about his death; all the more frequently it was asserted that he was still alive, and finally this is what they believed.' It was not only the Christians who made a myth of Nero, by turning him into the Anti-Christ: the Romans did so as well. There was obviously a 'mythical' receptiveness in the people who were ready to believe the best and the worst about the greatest, preferably both at the same time. Until Nero's Greek journey it was the minority rather than the majority who took offence at his behaviour, and the historians, who painted his picture, belonged to the minority.

In three areas Nero went too far in the opinion of the historians: in his artistic activities, his sexual activities and his brutality. The more harmless artistic liberties which he took led to far more indignation than the sexual liberties, which the Romans were used to from their emperors, and as for brutality, they were more than used to it. Let us now take a look at his achievements in all these spheres.

Nero as the artist and suffering hero

Ancient writers do not agree on Nero as a creative artist; Tacitus writes that his poems lack power and originality, Suetonius credits him with some talent as a poet, painter and sculptor; he himself had seen Nero's writing tablets and books, and confirms that he wrote his poems with great care and with his own imperial hand. Martial, who otherwise has nothing good to say about Nero, speaks approvingly of his poetry, and he was himself a man of the trade. The four lines of poetry which are still extant show that Nero wrote in the high-flown metaphorical style of his day; it is parodied in a satire by Persius, who was a few years older than Nero and a friend of Seneca's nephew Lucanus. As Persius makes fun of the bombastic poets who have maenads and Attis swimming around in their watering mouths, and as Nero is said to have written poems about 'Attis' and 'the bacchants', some writers have been of the opinion that this satire was directly aimed at the Emperor. Apart from Attis, the Syrian god who in ecstasy castrated himself, died and arose from the dead (and about whom Catullus had written a famous poem), it is known that Prince Paris appeared as the hero of a poem Nero wrote on the destruction of Troy. Traditionally, Paris was considered effeminate; in the effeminate Nero's poem fair Paris appeared as the victor in all sports and even as more than a match for Hector. Nero also went round nursing an extremely long epic poem on the whole of Rome's history, only he was in doubt as to how long it should be. Some were of the opinion that it could not fill fewer than 400 books, while the Stoic philosopher Annaeus Cornutus, who was also asked, thought this would be too many, and that no one would read them. Cornutus was later exiled. With this long poem Nero probably wanted to outdo Lucanus, who had written on the civil war; he had admittedly begun by loudly singing the praises of Nero: if the civil war was the price the Romans had to pay for Nero's principate, the price was not too high! But after having paid this entrance fee to Nero in his first canto, Lucanus later ignored him and became more and more obviously republican in his tendency and more and more antagonistic to Caesar — and at one time was forbidden to publish. Presumably Nero was less worried about Lucanus as a republican than as a poet; while he could still take a liberal view of other forms of lese-majesty, he tolerated no criticism of his artistic talents. The 'spies' of whom Nero made use in his last years were not only to prevent conspiracies, but also to make sure that his artistic achievements were received with suitable enthusiasm. A watch was kept on the public when he put in an appearance, and it is supposed almost to have cost the later Emperor Vespasian his life when he fell asleep during an imperial performance.

From the very beginning of his reign Nero had carefully worked on his voice, which was not naturally either very powerful or very beautiful; although he was otherwise unwilling to shoulder burdens, for this purpose he wore lead plates on his chest in order to strengthen his chest muscles. If it was only after the death of Agrippina that he appeared for the first time, before an invited audience, and only after the retirement of Seneca that he performed in public, it was probably not only because he was embarrassed, but also because he was afraid of what the public and the critics would say — though this was assured beforehand; he appears to have been so absorbed in his role as an actor that he forgot he was an emperor as well. When the Neronian games were held for the second time in 65 the Senate (!) awarded him the prize for rhetoric and poetry in advance in order to prevent him from taking part, but as his bodyguard echoed the wishes of the populace, he allowed himself to be persuaded to appear; he played Niobe weeping over her children, and he was not to be stopped. He observed all the rules of stagecraft, was humble before the judges and grateful for the applause he received — on the stage at least he lived up to the superior form of slavery which was the role of the king — according to Seneca: he was the humble servant of the people, its plaything, said Apollonius.

By his public appearances Nero got at cross purposes with the Senate nobility, but he won the affection of the people who without any doubt would rather see the Emperor drive a chariot at the races than hear him sing; Nero came to the conclusion that 'only the Greeks had an ear for music, and they were the only people worthy of benefitting from his art'. It was probably for 'artistic' rather than political reasons that Nero became more and more irritated with the Senate. In 58 he had refused a consulate for life and after 60 he was only once consul, in the catastrophic year 68, but to see in this a 'break' with the Senate and a consciously anti-conservative policy, as M.A. Levi has done, is to ignore the fact that after Seneca's retirement Nero showed no interest at all in state affairs and had no other policy than that of getting rid of those by whom he felt threatened. If there had been a conscious aim in replacing the bloodthirsty gladiatorial games with more peaceful forms of amusement, Nero also abandoned this political task in favour of his own career when he left Rome to have homage done to him in Greece.

It was the senators who were behind the first (Pisonian) conspiracy (p312), and it was military commanders who started the rebellion in 68 which cost Nero his power and his life. This rebellion was able to gain support in the provinces thanks to growing dissatisfaction with the increasing burden of taxation and with the imperial procurators, but it was not a social revolt or an attempt to gain independence from Rome: it was primarily the Emperor himself whom people were dissatisfied with and rebelled against. Now Nero's failure to show an interest in the army in the provinces rebounded on him, for the soldiers felt more loyalty to their generals than to the Emperor, to whom all had sworn allegiance but none had ever seen. By the previous year commanding Corbulo, the victor from the Armenian campaign, and the commanders from upper and lower Germania to take their own lives, Nero had increased the danger rather than reduced it. The first news of the revolt made no impression on Nero; the next made him lose his head. Nero could not tolerate not feeling loved; he had always been fêted and idolised, and it came as a shock to him to hear himself denounced by the leader of the rebellion in Gaul as a bad emperor — and a bad singer!

By acting with determination Nero would doubtless have been able to put down the rebellion, for most governors were still loyal, while the others were mutual rivals (as became apparent in the civil war after the death of Nero). But as usual in dangerous situations, Nero panicked and could think of nothing but his usual method: of executing those by whom he felt threatened. Only this time it was an impossible task. To achieve his object he would have had to have all senators and governors murdered; Suetonius writes that he did in fact consider something along these lines, and that at the same time he wanted to set fire to Rome and release wild animals, etc. etc.. But typically, he imagined that he could himself go to meet the armies unarmed and do nothing — but weep (as he had done so successfully in the part of Niobe), and when in this way he had touched the hardy soldiers he would sing songs of victory — which he ought now to start writing. Or he would appear in mourning in the Forum and ask for forgiveness and declare himself content with the post of governor in Egypt — Suetonius says he actually left a speech to this effect. At first he had made light of it all with the idea that a great artist can take care of himself anywhere — just think how well he had managed in Greece, the home of the arts! It had also been prophesied that he would become king in Jerusalem — obviously the messianic idea from Israel had made its way to Rome. Nero found it less difficult to accept that he was going to lose his empire than that the world was going to lose such a great artist. To the very end he thought himself more loved than he was: when he heard the soldiers coming to take him alive he plunged his sword into himself, and when they looked as though they would try to prevent him, he exclaimed, 'Too late ... That is loyalty for you.'

The general who started the rebellion in Gaul was very aptly called Vindex (the avenger); Dio Cassius knows what he said on that occasion to the Gauls: they should rebel: 'Because Nero has ruined

Roman society, eradicated the best in the Senate, seduced and killed his mother and lost everything resembling authority. Murder and robbery and rape have indeed been committed by others, but how shall we find words for all the other things he has done? I, my friends and companions, have with my own eyes seen (if you will believe me) that man (if he is a man, who has married Sporus and been married to Pythagoras) on the rostrum and on the stage, sometimes carrying a cither and wearing a tunic and buskins, sometimes in theatre boots and a mask. I have heard him sing, heard him as a herald and as an actor in tragedies; I have seen him in chains, seen him play the part of a villain, of a pregnant woman, indeed, even of a woman giving birth; I have seen him say and do everything and let people say to him and do to him the things that are told in the myths. Will anyone after this call such a man Caesar and princeps and Augustus? Never! No one shall abuse these lofty titles. They were suited to Augustus and Claudius, but he can more rightly be called Thyestes and Oedipus and Alcmeon and Orestes, for it is in these roles he has appeared and these names he has taken instead of the others. Rise therefore against him, help yourselves and help the Romans; free the whole of Roman society.'

Brutality and sexual urges

It is typical that Vindex should mention Nero's brutality but immediately add that others have been guilty of similar things; it is worth remembering, for Nero is remembered for more than he committed while many others are remembered for less; who remembers that Constantine the Great murdered his wife and son, his brother-in-law and his nephew for 'political' reasons? Tradition has been kind to Constantine; he established Christianity as the official religion, while Nero executed the Christians. He did so, however, because he needed a scapegoat in a critical situation, not because the Christians as such were repugnant to him; they were doubtless a matter of complete indifference to him. Nero was seen at the execution of the Christians, but there is nothing to indicate that he derived any personal pleasure from witnessing it; on the contrary, on another occasion Tacitus contrasts him with Domitian: 'In his day Nero at least turned his eyes away; he certainly gave orders for brutal actions, but he did not watch them.' Just as Nero did not wage aggressive wars, he was cruel only in self-defence, but it must certainly be added that with his lively imagination he was inclined to see dangers everywhere, and with his lack of realism he was inclined not to see them where they really did exist.

It was not Nero's brutality but his effeminacy, his artistic and sexual pursuits, which especially gave offence to Vindex and the more distinguished Romans whose dissatisfaction was not lessened by the fact that they themselves were, or felt they were, forced to take part in his games. The historians recall a public sex orgy which was arranged in 64 by Tigellinus on an artificial island surrounded by temporary brothels, where beautiful women of the best and worst society had to be prepared to bestow their favours on anyone who might want them, something which led to fighting. Nero obviously wanted to take the consequences of the fact that 'all men are lecherous' and give everyone the chance. He himself went as far in his depravity as it is possible to go, says Tacitus, adding that a few days after the sex orgy he had one of the boy prostitutes, Pythagoras (Suetonius calls him Doryphorus, but both names are Greek) married to him to the accompaniment of the entire marriage ritual; the Emperor wore a bridal veil, but otherwise nothing was veiled. After the death of Poppæa in 65 Nero not only married Statia Messalına, but also another boy, the castrated Sporus, who resembled Poppæa: the Emperor appeared as the bridegroom and did everything to make Sporus into a woman.

In this sphere Nero seems to have taken seriously his principle that nothing human should be unknown to him — or anything bestial, according to Suetonius' version: he invented a new game which consisted in his being sewn into the skins of wild animals and released from a cage; thus clothed, he thew himself upon condemned women and men standing tied to posts, and satisfied his desires on them. In his sex life Nero was also more imaginative than the other Roman emperors, with the possible exception of Elagabal, and the historians have scarcely invented everything of which they accuse him, even if indignation can be inventive.

As has already been said, there is nothing to indicate that Nero in general derived any sadistic pleasure from seeing people tortured, but Suetonius' account of how he appeared as a wild animal to his sexual victims could indicate a more particular tendency towards sexual sadism. If we are to believe that on several occasions he made sexual assaults on Brittanicus on the days before he murdered him, that he did the same with the young Aulus Plautius (about whom we know nothing else), that he was unusually tender with Agrippina when he took leave of her before the planned murder, and that he kicked his deeply loved Poppæa so viciously that she died of it, we cannot deny that there was some mysterious connection between Nero's tenderness and cruelty and — as it was obviously the thought of the death of the victims that excited him — between his sympathy and sexuality.

'That cruelty and sexual urges are closely connected is shown by the history of civilisation and is beyond any doubt, but in explaining this relationship we have not advanced beyond stressing the aggressive nature of the libido,' wrote Freud. Although more progress has perhaps been made now, we can here limit ourselves to the Stoic view: only a man who has his reason can love; when reason is discarded the personality disintegrates into passions, and of these anger, aggressiveness, is the most powerful. 'It conquers the most burning love, it has made the lover drive his sword through the body of the loved one, only to throw himself into the arms of his victim,' writes Seneca in 'On anger'; and in 'On good deeds' he writes of the tendency to wish evil on those whom you wish well: what your enemies wish for you, lovers can wish for each other. 'Thus hatred and senseless love lead to the same thing.' Just as you can make conquests in both love and war (so that the art of loving is portrayed by Ovid as an art of war), it is quite a common abnormity to associate the culmination of love with death, for where love is not an identification it is an urge to get rid of the other. Examples are the Liebestod of Tristan and Isolde, Don Juan's yearning for the woman whom he is about to repudiate, sexual murders and necrophilia — and Nero's attraction to those condemned to death can be mentioned in this context. In all cases passion is increased by the idea of the irrevocability of the relationship and perhaps by sympathy for the victim. Understood in this way sympathy is a passion, a mental suffering which, like all passions, is related to enjoyment, and it was perhaps not only for dogmatic reasons that Seneca warned Nero against sympathy. Nero had the ability of an actor to identify himself with someone else, and it was predominantly suffering heroes and heroines with whom he identified himself; the farewells in his own life, his hope of being able to awaken everyone's sympathy with his prayers and his tears shows also the dimensions of his self-pity. Suetonius' anecdote that as a schoolboy Nero complained because a green charioteer had been dragged perhaps reveals not only his interest in racing, but also in the suffering hero. It is not unlikely that the 16-17 year-old Nero wished with all his heart that he had not learned to write when he had to sign a death warrant. In 'On gentleness' Seneca expressed the wish that: 'What is now nature and a sudden inclination in you can be determined by reason': it was obviously from nervousness rather than the warmth of conviction that the young Nero was so gentle — and because of fear rather than evil that he subsequently became so brutal. A man who so to speak forcibly disregards his own sensitiveness loses his natural inhibitions and: 'The worst thing about cruelty is that it persists' — and that crime begets crime. It was probably because of the person it was intended for as well as its subject that Seneca wrote so much in his prince's mirror about the nervous prince who constantly punishes people in order to secure himself against his own fear — thereby producing the very thing he fears. At any event, his warnings now have a prophetic ring about them: 'Such a man is inevitably courting his own destruction . . . he is not only threatened by private conspiracies, but will soon be faced with general rebellion.'

That general rebellion has already been mentioned to anticipate the fatal outcome of events; Seneca was not to experience it or the culmination of Nero's licentiousness. The private conspiracy was the last he experienced.

Seneca on himself – and Nero

'A man comes with the intention of killing you. Wait a moment, why do you want to anticipate him?' writes Seneca in one of the epistles with death as its principal theme. He waited and made use of his time, disillusioned in the sense of entertaining no false hopes; apparently not only taking leave of court, but also taking leave of life gave him a sense of freedom. The only really free man is the one who 'lives after fulfilling his life'.

The man who has nothing to lose has more to give; the epistles to Lucilius are not exclusively deadly earnest, and they contain as much humour as pathos. When Seneca writes about himself it is not as an example to be followed, but always as an example of something or other, and especially as an example of how weak we all are. 'If I want to be amused at a fool I need not look for long: I laugh at myself,' he writes with reference to the custom of keeping half-wits and cripples as clowns in the larger houses — there was no other provision for taking care of those abnormal beings who had not been exposed as infants. Seneca had kept his first wife's servant girl Harpaste, who had gone blind in her old age but stubbornly maintained that there was no light in the house. In this way we are also blind to our own weaknesses and blame our surroundings, reasons Seneca — and as an example he mentions how irritated he was when the bailiff in his country mansion outside the city had acquired a decrepit slave who made himself known by his shouting: 'Don't you know me? I'm Felicio; you used to give me pictures and call me your favourite.' Thus reminded of his own old age Seneca quotes Vergil's Dido: 'I have lived and fulfilled the course my fate determined,' adding: 'If God gives us another tomorrow, we will rejoice at it.' Seneca appears to have taken seriously the Stoic precept that we should live every day as though it were our last.

Lucilius has asked how Seneca passes his time. Seneca has to admit that, although he used to start his day by jumping into the cold water in the Aqua Virgo aqueduct or the Tiber, he now ends up in a warm bath. Previously, despite his irony at the expense of devotees of physical exercise, he had run the race of the day together with a bright slave boy, but now the lad is getting too quick for Seneca, although he maintains that they are at the same stage in life, as both he and Seneca are losing their teeth. After the bath comes lunch, which only consists of bread, so that it is not necessary to wash his hands; then begins the day's work, undisturbed by the din from the Circus close by. In the summer of 64 when the fire broke out in *Circus maximus* Seneca's house must also have burned down, but he makes no mention of it, probably because he had just written about the fire in Lyons and used *that* as an example to show you can never feel safe, even if 'weapons rest and the whole world lives in security.' Nero's reign of terror only began with the living bonfires after the fire.

Seneca often speaks about his work, but he says little about his works; he mentions that he is writing a treatise on moral philosophy, but only once does he refer to one of his own works, the first book of 'On good deeds'. On the other hand he makes frequent reference to his reading: reading is an absolute necessity, as we must also take heed of what others are thinking; but he warns Lucilius against too much desultory reading: everything must serve a purpose. He himself is reading Epicure — in order to quote him in the first 29 epistles and to show that wisdom is not reserved for one way of thinking — or perhaps to beat his enemy on his own ground. Otherwise he is fond of quoting the poets Ovid and Vergil, and praises Cicero and Livy as the best writers of philosophy. And yet soon after this time Seneca was accused of departing from Cicero's path and criticised for his 'ordinary' — i.e. lively and pointed — style, behind which his champions claim to have discovered a conscious educational purpose: it was *not* Seneca's intention simply to argue and convince the intellect, but also to beguile and to appeal to the soul. But the more outstanding stylists usually have a more spontaneous sense of language than their critics (and champions), and it is noticeable that the only stylistic lesson they can draw from Seneca is that you should be more concerned with what you are writing about than with how you are writing about it. He knew that language changes with the state of society, and that style is an expression of a mental state: 'As your life, so your style'. Whether people insist on speaking only in the old style with words from the laws of the twelve tablets, or whether they will only use everyday, hackneyed or florid and poetical expressions, this indicates an inner weakness: 'Language which aims at the truth must be natural and simple.'

Seneca always took issue with those philosophers who were less concerned with reality than with their language. The first Stoics were responsible for a pioneering work in the linguistic field (many of our grammatical terms go back to them), and as his presentation of Stoic thought in the epistles to Lucilius proceeds, Seneca also has to pay attention to logic which, after ethics and physics, constituted the third area in philosophy, and which included grammar and the theory of knowledge. For instance Stoic monism gave Lucilius the opportunity of asking whether moral goodness is a material thing; Seneca replies that it is, but not without adding that that kind of question is more entertaining than useful. When the enemy is at the gate and everything is being mobilised it is disgraceful for philosophers to waste their time drawing conclusions such as: 'What you have not lost you have; you have not lost horns, therefore you have horns.' The philosophers of that time, who were also the spiritual guides of the age, were just as capable as the philosophers of a later era of giving people logical nuts to crack instead of intellectual food; Seneca could only express his surprise that philosophers, who are supposed to be lovers of wisdom and to seek the greatest understanding — find meaningless trifles.

When Seneca mentions the teachers of philosophy he had had in his youth (cf p78) that, too, is an example of the effect which can be achieved through a true philosophical discourse. He was more eager in those days — and he has not progressed so far that now in his old age he cannot settle down like a pupil at school and listen to the Stoic philosopher Metronax in Naples. It is asthma which has persuaded Seneca to leave the unhealthy air in Rome; this illness, which doctors then referred to as a 'foretaste of death', can also be used as an example in the letters to Lucilius, and at that point Seneca is not far from using himself as an example: follow the example of the man who dies without sorrow, even if he still rejoices in life! As in 'The Trojan Women' Seneca says here that there is nothing terrifying in death, for the state of the dead person is like that of the unborn child: death is one thing, and the dualistic concept of the immortality of the soul, which Seneca is sometimes a little bit inclined towards, is only a dream.

But although Seneca can cope with his foretaste of death, he cannot manage — seasickness. On a journey from Naples to Puteoli (Pozzuoli) nature goes wild both outside and inside; Seneca wants the skipper to sail closer to the coast, but it is too dangerous in a storm, and the almost seventy-year-old Seneca, with a supreme disdain for death, jumps into the waves and only with difficulty reaches the shore. From this experience he concludes that it was not fate but seasickness which constantly delayed Odysseus' return from Troy. Seneca has to emphasise that you cannot flee from your weaknesses and that peace of mind is not dependent on the place in which you find yourself; in the resort of Bajae, where he is lodged above the baths and gives a lively description of the sounds coming from the building, he has to challenge the view that concentration requires absolute silence. Nevertheless, he is anxious to get away from this fashionable town, to which nature has given so much, and which *luxus* has chosen as a setting for festivity. He makes no mention of the fact that it was also at Bajae that Agrippina was murdered and that what must have been the most gruesome conversation of his life took place there; he could not mention that any more than he could make any direct comments on his political experiences. There is no reference at all to Nero in the epistles, but without being mentioned by name his presence is felt on various occasions in the works from Seneca's last years.

In the seventh and final book in 'On good deeds', which was probably written in the last year of his life, Seneca went so far as to maintain that to kill a tyrant can be a benefit both to the tyrant and the people, though only in extreme cases; but Nero was an extreme case. In view of the fact that in 62 Nero and Seneca had thanked each other for their respective good deeds and that in 65 they stood as each other's enemies, it is tempting to see a personal motive when Seneca asks: 'What do you owe to the person who once was good to you? What should be your attitude to a person who has betrayed your friendship?' Nero must still have occupied a central place in Seneca's world, and even in less historical circumstances a hot friend cooling will lead one to take stock and think things over.

Seneca writes somewhere that the Emperor has everything, and yet there is a difference between his private purse and the state purse; to investigate what belongs to him and what to the State is not to encroach too much on his personal power. However, at this point Nero would probably have thought that it was, as he was bleeding Italy and the provinces dry and also plundering the temples. Seneca disagrees with the Sophist argument that plundering a temple is not sacrilege because it only means moving a few things from one place to another, and all places are the domain of the gods. According to Tacitus Seneca had left Rome because he did not want to be held partly responsible for sacrilege, but in this connection he did not specifically speak out against it or write about the Emperor's finances. He mentioned the Sophist defence of robbing the temples as an example of false argumentation, and mentioned the Emperor, who in a certain sense has everything and in a certain other sense does not have everthing, as an example of the wise man who has everything he needs and yet does not own everything. Therefore it is possible to do a wise man a service — and in the same way you can do an emperor a service! When Seneca specifically talks about the Emperor he does not usually mean Nero, but rather Augustus, the great example; after the deaths of

Agrippa and Maecenas even he had bewailed the fact that he did not have good advisors: 'That shows how difficult it is for a man who has many thousands of men at his disposal to find substitutes for *two!*' Could this also be applied to Seneca and Burrus? At all events Seneca's words could not be applied to Augustus when he wrote that the great often listen less to their consciences than to self-seeking advisors who compete to make lies attractive; that they believe themselves as great as they are told they are, and they are carried away by their anger which no one tries to stop; they ruin the harmony of society and spill the blood of many men — and finally their own! To give a man good advice and stop him on the slippery slope can be as beneficial a deed as giving houses and estates — and what had Seneca been able to give Nero in return for houses and estates? Things given on account of a high position and not from the goodness of the heart do not deserve the name of kindness, and a man who has been forced to accept them has merely done as he was told. The man who has given with a good heart but then shown himself to be arrogant, scornful, brutal, has forcibly suspended his own kindness. A man who has loudly proclaimed that he owes us the foundation for his position will often forget this when he is preoccupied with other things, for we are inclined to be more interested in what we do not have than what we have. When this happens a careful approach is called for, for we must take care not to turn a doubtful friend into a certain enemy. It happens that men turn against us not only *after*, but *because* we have done them a good service — even then it is best to maintain a show of friendship in order also to maintain the friendship should they change their minds.

Seneca says the gentle approach should always be tried as long as possible; this is what he himself had done with Nero, and he has been criticised for it. Seneca and Burrus, writes Dio Cassius, let Nero: 'follow his own desires in the hope that he would change once he had had enough, as though they were not aware that a young and wilful mind which has been brought up to total licence and unlimited self-assertion, far from getting enough by following his desires, on the contrary becomes more and more depraved by them.'

It was scarcely so simple. Nero and his instincts had been kept in check by Agrippina who, as she had cleared Nero's way to the throne, still had reason to believe that in him she had a compliant tool for her own desire for power. The young Emperor, who was enthusiastically received wherever he went, had to satisfy his interest in horse racing with models on a board and surreptitiously arrange his first erotic experiences with Acte, incidentally one of the few who kept Nero's sympathy and sympathy for Nero to the bitter end: she was given some vast estates in Sardinia and together with his two nurses arranged his funeral. It was not this loyal soul who led Nero on the path to damnation, and even if Seneca and Burrus had their presentiments about the kind of desires Nero had, they would certainly not have gained anything by depriving him of the more harmless ones, quite apart from the fact that it *was* Nero who was Emperor. If Nero had not been kept under such strict control by Agrippina he would scarcely have gone to such extremes in freeing himself from her; he discovered with delight that he could allow himself everything, but also with a fear which demanded its victims. But Nero would scarcely have allowed himself to be intimidated by Agrippina if he had not been and remained so tied to her that he could only free himself from her in desperation — and therefore not free himself at all.

At the end of his essay on good deeds Seneca appears to defend himself against the accusations of having been too easy-going with Nero: 'If he wants statues and fine garments no one is harmed by this sacrifice to his greed, but I will not give him soldiers or weapons.' To begin with, it is noticeable that Seneca as an example of a good friend who has become evil names a good prince who has become a tyrant; and then that he talks as one empowered to allow the tyrant to have statues and deny him weapons; very few people are in that position. Nero is notorious for collecting statues, much to the annoyance of the Greek cities he visited (the Laokoon group is presumed to have stood in his *Domus aurea*) — and for never wearing the same garments twice. Seneca appears to go even closer to the bone: 'If he appreciates being given stage artists and hetaeras and other things that can subdue his intemperance I will happily give them to him. I will deny him triremes with copper prows, but I will send him pleasure boats and Egyptian gondolas and other toys for the ocean of royal excesses.' Nero's sea-borne sex orgy had been celebrated shortly before this. Was Seneca with these somewhat unusual rules about how to deal with tyrants to whom one supplies the goods, trying to justify his own attitude and to point out that up to now the worst had after all been avoided? Nero had not tyrannised entire nations; he had not stepped in the bloody

311

footsteps of Xerxes or Alexander — though perhaps he had plans for doing so in his last year. Then, after the rules quoted, comes one more, a fatal one: 'And if there is no hope at all that he will see reason, I will with one and the same hand perform a good deed for all and repay his, for to such characters death is the only way out, and for the man who cannot recover it is best that he should depart.'

Fate caught up with Seneca before Nero.

The conspiracy: Seneca's death

It has already been mentioned (p189) that Seneca was under suspicion as a friend of Calpurnius Piso, something which Tacitus says gave Piso cause to be on guard — and led to the conspiracy against Nero. Apparently events confirmed Seneca's saying that fear leads to what it fears. The conspirators wished without doubt to free Rome from Nero's humiliating behaviour, his licentiousness and his cruelty, but the immediate cause was the danger threatening them themselves now that Nero had begun to exterminate those by whom he felt threatened.

Tacitus does not know who took the initiative in the conspiracy, only that Calpurnius Piso was its central figure. In a poem which was presumably written in praise of this Piso, 'Laus Pisonis', he is lauded as an orator, poet and player of draughts by a young man who would like to have Piso as his Maecenas; Piso appears also to have been on quite close terms with Nero. He was of a distinguished family, amiable and generous, good-looking and irresponsible; he sang and played the lyre and could be somewhat wanton; he lacked seriousness and self-control. In short, he was strangely reminiscent of Nero himself before he went off the rails, so much so that it is surprising the conspirators wanted to put him on the throne instead, all the more so as there were several hardened soldiers among them.

The only leaders mentioned by Dio Cassius are Faenius Rufus, the prefect of the praetorian guard, and Seneca. Once the plot had been uncovered because a couple of those involved had behaved in a suspicious manner in front of their slaves and had been betrayed and arrested, one of them, Antonius Natalis, betrayed Piso and Seneca — either because Natalis 'had carried on negotiations between him and Piso, or because he wanted to do a service to Nero, who hated Seneca and was looking for a way of crushing him.' So Tacitus does not really express an opinion as to whether Seneca was really implicated or not, but he mentions a rumour that the praetorian tribune Subrius Flavus had arranged with the centurions that at the right moment, 'in secret, but not without Seneca's knowing', they would put Calpurnius Piso out of action and make Seneca Emperor, as though they themselves were guiltless if a man so famous for his virtues was put on the throne.

It must have been obvious for the rebellious praetorians to seek help from Seneca at this critical moment. But can it be imagined that Seneca, who had been so relieved on giving up his state service, would give up his retirement and take on the burden of government, persuaded by his nephew Marcus like Thyestes by his sons? For Lucanus was also implicated, and it is improbable that Seneca had no information at all on the furtive undertaking — the failure of which cost both Lucanus and Seneca and his two brothers their lives. Tacitus writes of Seneca's last hours:

'Then followed the murder of Annaeus Seneca, a happy event for the Emperor, not because his implication in the conspiracy had been proven, but because now that poison had not worked he could turn to the sword. Admittedly, only Natalis had named him, and even then only said that he had been sent to Seneca during his illness to visit him and ask him to explain why he would not receive Piso: it was better that they should cultivate their friendship in intimate surroundings. And Seneca had replied that exchanges of opinions and regular conversations benefitted neither of them, but that his own welfare in fact was dependent on Piso's safety. Now a tribune of the guard, Gavius Silvanus, was ordered to take charge of the case and ask Seneca whether he admitted what Natalis had said to him and what he himself had replied. That very day — by chance or design — he had returned from the Campagna and had taken up residence on his estate twenty miles from Rome. The tribune reached him towards evening and had the villa surrounded by a platoon of soldiers; then he delivered the Emperor's message to Seneca, who was supping with his wife Pompeja Paulina and two friends.

Seneca replied that it was true that Natalis had been sent to him and had asked him why he had refused to receive Piso, saying that he had excused himself with his health and his need for peace and quiet. He had never had any reason to put the welfare of a private individual

313

above his own security, and he was not inclined to flattery; no one knew this better than Nero himself, who was better acquainted with his outspokenness than his submissiveness. When the tribune reported this to the Emperor in the presence of Poppæa and Tigellinus, who were his advisors in matters of life and death, he asked whether Seneca was making arrangements to die voluntarily. The tribune assured him that he had not observed any sign of fear or noted anything mournful in his words or expressions. So he was commanded to go back with the death order. Fabius Rusticus, however, says that he did not go back the same way, but sought out the prefect Faenius, placed the imperial orders before him and asked whether he should obey them; and that he was encouraged by him to carry them out, for fate had so willed it that they all lacked courage and bravery. Silvanus, of course, was himself one of the conspirators and now he played his part in making even more disgraceful the state of affairs which he had agreed to avenge. Nevertheless, he spared his voice and his eyes and sent one of the centurions in to Seneca with the last command.

Unafraid, he asked for his will; when the centurion forbade it, he turned to his friends and called them to witness that as he had been forbidden to thank them for their services and friendship he was leaving them the only thing and the most beautiful thing he had: the picture of his life; if they kept the remembrance of it they would as a reward for their loyal friendship gain the reputation of being just men. At the same time he tried, sometimes by conversing with them, sometimes by exhorting them, to get them to stem their tears and to show firmness of spirit; where, he asked, were their philosophical precepts now, and where was that reason in adversity in which they had encouraged each other for so many years? Who had not been aware of Nero's cruelty? After murdering his mother and brother he had no choice but to add his tutor and teacher to the list of his victims.

When he had said these words, which as it were were addressed to the general public, he embraced his wife, more tender in view of the danger that threatened her, and he begged and implored her to control her pain and not surrender herself to it for ever; may the thought of the life he had lived in the service of the good grant her true comfort and strength to bear the loss of her husband. However, she declared herself determined to die and refused to flee the hand of the murderer. Seneca, who would not prevent her from distinguishing herself, and who

314

feared leaving the one he loved most of all exposed to all kinds of assaults, then said, "I have shown you how to make your life tolerable, but you prefer an honourable death; I will not oppose the example you give. Let us then go to our deaths with the same courage and resolution; your reputation will be the greater."

Then they opened their arteries with a single stroke. Seneca, whose aged body, weakened by insufficient food, was slow to lose its blood, also cut the veins in his legs and knees; wearied by the searing pain and in order not to take away the courage of his wife and himself become weak at the sight of her sufferings, he persuaded her to go into another room; and as he had the power of speech right to the end he had scribes come, and he dictated many things which have been published in his own words, and which I will therefore refrain from repeating.

Meanwhile, Nero himself had no quarrel with Paulina, and so as not to increase resentment of his brutality he ordered her death to be prevented. At the command of the soldiers her slaves and freedmen bandaged her arms and stopped the bleeding. It is not clear whether this was without her knowledge: most people are inclined to believe the worst, and there were those who thought that she only wanted an honourable death together with her husband as long as she believed that Nero was implacable, and that the hope of a less cruel fate persuaded her to give in to her desire to live. This she did for a few more years, laudably faithful to her husband's memory, so deathly pale in her face and body that it was obvious how much of her vital strength she had lost.

Meanwhile, as time passed and death was slow in coming, Seneca asked his old and tried loyal friend and doctor, Statius Annæus, to take out the poison which had been procured long ago and which was the same as was given to condemned men in Athens; it was taken out, but he drank it in vain, for his limbs were already cold and his body unreceptive to the effect of the poison. So he climbed into a bath of hot water, sprinkled the slaves nearest to him and said that he was offering these drops of water to Jupiter Liberator. At last he was carried into a steam bath and suffocated in the steam and cremated without any funeral rites. This he had requested in the will he had written while he was still exceptionally rich and powerful and yet was giving thought to his last moments.'

315

EPILOGUE

Influence

Seneca was the only one of the great ancient writers to be both a poet and a philosopher, and his influence in both capacities has been considerable on the history of European intellectual history. A book of 400 pages has recently been published on his impact on the ancient world, but here we must be content with less. Mention has already been made of the attitude adopted to him by the earliest Christian writers; in the Middle Ages he was seen as the philosopher *par excellence*; he was believed to have had magical powers and was in general a legendary rather than an historical figure; various publications were spuriously ascribed to him, and the correspondence with St. Paul was thought to be genuine; legends obviously arose on his relationship with Nero, some of them showing that Seneca's former pupil wanted to take revenge on him because he had been beaten by him as a child. A distinction was drawn between the tragedian and the philosopher, though as a philosopher he was confused with his father, the author of the 'controversies' which formed the basis of the popular *Gesta Romanorum*. It was only when the later Renaissance rediscovered Tacitus that the historical truth began to appear. The 15th century saw a number of biographies of Seneca, and with the invention of printing he underwent a renaissance: the first edition of the philosophical works appeared in Naples in 1475, the first edition of the tragedies in Ferrara in 1484. The tragedies were of importance to English and Spanish Renaissance drama, German baroque drama and classical French tragedy; as a philosopher Seneca appealed first and foremost to the Renaissance humanists: Erasmus of Rotterdam was responsible for the first critical edition (Basel 1515), while the first philologist specialising in Seneca was also a Netherlander, Justus Lipsius, who finished his edition in 1605.

From the Renaissance to the Enlightenment Seneca was an influential figure; writers of very different persuasions made a thorough study of his work; for instance the Swiss reformer Zwingli put Seneca on a level with Plato, St. Paul and Moses, while Calvin saw him as the supreme representative of Roman philosophy and rhetoric and began his writing career with a commentary on 'On gentleness'; Montaigne the sceptic praised Seneca for 'inspiring and firing with enthusiasm' and learned from his conversational and inciting style; Descartes wrote a commentary on 'On the happy life' and did not find it sufficiently systematic, while Rousseau translated 'Apocolocyntosis.' Cicero's and Seneca's thinking on 'human law' and 'natural law' inspired the founders of modern thinking on international and natural law, Hugo Grotius and Samuel Pufendorf. Ludvig Holberg knew these writers and consequently, without having read Seneca, he could say in his 'Introduction to the understanding of natural and human law' (1716) that 'Seneca wrote at greater length on natural law than anyone else and can thus be said in this field to have surpassed both Greek and Roman philosophers.'

The Romantic age with its greater sense of history had a high opinion of the Greeks and a low one of the Romans. Seneca the statesman appears to have overshadowed Seneca the philosopher. 'Cicero and Seneca were despicable because of their hesitancy and indecision,' argues the Danish Romantic philosopher Henrik Steffens. 'His philosophical qualities must be considered very inferior,' was Hegel's assertion. Hegel's antithesis, Schopenhauer, naturally thought the opposite and stressed that Seneca's 'extremely energetic, witty and carefully thought out writings' were far superior to the 'dreary exercises' of the early Stoics. Schopenhauer considered the entire world to be will (and idea), and it was thus natural that he should be interested in the ancient philosopher who had placed the greatest emphasis on the will; he was also the most distinguished representative of the philosophical essay of which Seneca must be considered the originator.

Seneca was first published in Danish in 1658 by Birgitte Thott, who in her way began to prepare the Danish language for the writing of philosophy. In Holberg's day the young philosopher F. C. Eilschow, eager to philosophise in his mother tongue, continued this effort and translated 'On gentleness'. Holberg acquired Seneca's works in 1732, and: 'Seneca is a most important model when Holberg writes his 'Moral Essays' — 'It is for his "Moral Essays" that he chooses the greatest models; the seriousness with which he studies and imitates

317

them raises his artistry as an essayist to a new level which he fails to maintain in his "Epistles" as the importance of Seneca and Montaigne declines.' (F. J. Billeskov Jansen). Seneca was thus a major inspiration for Holberg's 'Moral Essays' from 1744, the fundamental idea of which is 'that there is a moral code founded on the light of nature'. Danish philosophy, which can be said to begin with the 'Moral Essays' — 'has essentially been pyschological and ethical in nature', and it has tended to be written in the form of essays rather than systematically and scientifically, and Seneca's importance for it has been greater than has hitherto been supposed. It might be well to admit this. 'Seneca's letters are essential nourishment,' asserted Kierkegaard, although he only made acquaintance with Seneca at a late stage in his life.

The criticism of Seneca

The first Danish work on Seneca, Marianne Alienus' 'Death and friendship. A study of Seneca's Epistles', was published in 1974! In it the author aims at 'contributing to the post-war rehabilitation of the philosopher and Stoic Seneca in the face of the traditional and still widespread presentation of him as a hypocrite and unimportant amateur philosopher'. It is true that Seneca, especially in the 19th century, was the object of widespread moral indignation which can easily be traced back to Suillius' accusations. The charges he made can be sensed behind Dio Cassius' or rather Xiphilinus' antitheses: Seneca spoke out against tyranny — and was the teacher of a tyrant. He spoke out against riches — and had a fortune of 300 million sesterces. He spoke out against flattery — and flattered Polybius. He entered upon an outstanding marriage — and whored with Julia, Agrippina and boy prostitutes. Somewhat less than two thousand years after Suillius, an American by the name of Th. W. Africa was quite convinced that Seneca whored with Julia in order to further his career. On the one hand Africa had to recognise that: 'few men have said wise things so well as Seneca', and that: 'the Roman Empire was never run so well as during the first five years of Nero's reign' — and on the other he quotes the Epistle of James: 'So with faith, if it does not lead to action, it is in itself a lifeless thing', despite the fact that running the Roman Empire was a kind of action. But Africa comments: 'Centuries earlier,

Socrates had demonstrated that morality was not a matter of eloquent words, but of difficult actions.' Correctly speaking, Seneca, the statesman in Rome, was in a somewhat more difficult situation than Socrates, the private individual in Athens, and Socrates can also scarcely be said to have had more success with Alcibiades than Seneca with Nero. No one seems to have given Socrates reponsibility for the fact that the young noblemen whom he 'taught true wisdom and true civic responsibility ... when they launched themselves into political life, turned out to be some of the worst rogues' (Peter P. Rohde). Meanwhile, Africa like others before him does not hesitate to make Seneca entirely responsible for Nero: 'Seneca set Nero an excellent example of duplicity and self-interest and encouraged the vices of the young ruler in order to keep power in his own hands ... An attentive pupil, Nero became an intellectual dabbler and a completely immoral man. Compromise was the least of Seneca's sins, and many of his deeds were motivated solely by a blind will to power.'

While Seneca (and Burrus) according to Dio Cassius were simply content to let Nero follow his instincts in the hope that he would soon have had enough, Africa maintains that Seneca consciously encouraged Nero's vices, which means that he did not forbid him to go to bed with Acte. On the one hand Africa reproaches Seneca for his desire for power — which was perhaps not entirely unjustified if he was to run the Roman Empire better than anyone else — and on the other he really reproves him for not forcefully enough using his power to realise his ideals, i.e. by using force. Seneca could have avoided compromises only if he had been able to avoid his position in court — which he was scarcely in a position to refuse. If we keep to Seneca's own words and the policy which according to the best sources was being followed in his day, there was not such a great difference between theory and practice as Africa's presentation of the case appears to indicate; indeed, in order to cover up the weakness of his argument he has to resort to the facile hypothesis that Seneca was a 'hypocrite' who did not mean what he wrote. This psychologically amateurish view of Seneca (and Nero) is, it should be noted, not found in any of the more serious works on Seneca, but it is commonly found as a stock assertion dragged from one second-hand work to another.

Nevertheless, there is a wider perspective to this kind of criticism of Seneca, which was particularly widespread in the Victorian age, when

319

imperialism was at its height, when power politics and (sexual) morals were glorified — and the idea of having a moral foundation for political acts was an abomination; so it still is for many Christians, who find it easier than Seneca to accept that the good is not of this world. 'Had he either been a true philosopher or purely and simply a courtier, he would have been happier and would have stood higher in men's estimation. To be both at the same time was unreasonable.' Such is the argument in a book on 'Heathen seekers of the truth' from 1913. The greatest of Seneca's failings was that in contrast to almost all other philosophers he was not content to interpret the world, but made an attempt to change it for the better: his activities as a statesman had a negative effect on the view of him as a philosopher — he became an 'amateur philosopher'.

Hellenism, the decline of Rome – and the West

Some of the most recent harsh comments on Seneca are to found in Vilhelm Grønbech's 'Hellenism' (1940). Grønbech, a distinguished Danish writer on the history of religion, is however not worried by the fact that Seneca was also a statesman and Nero's trusted tutor; Seneca's personal and political situations are no more an issue for him than those of the other 'hellenists', all of whom he dismisses together. Together is the right word for it, for: 'When we become familiar with people we find an ... amazing, almost deadly monotony in their intellectual lives.' This statement really is so amazing that it awakens a suspicion that Grønbech cannot have been *so* familiar with the people he is writing about. When Grønbech reproduces other authors, it is rarely in their own words, but usually in Grønbech's own, and when he recapitulates ideas, often with a ridiculous amount of exaggeration, they are never seen in their proper context, but always in Grønbech's. In this way Grønbech, who is fundamentally an ironist, can make the mistake of taking very seriously indeed something which Seneca meant ironically.

The essential point, however, is not the inessential things which Grønbech has to say about Seneca, whose writings he considers to be 'one vast case sheet', but his criticism of 'hellenism' in general, the cultural epoch stretching from some 300 years before Christ to 33 years after him, from the decline of the Greek city to the victory of Christianity. It is possible to consider this period either as the decline of civilisation or as the emergence of Europe, he writes, but it is essentially a 'cultural epoch on its own', which he therefore considers as something absolute, something divorced from what came before and afterwards. And just as he finds a monotonous streak in intellectual life, he comments that, 'There is no history in hellenism', adding: 'In this it resembles modern Europe, where nothing of fundamental importance has taken place for the last six hundred years.' One could perhaps venture to think that quite a lot has happened in that time, for instance the emergence of science and the development of technology, and Grønbech is indeed forced to recognise that there is: 'one essential difference between the two epochs: hellenism never made any discovery or invention which could get people going.' Those people never moved off the spot; their world had come to a halt or even 'been lost'; they were afraid of life, without contact with their neighbours, only concerned with the working of their own spirits and with their salvation. And Grønbech is so close to his subject that what he says of hellenism can also be said of 'Hellenism', in which the outer world does not exist. Grønbech is ironical about the hellenistic historians, especially Tacitus, who, in his opinion, knows of no other motive forces in history than virtues and vices; he entirely denies hellenism any historical sense, and like Roman historians he is content to note an absolute difference between then and now: 'Ancient peoples lived encompassed by a horizon which kept life together and gave it unity ... In hellenism that horizon has been broken through; there are no walls rounding off their experience to form a whole and to give tautness to their thinking.' As Grønbech correspondingly talks of: 'the time when Europe had a faith and a religion; when there was a background for all facets of life' — and compares that with 'now'. It is obvious that it is the 'hellenistic spirit in Europe' that his criticism of hellenism is directed at.

In this Grønbech is like Oswald Spengler who in his famous book 'The Decline of the West' also talks of the 'hellenism' of Europe and stresses the fact that the intellectual driving force in any culture is religious, while the people of the big cities are without religion; likewise he distinguishes between the 'cultural morals' which we have and the 'civilised morals' which we seek. It is at the critical stage when what has hitherto been taken for granted is no longer to be taken for granted that culture turns into civilisation; it is at this stage that Diogenes and Rousseau want to return to nature, and Zenon and Schopenhauer seek moral rules for something 'which is no longer guaranteed by the instincts'. It is well known that Spengler sees the various cultures as organisms germinating, blossoming, withering and dying: in urban civilisations they become organisations in which the intellect rules over the spirit, and the dictatorship of money and its tool, democracy, form the final transition to 'Caesarism'. Although Spengler finds parallels between all cultures, it is particularly the decline of Rome that he takes as his model and precedent for what is happening in Europe. Even before Rome finally fell, the decline had become an intellectual cross, a *memento mori*, and ever since it has resounded through most European historical thought. In Spengler's book it was given its most sensational formulation.

Even if regular patterns are identified in cultural developments, the differences are as striking as the similarities, and so Spengler's parallel between ancient Rome and modern Europe, in good 'hellenistic' fashion, is more contrived than obvious. But Spengler is particularly interesting in this connection because his view of history is strikingly reminiscent of that of the Romans themselves — in particular that of the elder Seneca who also (p67) talked of the childhood, manhood and old age of Rome — and pointed to the Caesarian character of the third stage. Spengler's cyclical view of history is yet another expression of the primitive opposition to history which asserted itself from the very start (Chapter I) and was still observable in the Romans, who *made* history (Chapter II); and although it says more about Spengler than about the history of the world, it also tells us something about the primitive manner of experiencing which may well have been modified but scarcely entirely changed by — history. So the disparity between the primitive mentality and city civilisation where Spengler believes history comes to a halt and where in Grønbech's view nothing much happens either, is perhaps in itself one of the contributory factors responsible for things going wrong.

It is striking that both for Spengler and Grønbech (as well as for Heidegger and Farrington (p24) it is a symptom of decline when man turns his attention to himself, to the unfulfilled ego seeking fulfillment. For Spengler Stoicism is the 'final phenomenon' in ancient culture like

Buddhism in Indian culture (to which Schopenhauer turned his attention when European culture began to wither) — and socialism in Europe! For Grønbech, too, Stoicism is a phenomenon of disintegration, and as he describes it it has become a sheer caricature; when, for instance he writes that: 'In order for an action to be virtuous it must be carried out exclusively for its own sake,' it is not only a distorted view but a wrong one. His own simple solution to the dissolution was that: 'We must find God in a religion of the people encompassing life in its entirety.' Meanwhile, in his complete acceptance of the course of history Spengler betrayed a certain Stoic tendency, and he ended his book on decline with a quotation from Seneca's oft-quoted translation of Cleanthes: *Ducunt volentem fata, nolentem trahunt*: the willing man leads fate, dragging the unwilling man along.

Hellenism, the 'dissolution of culture' means the same as the detachment of the individual from the community, which in its way of course can be seen as the emergence of the individual. The fact that the horizon is shattered and the old values lose their value leads to a search for new values which in the opinions of Spengler and Grønbech are more 'contrived' than obvious. This search, however, does not only begin with hellenistic philosophy, but with philosophy itself, with the recognition that there is a difference between the good things available and the good, and that there are other, generally valid values than those current. It is not only *metropolis* but *polis* itself which is based on law and reason instead of simply on custom and instinct; therefore to Hesiod the transition to urban society had been a decline, and therefore the first philosophers sought to found law on the natural order of things. But it is only in the metropolis, in Rome, that the decline in values becomes so far advanced that the Stoics and most consistently Seneca come to the epoch-making conclusion that the individual, irrespective of social status, has *a value in himself*. The formula for the revision of the old-established values or perhaps the disintegration of values, is that the measure for good and evil is moved from externals to the internal, from convention to conscience, a process which began with Protagoras' thesis that man is the measure of all things, and via Socrates' recognition that the individual is subject to a higher law than that of the state leads to Stoic teaching on the law which by nature is valid for all living beings. Where there is danger, there is also

323

salvation: to argue that growing humanist understanding is decadent, that Seneca's work, in which it receives its clearest expression, is a 'case sheet', is such a misconception that on that basis the search for symptoms should not stop at the decline of the city state but go back as far as the decline of tribal society. Indeed, it would really be necessary to go back to the transition from animal to *homo sapiens*, for the fatal thing is that reason takes the place of instinct — or rather that it does *not* do so, which Heraclitus had seen earlier as the problem of middle class democracy (p19).

Humane ideas could not prevent, but neither could they exactly cause, the decline of ancient culture and of Rome, which was due rather to the lack of ideas than the lack of instinct. The Romans did not set out to conquer the world, but they were led by their ambition (*gloria*) and short-term interests, until they were in possession of a world-wide empire which world-wide peace was necessary to maintain. After the Second World War, when it dawned on some that it was a question of 'one world or none', an Englishman called Lawrence Waddy wrote a book on 'Pax Romana and World Peace' in which Rome for once was not merely presented as a terrifying example: under the auspices of Rome peace reigned over a greater area and for a longer time than either before or since; this was admittedly on Rome's conditions, but then peace is usually dependent on the conditions of the great. At the height of the Empire — the period from Augustus to Hadrian — most of its population suffered less need than their successors in later centuries, and that is always something, unless, of course, one thinks that peace itself is not the best thing; at the end of this period a Greek writer like Plutarch could express the opinion that it was a good thing that Greece, which was suffering from internal divisions, was pacified by the Romans. But, Waddy argues: 'They were in fact a people who never saw ends clearly, but who handled with impressive success the means which could have led to the right ends.' Vergil saw that the peace which was the condition upon which the continued existence of the Empire depended had to be turned into a moral programme, and thus he saw further than the Roman historians who found the reason for the decline of the republic (and Empire) in the decline of the ancient (military) morals: what was needed was a new moral code; what was once a heroic deed (*virtus*) had now become a crime, said Seneca in his

324

epigram: to recreate social awareness requires a moral effort.

Modern, materialistic historians do not ascribe greater significance than Spengler and Grønbech to the moral, humane efforts; for them history is of course not guided by *fortuna* or fate, but by the economic laws of progress which Rome did not live up to, so that the stagnation of the Empire is explained by the fact that progress as such never got under way. The economic and technological progress which has given modern civilisation so much better remedies than were available to ancient civilisations is not, however, a guarantee in itself against the collapse of civilisation. Where the aim and the ideas are lacking, the means becomes an end in itself: in modern civilisation that is the productive and destructive growth, in Rome it was the army, which was and remained 'the decisive factor, not only in the political life of the Empire, but in its social and economic life as well.' (Rostovtseff). A social development cannot be entirely explained on the basis of an economic development which has *not* taken place; what in fact happened was that the entire Empire, which in principle the army was a means of keeping together, in the course of time became a means of keeping the army in existence, and in its turn the army turned the State into its tool; in the period of expansion the Romans had understood how to turn enemies into allies and even friends, but in the period of decline the State turned its citizens into its enemies whose only task was to serve the State with taxes and forced labour. From that time, i.e. about the time of Hadrian, the history of Rome becomes a terrifying example, as the state is no longer content to be a superstructure over the city authorities in Italy and the provinces, but grows into an all-embracing totalitarian bureaucracy which paralyses all initiative. A moral can be drawn from this story: it is not human ideas but brutal practice which undermines society; the life of a society is stifled not by organisation, but by organised force. It is no consolation that organised force cannot be maintained in the long run, for on the one hand the run is long, and on the other progress has produced far more sophisticated methods of oppression.

As has been pointed out, there are points of similarity between Spengler's view of history and that of the Stoics, but humanism makes the difference, and Cleanthes' and Seneca's words on allowing yourself to be guided by fate should not be misinterpreted as encouraging passive acceptance of a development which disregards man. In the view of Seneca a social organisation which does not allow (human) nature to develop its potential is not the work of fate but of *fortuna*, it is a deviation from the natural order of things and it is a challenge to fate or god or nature. It is not completely unreasonable to suppose that there are limits to how great a *dis*-harmony with nature men can tolerate: when the city of Rome had again become a village and cattle were grazing on the *Forum romanum*, nature had returned to the Romans — who had deviated too far from nature.

The rights of the state or of man

A parallel is still to be seen between Rome and modern civilisation in that we, too, have gone too far from nature. 'The optimistic picture of man engaged on subjugating surrounding nature' (p. 25) is beginning to look less optimistic: 'In his enthusiasm at his own scientific and technological progress modern man has constructed a system of production which is violating nature, and a social system which is violating man.' It is an economist, E. F. Schumacher, who makes this point. Economists otherwise usually advocate increased growth as the solution to social problems and the problems of resources and pollution, which actually increase with increased growth. They do so in deference to the words of the economist of economists, Keynes, who argued that 'greed and cupidity and calculation must be our gods for a time yet.' This economic view coincides in this respect with the Marxist concept in seeing morals as of secondary importance: progress brings about the attitude which it needs; only when the time is ripe will economic necessity transform inhumanity into its antithesis.

But the antithesis might be of the opposite kind: not one of plenty in contrast to a lack, but a lack in contrast to plenty, not greater humanity but greater inhumanity, because there was something lacking in the theory and therefore in the practice as well. For if the fault is that human attitudes are no more than a function of progress, a tool for history, then it is also wrong to suppose that theories on the nature of men have no effect on it.

E. F. Schumacher finishes his book on economics, sub-titled 'A Study of Economics as if People actually Mattered', by referring to 'the traditional wisdom of mankind' which puts human ends above inhuman means: 'But today this message is not only coming from wise men and saints, but from the actual course taken by physical events. It speaks to us in the form of terrorism, genocide, collapse, pollution and the exhaustion of natural resources. It is as though we are living through a phase in which all signals to a unique extent are pointing in the same direction.' Nature, *fysis*, confirms what the wise men said: that there are laws laid down by nature — not abstract laws of nature in a modern sense but moral laws which cannot be broken without challenging nature, fate, the gods — and what is true of external nature is also true of man who is a part of nature, for the transformation of nature's riches into articles of trade, which Seneca believed to be fatal, implies that artificial needs triumph over natural ones, that 'the desire to possess and the desire for power', in other words greed, cupidity and calculation, are the dominant forces.

In contrast to conventional wisdom Schumacher ascribes significance to men's own attitudes by linking the exploitation of nature to 'changes of a philosophical, not to say religious, nature, which have taken place in people's attitudes towards nature over the last three or four hundred years.' However, the change is older than science. Stoic humanism has without doubt made its mark on both Christianity and the humanism of the Renaissance and Enlightenment, but its concept of nature, its belief in the divinity of nature and in man's natural urge to achieve the good were lost first in the Christian belief that what is natural is sinful, the belief that passions, which get out of control and must therefore be castigated, *are* part of human nature — and then in modern science's objective picture of nature and man and in the kind of historical materialism which makes man a product of circumstances. The concept of men's natural rights cannot be founded on the kind of nature which science and 'scientific' socialism will recognise; and the liberalism which once founded its ideology on the old ideas of 'human rights' and 'the law of nature' thereby in reality turned them into a justification for the freedom to trade and compete and the right of private ownership which to Seneca symbolised a 'fall from nature' — and its 'declarations of human rights' ignored the fact that in the view of the ancients society is not based on personal interest but on a natural unity of interest.

This means that the only ideological basis for opposition to the 'legal' violence of governments has been the idea that there is 'something to which the law applicable to all living things forbids us to expose any human being': Humanist ideas can naturally be traced back to an historical and social situation (and thus be debased if we believe that in a given situation men can only reflect that situation and not give expression to innate human qualities, as they are nothing in themselves). In other words, they can be traced back to 'hellenism', when the individual was detached from a more 'organic' community and lost his immediate social significance and tried to find a meaning in himself, to the annoyance of Vilhelm Grønbech. It is still common to date individualism to a specific historical epoch and disparagingly call it 'bourgeois individualism', but the idea of the right of the individual does not reflect any historical epoch but rather stands in opposition to it: it is indignation at the violation of human dignity which finds its expression in the recognition that an individual is of value in himself. The alternative to a 'society of man' based on the rights of the individual and on natural needs, is the state with unrestricted rights over the individual, the state which uses the individual as a tool for its needs.

Stoic humanism

The Stoics were not content to maintain that man can and should be free, but maintained that in fact that is what he is — and that he is only himself when he *is* free. This might seem strange to us who are used to distinguishing between evaluation and knowledge, morals and science, but for an ancient philosopher it was absurd to preach a moral code not founded in nature. Philosophy arises as a result of the distinction between social conditions and nature — and with it evolves the idea of the emancipated, untrammelled individual.

If it is objected that circumstances in fact *do* rob man of his freedom, this already implies that man *is* free — the social order is only accepted as long as it is thought to reflect the order of nature, and we are not incensed at slavery as long as we find it 'natural'. Seneca asks whether in the criminal's situation we would not have acted in the same way, thus showing that he realised the extent to which crime is determined by society; and on the basis of this knowledge he was one of the first to advocate a purposive human legal system which does not merely take account of the crime but of the entire situation. This presupposes precisely the recognition of the fact that man is not by nature depraved, and it also presupposes that the man sitting in judgement is himself free. In short, passions can excuse the actions of others, but a man in the grip of passions cannot excuse them. It is only possible to understand the actions of others on their own terms, but if we only see our own actions as determined by circumstance, then we have surrendered ourselves.

Those who resort to the argument that we should not interpret but transform the circumstances of which man is a product forget that we are constantly interpreting circumstances and that we cannot improve them if we interpret them wrongly. And where would we get the idea of better conditions if our consciousness only reflected the conditions in which we find ourselves at present? Theories are human products, and if theories pay no attention to men, then men will be disregarded when they are put into practice.

More than other philosophies Stoicism has been characterised as an attitude — and more than other philosophies Stoicism stressed that it is the attitude which is important. In practice this means that we must all begin with ourselves — that it is a misconception to believe that we must qualify ourselves for every conceivable task other than that of improving the world.

Seneca must also be understood against the background of the world situation in which he lived, but there will be things in his philosophy which do not only point back.

NOTES

I

10   De ira II, 15, 2.

12   Mircea Eliade: Le mythe de l'éternel retour, 1949.

12–14   Hesiod: Works and Days, on journeys by sea 682–83, 236–237; inheritance 37–41; "House and family..." 245–247; conflicts between generations 182–184; "not knowing how much..." 40.

15   Robert Graves: The Greek Myths I, 1955, p 41–42.

15   Solon, fragment 3; Hesiod: Works and Days 320 ff.

16   Xenophon: fragments 24 & 15; Romans 5, 20; Plato: 293 c, Seneca: epistle 90, 6.

18   Anaximander, fr. 1; Heraclitus, fr. 30, 125 a, 121, 33, 114 and 2.

20   Socrates' defence speech 32 d, 29 d, 32 a, 41 c–d.

21   Hegel: Philosophie der Geschichte, Reclam 1961, p 378.

22   "Something particularly pernicious..." Plato: The Laws 797d. Mirciea Eliade op. cit.

22–23   Plato: The Laws 705 ab, 743 d, 797 c; Martin Heidegger: Platons Lehre von der Wahrheit, 1947; Benjamin Farrington: Greek Science 1944.

24   Democritus, fr. 125 (Farrington, p 69 ff); Aeschylus: Prometheus 436 ff.

25   Sophocles Antigone 323 ff, 338–339, trans. Niels Møller; Farrington op. cit. p 125, p 122.

26   Democritus: fr. 118.

28   Leo Hjortsø: De græske historikere (The Greek Historians), 1975, p 95.

29   "Being in harmony", cf Max Pohlenz: Die Stoa I, 4. ed. 1970, p 116 ff.

II

32–33   Polybios: I, 4 and VI, 57; Sallust: Catalina 10, 1 f.

33–34   Livy: Ab urbe condita pr. 11.

35   Cicero: De officiis III, 41; Livy I, 19.

36   On Pythagoras in Rome: Michael Grant: Roman Myths, 1971, p 138–139; Numa's Pythagorean writings: Livy 40, 29.

39   Seneca: De ira II, 7, 3; De cl. I, 15, 1; De br. vitæ 3, 1; Cicero: De
        inventione II, 161; De re pub. IV, 12.
39–40   On popular justice: J. A. Crook: Law and Life of Rome, 1967, p 251,
        and on taking the law into one's own hands in general A. W. Lintott:
        Violence in Republican Rome, 1968; Julius Cæsar: B. C. I, 22, 5.
40   Petronius: Satyricon 18.
42   "108 consuls. . ." H. Bengtson: Grundriss der römischen Geschichte, I,
        1967, p 146.
44–45   Seneca: de cl. I, 1, 3; I, 12, 2.
47   Tacitus: Hist. II, 38; Cato in Sallust: Catalina 52, 22 and 52, 5; Plutarch:
        Cato 30, 6; Cæsar in Sallust: Catalina 51, 13–14, and in Cicero: Att. IX,
        7, C. L.
48   Cicero: Deiot. 34; Philip. II, 45, 116; Seneca: De ben. I, 10, 14; Plutarch:
        Cato 66.
50   Cicero: De re pub. I, 25.
50   Erik Wistrand: Politik och litteratur i antikens Rom (Politics and lit. in
        ancient Rome), 1963, p 40.
52   Seneca: De br. vitæ 5, 1; Cicero: De re pub. I, 34; VI, 2.
52   Cæsar with the elder Pliny, 7, 30, 117.
53   "Homo Sum", cf Max Pohlenz: Die Stoa I, pp 137 & 273.
54   Rustic muses. . ." after Pollio, Vergil's fourth pastoral. Introduction.
        Translation. Retrospect. By Johannes Loft, 1941.
56   The Aeneid 6, 851 ff. On Vergil's concepts of *virtus* and *gloria*: D. Earl:
        The Moral and Political Traditions of Rome, 1967, p 66 ff.
56–57   The Aeneid 6, 792 ff, 1, 278 f. Polybios VI, 56; Ovid: The art of love I,
        637.
59   John Ferguson: The Religions of the Roman Empire, 1970, p 68.
60   Seneca: De cl. I, 14, 2.
61   H. H. Scullard: From the Gracchi to Nero, 3. ed. 1968, p 265.
63   Ronald Syme: The Roman Revolution, 1939.
64   Ovid: The art of love III, 121 ff.
66   On Ovid and Pythagorism: J. Carcopino: L'exil d'Ovid, poète
        néopythagoricien, in Rencontres de l'histoire et de la littérature
        romaines, 1963; Seneca: De ira II, 9, 2; Qu. nat. V, 15, 2; ep. 97, 1.
67   The elder Seneca quoted from Lactantius Inst. VII, 15, 14, after Santo
        Mazzarino: Den antikke verdens undergang.
68   Tacitus: Hist. I, 10; Ann. IV, 20.

III

69   Conference on philosophy, cf Actas del congreso internacional de
      filosofia en commemoracion de Seneca en el XIX centenario de su
      muerte, 1–3, Madrid, 1966. Seneca: Ad Helv. 17, 3–4.
71–72 The elder Seneca: Controv. VI, 8.
73   Seneca: De ben. V, 12, 2; J. Carcopino: La vie quotidienne à Rome à
      P'apogée de l'empire, 1947.
74   A.-M. Guillemin: Le public et la vie littéraire a Rome, 1937, p 62 f;
      Quintilian: Inst. 10, 1.
75   "vulgar style" Aulus Gellinus N. A. XII, 2, 1 and 12 ff; The elder
      Seneca: Controv. I, pr 11; I, pr 6 & 7; Suas. 2, 23; Controv. II, pr 3–4;
      Seneca: Ad Helv. 18, 2–3.
76   Tacitus: Ann. 16, 17; Acts of the Apostles 18, 12–17; "In a third..." Qu.
      nat. IV A, pr 9; Epigram 49 (Anthol. lat. 441) in Gli epigrammi
      attribuiti a L. Anneo Seneca, by Carlo Prato, Biblioteca degli scittori
      greci e latini, 1964.
77   Vergil: Georg. 3, 284, quoted in ep. 108, 24; ep. 108, 29 & 23; ep. 88, 42;
      Nietzsche: Werke in drei Bänden III, p 174; Ep. 106, 12; Fabianus: De
      brev. vitæ 10, 1; ep. 40, 12; ep. 100.
78   Attalus: ep. 108, 13–16; ep. 110, 14–20; Sextius: De ira III, 36; Sotion:
      ep. 108, 17–22.
78–79 Seneca: ep. 78, 1–3; Ad Helv. 19, 2; 19, 4.
81   "you, O Cæsar..." Suetonius: Tiberius, 59.
81–82 Seneca: De tr. an. 11, 11; De ben. III, 26, 1.
82   "It was the law and justice..." cf Ortega y Gasset, quoted by Per
      Krarup in Romersk Politik i Oldtiden (Roman Politics in the Ancient
      World), 1971, p 164 f; Acts. of the Apostles 25, 10–12; "Universal
      ombudsman": J. A. Crook: Law and Life of Rome, p 71.
84   Seneca: De ben. III, 7, 7; De ira II, 7, 3.
84   The Roman historians: Tacitus Ann. 14, 30; Suetonius: Claudius 25;
      Acts of the Apostles 22, 25–29.
85   "Jus animantium" De cl. I, 18, 2; Seneca: Ad Marc. 20, 2; Ad Helv. 19,
      2.

IV

87   Philo: De legatione 13, 22.
87   Suetonius: Gajus Cæsar Caligula 14 & 27.
89   Philo 76, 352 ff.

90   "No mortar in his sand" Suetonius: Caligula 53; Dio Cassius 59, 19, 7–8; An epistle: 78, 6; Ad Marc. 22, 1; 20, 3 et passim.

91   Tacitus: Ann. 4, 34; Ad Marc. 15, 1; Ad Pol. 17, 4.

92   Seneca on Caligula: Ad Helv. 10, 4; De ira II, 33, 6; III, 19, 1; De con. sap. 18, 1; Suetonius: Caligula 50.

93–94   De con. sap. 18, 5; 2, 3; De ben. LL, 12; De ira III, 16, 2.

94   Dio Cassius 59, 16.

95   Suetonius: Caligula 24.

96   Tacitus: Ann. 14, 2; Suetonius: Caligula 45; Seneca: Qu. nat. IV A, pr 15; ep. 4, 7.

97   J. P. V. D. Balsdon: The Emperor Gajus, 1934, p 72; De ira III, 19, 5.

98   On the Seneca tradition: Paul Faider: Etudes sur Sénèque, 1921; H. V. Morton: The Magic of Rome, 1962; Seneca: ep. 95, 2.

99   Konrad Lorenz: Das sogenannte Böse, 1963; English version: On Agression 1966; De ira II, 17.

101–02   De ira II, 8, 3; I, 8, 2–3; II, 9, 4; II 21, 7; II, 5, 2 & 3; II, 31, 8.

103   Alf Ross: Skyld, ansvar og straf (Guilt, responsibility and punishment) 1970, p 46–47.

103–04   Seneca: ep. 7, 7; De ira II, 31, 5; II, 32, 1; II, 10, 2; II, 21, 11.

105   Jesus: Matth. 7, 14; Hesiod: Works and Days 291; Seneca: De ira II, 13, 1–3.

106   De con. sap. passim.

107   De ira II, 34, 4.

                                    V

110   Acts of the Apostles 24; Suetonius: Claudius 28–29.

111   "a shameless..." Gyldendals fremmedordbog (Gyldendal's Dictionary of Foreign Words), 1963; Dio Cassius 60, 8, 5.

112–113 Seneca: Qu. nat. IV A, pr 15; De con. sap. 9, 2; 8, 3; 14, 1; Ad Pol. 13, 2; Suetonius: Claudius 29; Tacitus: Ann. 11, 1–3.

114   Epigr. 19 (Anth. lat. 410).

114   Epigr. 3 (Anth. lat. 237).

115–117 Ad Helv. 10, 3; 8, 3–4; 20, 2; Epigr. 1 (Anth. lat. 232).

118   Ad Pol. 13, 3 et passim.

120   Pliny the Younger: ep. 5, 3; Quintilian: Inst. 10, 1 & 129; Epigr. 71 (Anth. lat. 667); Xerxes, epigr. 5, 8 (Anth. lat. 396).

122   Two epigrams, 69 & 70 (Anth. lat. 462–63); Pasienus Crispus, Qu. nat. IV A, pr 6; De ben. I, 15, 5.

123   Ronald Syme: The Roman Revolution; Domitia, Quintilian Inst. VI, 3, 74; VI, 1, 50.

124   Tacitus: Ann. 11, 11–12; Suetonius: Claudius 29.

127   De brev. vitæ 15, 5; 10, 5; 10, 4 et passim.

127   "It has therefore been suggested..." cf Miriam T. Griffin: De brevitate vitæ, JRS, 1962, p 104–13; Epigr. 72 (Anth. lat. 804).

128   Dio Cassius 61, 10, 3; J. Carcopino: Daily Life ..., p 101 ff.

129   St Jerome: Ad Jovin. I, 40–49; Seneca: epistle 9; Ad helv. 13.3.

129–130 Epigr. 38 (Anth. lat. 430); Dio Cassius 60, 8, 5 & 61, 10, 1; Suetonius: Claudius 29; Epigr. 59 (Anth. lat. 453).

130   "artless nature" (inornata simplicitas), epigr. 65, 6 & De tr. an 17. 2; Pompeja Paulina, ep. 104, 2; "It is said..." Scoliast Juvenal ad sat. V, 109.

VI

132   Tacitus: Ann. 12, 7.

133   Seneca: De otio 6, 6; Suetonius: Nero Claudius Cæsar 60, 35.

134–136 Suetonius: Nero 6 & 52; Tacitus 13, 3; Dio Cassius 60, 35.

136   "The moral arguments", cf A. Stahr: Agrippina, die Mutter Neros, 1867, pp 330–43; M. C. Gertz: Senecas Breve og andre Skrifter til Lucilius (Seneca's letters and other writings to Lucilius) 1927, I, p VI, – and counter arguments in Otto Weinrich: Römische Satiren, 1962, pp 332–37.

138   Apocol. 10, 3 et passim; "But only twice..." De cl. I, 23, l; De ben. I, 15, 5; "attempts have admittedly been made to deny..." (cf Carlo Pascal: Nerone, 1923, s. 181–85.

138   Odyssey 1, 170; 9, 35 f; Apocol. 5, 4; "Even if my sister..." Apocol. 10, 3; Konrad Kraft: Der politische Hintergrund von Senecas Apocolocyntosis. Historia 15, 1966.

140   Apocol. 4, 1; De cl. II, 2, 2; I, 10, 3.

141   Tacitus 13, 2; Suetonius: Nero 10.

141   Tacitus 13, 11; Trajanus: Vict. Aur. Epit. 5; Epistle to the Romans, 13, 3–4, 6–7.

142   Tacitus 13, 4; Suetonius: Nero 10; Tacitus 13, 5; De cl. I, 25, 5.

143   Inscription: Corpus Inscriptionum Latinarus IV, 4418.

145   Suetonius, Nero 12.

146   Augustus: Res gestæ 22–23.

148   Augustin: Conf. VI. VI, 8; "Proof of the worst...", De vita beata, r, 1;

Seneca: De cl. I, 18, 2; I, 15, 1; I, 26, 3.

149 "Three times. . ." De cl. I, 12, 4; I, 25, 3; I, 26, 1; "It is I. . ." De cl. I, 1, 2 ff.

150 "A catastrophe. . ." De cl. I, 4, 2; De ira II, 23, 3–4; "To own the State. . ." ep. 14, 13; Brutus, De ben. II, 20, 2.

151 Caesar, De ira III, 30; M. Rostovtzeff: Social and Economic History of the Roman Empire, 1926, p 85.

151 De cl. I, 19, 1; I, 19, 4; 1, 20, 3; I, 10, 3; I, 22, 1–2.

153 Suetonius: Claudius 34; Nero 15; De cl. I, 8, 1 ff; Jesus: Matthew 20, 26–27; Luke, 22, 25; Mark 10, 44.

154 De cl. I, 18, 3; K. E. Løgstrup: Norm og spontaneitet (Norm and spontaneity), 1972, p 18; De cl. I, 1, 2; I, 1, 6.

155 "This conventional Augustus. . ." Henry Bardon: Les empéreurs et les lettres latines d'August à Hadrien, 1940, p 185; De cl. I, 11, 2; I, 8, 7; II, 1, 4.

156 Tacitus 13, 14; "Abdicere", Suetonius: Nero 34.

157 Tacitus 13, 17; Adolf Stahr: Agrippina, 1867, p 248.

158 B. H. Warmington: Nero. Reality and Legend, 1969, p 42.

160 De ben. I, 9, 5.

160 Ludwig Friedlaender: Darstellungen aus der Sittengeschichte Roms, I, 7. Auflage, 1901, p 330; M. Rostovtzeff, op cit. p 513; Seneca: Ad Helv. 10, 5; Medea 329 ff, 364–65, 368 ff.

162 Lucretia: De rerum natura II, 1150 ff; Columella: De re rustica III, 3, 3; The elder Pliny 14, 51; Tacitus 13, 18; Seneca: ep. 12 & 86.

162 The older Pliny 18, 35; cf Jens Erik Skydsgaard: Den romerske Villa Rustica (The Roman Villa Rustica), 1961, p 90 ff; Seneca: ep. 89, 20; ep. 87, 41; "Placed limits. . ." Suetonius: Nero 16; Hartvig Frisch: Kulturhistorie (History of Culture) II, 4th ed. 1964, p 75 f.

164 M. Rostovtzeff: Geschichte der alten Welt. Rom, 5th ed. 1970, p 386 & 387.

166 Tacitus 13, 8; 13, 41; L. Friedlaender, op cit. I. p 145; Tacitus 14, 51; "Coins", cf Michael Grant: Gladiators, 1976, p 37.

166 Tacitus 13, 42.

168 M. Heidegger: Sein und Zeit, 1927, §27; Seneca: De vita beata; De vita beata 7, 3; 2, 2; 24, 3; 2, 1; 1, 1; 9, 4; 8, 6.

169 15, 7; 17, 1–4.

170 23, 1; 2, 4.

171 Tacitus 13, 45; 14, 1; Plutarch: Galba 20.

171   Tacitus 14, 3 ff; Tacitus 14, 14 ff.
173   Suetonius: Nero 22.
175   "All sources..." Suetonius 12, Tacitus 15, 32; Dio Cassius 62, 17, 3; 62, 20, 3; 61, 10, 5.
176   Herc. fur. 468–70; Tacitus 14, 52.
177   "Seneca is said..." Dio Cassius 62, 18, 3; De cl. I, 18, 2.
178   De ben. III, 6–17; III, 22, 3; Tacitus 14, 42–45; 12, 12.
179   De ben. III, 18, 2; III, 28, 1; Ep. 47, 18.
180   De tr. an. 5, 5.
181   De tr. an. 2, 7; 2, 10.
182   De tr. an. 2, 4; 1, 10.
183   De tr. an. 4, 1; 4, 6; 11, 3; 15, 1.
184   De tr. an. 2, 5; 10, 6; De otio 8, 3.
185   The elder Pliny 22, 23; ep. 63, 14; Tacitus 14, 51; "hypothesis": René Waltz: Vie de Sénèque, 1924, p 384.
186   Tacitus 14, 53–56.
188   Tacitus 14, 57; 15, 23; 14, 65.

VII

190   "It was now a case of..." Ep. 8, 3; Qu. nat. III pr. 2.
191   Ep. 20, 5; 71, 36; 16, 1.
192   Ep. 80, 4; 81, 13; 94, 54 f. De ben. IV, 17, 2; ep. 59, 11; 43, 3 f; 41, 7; 20, 2.
193   Ep. 102, 17; M. Pohlenz: Die Stoa, p 314; ep. 32, 4 f; 59, 14; 48, 3.
193   Ep. 6, 1; 75, 1 & 5; 52, 8 f. Lucilius: ep. 34, 2; 21, 5; Cato: ep. 14, 3. Demetrius: De vita beata 18, 3; De ben. VII, 8, 2 f.
194   Ep. 62, 3; De ben. VII, 11; ep. 5, 4; 29, 1; Qu. nat. IV pr. 7; ep. 20, 9
195   Ep. 87, 41; 115, 10; De ben. VII, 2–5.
196   Suetonius: Nero 31; Tacitus 15, 45; ep. 87.
197   De prov. 6, 7.
198   Ep. 70, 8–9; Tacitus 15, 45; De ben. IV, 7, 2; Phaedra 972–80.
200   De prov. 1, 1; 2, 9; J. Ferguson: The Religions of the Roman Empire, p 78.
200   Fortuna, De ben. IV, 8, 3; De prov. 3, 4; 6, 3.
201   Ep. 120, 14 f; 102, 2.
202   The elder Pliny 2, 22; Livy I, 16.
203   J. Carcopino: op. cit. Cato, De con. sap. II, 2; Dio Cassius 56, 36.
204   Lucanus II, 306–13.
204   NF, cf J. Ferguston op cit. p 136; Thyestes 875–84.

206	Hebrews 9, 25–28; Dio Cassius 62, 17, 3.
206	Tacitus 15, 44.
207	Ep. 95, 30 ff; 4., 1; 96, 2; Augustine: De civ. Dei 6, 10–11; 20, 19; Tertullian: De anima 20, 1; Apol. 17, 6; Lactantius: Inst. 2, 8, 23; 6, 24, 13 f.
208	Philippians 4, 22; Lactantius: De mort. pers. c 2.
209	Lactantius: Inst. 3, 8 & 18 & 23.
210	Seneca: De ben. V, 17, 4; Compassion, De ira II, 15, 3; De ben. III, 7, 5; V. 9, 2.
212	Friendship, sp. 6, 4; ep. 9; Dionysios 2, 10, 3; Per Krarup: Romersk politik i oldentiden, 1971, p 79.
212	Ep. 81, 32; De ben. III, 28, 1.
213	Kant: Grundlegung zur Metaphysik der Sitten, 1785, I. Abschnitt; De ben. 15, 4; II, 16, 1.
214	Kant: Kritik der praktischen Vernunft, 1788, I. Teil, 1. Buch, § 7; Grundlegung..., II. Abschnitt; "Seneca said..." ep. 88, 30. Galatians, 3, 28; De vita beata, 24, 3; De ben. IV, 18, 2; I, 4, 2; Hermann Broch, cf. eg. Die Schlafwandler, 1888–1918, Vol III, chap. 44.
215	De ben. VI, 38, 2 f; Augustine: De vic. Dei 12, 28; De ben. VI, 3, 4.
216	"Perdidi" VII, 19, 9; IV, 26, 1; VII, 31–32; Jesus: Matth. 5, 44–46.

VIII

218	De otio 5, 8; Qu. nat. I, 5, 6; VII, 17, 2.
219	Qu. nat. VI, 8, 3; II, 43, 2; III pr. 9 & 5; I pr. 9 & 11.
220	Qu. nat. I pr. 3–5; IV B 6, 2 f.
221	Qu. nat. VI, 3, 4.
222	Epicure: Ad Menoec. 134 Us; fr. vaticam. 9; divinatio: Qu. nat. II, 32–38.
223	Ep. 41, 9; Phaedra 483–557.
224	Ep. 90, 38 f.
225	Qu. nat. III, 30, 7.
225	Qu. nat. VII, 25, 5; De ben. VII, 1: Salutare: Qu. nat. II, 59, 1.
226	Qu. nat. V, 18, 13 f and 4; Poseidonios: ep. 90, 19 & 25.
227	Petronius: Satyricon 68; Tacitus 16, 18.
228	Friedrich Engels: Marxismen-leninismens grundlag (The basis of Marxism-Leninism), 1961, p 134 f; Seneca: De brev. vitæ 20, 5.
229	Paul Louis: Le travail dans le monde romain, 1912; Pliny 14, 4; 2, 118; Dio Cassius 63, 16.

230   Pliny 11, 198; 11, 150; 9, 22; 2, 137; Lucretius: De rerum natura VI, 230; Qu. nat. II, 31, 1.
232   Qu. nat. I, pr. 15; II, 6, 2; Jacques Monod: Le hasard et la nécessité, 1970.
233   Qu. nat. II, 32, 2; De ira II, 27.
234   Democritus fr. 125.-
235   Zenon, quoted by Diogenes Laertius.
236   Qu. nat. VI, 18, 1; V, 5; II, 5, 1.
237   Qu. nat. VII, 27, 4; III, 13, 3; III, 28. Fortuna: VI, 1, 4; III, 29, 9; III, 27, 12.
238   Qu. nat. III, 30, 7 f; Goethe: Sämtliche Werke, Jubliäums-Ausgabe, 40, p 142–46; Qu. nat. VII, 1, 2.
238   Qu. nat. II, 46; VII, 23, 1.
239   Qu. nat. VII, 25 ff; ep. 64, 7.

IX

240   Arthur Janov: The primal scream, 1970.
241   De tr. an. 17, 1 f; 17, 10 f; Mircea Eliade: Le mythe de l'éternel retour.
243   Carcopino: op cit. "payments to authors" cf Heinz Kindermann: Theatergeschichte Europas, 1966, I, p 198; Livy 7, 2.
244   Mimen, De br. vitæ, 12, 8; Publilius, ep. 8, 8; 9, 21; De tr. an. 11, 8.
244–245 Paris, Lukian: De salt. 63; Ovid: Tr. 2, 519; Seneca: ep. 47, 17; Tacitus: Ann. 13, 25; Aristotle: Poetics, 13, 5–11.
246   "Of its own accord" cf Gerald F. Else: The Origin and early Form of Greek Tragedy, 1967.
247   Iliad, 19, 86 ff & 19, 137 f; Aischylos: Ag. 750 ff, Ch. 910–11.
249   Plato: Republic 380 a.
249   Aischylos: Ag. 177 f.
250–251 Seneca: Agamemnnon 297, 76, 798 f, 132 ff, 141 ff.
255   Oedipus 875, 1019, 1035 f; Phoenicians 134–37.
256–257 Phoenician Women 334–39, 45 1 ff, 216–17.
259–260 Hercules 250–53, 362–69.
261   "elsewhere", Qu. nat. III, pr. 10; ep. 113, 30.
262   Herc. 739–47.
263   Euripedes: Hippolitus 1433 ff..
265   Phaedra 195–215
266   De ira II, 21, 7.
267   "Hippolytus lists. . ." Phaedra 555 ff; Medea 375 ff.
267   Euripides: Medea 267 f.

339

269   Medea 199–200, 417–21.

271   "The great villains..." cf Robert Graves: The Greek Myths, II, p 29.

272–273 Thyestes 446–56, 468–70; 607–14; 878–80.

276   "Let them hate me..." Suetonius: Tiberius 59, Caligula 30; De cl. II, 2, 2.

276   Ep. 80, 7 f. – "Marionette tragedy": Th. Thomann in Seneca: Tragödien II, p 12.

277   Polybius 38, quoted from S. Mazzarino: La fine del mondo antico.

277   The Trojan Women 298, 330–36, 792, 1016–23, 1–6, 371–77.

282   Léon Herrmann: Le théatre de Sénèque, 1924, p 133; Medea 163; ep. 5, 7; The Trojan Women 425; Phaedra 164; Epicure fr. 532.

283   Ep. 97, 13; ep. 105, 8; Quintilian: Inst. VIII, 3, 31; Tacitus: Ann. 11, 13; 14, 52; "Oedipus and Agamemnon..." cf I Wight Duff: A Literary History of Rome in the Silver Ages, 3rd ed. 1964 (1927), p 205; Oedipus 911–14; Hercules 202–4.

283   "incredible that Seneca..." W. Beare: The Roman State, 3rd. ed. 1964, p 224; Seneca: ep. 108, 9 f; 94, 27.

284   Theodor Thomann: Seneca Sämtliche Tragödien, 1961, Einführung.

285   "It has even been said that Seneca..." Peter D. Arnott: An Introduction to the Roman World, 1970, ch. 7 The Rome of Seneca, p 223;

286   Antonin Artaud:Grusomhedens teater (The theatre of cruelty) (1932), trans. Christian Ludvigsen in Vindrosen, 1959, p 487.

286   Seneca: p. 9, 7; De prov. 5, 11.

287   Suetonius: Nero 37; Tacitus: Ann. I, 6; 13, 17.

288   Thyestes 213–17; Oedipus 703–6; Phoenician Women 659–60.

289   Octavia 574–75, 579–80, 185.

290   Curiatus maternus, cf. H. Bardon: Les empéreurs... p 299.

X

291   Philostrates: Apollonius IV, 36.

292   Dittenberger: Sylloge Inscriptionum Graecarum, 3rd ed., 814, 10–26.

294   Dio Cassius 63, 5.

294   E. M. Smallwood, ed. Documents (of Gajus, Claudius and Nero), 1967; 391.

295   Dio Cassius 61, 4, 1.

296   Suetonius: Nero 53; the elder Pliny 30, 5–6; Suetonius: Nero 29; 37; Dio Cassius 61, 5, 1; Søren Kierkegaard: Collected Works (in Danish) II, 1st ed. p 167; Seneca: ep. 42, 4.

297   Dio Cassius 63, 9; "It is told about Nero": Tacitus: Ann. 13, 17; 14, 2; Suetonius: Nero 21, 28, 33, 35.

297   Oedipus monologue; Suetonius: Nero 46; Dio Cassius 63, 28, 5; Suetonius: Nero 46; Tacitus: Historia II, 8, 1.

298   Nero as artiste. Tacitus: Ann. 14, 16; Suetonius 52; Martial VIII, 70, 8; Persius: sta. I, 105; Cornutus, Dio Cassius 62, 29, 3.

298   Seutonius: Nero 22.

300   M. A. Levi: Nerone e i suoi tempi, 1949.

301   Suetonius: Nero 49; Dio Cassius 63, 22.

302–303 Tacitus: Agricola 45; Ann. 15, 37; Suetonius: Nero 29, 35.

304   S. Freud: Three essays on the sexual theory; Seneca: De ira II, 36, 6; De ben. VI, 27, 4; Suetonius: Nero 22.

305   Seneca: De cl. II, 2, 2; I, 13, 2; I, 25, 3; ep. 70, 8, 32, 5.

305   Ep. 32, 5; 50, 2; 12, 3; Vergil: Aeneid 4, 653; ep. 12, 9; 83, 4 f; 91, 2.

307   81, 3; 84, 1 & 45, 1 (reading); I. Hadot: Seneca und die griechischrömische Tradition der Seelenleitung, 1969, p 184 ff; Language, ep. 115, 1; 114, 1 & 13–14; 40, 4.

307   "That kind of question..." ep. 106, 3; 49, 8; Ep. 76, 4 (Metronax), 54 (asthma), 53 (seasickness).

308   Ep. 56 & 51 (Bajæ); De ben. VI, 32, 2 et passim.

310   Dio Cassius 61, 4, 2; De ben. VII, 20, 2 f.

312   Tacitus: Ann. 15, 48 ff; Dio Cassius 62, 24, 1.

313   Tacitus: Ann. 15, 60–64.

Epilogue

316   W. Trillitzsch: Seneca im literarischen Urteil der Antike. Darstellung und Sammlung der Zeugnisse, I–II, Amsterdam, 1971. Middle Ages, cf. Carlo Pascal: Nerone nella storia aneddotica e nella leggenda, 1923, p. 199–208.

316   Zwingli: Prov. 2, 3; Calvin: pr. to De clementia; Montaigne: Essais II, 31; Descartes: ep. 397 ff; Holberg: Collected Works I, p. 522; Hegel: Vorlesungen über die Geschichte der Philosophie, XIV, p. 435; Schopenhauer: Parerga und Paralipomena, Fragmente zur Geschichte der Philosophie, § 6.

318   F. J. Billeskov Jansen: Holberg som Epigrammatiker og Essayist
       (Holberg as epigrammatist and essayist), 1938–39, I, p. 200, II, p. 231;
       Harald Høffding: Danske Filosoffer (Danish philosophers), 1909, p. 8
       & 2; Søren Kierkegaard: Papers X, 3 A 35; Marianne Alenius: Døden
       og venskabet. En studie i Senecas breve, (Death and friendship. A
       study of Seneca's letters), Studier fra Sprog- og Oldtidsforskning,
       1974, p. 7; Dio Cassius 61, 10.

319   Th. W. Africa: Rome of the Caesars, 1965, p. 94, p. 100; Epistle of
       James 2, 17; Peter P. Rohde: Den store Moders genkomst (The return
       of the great mother) 1966, p. 77.

320   F. W. Farrar: Seekers after God, 1868..

321   Vilhelm Grønbech: Hellenismen, 1940, I, p. 421 ("record of illness"),
       abridged ed. 1953, p. 18, 7, 273, 61, 14f, 283, 9.

321ff Oswald Spengler: Untergang des Abendlandes; "Memento mori",
       cf. Walther Rehm: Der Untergang Roms im abendländishchen
       Denken, 1930.

323   V. Grønbech: Hellenismen, 1953, p. 50, p. 291; Seneca: ep. 107, 11.

324   Lawrence Waddy: Pax Romana and World Peace, 1950, p. 9;
       Plutarch, cf. Leo Hjortsø: De græske historikere, 1975, p. 159;
       Seneca: epigr. 69 (Anth. lat. 462), 19; M. Rostovtzeff: Social and
       Economic History, p. 121.

326   E. F. Schuhmacher: Vækst eller velfærd (Small is Beautiful, 1973).

328   "The law..." De cl. I, 18, 2.

SENECA'S WORKS

LIST OF NAMES

Athenodorus 182f
Attalus 78
Augustine, St. 148, 208, 215
Augustus 33, 36, 37, 51f, 53, 54–57, 59, 60–66, 67, 80ff, 92, 96, 111, 112, 123, 124, 126, 127, 135, 136, 137f, 139, 140, 143, 146, 149, 150, 153f, 155, 163, 164, 177, 183, 186, 187, 203, 204, 212, 244, 274, 287, 294, 302, 309, 310, 324

Balsdon, J.P.V.D. 97
Beckett, S. 255
Billeskov Jansen, F.J. 318
Britannicus 111, 124, 133, 135, 137, 139, 156ff, 162, 170, 287, 294, 297, 304
Broch, Hermann 57, 215
Brook, Peter 285
Brutus 49, 50, 51, 53, 91, 150
Burrus 133, 140, 154, 156, 157ff, 172, 174, 185, 294, 310, 311, 319

Caesar, see Julius
Caesonius Maximus 197
Caligula 67, 81, 86, 87–89, 90, 92–98, 102, 109, 111, 113, 119, 127, 133, 135, 136, 137, 138, 146, 148, 150, 151, 155, 174, 183, 194, 203, 287
Calpurnius Piso 189, 312–313
Calpurnius Siculus 155, 282
Calvin 317
Carcopino, J. 73, 128, 229, 243
Cassius 50, 51, 53, 91, 179
Cassius Chaerea 93f, 98
Cassius Longinus 165, 178ff
Catalina 48, 51
Cato the Younger 47–49, 68, 72, 94, 106f, 112, 122, 150, 194, 201, 203, 204, 241
Cato the Elder 42, 162
Catullus 299
Chaeremon 134
Chrysippos 30, 182, 184, 236
Cicero 35, 39, 48, 50, 51, 52, 53, 74, 77, 80, 106, 108, 129, 214, 307, 317
Claudius 37, 85, 109–111, 113, 118, 119, 121, 123, 124, 125, 127, 132, 133, 135–140, 143, 144, 146, 150, 153, 156, 159, 165, 166, 178, 187, 203, 238, 282, 287, 294, 297, 302
Cleanthes 30, 182, 323, 325

Julia Livilla 95, 97, 100f, 111ff, 133, 137, 318
Julius Caesar 33, 34, 35, 37, 40, 46, 47-51, 52, 56, 60, 62, 63, 65, 68, 92, 111, 136, 145, 149, 150ff, 194, 204, 241, 299

Kant 213ff
Keynes 326
Kierkegaard 47, 125, 296, 318
Kraft, Konrad 139
Krarup, P. 212
Krates 29

Lactantius 208-210, 225
La Rochefoucauld 192
Leibniz 199
Lepidus 51
Levi, M.A. 300
Lipsius 316
Livia 60, 80, 96
Livy 33ff, 35, 92, 202, 243, 307
Lorenz, K. 99
Lucanus 76, 115, 174, 177, 204, 245, 285, 298, 299, 313
Lucilius 77, 97, 111, 190-198, 208, 211, 218, 287, 305ff
Lucretius 162, 219, 229, 230, 231
Lucullus 46

Machiavelli 192
Maecenas 64, 111, 186, 187, 310, 312
Marcia 90-92, 117f
Marcus Antonius, see Antonius
Marcus Aurelius 195
Marius 44ff, 115
Martial 298
Mela 75ff
Menander 53
Messalina 109-113, 123, 124, 132, 137, 166
Metronax 308
Miliboeus 282
Mill, J.S. 168

348

Monod, J. 232ff
Montaigne 317
Morton, H.V. 98